LATIN GRAMMAR

D1562551

LATIN GRAMMAR

Grammar, Vocabularies, and Exercises
in Preparation for
the Reading of the Missal and Breviary

CORA CARROLL SCANLON, A.M.

Milwaukee State Teachers College

AND

CHARLES L. SCANLON, A.M.

Marquette University

EDITED BY

REV. NEWTON THOMPSON, S.T.D.

TAN BOOKS AND PUBLISHERS, INC.
Rockford, Illinois 61105

PREFACE

This Latin grammar is intended for students who are entering seminaries or religious novitiates without previous study of Latin, for sisters in communities that recite the breviary, and for the growing number of lay people who use the Roman missal and the Roman breviary. Its twenty lessons, divided into fifty units, cover all the grammatical essentials for the intelligent reading of these two books. The vocabulary comprises the 914 words that make up the Ordinary of the Mass and the three Requiem Masses with their additional Collects, since these are the words that a daily user of the missal will encounter most frequently. However, to make the work as valuable as possible for those who use the missal in its entirety, as well as for those who wish to undertake the daily reading of the breviary, the Latin-English vocabulary at the end of the book includes not only all the words of the Roman missal, but also the complete vocabulary of the Roman breviary.

Of the 914 words used throughout the twenty lessons, 476 have been distributed as regular lesson vocabularies. The remaining 438 words have been grouped in those sections included in each lesson that are devoted to the study of cognates, derivatives, and compounds.

Beginning with Lesson IV and continuing through Lesson XX, the Latin text of each lesson (translation from Latin into English) has been divided into two parts. The second part consists at first of isolated words and short phrases taken from the Ordinary of the Mass and utilizes the vocabulary given up to that point. Later, as the vocabulary increases, these phrases are expanded into complete sentences and finally whole paragraphs are presented. In this way the entire Ordinary and the complete Requiem Masses have been given by the time the twentieth lesson is completed. Extra reading is provided by nine Reading Lessons, one inserted after each lesson from XII to XX inclusive. These are taken from the Vulgate text of the New Testament and have been selected to give a short presentation of the life of Christ from His birth to the Resurrection.

The Appendix contains irregular declensions, cardinal and ordinal numerals, the four regular conjugations complete, and the conjugations of the common irregular verbs.

PRONUNCIATION

1. Vowels. The pronunciation of the vowels is shown in the following table:

Vowel	Pronunciation	Example
a	as in *arm*	*ad, mater*
e	as *a* in *fate*	*me, video*
i	as in *machine*	*qui, ire*
o	as in *or*	*porta, omnis*
u	as in *tutor*	*cum, sumus*

2. Diphthongs. The diphthongs are pronounced as follows:

Diphthong	Pronunciation	Example
ae	as *a* in *fate*	*prae, illae*
oe	as *a* in *fate*	*coelum, coepi*
au	as *ou* in *out*	*aut, laudo*

In a few instances the individual vowels of *ae* and *oe* are pronounced separately. In the vocabularies these instances will be shown by a diaeresis (··) over the second vowel. *Míchaël, poëma.*

3. Consonants. They are pronounced as in English, with the following exceptions:

Consonant	Pronunciation	Example
c (before *e* or *i*)	as *ch* in *church*	*certus, cibus*
ch	as in *ache*	*Christus*
g (before *e* or *i*)	as in *gentle*	*gens, agit*
g (before other letters)	as in *go*	*gratis, glória*
gn	as *ny* in *canyon*	*agnus, ignis*

Consonant	Pronunciation	Example
j (or consonant *i*)	as *y* in *yes*	*Jesus, justus*
s	as *s* in *sing* (never as *s* in *raise*)	*miser, fides*
sc (before *a, o, u,* or a consonant)	as *sc* in *scope*	*scutum, Pascha*
sc (before *e* and *i*)	as *sh* in *shall*	*ascéndere, scio*
th	as *t* in *ten*	*Thomas*
ti (when followed by a vowel and preceded by any letter except *s, t,* or *x*)	as *tsee*	*gratia, totius*
x (in words beginning *ex* followed by a vowel, *h,* or *s*)	as *gs*	*exaudíre*
x (in all other cases)	as *ks*	*pax, excusáre*

CONTENTS

LESSON I

Mea culpa, mea culpa, *Through my fault, through my fault,*
mea máxima culpa. *through my most grievous fault.*

Vocabulary

aqua, -ae,[1] f., *water*
ánima, -ae, f.,[2] *soul*
terra, -ae, f., *earth, land*
tuba, -ae, f., *trumpet*
via, -ae, f., *way, road*
vita, -ae, f., *life*
María, -ae f., *Mary*
Lúcia, -ae, f., *Lucy*
culpa, -ae, f., *fault, guilt*
et, *and*
a (ab) [3] (with abl.), *from, by*
e (ex) [3] (with abl.), *out of, from*
cum (with abl.), *with*
in (with abl.), *in, on*
in (with acc.), *against, into, unto*
ad (with acc.), *to, toward, near*

1. Declension. In English a noun changes its form only to indicate possession (the possessive case) or to express plural number. In form the nominative and objective cases are the same.

---

[1] The genitive ending is given after the nominative to show the declension.

[2] For the dative and ablative plural, besides the regular form in -is, the form animabus is also used.

[3] The forms ab and ex must be used before a vowel or h; all four forms may be used before consonants.

I

The *man* is here.	I saw the *man*.
The *man's* hat.	The *men* are here.

In Latin the noun usually changes its form for each case and there are five of these: nominative (nom.), genitive (gen.), dative (dat.), accusative (acc.), and ablative (abl.). In addition, adjectives, as well as nouns, in Latin change their forms to indicate their case, gender, or number, for all adjectives must be made to agree in case, gender, and number with the noun modified. To decline a noun or adjective means to give its forms in the right order and all these forms taken together constitute what is called a declension. There are five declensions in Latin, that is, all nouns may be assembled into five distinct classes or groups, which are distinguished from one another by the ending of the genitive singular.

2. Gender. In English the gender of a noun depends upon the sex to which it refers. The noun *prince* is masculine gender because it refers to a male; the noun *women* is feminine gender because it indicates females; all sexless objects (for example, *chair*) are said to belong to the neuter gender. Many nouns that are classified in English as neuters may be masculine or feminine in Latin.

3. First declension. All nouns that have the genitive singular ending -ae belong to the first declension. Most of the nouns of this declension are of the feminine gender. The following case endings are added to the base:

	Singular	Plural
Nom.	-a	-ae
Gen.	-ae	-arum
Dat.	-ae	-is
Acc.	-am	-as
Abl.	-a	-is

The ablative may have various meanings: by, from, out of, with, in, etc.

aqua (base, **aqu-**), *water*

	Singular		Plural	
Nom.	**aqua**	*the water*	**aquae**	*the waters*
Gen.	**aquae**	*of the water*	**aquárum**	*of the waters*
Dat.	**aquae**	*for the water*	**aquis**	*for the waters*
Acc.	**aquam**	*the water*	**aquas**	*the waters*
Abl.	**aqua**	*in the water*	**aquis**	*in the waters*

aqua bona, *the good water*

Nom.	**aqua bona**	**aquae bonae**
Gen.	**aquae bonae**	**aquárum bonárum**
Dat.	**aquae bonae**	**aquis bonis**
Acc.	**aquam bonam**	**aquas bonas**
Abl.	**aqua bona**	**aquis bonis**

Note the following:

a) The base is obtained by dropping the ending of the genitive singular. The case endings are added to this base.

b) There are no articles in Latin. **Aqua** means *water* or *the water*.

c) The genitive case corresponds to the possessive case in English. **Aquae** means *of the water* or *the water's* (*color*).

d) The dative case corresponds to the English indirect object. He gives an apple *to the boy*.

e) The accusative case is the English objective case. The direct object of a verb (or the object of certain prepositions) is put in the accusative case.

f) The ablative case is used after most prepositions.

g) In Latin the adjective frequently follows the noun.

EXERCISES

A. Cognates. Nouns ending in *-ance* and *-ence* in English end in *-antia* and *-entia* in Latin. Pronounce and give the meaning for the following.

1. indulgéntia. 2. negligéntia. 3. sciéntia. 4. senténtia. 5. sequéntia. 6. substántia. 7. temperántia. 8. arrogántia. 9. diligéntia. 10. innocéntia. 11. benevoléntia. 12. prudéntia. 13. imprudéntia. 14. consciéntia. 15. abundántia. 16. petulántia. 17. perseverántia.

B. Read the Latin and give the meaning in English.

1. María et Lúcia. 2. Ad Maríam. 3. In terra. 4. Ex tuba. 5. Terra Maríae. 6. In via. 7. Vita ánimae. 8. Ab Lúcia. 9. Ad vitam. 10. Cum tubis. 11. Terrárum bonárum. 12. Vitae. 13. In ánima. 14. Ad vias. 15. A terris. 16. In aquam. 17. Ad Lúciam. 18. Ad terram Maríae. 19. Ex María. 20. Ad vitam Lúciae. 21. Ex terris. 22. A terra Maríae. 23. A terris bonis. 24. Tuba bona. 25. Tubae bonae. 26. Cum tubis bonis. 27. Ex aquis bonis. 28. Ad vitam bonam.

UNIT TWO

A. Make the adjective *bona* agree in case and number with each of the following nouns.

1. terram...... 2. tubas...... 3. vitae...... 4. animárum...... 5. terris...... 6. aquae...... 7. via...... 8. vitam...... 9. tubárum...... 10. aquas...... 11. viae...... 12. vita...... 13. tubis...... 14. animábus...... 15. ánimas......

B. Decline *terra* and *tuba*. Then decline each of them with the adjective *bona*. (See the declension of *aqua bona* above.)

C. Vocabulary building.

a) **Derivations.** Find in sections A and B of Unit One the words that have the same derivation as the following:

1. terrénus (earthly). 2. vívere (to live). 3. indulgére (to pardon). 4. scire (to know). 5. prudens (prudent). 6. bene (well). 7. vivus (living). 8. terréna (earthly things). 9. dilígere (to love). 10. sequi (to follow). 11. stare (to stand). 12. ínnocens (innocent). 13. volo (I wish). 14. témperans (temperate). 15. arrogánter (arrogantly).

b) Note the relation between the following Latin and English words.

Latin	English
aqua	aqueous
ánima	animation
vita	vital
terra	territory
via	viaduct
terra	terrestrial
aqua	aquarium

c) Observe the relation of

these adjectives to	*these nouns*
terrénus (earthly)	terra
vitális (vital)	vita
animósus (high-spirited)	ánima
ínnocens (innocent)	innocéntia
prudens (prudent)	prudéntia

d) Note the relation of

these verbs to	*these nouns*
indulgére (to forgive)	indulgéntia
abundáre (to abound)	abundántia
scire (to know)	sciéntia
perseveráre (to persevere)	perseverántia

Glória in excélsis Deo. *Glory to God in the highest.*

Vocabulary

servus, -i, m., *servant, slave*
Deus, -i, m., *God*
apóstolus, -i, m., *apostle*
inimícus, -i, m., *enemy*
fílius, -ii or -i, m., *son*
regnum, -i, n., *kingdom, reign*
caelum,[1] -i, n., *heaven, sky*
princípium, -i, n., *beginning*
glória, -ae, f., *glory*
bonus, bona, bonum, *good, kind*
beátus, beáta, beátum, *blessed*
sanctus, sancta, sanctum, *holy, saintly* (as a noun, *saint*)
esse, *to be*
posse, *to be able, can*
semper (adv.), *always, ever*

4. **Second declension.** All nouns that end in -i in the genitive singular belong to the second declension. Those that end in -us, -er, or -ir in the nominative singular are masculine. Those that end in -um are neuter. In this declension the following case endings are added to the base:

---

[1] The plural is usually caeli.

6

	Singular		Plural	
	Masculine	*Neuter*	*Masculine*	*Neuter*
Nom.	-us (-er, -ir)	-um	-i	-a
Gen.	-i	-i	-orum	-orum
Dat.	-o	-o	-is	-is
Acc.	-um	-um	-os	-a
Abl.	-o	-o	-is	-is

	Singular		Plural	
Nom.	servus	regnum	servi	regna
Gen.	servi	regni	servórum	regnórum
Dat.	servo	regno	servis	regnis
Acc.	servum	regnum	servos	regna
Abl.	servo	regno	servis	regnis

Singular

Nom.	servus bonus	regnum bonum
Gen.	servi boni	regni boni
Dat.	servo bono	regno bono
Acc.	servum bonum	regnum bonum
Abl.	servo bono	regno bono

Plural

Nom.	servi boni	regna bona
Gen.	servórum bonórum	regnórum bonórum
Dat.	servis bonis	regnis bonis
Acc.	servos bonos	regna bona
Abl.	servis bonis	regnis bonis

Note that the adjective has a different form for each gender: **bonus** (masculine), **bona** (feminine), **bonum** (neuter). The feminine form is declined according to the first declension; the masculine and neuter are declined according to the second declension.

5. **Conjugation of verbs.** To conjugate a verb means to give all its forms (persons, tenses, moods, etc.) in their proper order.

Present Indicative of

	esse, *to be*	posse, *to be able*
(ego)	sum, *I am*	possum, *I am able, I can*
(tu)	es, *thou art*	potes, *thou art able, thou canst*
(is, ea, id)	est, *he (she, it) is*	potest, *he (she, it) is able, he can*
(nos)	sumus, *we are*	póssumus, *we are able, we can*
(vos)	estis, *you are*	potéstis, *you are able, you can*
(ei, *m.*, eae, *f.*, ea, *n.*)	sunt, *they are*	possunt, *they are able, they can*

NOTE. Since in Latin the form of the verb changes for each person, the subject pronouns are not necessary. They may be and usually are omitted.

EXERCISES

A. Cognates. Many Latin adjectives ending in -ius and nouns ending in -ium, end in -y in English. Pronounce and give the meaning of:

1. anniversárius. 2. voluntárius. 3. necessárius. 4. legionárius. 5. contrárius. 6. mystérium. 7. remédium. 8. testimónium. 9. stúdium. 10. collóquium. 11. subsídium. 12. augúrium. 13. matrimónium. 14. seminárium.

B. Read the Latin and give the meaning in English.

1. Servus bonus est.[1] 2. Fílii boni esse possunt. 3. Sanctis apóstolis. 4. Beátae Maríae. 5. Apóstoli sancti sunt. 6. María semper beáta est. 7. Boni semper esse póssumus. 8. Fílius Maríae est. 9. Glóriae caeli. 10. Regna terrae. 11. Ad Dei glóriam. 12. In terra apostolórum sumus. 13. Ad terram sanctam. 14. Lúcia cum servo est. 15. Fílius servis bonus est. 16. María semper bona fíliis est. 17. Terra beáta est. 18. Servi

---

[1] In Latin the usual order of words is: subject, object or predicate complement, verb.

boni esse potéstis. 19. In princípio. 20. Regnum beátum esse potest.
21. Ego sum fílius servi. 22. Semper inimícus regni est. 23. María et
Lúcia beátae sunt. 24. Lúcia semper bona est. 25. Ad terras bonas et
beatas. 26. María cum Lúcia est. 27. Lúcia bona esse potest. 28. Apóstoli sumus. 29. Apóstoli boni esse póssumus. 30. Ad glóriam apostólo-
rum beatórum. 31. Princípium caeli et terrae. 32. Princípium glóriae
sanctórum. 33. Ad glóriam caeli. 34. Caelum regnum sanctórum est.
35. Sancti Dei servi boni sunt.

Unit Two

A. Decline in the singular and plural.

1. regnum beátum. 2. fílius bonus. 3. sanctus apóstolus. 4. servus
bonus.

B. Give the English meaning of:

1. ego sum. 2. potes. 3. esse possum. 4. potéstis. 5. id est. 6. possunt.
7. es. 8. esse potest. 9. vos estis. 10. sumus. 11. sunt. 12. póssumus.

C. Make the adjective in parentheses agree with the noun.

1. (sanctus) apóstoli. 2. terris (sanctus). 3. filiórum (bonus). 4.
(beatus) Maríae. 5. terrae (beatus). 6. servos (bonus). 7. fílium (bonus). 8. regna (beatus). 9. in terram (sanctus). 10. vita (beatus) 11.
viae (sanctus). 12. tubis (bonus). 13. aquas (bonus). 14. ánimae
(beatus). 15. terrárum (sanctus).

D. Vocabulary building.

a) **Derivations.** Find, in sections A and B of Unit One, words that
have the same derivation as the following:

1. fília [1] (daughter). 2. apostólicus (apostolic). 3. dea [2] (goddess).
4. serva (woman servant). 5. caeléstis (heavenly). 6. rex (king). 7.
gloriósus (glorious). 8. regína (queen). 9. principális (perfect). 10

---

[1] Dative and ablative plural, filiábus.
[2] Dative and ablative plural, deábus.

glorificáre (to glorify). 11. sérvitus (servitude, service). 12. annus (year). 13. légio (legion). 14. loqui (to speak). 15. regnáre (to reign). 16. servíre (to serve). 17. amícus (friend). 18. régere (to rule, to govern). 19. bona (good things). 20. sancte (holily). 21. bene (well). 22. beatitúdo (happiness). 23. beáte (happily). 24. sempitérnus (everlasting).

b) Observe the relation between these English and Latin words.

Latin	English	Latin	English
servus	servitude	beátus	beatitude
posse	possible	inimícus	inimical
fílius	affiliate	caelum	celestial
sanctus	sanctuary	fílius	filial
Deus	Deity	annus	annual

c) Observe the relation between

these verbs	and	these nouns	these adjectives	and	these nouns
servíre (to serve)		servus	gloriósus (glorious)		glória
regnáre (to reign)		regnum	apostólicus (apostolic)		apóstolus
sanctificáre (to sanctify)		sánctitas	caeléstis (heavenly)		caelum
glorificáre (to glorify)		glória	anniversárius		annus (year)
			voluntárius		volúntas (will)
			legionárius		légio (legion)

LESSON III

Unit One

Hosánna in excélsis. *Hosanna in the highest.*

Vocabulary

homo, hóminis, m., *man*
virgo, vírginis, f., *virgin, maiden*
calix, cálicis, m., *chalice*
corpus, córporis, n., *body*
cor, cordis, n. (gen. pl., **córdium**), *heart*
auxílium, -ii, n., *help*
magnus, magna, magnum, *big, great*
acer, acris, acre, *sharp, ardent, bitter*
omnis (m. and f.), **omne** (n.), *all, every, every one;* **ómnia,**[1] *all things*
non, *not*
nunc, *now*

6. Third declension. All nouns and adjectives with the genitive singular in -is belong to this declension.

homo (base, **homin-**), m., *man*   **corpus** (base, **corpor-**), n., *body*

	Singular			Plural	
Nom.	homo	corpus	Nom.	hómines	córpora
Gen.	hóminis	córporis	Gen.	hóminum	córporum
Dat.	hómini	córpori	Dat.	homínibus	corpóribus
Acc.	hóminem	corpus	Acc.	hómines	córpora
Abl.	hómine	córpore	Abl.	homínibus	corpóribus

[1] Latin adjectives are frequently used as nouns, especially in the neuter: **bonum,** *something good;* **bona,** *good things;* **caeléstia,** *heavenly things.*

11

Most masculine and feminine nouns belonging to this declension are declined like **homo.**

All neuter nouns and adjectives, no matter what declension they may belong to, always have their nominative and accusative alike and always end in -a in the nominative and accusative plural.

7. Declension of adjectives. All adjectives fall into two main groups, the first group belonging to the -us, -a, -um type (**bonus, bona, bonum**); these are declined according to the first and second declensions. The second group, declined according to the third declension, contains three classes of adjectives:

those that have three forms in the nominative singular, one for each gender:

masc., **acer**   fem., **acris**   neuter, **acre**

those that have two forms in the nominative singular, one for the masculine and feminine, and one for the neuter:

masc. and fem., **omnis**   neuter, **omne**

and those that have one form in the nominative singular for all three genders:

masc., fem., and neuter, **clemens**

Almost all third declension adjectives (as well as some nouns) end in -i in the ablative singular, have -ium in the genitive plural, either -is or -es in the accusative plural of the masculine and feminine, and -ia in the nominative and accusative plural of the neuter.

Examples:

hóminum ómnium, *of all men*
vírgines cleméntes, *merciful virgins*
córpora ómnia, *all bodies*
culpas omnes, *all faults*
córdium cleméntium, *of merciful hearts*

corda cleméntia, *merciful hearts*
in omni córpore, *in every body*

A. Cognates. Many Latin words may be turned into English by dropping the last letter or the last two letters. Pronounce the following and give the English equivalent of each.

1. ángelus. 2. baptísma. 3. altáre. 4. cathólicus. 5. christiánus. 6. consubstantiális. 7. diréctus. 8. holocáustum. 9. hóstia. 10. humánus. 11. hymnus. 12. hyssópus. 13. judiciális. 14. justus. 15. signum. 16. persóna.

B. Read the Latin and give the meaning in English.

1. Ad altáre Dei. 2. Hómines cleméntes. 3. Calix magnus est. 4. Cálices magni in altári sunt. 5. In princípio et nunc et semper. 6. Ad vitam aetérnam. 7. Beátae Maríae semper vírgini. 8. Glória Fílio. 9. Culpa servi non est. 10. Hómines omnes non cleméntes sunt. 11. Flammis ácribus. 12. Omnes sanctos. 13. Auxílium ómnium sanctórum. 14. Glória Dei magna est. 15. Fílii hóminis non sumus. 16. Ex María Vírgine. 17. In caelum. 18. Regnum caeli aetérnum est. 19. Resurréctio córporis. 20. Cor Maríae clemens est. 21. Ómnibus christiánis. 22. In vitam aetérnam. 23. Ego sum resurréctio et vita. 24. Beátae Maríae semper vírginis. 25. In caelis; in terris. 26. Justum est. 27. Homo servis bonus esse potest. 28. María et Lúcia nunc cum fíliis sunt. 29. Culpa filiórum non est. 30. Elevátio cálicis. 31. Virgo non magna est. 32. María et Lúcia magnae sunt. 33. Culpa Maríae non est; culpa Lúciae est. 34. Flammae acres et aetérnae sunt. 35. Omnes cálices non semper magni sunt. 36. In princípio auxílium hóminum magnum est. 37. Aqua nunc in cálice est. 38. Córpora hóminum magna sunt. 39. Cor in córpore est. 40. Omnes hómines boni in corde Dei sunt. 41. Omnes vírgines bonae et cleméntes esse possunt. 42. Bona es, María. 43. Beáta esse potes. 44. Servi boni, cleméntes estis. 45. Nos sumus servi hóminis. 46. Calix magnus non in flammis est. 47. Tu es

homo. 48. Deus aetérnus est. 49. Hómines terrae non aetérni sunt.
50. Ángeli et sancti aetérni sunt.

Unit Two

A. Give the genitive singular and the nominative plural of the
following:

flamma magna	homo bonus	omnis homo
bonum auxílium	corpus omne	sanctus ángelus
vita aetérna	virgo clemens	corpus magnum
beáta María	calix magnus	omnis ángelus
beátus sanctus	sancta virgo	aqua acer

Examples:

Nom. sing.	Gen. sing.	Nom. pl.
bonus homo	**boni hóminis**	**boni hómines**
auxílium magnum	**auxílii magni**	**auxília magna**

B. Decline in the singular and plural:

corpus bonum	via magna	sanctus beátus
beáta virgo	omnis homo	cor bonum
homo magnus	bona vita	omnis fílius

C. Make the adjective in parentheses agree with the noun.

1. (omnis) corpóribus. 2. (beátus) sancti. 3. Deus (clemens). 4. vírgines (bonus). 5. fíliis (magnus). 6. (omnis) corda. 7. córporum
(bonus). 8. hóminum (clemens). 9. flamma (acer). 10. vitam (aetérnus). 11. vias (magnus). 12. ex flamma (acer). 13. cálices (omnis).
14. Deum (bonus). 15. (sanctus) apóstolos. 16. (sanctus) virgínibus.
17. auxílii (bonus). 18. aquas (bonus). 19. regiónes (terrénus). 20.
ánimae (vivus). 21. homo (justus). 22. servos (inimícus). 23. regna
(caeléstis). 24. aquam (clarus). 25. regnum (gloriósus). 26. (unus)
Deum.

D. Vocabulary building.

a) **Derivations.** Find, in sections A and B of Unit One, the words that have the same derivation as the following:

1. angélicus (angelic). 2. judex (judge). 3. juste (justly). 4. humánitas (humanity). 5. justítia (justice). 6. judicáre (to judge). 7. dirígere (to direct). 8. cleménter (mercifully). 9. judícium (judgment). 10. principális (principal). 11. justificáre (to justify). 12. conglorificáre (to glorify). 13. altus (high). 14. omnípotens (omnipotent). 15. cleméntia (clemency). 16. caeléstis (heavenly). 17. terrénus (earthly). 18. regnáre (to reign). 19. corporális (corporal). 20. magnópere (greatly). 21. corpuléntus (fat). 22. signáculus (little seal). 23. sígnifer (standard bearer). 24. insignítus (signed). 25. rectus (right).

b) Observe the relation between these Latin and English words.

Latin	English	Latin	English
homo	homicide	flamma	inflammation
culpa	culprit	corpus	corporal
magnus	magnitude	acer	acerbity
omnis	omnipotent	auxílium	auxiliary
cor	cordial	virgo	virginity
ángelus	angelic	diréctus	direction

c) Observe the relation between

these adverbs and these adjectives		these adjectives and these nouns	
bene (well)	bonus	corporális	corpus
sancte (piously)	sanctus	(corporal)	
juste (justly)	justus	angélicus (angelic)	ángelus
dirécte (directly)	diréctus	altus (high)	altáre
humáne (humanly)	humánus	humánus (human)	homo

LESSON IV

Sanctus, sanctus, sanctus, *Holy holy, holy,*
Dóminus Deus Sábaoth. *Lord God of hosts.*

Vocabulary

monére, *to warn, advise, teach*
habére, *to have, hold, consider*
dare, *to give*
vocáre, to call
salváre, *to save*
intráre, *to enter*
laudáre, *to praise*
pónere, *to set, put*
dúcere, *to lead*
míttere, *to send*
dícere, *to say, speak, tell*
audíre, *to hear*
servíre, *to serve* (takes its personal object in the dative)
imploráre, *to implore*
convértere, *to convert*
excusáre, *to excuse*
liberáre, *to free*
pássio, passiónis, f., *suffering*
sancta sanctórum, n. pl., *holy of holies*
nomen, nóminis, n., *name*
pater, patris, m., *father*
gens, gentis (-ium), f., *nation*
tristis (m. and f.), triste (n.), *sad, sorrowful*
omnípotens (m., f., n.); gen. omnipoténtis, *almighty*
de (prep. with abl.), *from, down from, about, concerning*

8. Verbs. In Latin all verbs, except a few that cannot be classified, may be assembled into four distinct groups or conjugations that are distinguished from each other by the ending of the infinitive. Verbs ending in -are are said to belong to the first conjugation (laudáre, *to praise*). Those ending in -ere and stressed on the next to the last syllable belong to the second conjugation (monére, *to warn*). Those having the infinitive ending in -ere and stressed on the third syllable from the end belong to the third conjugation (dúcere, *to lead*). Those that end in -ire are grouped together as a fourth conjugation (audíre, *to hear*).

The following are the forms of all four conjugations in the present indicative:

Active Voice

I
laudáre, *to praise*

laudo	*I praise*
laudas	*thou praisest*
laudat	*he (she, it) praises*
laudámus	*we praise*
laudátis	*you praise*
laudant	*they praise*

II
monére, *to warn*

móneo	*I warn*
mones	*thou warnest*
monet	*he (she, it) warns*
monémus	*we warn*
monétis	*you warn*
monent	*they warn*

III
dúcere, *to lead*

duco	*I lead*
ducis	*thou leadest*
ducit	*he (she, it) leads*
dúcimus	*we lead*
dúcitis	*you lead*
ducunt	*they lead*

IV
audíre, *to hear*

áudio	*I hear*
audis	*thou hearest*
audit	*he (she, it) hears*
audímus	*we hear*
audítis	*you hear*
áudiunt	*they hear*

Passive Voice

I

laudor	*I am praised*
laudáris [1]	*thou art praised*
laudátur	*he (she, it) is praised*
laudámur	*we are praised*
laudámini	*you are praised*
laudántur	*they are praised*

II

móneor	*I am warned*
monéris	*thou art warned*
monétur	*he (she, it) is warned*
monémur	*we are warned*
monémini	*you are warned*
monéntur	*they are warned*

III

ducor	*I am led*
dúceris	*thou art led*
dúcitur	*he (she, it) is led*
dúcimur	*we are led*
ducímini	*you are led*
ducúntur	*they are led*

IV

áudior	*I am heard*
audíris	*thou art heard*
audítur	*he (she, it) is heard*
audímur	*we are heard*
audímini	*you are heard*
audiúntur	*they are heard*

Note the following:

a) The infinitive ending (-are, etc.) is dropped before adding the personal endings.

b) The distinguishing vowel of the first conjugation is -a, of the second, -e, and of the third and fourth, -i.

c) Most verbs of the first conjugation are regular, that is, they will be conjugated in all moods and tenses like laudáre.

d) All verbs of the third conjugation are partly irregular and this irregularity will occur in the perfect tenses and in the past participle. More will be said of this in later lessons.

e) There are no progressive or emphatic forms in Latin. laudo means *I praise, I do praise, I am praising.*

---

[1] In the present, imperfect, and future, the second person singular of the passive has another form, with the ending -re. Thus: laudáre, monére, dúcere, audíre.

A. Cognates. (a) Many verbs ending in -are in Latin have the ending *-ate* in English. Pronounce the following and give the English equivalent.

1. separáre. 2. eleváre. 3. resuscitáre. 4. supplicáre. 5. venerári (pass. inf.). 6. illumináre. 7. immoláre. 8. liberáre. 9. commemoráre. 10. communicáre. 11. celebráre. 12. cooperáre. 13. creáre. 14. decoráre. 15. cremáre (burn). 16. donáre (give, grant). 17. expiáre. 18. cogitáre (think). 19. congregáre.

b) Many verbs ending in -are or -ere in Latin end in *-e* in English. Pronounce the following and give the English equivalent.

1. observáre. 2. praeparáre. 3. excusáre. 4. imploráre. 5. inclináre. 6. evádere. 7. intercédere. 8. praecédere. 9. praesúmere. 10. absólvere. 11. adoráre. 12. deputáre (appoint). 13. salutáre. 14. consolári. 15. adhaerére. 16. residére.

c) Many verbs become English when the infinitive ending is dropped. What is the English equivalent of?

1. manifestáre. 2. visitáre. 3. commendáre. 4. confirmáre. 5. consideráre. 6. expectáre. 7. honoráre. 8. convértere. 9. descéndere. 10. discérnere. 11. ascéndere. 12. comprehéndere. 13. respondére. 14. formáre. 15. reformáre.

d) Verbs ending in -ficare in Latin have the ending *-fy* in English. Pronounce and give the English for:

1. glorificáre. 2. justificáre. 3. pacificáre. 4. sanctificáre. 5. vivificáre (to bring to life).

B. Read and give the English meaning of the following:

1. Pater fílios in aquam ducit. 2. Fílius a patre non monétur. 3. Sancti ab ómnibus laudántur. 4. Vírginem bonam semper laudámus. 5. Nunc a fíliis audímur. 6. Magnum cálicem in altáre ponit. 7. Deus

pater omnípotens géntium ómnium terrae est. 8. Fílii in nómine patrum dicunt. 9. Servi auxílium inimicórum non implórant. 10. Hómines vírgines in via praecédunt. 11. In omnes regiónes terrae apóstoli mittúntur. 12. Hómines boni et cleméntes inimícos convértunt. 13. Ángeli descéndunt de caelis. 14. Virgo culpas servi excúsat. 15. Virgo tristis a magnis difficultátibus non liberátur. 16. Homo corpus et ánimam habet. 17. Lúcia tubam fílio dat. 18. Servímini a servis bonis. 19. Hómines in terras inimícas intrant. 20. Virgo dicit; patrem vocat. 21. Calix a fílio habétur. 22. In princípio inimíci gentis non monéntur. 23. Omnes servi ab homínibus bonis ducúntur. 24. Pater Maríae nunc dicit: Tu es semper virgo bona et clemens. 25. Auxílium ab ómnibus géntibus implorátur. 26. Cálices in altári a fíliis bonis ponúntur. 27. Nomen servi a María non audítur. 28. Omnes gentes terrae ab apóstolis vocántur. 29. Nómina filiórum a patre non dantur. 30. In princípio servi boni et tristes ab inimícis non liberántur. 31. Omnes culpae servórum a vírgine cleménti excusántur.

1. In nómine Patris et Fílii. 2. Ad altáre Dei. 3. De gente non sancta. 4. Tristis es. 5. Omnípotens Deus. 6. Ad vitam aetérnam. 7. Beáta María semper Vírgo. 8. Ad sancta sanctórum. 9. Ómnium sanctórum. 10. Laudámus, adorámus, glorificámus. 11. Deus Pater omnípotens. 12. Magna glória. 13. Fílius Patris. 14. In glória Dei Patris. 15. In corde. 16. Pater omnípotens. 17. Caeli et terrae. 18. Ex Patre. 19. Deus de Deo. 20. Consubstantiális Patri. 21. Ex María Vírgine. 22. Cum Patre et Fílio adorátur et conglorificátur. 23. Ecclésia sancta, cathólica et apostólica. 24. In remíssionem peccatórum. 25. Expécto resurréctionem. 26. Divínae majestátis. 27. Sancta Trínitas. 28. Passiónis, resurrectiónis et ascensiónis. 29. Ad glóriam nóminis. 30. Laudant ángeli.

Unit Two

A. Decline the following in the singular and plural:

1. nomen sanctum. 2. pater omnípotens. 3. gens tristis.

B. Add the third person singular ending to each of these verbs (first of the active, then of the passive voice), and give the meaning in English.

1. mon _____. 2. separ _____. 3. duc _____.
4. aud _____. 5. convert _____. 6. dic _____.
7. voc _____. 8. hab _____. 9. serv _____.

C. Add the first person plural ending to these verbs (first of the active and then of the passive voice); give the meaning of each form.

1. pon_____. 2. aud_____. 3. observ_____.
4. salv_____. 5. mon_____. 6. comprehend_____.
7. mitt_____. 8. expect_____. 9. liber_____.

D. Change the infinitive in parentheses to the correct form of the verb (first active, then passive voice), and give the meaning of each form.

1. ego (laudáre). 2. is (imploráre). 3. nos (commendáre). 4. ei (evádere). 5. vos (adoráre). 6. tu (dare). 7. ea (monére). 8. ego (habére). 9. id (salváre). 10. nos (honoráre). 11. eae (audíre). 12. vos (servíre).

E. Vocabulary building.

a) Derivations. Find, in sections A and B of Unit One, words that have the same derivation as the following:

1. liber (free). 2. creatúra (creature). 3. excusátio (excuse). 4. supplex (suppliant). 5. venerábilis (venerable). 6. lumen (light). 7. memória (remembrance). 8. opus (work). 9. libértas (liberty). 10. intercéssio (intercession). 11. honor (honor). 12. glória (glory). 13. vivus (living). 14. pax (peace). 15. justítia (justice). 16. mónitum (precept). 17. patriárcha (patriarch). 18. serva (woman servant). 19. sérvitus (service). 20. audítio (hearing). 21. pátria (fatherland). 22. laus (praise). 23. salvus (safe). 24. dictum (word). 25. dux (leader). 26.

exaudíre (to hear). 27. contristáre (to be sorrowful). 28. **donum** (gift). 29. circumdáre (to encompass). 30. declináre (to incline). 31. inhaerére (to adhere to). 32. **datum** (gift). 33. aggregáre (to join, to add to).

b) Observe the relation between these Latin and English words.

Latin	English	Latin	English
monére	admonish	vocáre	vocation
salváre	salvation	intráre	entrance
laudáre	laudatory	dúcere	conductor
pónere	component	míttere	admit
audíre	auditorium	benedícere	benediction
servíre	service	nomen	nomination
pater	paternal	míttere	missive
laudáre	laudable	aggregáre	aggregate

c) Note the relation of

these nouns	to	these verbs	these nouns	to	these verbs
mónitum (precept)		monére	datum (gift)		dare
dictum (word)		dícere	dux (leader)		dúcere
servus (servant)		servíre	elevátio (elevation)		eleváre
lumen (light)		illumináre	creátor (creator)		creáre
separátio (separation)		separáre	descénsus (descent)		descéndere
absolútio (absolution)		absólvere	justítia (justice)		justificáre
sanctificátor (sanctifier)		sanctificáre	honor (honor)		honoráre

LESSON V

Unit One

Per ómnia saécula saeculórum. *World without end.*

Vocabulary

vidére, *to see* (the passive voice also means *to seem*)
audére, *to dare, to venture, to make bold*
clamáre, *to shout, to cry out*
ire, *to go*
introíre (*like* ire), *to enter, to go within*
laváre, *to wash*
manducáre, *to eat*
acceptáre, *to receive, to accept*
lamentáre, *to lament, to weep*
venerári, *to venerate*
respondére, *to answer, to respond*
bíbere, *to drink*
cádere, *to fall*
Dóminus, -i, m., *Lord;* **dóminus,** *master, lord*
orátio, oratiónis, f., *prayer*
juvéntus, juventútis, f., *youth*
pax, pacis, f., *peace*
dolósus, -a, -um, *deceitful*
iníquus, -a, -um, *unjust*
miséricors (m., f., n.); gen., **misericórdis,** *merciful*
quare? *why?*
pro (prep. with abl.), *for, for the sake of, in behalf of*
mecum, *with me*
vobíscum, *with you*

23

9. Personal pronouns.

First Person

Singular	Plural
Nom. ego, *I*	nos, *we*
Gen. mei, *of me, of myself*	nostrum (nostri), *of us, of ourselves*
Dat. mihi, *to me, to myself*	nobis, *to us, to ourselves*
Acc. me, *me, myself*	nos, *us, ourselves*
Abl. me, *by, with me, myself*	nobis, *by, with us, ourselves*

Second Person

Nom. tu, *thou*	vos, *you*
Gen. tui, *of thee, of thyself*	vestrum (vestri), *of you, of yourselves*
Dat. tibi, *to thee, to thyself*	vobis, *to you, to yourselves*
Acc. te, *thee, thyself*	vos, *you, yourselves*
Abl. te, *by, with thee, thyself*	vobis, *by, with you, yourselves*

Third Person

Nom. is [1] (ea, id), *he* (*she, it*)	ei (eae, ea), *they*
Gen. ejus, *of him* (*of her, of it*)	eórum (eárum, eórum), *of them*
Dat. ei, *to him* (*to her, to it*)	eis, *to them*
Acc. eum (eam, id), *him*	eos (eas, ea), *them*
Abl. eo (ea, eo), *by, with him*	eis, *by, with them*

Reflexive of the Third Person

Gen. sui, *of himself, of herself, of itself, of themselves*
Dat. sibi, *to himself, to herself, to itself, to themselves*
Acc. se or sese, *himself, herself, itself, themselves*
Abl. se or sese, *by, with himself, herself, itself, themselves*

---

[1] This form is really the demonstrative pronoun *that*, but is used in Latin to supply the third person of the personal pronoun.

Note. The preposition **cum** is added to the forms **me, te, se, nobis,** and **vobis: mecum, tecum, secum, nobíscum, vobíscum** (*with me,* etc.).

10. Present indicative of **ire,** *to go.*

eo, *I go*	**imus,** *we go*
is, *thou goest*	**itis,** *you go*
it, *he goes*	**eunt,** *they go*

EXERCISES

A. Cognates. Adjectives in -**bilis** have the nominative and accusative neuter in -**e** (sing.) and -**ia** (pl.). They have the ending *-ble* in English. Pronounce the following and give the English equivalent:

1. acceptábilis. 2. ineffábilis. 3 innumerábilis. 4. invisíbilis. 5. venerábilis. 6. visíbilis. 7. nóbilis. 8. miserábilis. 9. terríbilis. 10. lamentábilis. 11. memorábilis. 12. horríbilis. 13. affábilis. 14. incredíbilis. 15. insuperábilis.

B. Read the following and translate into English:

1. Fílii in aquam intráre non audent. 2. Pater nos semper laudat. 3. Mihi tubam magnam dat. 4. Quare eos de inimícis non monétis? 5. Virgo bona et miséricors patrem implórat pro servis trístibus. 6. Eum vidémus; nos vidére non potest. 7. María ei aquam dat et Lúcia eam bibit. 8. Quare tibi nunc dícere non póssumus? 9. Hómines iníqui et dolósi a flammis ácribus non salvántur. 10. Pax in ómnibus géntibus terrae esse potest. 11. Aqua nos lavámus. 12. Fílius tubam habet; nunc mihi eam dat. 13. Omnes inimíci clamant et in aquam cadunt. 14. Pater cum fíliis et virgínibus in habitatiónem íntroit. 15. Se salvant; me salváre non possunt. 16. Nobis sérviunt et nos manducámus. 17. Juvéntus hóminis non semper beáta est. 18. Quare me vocant? Eas non aúdio. 19. Vos in aqua vidétis. 20. Non nobis acceptábilis est. 21. Deus oratiónes juventútis audit. 22. Deus miséricors est; nunc pacem ómnibus géntibus dat. 23. Quare iníqui et dolósi estis? 24. Homo bonus semper pro inimícis implórat. 25. Quare aquam fílio

non das? 26. Aquam bíbere non audémus. 27. Quare non audétis in fines inimicórum introíre? 28. Me lavo; se laudant; te vides; vos salvátis. 29. Nunc aquam do tibi. 30. Quare mihi aquam non das?

1. Dóminus vobíscum. 2. Ad sancta sanctórum. 3. Et in terra pax homínibus. 4. Laudámus te. 5. Adorámus te. 6. Glorificámus te. 7. Fílius Patris. 8. In glória Dei Patris. 9. Glória tibi, Dómine. 10. Visibílium omnium et invisibílium. 11. Descéndere de caelis. 12. Pro nobis. 13. Ascéndere in caelum. 14. Cum Patre et Fílio adorátur et conglorificátur. 15. Pro ómnibus christiánis. 16. In vitam aetérnam. 17. Pax Dómini. 18. Tecum. 19. Sancto nómini. 20. Ascéndere ad te. 21. In nobis. 22. Dómine sancte,[1] Pater omnípotens, aetérne Deus. 23. In nómine Dómini. 24. Pro se. 25. Pro redemptióne animárum. 26. Ego te absólvo. 27. Pro vobis. 28. Gloriósae ascensiónis. 29. Hóstia sancta. 30. Omnis benedíctio caeléstis. 31. Divína institútio. 32. Audémus dícere. 33. Consecrátio córporis. 34. Pacem do vobis. 35. Ego praesúmo. 36. Cum Deo Patre. 37. Ab inimícis. 38. Pro me. 39. Corpus Dómini. 40. In pace.

UNIT TWO

A. Translate into English.

1. María nos videt. 2. Ei clamant. 3. Aquam tibi do. 4. Nos lavámus. 5. In eam cáditis. 6. Eo vobíscum. 7. Implórant pro nobis. 8. Eunt mecum. 9. Nos ea preparámus. 10. Mihi non acceptábilis. 11. Ea me vísitat. 12. Id nobis dant. 13. Eas mihi das. 14. Ego tibi dico. 15. Nos ea manducámus. 16. Ei eam bibunt. 17. Ego eum honóro. 18. Pacem do vobis. 19. María et Lúcia eis eas mittunt. 20. Eam audítis. 21. In aqua id ponit. 22. Ea non hábeo. 23. Eae te vocant. 24. Pater eum laudat. 25. Nos vos monémus.

---

[1] There are two other cases in Latin besides those already given: the vocative and the locative. The former is used in direct address and usually has the same form as the nominative. Adjectives and nouns of the second declension, however, usually have the ending -e instead of -us. The locative, used in expressions of place, is like either the genitive or the ablative.

B. Give the meaning of these forms of *ire.*

1. ego eo. 2. is it. 3. vos itis. 4. ei eunt. 5. tu is. 6. nos imus. 7. eae eunt. 8. ea it. 9. id it.

C. Give the meaning of these forms of *introíre.*

1. nos introímus. 2. ei introéunt. 3. tu intróis. 4. ego introéo. 5. vos introítis. 6. is intróit. 7. ea intróit. 8. eae introéunt. 9. id intróit.

D. Conjugate in the present tense, active and passive voice:

    vidére   lav
áre

Conjugate in the present tense:

    audére   manducáre   bíbere

E. Decline in the singular and plural:

    orátio bona   homo dolósus

Give the accusative singular of:

Dóminus sanctus	omnis orátio	virgo miséricors
pax iníqua	homo fidélis	juvéntus beáta

F. Vocabulary building.

a) Find, in sections A and B of Unit One, the words that have the same derivation as the following:

1. accípio (to take, to accept). 2. venerári [1] (to venerate). 3. vidére (to see). 4. miser (wretched). 5. accéptus (welcome, agreeable). 6. memoráre (to remember). 7. crédere (to believe). 8. super (over). 9. invisíbilis (invisible). 10. clamor (shout, cry). 11. domnus (sir, master). 12. oráre (to pray). 13. pacificáre (to pacify). 14. iníquitas (iniquity). 15. misericórdia (mercy). 16. miséria (wretchedness). 17. memória (remembrance). 18. súperus (supreme). 19. dómina (mistress). 20. miseréri (to have mercy). 21. exíre (to go out). 22. júvenis

[1] Some Latin passive forms are translated by an English active verb.

(young). 23. aéquus (right, just). 24. dolóse (deceitfully). 25. miserátio (mercy).

b) Observe the relation between these Latin and English words.

Latin	English	Latin	English
cádere	decadent	ire	exit
clamáre	exclamation	vidére	vision
laváre	lavatory	bíbere	bibulous
orátio	oration	juvéntus	rejuvenate
iníquus	equity	dóminus	dominate

c) Note the relation of

these adverbs to	these adjectives
cleménter (mercifully)	clemens
innumerabíliter (innumerably)	innumerábilis
nobíliter (nobly)	nóbilis
miserabíliter (miserably)	miserábilis
incredibíliter (incredibly)	incredíbilis
supplíciter (humbly)	supplex

these verbs to	these nouns and adjectives
pacificáre (to pacify)	pax
oráre (to pray)	orátio
domistári (to rule)	Dóminus
miseréri (to have mercy on)	miséricors
accípere (to receive, to accept)	acceptábilis
crédere (to believe)	incredíbilis

REVIEW LESSON NUMBER I

A. Give the English for these phrases.

1. in caelo et in terra. 2. regnum bonum. 3. in princípio. 4. ex María.
5. in via. 6. vitae sanctórum. 7. Sancta María. 8. sanctis apóstolis.
9. regnum Dei. 10. beátae Mariáe. 11. ego sum. 12. vos estis. 13. cum
Lúcia. 14. benedíctio aquae. 15. in glória Dei. 16. redémptio animárum. 17. beatórum apostolórum. 18. glória Dei. 19. caeli et terrae.
20. cum glória.

B. What Latin words do the following remind you of?

gloriósus, regnáre, caeléstis, terrénus, servíre, vivus, apostólicus,
sánctitas, ascéndere, beatitúdo.

C. Find in the list of English words the meaning of each Latin
word.

et	always	esse	to be
ab	life	apóstolus	protection
semper	man	protéctio	majesty
homo	and	Deus	apostle
vita	from	majéstas	God
salvátio	heaven	magnus	help
ex	salvation	cor	chalice
caelum	servant	calix	great
cum	out of	corpus	heart
servus	with	auxílium	body
princípium	flame	fílius	holy
inimícus	all	sanctus	everlasting
omnis	beginning	nunc	glory
flamma	way	aetérnus	son
via	enemy	glória	now

virgo	merciful	culpa	remedy
regnum	blessed	ánima	to
posse	virgin	ad	fault
beátus	to be able	terra	soul
clemens	kingdom	remédium	land

D. Translate the following into English.

1. Virgo clemens est. 2. Sancti beáti sunt. 3. Sancti non sumus. 4. Ego non sum apóstolus. 5. Cor in córpore est. 6. Possunt esse sancti. 7. Possum esse apóstolus. 8. Hómines possunt boni esse. 9. Potéstis esse boni. 10. Fílius cum servo esse potest. 11. Nos in terra sumus. 12. Vos apóstoli potéstis esse. 13. Ego non sum inimícus Dei. 14. Tu es fílius bonus. 15. Is potest esse in via.

E. Translate these phrases into English.

1. Salvátio hóminum.
2. Corpus hóminis.
3. Fílius servi.
4. Fílii Dei.
5. Princípium terrae.
6. Ex corde.
7. In terra.
8. Ad terram.
9. A terra.
10. In princípio.
11. Ab homínibus.
12. In caelo.
13. Cum sanctis.
14. Ex córpore.
15. Ab apóstolis.
16. Ad Maríam.
17. Cum inimícis.
18. Ad caelum.
19. In caelum.
20. In regno Dei.
21. Ad regnum caelórum.
22. Ab inimícis Dei.
23. Cum bonis homínibus.
24. Ad Dei cleméntis servos.
25. Ab ómnibus apóstolis.
26. Cum Dei servis.
27. In glória sanctórum.
28. Sancti in regno Dei.
29. Ad terram bonam.
30. Cum sanctis apóstolis.

F. Give the meanings of these words.

semper	virgo	audíre	régio	dare
dúcere	nunc	gens	ángelus	de
nomen	esse	ab	dígnitas	posse

G. Give the meaning of each of these verb forms.

1. laudáris. 2. eunt. 3. estis. 4. habet. 5. élevat. 6. ducit. 7. intróit. 8. imus. 9. audiúntur. 10. dico. 11. potes. 12. do. 13. adorámus. 14. conglorificátur. 15. ponunt.

LESSON VI

UNIT ONE

Credo in unum Deum. *I believe in one God.*

Vocabulary

laetificáre, *to give joy to*
judicáre, *to judge*
afflígere, *to afflict*
erúere, *to deliver*
incédere, *to go, walk*
speráre, *to hope*
causa, -ae, f., *cause*
fortitúdo, fortitúdinis, f., *strength*
lux, lucis, f., *light*
véritas, veritátis, f., *truth*
mons, montis (-ium), m., *hill, mountain*
saéculum, i, n., *time, age, world;* in saécula saeculórum, per ómnia saécula saeculórum, *world without end;* a saéculo, *from the beginning.*
sicut (sícuti), adv., *as, just as*
per (prep. with acc.), *through, by*
quia, quóniam, conj., *for, because, that*
meus, -a, -um, *my, mine*
tuus, -a, -um, *thy, thine; your, yours* (sing.)
suus, -a, -um, *his, her, hers, its, their, theirs*
noster,[1] nostra, nostrum, *our, ours*

---

[1] In noster the -e is retained only in the nominative singular masculine. Vester is declined like noster.

vester, vestra, vestrum, *your, yours* (pl.)
qui, *who* (relative)

11. **The imperfect tense.** This is formed by adding the following personal endings to the base:

Active		Passive	
Singular	Plural	Singular	Plural
-bam	-bámus	-bar	-bámur
-bas	-bátis	-báris	-bámini
-bat	-bant	-bátur	-bántur

Thus for the first conjugation we have the following:

Active

Singular		Plural	
laudá-bam,	*I praised*	lauda-bámus,	*we praised*
laudá-bas,	*thou praisedst*	lauda-bátis,	*you praised*
laudá-bat,	*he praised*	laudá-bant,	*they praised*

Passive

Singular		Plural	
laudá-bar,	*I was praised*	lauda-bámur,	*we were praised*
lauda-báris,	*thou wast praised*	lauda-bámini,	*you were praised*
lauda-bátur,	*he was praised*	lauda-bántur,	*they were praised*

For the other conjugations the imperfect tense is formed in a similar manner. Thus we have:

moné-bam,	*I warned*	monébar,	*I was warned*
ducé-bam,	*I led*	ducé-bar,	*I was led*
audié-bam,	*I heard*	audié-bar,	*I was heard*

NOTE. Since there are no progressive tenses in Latin, **laudábam** means *I praised* or *I was praising*.

12. **The imperative.** The common imperative forms are two in number: a singular form corresponding to the pronoun **tu**, and a plural form corresponding to **vos**.

I	II
(laudáre, *to praise*)	(monére, *to warn*)
lauda, *praise (thou)*	mone, *warn (thou)*
laudáte, *praise (ye, you)*	monéte, *warn (ye, you)*

III	IV
(dúcere, *to lead*)	(audíre, *to hear*)
duc, duce, *lead (thou)*	audi, *hear (thou)*
dúcite, *lead (ye, you)*	audíte, *hear (ye, you)*

13. The irregular verbs esse, posse, ire.

Imperfect

(esse, *to be*)	(posse, *to be able*)	(ire, *to go*)
eram, *I was*	póteram, *I was able*	ibam, *I went*
eras, *thou wast*	póteras, *thou wast able*	ibas, *thou wentest*
erat, *he was*	póterat, *he was able*	ibat, *he went*
erámus, *we were*	poterámus, *we were able*	ibámus, *we went*
erátis, *you were*	poterátis, *you were able*	ibátis, *you went*
erant, *they were*	póterant, *they were able*	ibant, *they went*

Imperative

es,[1] *be (thou)*	(posse has no imperative)	i, *go (thou)*
este,[2] *be (ye, you)*		ite, *go (ye, you)*

EXERCISES

A. Cognates. Many Latin words become English when the last letter or the last two letters are dropped.

1. mortális. 2. orthodóxus. 3. patriárcha. 4. patrónus. 5. pontificális. 6. prophéta. 7. sacerdotális. 8. sacraméntum. 9. spíritus. 10. strictus.

---

[1] The form esto is more usual.
[2] The form estote is sometimes used instead of este.

11. temporális. 12. testaméntum. 13. apostólicus. 14. archángelus. 15. firmaméntum. 16. méritum. 17. Christus. 18. eléctus. 19. praecéptum. 20. singuláris.

B. Read the Latin and give the meaning in English.

1. Non est culpa mea; est culpa ejus. 2. Pater suus ei dat tubam magnam. 3. Júdicant inimícos suos. 4. Mérita nostra consíderat quóniam justus est. 5. Fílii nostri in monte incédunt. 6. In habitatióne nostra lucem non habémus. 7. Date virgínibus auxílium vestrum. 8. Fortitúdo sua magna est, quia causa sua bona est. 9. Dic semper veritátem. 10. Servi nostri ibant ad montes nobíscum. 11. Vírgines miserábiles ab calamitátibus suis eruebántur. 12. Homo dolósus et iníquus non laetíficat nos. 13. Pater tristis erat quia ab fíliis suis affligebátur. 14. Duc eos ad montem. 15. Audíte, fílii. 16. Lauda patrem tuum quóniam bonus et clemens est. 17. Prophéta genti dicébat. 18. Calix in altáre ponebátur. 19. Nomen suum María erat. 20. Nos vidére non póterant. 21. Beátus erat quóniam bonus erat. 22. A flammis ácribus eruebántur. 23. Servi lucem in monte vidébant. 24. Sperabámus in fortitúdine hóminum bonórum. 25. Quare non dícitis semper veritátem? 26. Vírgines sperábant in fortitúdine patrum suórum. 27. Servi nostri manducábant et bibébant. 28. Apóstoli sancti pacem et lucem et veritátem géntibus miserabílibus ducébant. 29. Quare servi ejus ad montes mittebántur? 30. Fortitúdo mea non magna est. 31. Per vias miserábiles ad montes magnas ducebámur. 32. Quare sperábas in causa hóminis iníqui et dolósi? 33. Ab inimícis nostris judicabámur. 34. Aquam bonam in móntibus non vidébam. 35. Sicut erat in terris sanctis.

1. Ad Deum qui laetíficat juventútem meam. 2. Júdica me, Deus, et discérne causam meam de gente non sancta. 3. Ab hómine iníquo et dolóso érue me. 4. Quia tu es, Deus, fortitúdo mea. 5. Quare tristis incédo? 6. Afflígit me inimícus. 7. Lucem tuam et veritátem tuam. 8. In montem sanctum tuum. 9. Quare tristis es, ánima mea? 10. Spera

in Deo. 11. Sicut erat in princípio et nunc et semper, et in saécula saeculórum. 12. Omnípotens Deus. 13. Deo omnipoténti. 14. Beáto Michaéli Archángelo. 15. Et tibi, Pater. 16. Mea culpa. 17. Beáta María semper Virgo. 18. Oráre pro me ad Dóminum Deum nostrum. 19. Misericórdia tua. 20. Da nobis. 21. A nobis. 22. Iniquitátes nostrae. 23. Per Christum Dóminum nostrum. 24. Orámus te, Dómine, per mérita sanctórum tuórum. 25. Magna glória tua. 26. Cor meum. 27. In corde tuo. 28. In corde meo. 29. Glória tibi, Dómine. 30. Ómnia saécula. 31. Humanitátis nostrae. 32. Dóminus noster. 33. Per ómnia saécula saeculórum. 34. Divínae majestátis tuae. 35. Per intercessiónem beáti Michaélis Archángeli. 36. Ómnium electórum suórum. 37. Misericórdia tua. 38. Orátio mea. 39. Altáre tuum. 40. Ánima mea et vita mea.

Unit Two

A. Conjugate in the imperfect tense, active voice: **dare; habére; dícere; servíre.**

Conjugate in the imperfect tense, passive voice: **salváre, monére, míttere, audíre.**

B. Give two imperative forms for each of these verbs: **vocáre; dúcere; vidére; audíre; introíre; bíbere; esse; judicáre.**

C. Change the infinitive to the correct form of the imperfect indicative tense.

1. ego (esse). 2. tu (posse). 3. ei (ire). 4. vos (ire). 5. nos (esse). 6. ea (posse). 7. id (esse). 8. ego (ire). 9. ego (posse). 10. is (ire). 11. nos (posse). 12. vos (esse).

D. Change the possessive adjective in parentheses to the correct case, gender, and number.

1. ánimae (meus). 2. terris (suus). 3. via (noster). 4. regno (tuus). 5. fílii (vester). 6. lucem (meus). 7. saéculi (noster). 8. corpus (suus). 9. pátribus (suus). 10. juventúti (tuus). 11. (meus) culpa. 12. montes

(noster). 13. nóminum (vester). 14. servórum (suus). 15. patris (noster).

E. Vocabulary building.

a) **Derivations.** Find, in sections A and B of Unit One, the words that have the same derivation as the following:

1. **exaudíre** (to hear favorably). 2. **benedícere** (to bless). 3. **con-cédere** (to grant). 4. **dedúcere** (to lead). 5. **dispónere** (to dispose, to order). 6. **laetítia** (joy). 7. **judícium** (judgment). 8. **exúere** (to free from). 9. **spes** (hope). 10. **fortis** (strong, valiant). 11. **lucére** (to shine). 12. **verus** (true). 13. **mónitum** (precept). 14. **christiánus** (Christian). 15. **merére** (to be worthy). 16. **mori** (to die). 17. **pátria** (fatherland). 18. **póntifex** (pope, bishop). 19. **pater** (father). 20. **sacérdos** (priest). 21. **sacer** (sacred). 22. **tempus** (time). 23. **apóstolus** (apostle). 24. **sacrifícium** (sacrifice). 25. **sacrosánctus** (most holy). 26. **mors** (death). 27. **elígere** (to elect).

b) Observe the relation between these Latin and English words.

Latin	English	Latin	English
saéculum	secular	véritas	veritable
lux	lucid	fortitúdo	fortify
cáusa	causation	speráre	desperation
incédere	recede	afflígere	affliction
judicáre	judgment	dúcere	reduction

c) Note these verbs with their compounds.

míttere (to send)
- **admíttere**, to send to, to join, to admit
- **commíttere**, to send with or together, to unite, to commit
- **emíttere**, to send out, to emit
- **permíttere**, to send through, to suffer, to permit
- **promíttere**, to send forth, to promise
- **dimíttere**, to send away, to forgive, to dismiss

dúcere (to lead)

- **dedúcere,** to conduct, to deduce
- **edúcere,** to lead out, to bring forth, to educe
- **indúcere,** to lead in, to lead, to induce
- **perdúcere,** to lead to or through, to bring, to prolong
- **addúcere,** to lead to, to bring, to adduce

LESSON VII

In nómine Patris et Fílii et   *In the name of the Father and of the*
Spíritus Sancti. Amen.   *Son and of the Holy Ghost. Amen.*

Vocabulary

cornu, us, n., *horn*
spíritus, us, m., *spirit;* Spíritus Sanctus, *Holy Ghost*
manus, us, f., *hand*
domus,[1] us, f., *house*
cívitas, civitátis, f., *city*
ecclésia, ae, f., *church*
frater, fratris, m., *brother*
laus, laudis, f., *praise*
puer, púeri, m., *boy, servant*
pars, partis (-ium), f., *part*
crux, crucis, f., *cross*
liber, libri, m., *book*
léctio, lectiónis, f., *lesson*
mater, matris, f., *mother*
fortis (m. and f.), forte (n.), *strong, brave*
miser, mísera, míserum, *wretched*
pauper (m., f., n.), gen., páuperis, *poor*
malus, -a, -um, *bad, evil, wicked*
crédere, *to believe*
stare, *to stand*
veníre, *to come*
movére, *to move*

---

[1] See Appendix for irregular declensions.

39

nocére, *to harm*
judicáre, *to judge*
dolósus, -a, -um, *deceitful*
orátio, oratiónis, f., *prayer*
malítia, -ae, f., *wickedness*
sanctus, -i, m., *a holy man*
ergo, *therefore*
ídeo, *therefore*
ígitur, *therefore*

14. **Fourth declension.** All nouns having the genitive singular ending -us belong to this declension. Most of them are masculine.

spíritus (base, spirit-), m., *spirit*

	Singular	Plural
Nom.	spíritus	spíritus
Gen.	spíritus	spirítuum
Dat.	spirítui	spirítibus
Acc.	spíritum	spíritus
Abl.	spíritu	spirítibus

15. **The future tense.** In the first and second conjugations this is formed by adding the following personal endings:

Active		Passive	
Singular	Plural	Singular	Plural
-bo	-bimus	-bor	-bimur
-bis	-bitis	-beris	-bímini
-bit	-bunt	-bitur	-búntur

Thus for the first conjugation we have the following:

Active

Singular	Plural
laudá-bo, *I shall praise*	laudá-bimus, *we shall praise*
laudá-bis, *thou wilt praise*	laudá-bitis, *you will praise*
laudá-bit, *he will praise*	laudá-bunt, *they will praise*

Passive

laudá-bor, *I shall be praised*   laudá-bimur, *we shall be praised*
laudá-beris, *thou wilt be praised*   lauda-bímini, *you will be praised*
laudá-bitur, *he will be praised*   lauda-búntur, *they will be praised*

For the second conjugation the future tense is formed in a similar manner. Thus we have:

moné-bo, *I shall warn*   moné-bor, *I shall be warned*

In the third and fourth conjugations the future tense is formed by adding the following personal endings to the base:

Active		Passive	
Singular	Plural	Singular	Plural
-am	-émus	-ar	-émur
-es	-étis	-éris	-émini
-et	-ent	-étur	-éntur

Thus for the third conjugation we have the following:

Active

Singular	Plural
dúc-am, *I shall lead*	duc-émus, *we shall lead*
dúc-es	duc-étis
dúc-et	dúc-ent

Passive

duc-ar, *I shall be led*	duc-émur, *we shall be led*
duc-éris	duc-émini
duc-étur	duc-éntur

In the fourth conjugation the future tense is formed in a similar manner. Thus we have:

áudi-am, *I shall hear*   áudi-ar, *I shall be heard*

16. The future tense of esse, posse, and ire.

(esse, *to be*)	(posse, *to be able*)	(ire, *to go*)
ero, *I shall be*	pótero, *I shall be able*	ibo, *I shall go*
eris, *thou shalt be*	póteris, *thou shalt be able*	ibis, *thou shalt go*
erit, *he will be*	póterit, *he will be able*	ibit, *he will go*
érimus, *we shall be*	potérimus, *we shall be able*	íbimus, *we shall go*
éritis, *you will be*	potéritis, *you will be able*	íbitis, *you will go*
erunt, *they will be*	póterunt, *they will be able*	ibunt, *they will go*

EXERCISES

A. Cognates.

a) Many nouns ending in -ia in Latin end in -y in English. Pronounce and give the English for the following:

1. família. 2. glória. 3. memória. 4. miséria. 5. victória. 6. ignomínia.
7. custódia. 8. perfídia.

b) Nouns and adjectives ending in -ens in Latin end in -*ent* in English. Pronounce and give the English for the following:

1. óriens. 2. clemens. 3. parens. 4. ínnocens. 5. omnípotens. 6. cómpetens. 7. praesens.

B. Read and give the English meaning of the following:

1. Omnes hómines in civitátem introíbunt cum tubis et córnibus.
2. Non credémus in inimícum iníquum et dolósum. 3. Mater bona et justa ab fíliis suis semper laudábitur. 4. Ad ecclésiam ibit; Deum laudábit et auxílium ejus supplicábit. 5. Puer ad domum nostram véniet et famíliam suam expectábit. 6. Servi mei páuperes sunt, non mali. 7. Libros non hábeo; ergo lectiónes meas non praeparábo. 8. Manus pars córporis est. 9. Virgo pro frátribus míseris suis intercédet. 10. Ínvoca Dóminum et tibi fortitúdinem, lucem et veritátem dabit. 11. Date servis vestris laudem et bene vobis sérvient. 12. Puer fortis

est; nos salváre póterit. 13. Clamáte; nos áudient. 14. Eum vidébis quóniam cum fratre meo incédet. 15. De cruce non descéndet. 16. Crux magna non movébitur. 17. Vocábor et respondébo. 18. Vírgines stabant cum matre sua. 19. Pater et mater paréntes famíliae sunt. 20. Memóriae juventútis nostrae laetificábunt nos. 21. Vírgines bonae erant; ergo beátae erant. 22. In inimicórum civitátes magnas introíbunt et matres suas et omnes vírgines éruent. 23. Matres servórum semper míserae et páuperes erant. 24. Crux in ecclésia stabit. 25. Hómines mali et dolósi non in lectiónes apostolórum credébant. 26. Púeri páuperes et míseri ad nostram civitátem non vénient. 27. Laudes servórum páuperum Deum laetificábunt. 28. In princípio auxília ad gentes non ducéntur. 29. Non crédimus in libros malos. 30. Pars crucis in ecclésia stat. 31. Fílii boni et fortes erunt; ígitur mater eorum beata erit. 32. Quare míseri estis, servi mei? 33. Páuperes non semper mali sunt; mali non semper páuperes sunt. 34. Fratres nostri, quare estis míseri? 35. Mater bona in ecclesia erit cum ómnibus fíliis suis.

1. Mater mea. 2. Lavábis me. 3. Omnes iniquitátes meas. 4. Spíritus sanctus tuus. 5. Líbera me. 6. Oratióne mea. 7. In manus inimíci. 8. A sanctis ángelis. 9. Vobis dícimus. 10. Descéndet de caelo. 11. Semper cum Dómino érimus. 12. In memoria aetérna erit justus. 13. Lucis aeternae. 14. Salva me. 15. Sum causa tuae viae. 16. Flammis ácribus. 17. Voca me. 18. Frater meus. 19. Dabit tibi Deus. 20. Frater tuus. 21. Dicit ei Martha. 22. In resurrectióne. 23. Ego sum resurréctio et vita. 24. Omnis qui credit in me. 25. Tu es Christus Fílius Dei. 26. Líbera eas. 27. In lucem sanctam. 28. Pro animábus. 29. Cum sanctis tuis. 30. Cum servo tuo. 31. Judicáre saéculum. 32. Ánima ejus.

Unit Two

A. Decline in the singular and plural: **cornu magnum; manus fortis; domus mísera.**

B. Decline in the singular: **Spíritus Sanctus; laus tua; ecclésia cathólica.**

C. Give the nominative, genitive, and dative plural of the following: puer ínnocens; mater pauper; cívitas nóbilis; frater miséricors; liber malus.

D. Vocabulary building.

a) Derivations. Find, in sections A and B of Unit One, words that have the same derivation as the following:

1. audítus (hearing). 2. malum (evil). 3. domínátio (dominion). 4. civis (citizen). 5. laudábilis (praiseworthy). 6. párticeps (partaker). 7. crucifíxus (crucified). 8. fortitúdo (strength). 9. miséria (wretchedness). 10. dóminus (lord, master). 11. laudáre (to praise). 12. malítia (malice). 13. advéntus (coming, advent). 14. credíbilis (credible). 15. circumstáre (to stand around, to be present). 16. fámulus (servant). 17. glorificáre (to glorify). 18. memoráre (to remember). 19. victus (conquered). 20. ignoráre (to be ignorant). 21. custos (guard). 22. cleménter (mercifully). 23. innocéntia (innocence). 24. custodíre (to guard). 25. male (badly). 26. compétere (to be capable of, to be fit for). 27. nocens (harmful). 28. nocére (to harm). 29. conglorificáre (to glorify).

b) Observe the relation between these Latin and English words.

Latin	English	Latin	English
cornu	cornucopia	manus	manipulate
domus	domicile	laus	laudable
ecclésia	ecclesiastical	crédere	credence
stare	station	veníre	circumvent
movére	remove	pauper	pauperize
malus	malediction	fortis	fortify
crux	crucial	puer	puerile
liber	library	frater	fraternity
cívitas	civic	pars	partial
mater	maternity	manus	maniple

c) Observe these verbs with their compounds.

stare (*to stand*)
- circumstáre, to stand around, to be present, to surround
- praestáre, to stand before, to excel, to accomplish, to bestow
- exstáre, to stand out or forth

pónere (*to put*)
- dispónere, to put in different places, to order, to dispose
- impónere, to put upon, to impose
- expónere, to put out, to expose

esse (*to be*)
- adésse, to be at or near, to be present
- abésse, to be away from, to be absent
- prodésse,[1] to be for, to benefit, to avail

[1] The **d** is omitted in all forms where it would be immediately followed by a consonant.

LESSON VIII

Glória Patri et Fílio et Spirítui Sancto.	*Glory be to the Father and to the Son and to the Holy Ghost.*

Vocabulary

dies, diéi, m. and f., *day;* in novíssimo die, *on the last day*

fides, fídei, f., *faith*

fácies, faciéi, f., *face*

missa, -ae, f., *Mass;* missa est, *the Mass is finished*

panis, panis, m., *bread*

discípulus, -i, m., *pupil, disciple*

tectum, -i, n., *roof*

nox, noctis (-ium), f., *night*

murus, -i, m., *wall*

somnus, -i, m., *sleep*

grátia, -ae, f., *grace, thankfulness*

ágere, *to act, to put in motion;* grátias ágere, *to give thanks*

dormíre, *to sleep*

scríbere, *to write*

docére, *to teach*

peccáre, *to sin*

novus, -a, -um, *new*

aequus, -a, -um, *right*

dignus, -a, -um, *meet, worthy*

potens (m., f., n.), gen., poténtis, *powerful*

ecce (interject.), *behold*

sic (adv.), *so, thus*

hódie (adv.), *today, this day*

46

item (adv.), *also, likewise*
simul (adv.), *together*
sed (conj.), *but;* sed et, *as also*

17. **Fifth declension.** It comprises nouns with the genitive singular ending -ei. They are feminine in gender.[1]

dies (base, di-), *day*			res, f., *thing*		
	Singular	Plural		Singular	Plural
Nom.	dies	dies	Nom.	res	res
Gen.	diéi	diérum	Gen.	rei	rerum
Dat.	diéi	diébus	Dat.	rei	rebus
Acc.	diem	dies	Acc.	rem	res
Abl.	die	diébus	Abl.	re	rebus

18. **Participles.** The participles of the four conjugations are the following:

Present (active)	Past (passive)
laudans, *praising*	laudátus, *praised*
monens, *warning*	mónitus, *warned*
ducens, *leading*	ductus, *led*
áudiens, *hearing*	audítus, *heard*

Future (active)	Gerundive (passive)
laudatúrus, *about to praise*	laudándus, *must be praised*
monitúrus, *about to warn*	monéndus, *must be warned*
ductúrus, *about to lead*	ducéndus, *must be led*
auditúrus, *about to hear*	audiéndus, *must be heard*

NOTE. (a) A participle, like an adjective, agrees with the noun modified or the noun referred to.

b) The present participle is declined according to the third declension: laudans (m., f., n.); gen., laudántis.

---

[1] Exception: dies is sometimes masculine in the singular, always masculine in the plural.

c) The rest are declined in the first and second declensions: laudátus, laudáta, laudátum.

d) The gerundive is used to express necessity or obligation.

Examples:

Present: Puerum fratrem laudán-   *I heard the boy praising his*
tem audiébam.   *brother.*

Ad civitátem servos du-   *They came to the city leading the*
céntes veniébant.   *slaves.*

Past: A matre sua vocáti, fílii in   *Having been called by their*
domum introíbant.   *mother, the sons went into the*
                                   house.

Vírgines afflíctas pacificá-   *They will pacify the afflicted*
bunt.   *maidens.*

Future: Ad montem itúri sunt.[1]   *They are about to go to the hill.*
Nos monitúrus erat.   *He was about to warn us.*

Gerundive: Domus nostrae sal-   *Our homes must be saved.*
vándae sunt.[2]

Libri movéndi erant.   *The books had to be moved.*

19. Participles of esse, posse, and ire.

(esse, *to be*)   (posse, *to be able*)

Future: futúrus, *about to be*   Present: potens (used as an adjective), *powerful*

(ire, *to go*)

Present: iens (eúntis), *going*

Future: itúrus, *about to go*

[1] This form is also referred to as the active periphrastic.
[2] This form is sometimes called the passive periphrastic.

LATIN GRAMMAR

A. Cognates. Many Latin adjectives ending in -us and -osus become -ous in English. Pronounce and give the English for the following:

1. copiósus. 2. gloriósus. 3. laboriósus. 4. religiósus. 5. perniciósus. 6. furiósus. 7. studiósus. 8. invidiósus. 9. injuriósus. 10. insidiósus. 11. ímpius. 12. pius. 13. propítius. 14. treméndus. 15. supérfluus.

B. Verbs with the prefix, a-, ab-, or abs- convey the idea of *from* or *away from*.

1. abésse (to be away, to be absent). 2. abdúcere (to lead away, to abduct). 3. avértere (to turn away, to avert). 4. abstinére (to hold from, to abstain). 5. abstráhere (to draw from, to abstract). 6. amíttere (to send away). 7. abíre (to go away). 8. amovére (to move from). 9. avocáre (to call away from). 10. abrúmpere (to break away from). 11. abstergére (to wipe away). 12. absólvere (to loose from, to absolve).

C. Read and translate into English.

1. Domus muros et tecta habent. 2. Nox pars diéi est. 3. Ad muros civitátis veniebámus. 4. Dignum est nostris mátribus bonis grátias ágere. 5. In somno justórum dórmiunt. 6. In manus tuas libros datúri erámus. 7. Homo potens est, sed Deus omnípotens est. 8. Omnes discípuli lectiónes bonas hódie habébant. 9. Fácies vírginis bona et clemens erat. 10. Sancta Fides nomen civitátis est. 11. Panis manducándus est. 12. Púeri domum mitténdi sunt. 13. Deo grátiae agéndae sunt. 14. Vobis item scribam de ecclésia nova. 15. Mater cum púeris simul salvátur. 16. Audi, dictúrus est. 17. Vírgines nobis servitúrae erant. 18. Frater meus in domum clamans intrat. 19. Ab dómino laudáti servi beáti sunt. 20. Civitátem magna luce illuminátam vidébant. 21. Crédere non póssumus in fidem géntium malárum. 22. Aequum est pro pace intercédere. 23. Calix a flammis salvándus est. 24. Eos in monte stantes vidémus. 25. Eos docébit et non peccábunt.

26. Ecce homo! 27. Omnes libros salvátos a flammis habémus. 28. In monte stans eos júdicat. 29. Crucem magnam a patre suo datam videt puer. 30. Nobis erat dictúrus nomen suum. 31. Fides patrum nostrórum fortis erat. 32. Vírgines fratres suos vocántes audiébam. 33. Nos monitúri erant quia flammas ascendéntes de tecto domus vidébant. 34. Homo pauper et miser erat, sed auxílium non implorábat. 35. Auxílium ad civitátem mitténdum est.

1. Emítte lucem tuam et veritátem tuam. 2. Et introíbo ad altáre Dei, ad Deum qui laetíficat juventútem meam. 3. Tu vivificábis nos. 4. Dómine, exáudi oratiónem meam. 5. Dómine Deus, Rex caeléstis, Deus Pater omnípotens. 6. Cum Sancto Spíritu in glória Dei Patris. 7. Deo grátias. 8. In corde meo. 9. In nómine Patris et Fílii, et Spíritus Sancti. 10. Glória tibi, Dómine. 11. Laus tibi, Christe. 12. Credo in unum Deum. 13. Visibília ómnia, et invisibília. 14. Ómnia saécula. 15. Deus de Deo. 16. Nos hómines. 17. Ventúrus est cum glória. 18. Qui cum Patre et Fílio simul adorátur et conglorificátur. 19. Una, sancta, cathólica, et apostólica ecclésia. 20. Unum baptísma. 21. Exspécto vitam ventúri saéculi. 22. Dóminus vobíscum. 23. Et cum spíritu tuo. 24. Dóminus noster. 25. In spíritu humilitátis. 26. Veni, sanctificátor, omnípotens, aetérne Deus. 27. Misericórdia tua. 28. Lavábo manus meas. 29. Domus tuae. 30. Cum ímpiis. 31. Ánima mea. 32. In mánibus iniquitátes sunt. 33. In ecclésiis benedícam te, Dómine. 34. In honórem beátae Maríae semper Vírginis. 35. Pro nobis intercédere. 36. De mánibus tuis. 37. Ad laudem et glóriam nóminis sui. 38. Ecclésiae suae sanctae. 39. Dignum et justum est. 40. Cathólicae et apostólicae fidéi. 41. Pater noster, qui es in caelis. 42. Panem nostrum da nobis hódie. 43. Elevátio mánuum meárum. 44. Dórmiunt in somno pacis. 45. Omni benedictióne caelésti et grátia. 46. Ite, missa est.

UNIT TWO

A. Decline in the singular and plural: **dies gloriósus; fácies tristis.**

B. Give the four participles of the following:

1. dare. 2. dícere. 3. servíre. 4. habére. 5. speráre. 6. monére. 7. audíre. 8. addúcere. 9. exaudíre. 10. indúcere. 11. dormíre. 12. laváre.

C. Vocabulary building.

a) **Derivations.** Find, in sections A and B of Unit One, the words that have the same derivation as the following:

1. scriptúra (writing, Scripture). 2. peccátor (sinner). 3. novíssimus (newest, last). 4. indígnus (unworthy). 5. iníquus (unjust). 6. omnípotens (almighty). 7. peccátum (sin). 8. doctrína (doctrine). 9. fidélis (faithful). 10. dormítio (sleep). 11. gratus (gracious). 12. dignári (to vouchsafe, to grant). 13. pie (mercifully). 14. propitiátio (merciful forgiveness). 15. píetas (piety). 16. trémere (to tremble). 17. convértere (to turn, to convert). 18. propitiábilis (propitious). 19. tremor (fear). 20. tenére (to hold). 21. propitiáre (to be merciful). 22. adscríptus (approved). 23. aequálitas (equality). 24. innováre (to renew). 25. gratis (without recompense). 26. digne (worthily).

b) Observe these Latin and English words and their similarities.

Latin	English	Latin	English
discípulus	discipline	nox	nocturnal
dormíre	dormitory	somnus	somnolent
murus	mural	fácies	facial
ágere	agent	fides	fidelity
scríbere	inscription	docére	docile
peccáre	impeccable	dignus	dignitary
aéquus	equality	novus	renovate
potens	potential	servíre	servitude

c) Observe these verbs with their compounds.

ire, to go
- introíre, to go within, to enter
- praeíre, to go before
- redíre, to go back, to return
- transíre, to go through

veníre, to come
- adveníre, to come (to)
- inveníre, to come upon, to find
- perveníre, to come through, to attain
- praeveníre, to come before, to prevent
- proveníre, to come for
- subveníre, to come under, to come up to, to assist

LESSON IX

Unit One

Dóminus vobíscum. *The Lord be with you.*
Et cum spíritu tuo. *And with thy spirit.*

Vocabulary

repéllere (répuli, repúlsus), *to cast from, to repel*
conturbáre, *to disturb*
osténdere (osténdi, osténsus), *to show*
sedére (sedi, sessus), *to sit*
tóllere (sústuli, sublátus), *to take away*
mundáre, *to cleanse*
salutáre, salutáris, n. (noun), *health, salvation*
salutáris, -e, adj., *saving, salutary*
vultus, vultus, m., *countenance*
cogitátio, cogitatiónis, f., *thought*
verbum, -i, n., *word*
opus, óperis, n., *deed, work*
indulgéntia, -ae, f., *pardon, forgiveness*
plebs, plebis, f., *people*
mens, mentis, f., *mind*
volúntas, voluntátis, f., *will*
adjutórium, adjutórii, n., *help*
agnus, -i, m., *lamb*
mundus, -i, m., *world*
deprecátio, deprecatiónis, f., *prayer*
spes, spei, f., *hope*
dexter, dextra (déxtera), dextrum (déxterum), *right, right hand*

53

solus, -a, -um, *only, alone, sole*
excélsus, -a, -um, *high;* in excélsis, *in the highest*
hic, *here*
nimis, *exceedingly*
dum (conj.), *while, when, until*

20. The perfect tense. In the active voice this tense is formed by the following personal endings added to the perfect stem of the verb:

Singular	Plural
-i	-imus
-ísti	-ístis
-it	-érunt

Thus for the first conjugation we have the following:

Singular	Plural
laudáv-i, *I have praised*	laudáv-imus, *we have praised*
laudav-ísti	laudav-ístis
laudáv-it	laudav-érunt

In the passive voice the perfect tense is formed by adding the present tense of the verb **esse** to the past participle. Thus we have:

Singular	Plural
laudátus sum, *I have been praised*	laudáti sumus, *we have been praised*
laudátus es	laudáti estis
laudátus est	laudáti sunt

In the other conjugations the perfect tense is formed in a similar manner. Thus we have:

Active	Passive
mónu-i, *I have warned*	mónitus sum, *I have been warned*
dux-i, *I have led*	dúctus sum, *I have been led*
audív-i, *I have heard*	audítus sum, *I have been heard*

21. Perfect tense of **esse, posse,** and **ire.**

(esse, *to be*)   (posse, *to be able*)   (ire, *to go*)

fui, *I have been*   **pótui,** *I have been able*   **ivi (ii),** *I have gone*

NOTE. (a) All other perfect tenses (the pluperfect and future perfect indicative and the perfect and pluperfect subjunctive) are formed on the perfect stems as given above. Only the endings will differ. For these tenses, see the Appendix.

b) Many verbs are irregular in the perfect. But, if the first person singular of the perfect is known, all other forms of the perfect active tenses can be formed on the stem of this one.

c) Past participles are frequently irregular. Hereafter, whenever verbs are given in the vocabularies the first person singular of the perfect and the past participle of all irregular verbs will be given also.

d) The **vi** of the second person singular and plural of first conjugation verbs is frequently dropped: **laudásti** and **laudástis** for **laudavísti** and **laudavístis.**

22. Prepositions.

a) The following prepositions govern the accusative:

ad, *to, toward, near*
ante, *before*
apud, *to, with, in the presence of*
circum, *around*
contra, *against*
inter, *between, among*
intra, *within*
ob, *for, in consideration of*
per, *through, by*
post, *after*
propter, *for, because of*
secúndum, *according to*

supra, *over, above, upon*
trans, *through, across*

b) The following prepositions govern the ablative:

a, ab, *from*
coram, *in the presence of*
cum, *with*
de, *from, down from*
e, ex, *out of*
prae, *before*
pro, *for, through, in behalf of*
sine, *without*

c) In (*in* or *into*), sub (*under*), super (*above*), govern the accusative when they indicate motion towards a place, but govern the ablative when they denote rest in a place.

EXERCISES

A. **Cognates.** Many nouns ending in -io in Latin have the ending -ion in English. They are feminine in Latin. Pronounce the following and give the English equivalent.

1. absolútio. 2. ascénsio. 3. benedíctio. 4. conféssio. 5. congregátio. 6. consecrátio. 7. contágio. 8. damnátio. 9. devótio. 10. dispósitio. 11. elevátio. 12 habitátio. 13. institútio. 14. intercéssio. 15. oblátio. 16. protéctio. 17. pássio. 18. redémptio. 19. régio. 20. remíssio. 21. resurréctio. 22. salvátio. 23. supplicátio. 24. condítio. 25. conversátio.

B. Verbs having the prefix ad- convey the idea of *at, toward, to,* or *against*.

1. adésse (to be at, to be present). 2. addúcere (to lead to). 3. advértere (to turn toward). 4. adíre (to go to). 5. adoráre (to pray to, to adore). 6. admovére (to move to). 7. adjuváre (to help toward). 8. admonére (to warn against, to admonish). 9. addícere (to assent to). 10. adveníre (to come to).

C. Translate into English.

1. Inimícus repelléndus erat. 2. Discípuli nostri ab puéris clamántibus conturbáti sunt. 3. Verba sua nobis ostendérunt fidem suam in causam suam. 4. Virgo ad déxteram matris sola stabat. 5. Cogitátio verbum praecédit. 6. Fortis fuit, quóniam spem et fidem in corde hábuit. 7. Hódie in ecclésia non fuerunt; absunt. 8. Hic sédimus adjutórium vestrum sperántes. 9. Virgo domum mundábat, dum mater ejus dormiébat. 10. Volúntas in mente est. 11. Vultus hóminis conturbátus est, quóniam spíritus ejus miser est. 12. Non dícimus dum manducámus. 13. Pater filio suo agnum dabit. 14. Verba sua laetificavérunt omnes qui audivérunt. 15. Arrogántiam inimicórum nostrórum observávimus. 16. Dícitur: volúntas plebis volúntas Dei est. 17. Eum monuísti, sed non audívit. 18. Quare eos ad montem adduxérunt? 19. Domus nostrae ab mánibus hóminum malórum liberátae sunt. 20. Omnes servi vocáti sunt, sed non respondérunt. 21. Frater meus non dormívit hódie. 22. Mater tua indulgéntiam osténdit tibi. 23. Eos nimis laudávimus, et nobis bene servivérunt. 24. Agnum in altári immolavérunt. 25. Ópera plebis innocéntis Deum laetíficant. 26. Frater tuus non hic fuit. 27. Ea ad matris domum fuit. 28. Auxílium nostrum imploravérunt. 29. Mater ejus introívit dum hic erámus. 30. Verba indulgéntiae sperávit. 31. Ópera sua in terra magna fuérunt. 32. Volúntas Dei volúntas sanctórum est. 33. Cogitatiónes nostrae se osténdunt in vultu. 34. Hic sedérunt dum domum mundabámus. 35. Inimícos suos repulérunt et nunc non conturbántur.

D. 1. Quare me repulísti, et quare tristis incédo, dum afflígit me inimícus? 2. Me deduxérunt et adduxérunt in montem sanctum tuum. 3. Quare contúrbas me? 4. Salutáre vultus mei. 5. Adjutórium nostrum in nómine Dómini. 6. Quia peccávi nimis cogitatióne, verbo, et ópere. 7. Mea culpa, mea culpa, mea máxima culpa. 8. Indulgéntiam, absolutiónem, et remissiónem peccatórum nostrórum. 9. Deus, tu convérsus vivificábis nos. 10. Osténde nobis, Dómine, misericórdiam tuam. 11. Et salutáre tuum da nobis. 12. Ómnia peccáta mea. 13. Glória in excélsis Deo. 14. Et in terra pax homínibus bonae voluntátis. 15. Benedícimus te. 16. Grátias ágimus tibi propter magnam glóriam tuam. 17. Qui tollis peccáta mundi. 18. Deprecatiónem nostram. 19. Qui sedes ad déxteram Patris. 20. Quóniam tu solus sanctus. 21. Tu solus Dóminus. 22. Munda cor meum. 23. Ante ómnia saécula. 24. Qui propter nos hómines. 25. Sub Póntio Piláto. 26. Secúndum Scriptúras. 27. Sedet ad déxteram Patris. 28. Non erit. 29. Per prophétas. 30. In remissiónem peccatórum. 31. Pro innumerabílibus peccátis, et offensiónibus, et negligéntiis meis et pro ómnibus circumstántibus, sed et pro ómnibus fidélibus christiánis. 32. Tecum. 33. In unitáte Spíritus sancti. 34. Bénedic hoc sacrifícium tuo sancto nómini praeparátum. 35. Per intercessiónem beáti Michaélis Archángeli, stantis a dextris altáris.

Unit Two

A. Learn the perfect indicative and the past participle (if irregular) of these partly irregular verbs.

Infinitive	Perfect Indicative	Past Participle
dare	dedi	datus
míttere	misi	missus
pónere	pósui	pósitus
dícere	dixi	dictus
vidére	vidi	visus
bíbere	bibi	bíbitus
cádere	cécidi	casus
afflígere	afflíxi	afflíctus
erúere	érui	érutus
incédere	incéssi	incéssus
crédere	crédidi	créditus
stare	steti	status
veníre	veni	ventus
movére	movi	motus
ágere	egi	actus
scríbere	scripsi	scriptus

docére	docui	doctus
evádere	evási	evásus
respondére	respóndi	respónsus
convértere	convérti	convérsus
descéndere	descéndi	descénsus
discérnere	discrévi	discrétus
súrgere (to arise)	surréxi	surréctus

B. Give the perfect and the past participle

a) of these verbs which are like **pónere:**
    dispónere; impónere

b) of these verbs which are like **míttere:**
admíttere; commíttere; emíttere; permíttere; dimíttere; promíttere

c) of these verbs which are like **dícere:**
    addícere; benedícere

d) of these verbs which are like **dúcere:**
   dedúcere; edúcere; indúcere; perdúcere; addúcere

e) of these verbs which are like **incédere:**
concédere; intercédere; praecédere; procédere; recédere (to go back);
    secédere (to withdraw)

f) of these verbs which are like **veníre:**
adveníre; inveníre; perveníre; praeveníre; proveníre; subveníre

g) of these verbs which are like **convértere, descéndere,** and **dare**
respectively:
   revértere (to go back), avértere; ascéndere; circumdáre

h) of these verbs which are like **súrgere:**
    resúrgere; consúrgere (to rise up)

C. Change the word in parentheses to the right case. The forms
given are all nominative.

 1. inter (ei). 2. coram (Deus). 3. secúndum (Scriptúrae). 4. cum

(agnus). 5. trans (muri). 6. pro (vos). 7. ad (dexter). 8. in (ecclésiae). 9. ab (puer). 10. ex (cívitas). 11. contra (inimícus). 12. sine (spes). 13. cum (laus). 14. per (intercéssio). 15. de (caela). 16. pro (pax). 17. post (is). 18. cum (ego). 19. de (Deus). 20. e (domus). 21. intra (muri). 22. a (flammae). 23. propter (véritas). 24. circum (mons). 25. ante (ómnia saécula). 26. prae (miséria). 27. ob (ópera). 28. sine (ei). 29. inter (nos). 30. contra (tu).

D. Vocabulary building.

a) **Derivations.** Find in sections A, B, and C of Unit One the words that have the same derivation as the following:

1. turba (multitude, crowd). 2. sedes (seat). 3. salus (salvation). 4. cogitáre (to think). 5. indulgére (to forgive, to grant). 6. adjuváre (to aid). 7. deprecári (to beseech). 8. benedíctus (blessed). 9. devótus (devoted). 10. absólvere (to absolve). 11. eleváre (to lift up). 12. habitáre (to dwell). 13. resúrgere (to rise again). 14. ascéndere (to ascend). 15. salváre (to save). 16. salvus (safe). 17. intercédere (to intercede). 18. redímere (to redeem). 19. supplicáre (to beseech). 20. redémptor (redeemer). 21. protégere (to protect). 22. perturbátio (disturbance).

b) Observe the relation between these Latin and English words.

Latin	English	Latin	English
volúntas	volunteer	mundus	mundane
excélsus	excellent	adjutórium	adjutant
mens	mentality	plebs	plebeian
opus	operatic	verbum	verbal
sedére	sedentary	osténdere	ostentation
dexter	dexterity	solus	solitary

c) Note these verbs with their compounds.

dícere (to speak) { addícere, to speak against, to assent to, to doom to, to adjudge
benedícere, to speak well, to bless

vértere (to turn) { **convértere**, to turn together or toward, to convert
avértere, to turn away, to avert

d) Observe the formation of

these adverbs	from	*these adjectives*
negligénter (negligently)		négligens
arrogánter (arrogantly)		árrogans
temperánter (temperately)		témperans
diligénter (diligently)		díligens
innocénter (innocently)		ínnocens
prudénter (prudently)		prudens
abundánter (abundantly)		abúndans
petulánter (petulantly)		pétulans
supplíciter (humbly)		supplex

LESSON X

| Per eúmdem Christum Dóminum nostrum. | *Through the same Christ our Lord.* |

Vocabulary

sólvere (solvi, solútus), *to fulfill, to loose*
súmere (sumpsi, sumptus), *to receive*
tribúere (tríbui, tribútus), *to grant*
valére, *to be worthy, to avail*
nuntiáre, *to announce, to proclaim*
delére (delévi, delétus), *to blot out*
dirígere (diréxi, diréctus), *to direct*
Evangélium, ii, n., *Gospel*
lábium, ii, n., *lip*
dictum, i, n., *word*
delíctum, i, n., *crime, sin*
conspéctus, us, m., *sight*
os, oris, n., *mouth*
óstium, ii, n., *door*
malítia, ae, f., *evil, malice*
malum, i, n., *evil*
verus, -a, -um, *true*
vivus, -a, -um, *living*
salvus, -a, -um, *safe*
sursum (adv.), *upward;* sursum corda, *lift up your hearts*
étiam (adv.), *also*
íterum (adv.), *again*
ac, atque, -que (added to a word), *and*

ut (uti), *that, in order that*
ne, *that not, lest*

23. The present subjunctive. Its forms are as follows:

Active Voice

I	II	III	IV
laudem	móneam	ducam	aúdiam
laudes	móneas	ducas	aúdias
laudet	móneat	ducat	aúdiat
laudémus	moneámus	ducámus	audiámus
laudétis	moneátis	ducátis	audiátis
laudent	móneant	ducant	áudiant

Passive Voice

lauder	monear	ducar	áudiar
laudéris	moneáris	ducáris	audiáris
laudétur	moneátur	ducátur	audiátur
laudémur	moneámur	ducámur	audiámur
laudémini	moneámini	ducámini	audiámini
laudéntur	moneántur	ducántur	audiántur

NOTE. In the present subjunctive the first conjugation is characterized by the vowel e and the rest by the vowel a.

24. Present subjunctive of esse, posse, and ire.

(esse, *to be*)	(posse, *to be able*)	(ire, *to go*)
sim	possim	eam
sis	possis	eas
sit	possit	eat
simus	possímus	eámus
sitis	possítis	eátis
sint	possint	eant

25. Uses of the subjunctive. (a) A common use of the subjunctive is to express a hope, a wish, or a command in the first and third per-

sons if affirmative. We have already learned that the imperative is
used to express a command in the second person singular and plural
when affirmative. If the command is negative, all persons may take
the subjunctive. Negative commands are introduced by the word **ne.**

Let them be warned.	Moneántur.
May we be heard.	Audiámur.
May they be happy.	Beáti sint.
Let us pray.	Orémus.
Let us not stand here.	Ne hic stemus.
Let it not be said.	Ne dicátur.
Do not disturb them.	Ne eos contúrbes.

b) The subjunctive is also used in subordinate clauses introduced
by the conjunction **ut** or **uti** (negative, **ne**) to express purpose.

I shall put the books here in order that he may have them.	Libros hic ponam, ut eos hábeat.
They are coming to the house in order that we may see them.	Ad domum véniunt, ut eas videámus.
He sends them away in order that they may not (lest) disturb us.	Eos dimíttit, ne nos contúrbent.

26. Other ways of expressing purpose.

a) Subjunctive with relative pronoun.

The boys come in order to see the lamb.	Púeri véniunt qui agnum vídeant.

b) Gerundive with the preposition **ad.**

He shouts in order to warn the men.	Clamat ad hómines monéndos.

c) Gerundive with **causa** (*abl.*, for the purpose of).

He comes to give thanks.	Venit gratiárum agendárum causa.

d) With the infinitive.

He shall come again with glory to judge both the living and the dead.	**Et íterum ventúrus est cum glória judicáre vivos et mórtuos.**

A. Many Latin words become English if the last letter or the last two letters are changed to *-e*. Pronounce and give the English for the following:

1. Apocalýpsis. 2. contrítus. 3. creatúra. 4. causa. 5. divínus. 6. futúrus. 7. immaculátus. 8. incarnátus. 9. incénsum. 10. ira. 11. medicína. 12. modus. 13. natúra. 14. obscúrus. 15. offénsio.

B. Con (com) is the commonest of the prefixes. Compounded with verbs it has the meaning of *together* (*with*).

1. **continére** (to hold together, to contain). 2. **conveníre** (to come together, to convene). 3. **condúcere** (to lead together, to conduct). 4. **commíttere** (to send together, to unite, to commit). 5. **convocáre** (to call together, to convoke). 6. **convértere** (to turn together, toward, with, to convert). 7. **compónere** (to put together, to compose). 8. **comprímere** (to press together, to compress). 9. **congregáre** (to gather together, to congregate). 10. **confídere** (to trust with, to confide). 11. **conjuráre** (to swear together, to conjure). 12. **consentíre** (to feel together, to agree).

C. Read and translate into English.

1. Ne intret homo ímpius. 2. Dicta sua nuntiáta sunt, ut audiámus. 3. Ne absint servi dum dóminus in civitáte est. 4. Verba deleántur, ne mater tua vídeat. 5. Quare vírgines non mones, ne in aquam cadant? 6. Non dico, ne júdicer. 7. Vocant, ut eos expectétis. 8. Ne judicétur suis verbis malis, sed opéribus bonis. 9. Deprecatiónes mundi ad caelum ascéndant, ut Deus pacem ad plebem suam mittat. 10. In

domum intróeunt, ut mandúcent et dórmiant. 11. Aquam mihi dant
ad manus meas lavándas. 12. Venit cálicis tolléndi causa. 13. Sedeámus
cum matre nostra. 14. Véniant, ut nos dóceant veritátem. 15. Ne
moveátur crux. 16. Discípuli studiósi sunt, ut laudéntur. 17. Hómines
fortes adjutórium addúcunt, ut cívitas salvétur. 18. Introímus in
ecclésiam ad dicta ejus audiénda. 19. Nos vocat qui osténdat nobis
libros novos. 20. Sedet cogitatiónis scribéndae causa. 21. Dic eis veritátem, ut credant in te. 22. Dírigat nos ad montem. 23. A peccátis suis
solvántur. 24. Lábia pars oris sunt. 25. Ne stent in óstio. 26. Evangélia
homínibus iníquis nuntiáta sunt, sed non audivérunt. 27. Intróeant
íterum in domum ne ab inimícis videántur. 28. Deleántur verba
nostra mala et ópera nostra iníqua. 29. Salvi sint fílii, étiam vírgines.
30. Nos dirigámus Romam, dixérunt. 31. Hic sumus ut géntibus
dicta sancta Evangélii nuntiémus. 32. Malítia inimíci ad gentes bonas
malum magnum addúxit. 33. Váleant ópera sua. 34. Libertátem
tribuámus servis bonis et fórtibus. 35. Credant servi páuperes in verba
dómini sui.

D. 1. Perdúcat te ad vitam aetérnam. 2. Indulgéntiam, absolutiónem
et remissiónem peccatórum nostrórum, tríbuat nobis omnípotens et
miséricors Dóminus. 3. Orémus. 4. Munda cor meum ac lábia mea,
omnípotens Deus, qui lábia Isaíae prophétae mundásti. 5. Ut sanctum
Evangélium tuum digne váleam nuntiáre. 6. Dóminus sit in corde
meo et in lábiis meis, ut digne et competénter annúntiem Evangélium
suum. 7. Sequéntia sancti Evangélii secúndum Lucam. 8. Laus tibi,
Christe. 9. Per evangélica dicta deleántur nostra delícta. 10. Credo in
unum Deum. 11. Deum verum de Deo vero. 12. Deo meo vivo et
vero. 13. Ut in conspéctu divínae majestátis tuae ascéndat. 14. Incénsum ascéndat ad te. 15. Et descéndat super nos miséricordia tua. 16.
Dirigátur, Dómine, orátio mea, sicut incénsum in conspéctu tuo.
17. Pone, Dómine, custódiam ori meo, et óstium circumstántiae lábiis
meis. 18. Ut non declínet cor meum in verba malítiae, ad excusándas
excusatiónes in peccátis. 19. Ut aúdiam. 20. Grátias agámus Dómino
Deo nostro. 21. Sursum corda. 22. Vere dignum et justum est, aequum

et salutáre, nos tibi semper grátias ágere. 23. Ac beáta Séraphim. 24. Confessióne dicéntes. 25. Benedíctus qui venit in nómine Dómini. 26. Hosánna in excélsis. 27. Uti accépta hábeas, et benedícas. 28. Qui nos praecessérunt. 29. Ut indúlgeas. 30. Creas, sanctíficas, vivíficas, benedícis, et praestas nobis. 31. Praecéptis salutáribus móniti. 32. Sanctificétur nomen tuum. 33. Advéniat regnum tuum. 34. Sed líbera nos a malo. 35. Da propítius pacem in diébus nostris. 36. Per ómnia saécula saeculórum. 37. Pax Dómini sit semper vobíscum. 38. Agnus Dei, qui tollis peccáta mundi, dona nobis pacem. 39. Dómine Jesu Christe, qui dixísti apóstolis tuis. 40. Secúndum voluntátem tuam.

Unit Two

A. Give the present active subjunctive of **clamáre, posse**, and **introíre**. Give the present passive subjunctive of **audíre, crédere**, and **habére**.

B. Give the perfect active indicative of **sólvere, súmere**, and **tribúere**. Give the perfect passive indicative of **delére** and **dirígere**.

C. Give the English for:

1. Eant. 2. Intrémus. 3. Ne tríbuat. 4. Ne laudes. 5. Áudiar. 6. Intróeat. 7. Ne ponas. 8. Stet. 9. Adsint. 10. Moneátur. 11. Sit. 12. Prosit. 13. Ne cadámus. 14. Mandúcent. 15. Bibam. 16. Áudeat. 17. Ne vídear. 18. Ne dicátis. 19. Lavémus. 20. Ducátur.

D. Change the infinitive in parentheses to the right form of the present subjunctive.

1. Puérum monémus, ne (cádere). 2. Panem dat nobis, ut (manducáre). 3. Venit, ut domum (mundáre). 4. Íntroit in ecclésiam, ut grátias (ágere). 5. Ábstinet, ne (peccáre). 6. Ad terram novam it, ut plebem (docére). 7. Venímus, ut vos (vidére). 8. Frater eum vocat, ne (movére). 9. Intrant, ut nobis (servíre). 10. Dat cornu fílio, ut bonus (esse).

E. Change the infinitive in parentheses to the right form of the gerundive.

1. Ad dicta (delére). 2. Verbi (dícere) causa. 3. Ad veritátem (nuntiáre). 4. Tubae (dare) causa. 5. Ad fratres suos (salváre). 6. Lucis (vidére) causa. 7. Ad spíritus nostros (laetificáre).

F. Vocabulary building.

a) **Derivations.** What words in sections A, B, C, and D of Unit One have the same derivation as the following?

1. absólvere (to absolve). 2. repósitus (laid up). 3. annuntiáre (to announce). 4. diréctus (direct). 5. evangélicus (of the Gospel). 6. dícere (to say). 7. malus (bad). 8. véritas (truth). 9. vívere (to live). 10. salváre (to save). 11. creáre (to create). 12. divínitas (divinity). 13. salvátio (salvation). 14. creátor (creator). 15. mácula (stain). 16. caro (flesh). 17. natus (born). 18. tenére (to hold). 19. veníre (to come). 20. fidélis (faithful). 21. grex (flock). 22. jusjurándum (oath). 23. ámodo (from henceforth). 24. médicus (physician). 25. erígere (to erect).

b) Observe the relation between these Latin and English words.

Latin	English	Latin	English
sólvere	resolve	súmere	presumption
tribúere	contribute	valére	value
nuntiáre	annunciation	delére	delete
lábium	labial	dictum	dictate
os	oral	malítia	malicious
verus	veritable	vivus	vivid
salvus	salvage	natus	native
grex	gregarious	mácula	immaculate
médicus	medical	creáre	creative
tenére	tenacious	caro	incarnate
dícere	dictate	ecclésia	ecclesiastical

c) Note the formation of

these adverbs	from	*these adjectives*
recte (rightly)		rectus (right)
pure (purely)		purus (pure)
aeque (equally)		aequus (equal)
benígne (favorably)		benígnus (favorable)
digne (worthily)		dignus (worthy)
pie (mercifully)		pius (merciful)
juste (justly)		justus (just)
male (badly)		malus (bad)
vere (truly)		verus (true)
secúre (securely)		secúrus (secure)
divíne (divinely)		divínus (divine)
mire (wonderfully)		mirus (wonderful)
alte (highly, on high)		altus (high)

REVIEW LESSON NUMBER II

A. Translate these imperfect tenses into English.

1. monébam. 2. dabat. 3. vocabántur. 4. habébas. 5. ponebántur.
6. audiebátis. 7. serviébam. 8. vidébat. 9. audiébant. 10. manducabá-
mus. 11. bibébas. 12. ibat. 13. introíbant. 14. erant. 15. potéram. 16. ju-
dicabámini. 17. cadébas. 18. affligebámini.

B. Give the meaning of each of these verb forms.

1. movébit. 2. vénio. 3. stabat. 4. credis. 5. laetificabántur. 6. érue.
7. judicáris. 8. cadébat. 9. afflígit. 10. manducáte. 11. bíbimus. 12. dic.
13. serviéntur. 14. mittunt. 15. ducam. 16. ite. 17. erat. 18. incédo. 19.
sperabámus. 20. lavábo. 21. íntroit. 22. vidétis. 23. clamábant. 24. servié-
mini. 25. ponet.

C. Of what verbs are the following verbs compounds?

1. circumstáre. 2. introíre. 3. indúcere. 4. benedícere. 5. permíttere.
6. dispónere. 7. adésse. 8. adveníre.

D. Give the meaning of each of these words.

1. faciébus. 2. domum. 3. vocáris. 4. vobíscum. 5. fratrem. 6. saécula.
7. fílii. 8. animábus. 9. tibi. 10. sese. 11. cívitas. 12. míserum. 13. introíbo.
14. júdica. 15. ácria. 16. cordi. 17. córporum. 18. terris. 19. visibílium.
20. majestátis. 21. discípulos. 22. puer. 23. crucis. 24. omnipoténtes. 25.
spirítui. 26. incédent. 27. vidébam. 28. móniti. 29. lavábimus. 30. ab-
dúcam. 31. peccátis. 32. sérviens. 33. adorámus. 34. creátur. 35. affligí-
mini. 36. este. 37. duc. 38. docébant. 39. audíte. 40. grátias. 41. ecclésiae.
42. pace. 43. hábeo. 44. credis. 45. stabat. 46. mihi. 47. ejus. 48. nostris.
49. monébimur. 50. eam.

E. Select from column B an adjective that correctly describes a
noun in column A.

A	b	A	B
regno	meis	libri	beátae
Deum	christiánas	púerum	tristis
spíritus	meum	fratris	perniciósi
mánibus	aetérno	vírgini	cleméntis
ecclésias	sancti	ánima	studiósum
orátio	justas	saeculórum	fortes
matrum	nova	hómines	claram
grátias	nostra	dómui	bonae
pars	suae	juventútis	magno
humilitátis	bonárum	lucem	ómnium
habitatiónem	tua	ecclésiam	diffícilis
famíliae	nostram	frátribus	páuperis
discípulo	divínae	léctio	suus
flammis	pio	hóminis	cathólicam
auxília	ácribus	panis	nostris

F. What Latin nouns do these verbs recall?

1. pacificáre. 2. servíre. 3. ascéndere. 4. absólvere. 5. sanctificáre. 6. benedícere. 7. salváre. 8. glorificáre. 9. eleváre.

G. Give

a) Four compounds of **míttere** with their meanings.

b) Three compounds of **dúcere** with their meanings.

c) Four compounds of **veníre** with their meanings.

H. Like what verbs are the following verbs conjugated?

1. benedícere. 2. dispónere. 3. avértere. 4. circumdáre. 5. adésse. 6. praestáre. 7. procédere. 8. ascéndere. 9. transíre. 10. exaudíre.

I. Combine the following word groups to form complete sentences and translate each sentence into English.

1. Hómines fortes	in monte	vírginis bonae
2. Púeri páuperes	mater	dormiébant
3. Ego sum	ad civitátem	missi sunt
4. Fratres mei	a nobis	lavavérunt
5. Servi mali	se	non salvabúntur
6. Domus nostra	in civitáte	in manus tuas
7. Discípuli sui	non hic	est
8. Libros	vobis	fuérunt hódie
9. Cornua	bonos	non habébo
10. Pono	eos	data sunt
11. Pater miser	te	móniti sumus
12. Pax in terra	bonum	vocábimus et véniet
13. Non	a Deo	credunt
14. Púerum	nos	laetíficat
15. Nos	in domum	introívit

J. Give the meaning of the following:

peccábo	docéo	scribam	dórmiam
pecco	docéam	scribo	dormiébam
peccem	docébam	scribébam	dórmio
peccábam	dócui	scripsi	dormívi
peccávi	docébo		

moveátur	créditur	judicábitur	serviebátur
movébitur	credebátur	judicabátur	servítur
motus est	créditus est	judicátus est	servítus est
movebátur	credétur	judicétur	serviátur
movétur	credátur	judicátur	serviétur

dabámini	hábiti estis	amittímini	audiémini
dámini	habebímini	amittémini	audíti estis
démini	habeámini	amittámini	audiámini
dabímini	habémini	amíssi estis	audiebámini
dati estis	habebámini	amittebámini	audímini

stabis	dírigis	delébas	vénias
stas	dirigébas	déleas	veniébas
stetísti	direxísti	delevísti	venísti
stabas	dírigas	delébis	venis
stes	díriges	deles	vénies

LESSON XI

Pax Dómini sit semper vobíscum.	*The peace of the Lord be always with you.*

Vocabulary

regnáre, *to reign*
timére, *to fear, to be afraid*
pérdere (like crédere), *to lose, to destroy, to waste*
muníre, *to defend, to fortify*
sonus, -i, m., *sound*
sanguis, sánguinis, m., *blood*
vinum, -i, n., *wine*
rex, regis, m., *king*
lex, legis, f., *law*
auris, auris (-ium), f., *ear*
pes, pedis, m., *foot*
finis, finis (-ium), m. and f., *end, border*
ignis, ignis (-ium), m., *fire*
cáritas, caritátis, f., *charity, love*
locus, -i, m., *place*
lumen, lúminis, n., *light*
munus, múneris, n., *gift*
óculus, -i, m., *eye*
porta, -ae, f., *gate*
lacus, lacus, m., *lake, pit*
vir, viri, m., *man*
altus, -a, -um, *high*

bene, *well*
autem, *however*
prídie (adv.), *on the day before*

27. **Demonstratives.** These are both pronouns and adjectives.

hic, *this*

Singular	Plural
Nom. hic (haec, hoc)	hi (hae, haec)
Gen. hujus	horum (harum, horum)
Dat. huic	his
Acc. hunc (hanc, hoc)	hos (has, haec)
Abl. hoc (hac, hoc)	his

ille, *that*

Nom. ille (illa, illud)	illi (illae, illa)
Gen. illíus	illórum (illárum, illórum)
Dat. illi	illis
Acc. illum (illam, illud)	illos (illas, illa)
Abl. illo (illa, illo)	illis

iste, *this, that, that of yours*

Nom. iste (ista, istud)   (The plural is regular, like that of
Gen. istíus   ille.)
Dat. isti
Acc. istum (istam, istud)
Abl. isto (ista, isto)

28. **Ipse,** *self.* This pronoun is intensive or emphatic, not reflexive. The plural is regular.

Nom. ipse (ipsa, ipsum), *he himself,* etc.
Gen. ipsíus
Dat. ipsi
Acc. ipsum (ipsam, ipsum)
Abl. ipso (ipsa, ipso)

A. Cognates. Many Latin words become English by changing the last letter or the last two or three letters to *-e*. Pronounce and give the English for the following:

1. paradísus. 2. serénus. 3. replétus. 4. secúrus. 5. purus. 6. solus. 7. suavis (sweet, gentle). 8. sublímis (on high). 9. thronus. 10. virtus (also power). 11. scriptúra (writing). 12. doctrína. 13. disciplína. 14. sacrifícium. 15. offícium (favor, kindness).

B. The prefix **de-** means *from* or *down from* and may also indicate the cessation or removal of the usual idea of the word with which it is compounded.

1. **dedúcere** (to lead from, to deduce). 2. **depónere** (to put down or aside, to deposit). 3. **denuntiáre** (to denounce). 4. **detinére** (to hold from, to detain). 5. **desperáre** (to be without hope, to despair). 6. **despícere** (to look down upon, to despise). 7. **deésse** (to be lacking). 8. **dependére** (to hang from, to depend). 9. **demens** (lack of mind, demented). 10. **deprímere** (to press down, to depress).

C. Translate into English.

1. Vídeo domum magnam in illo monte. 2. Ipse dixit. 3. Venímus ad finem istíus viae. 4. Vitam suam in malítia pérdidit. 5. Venerunt autem prídie, ad nobis múnera danda. 6. Cathólici dedérunt beátae Maríae Vírgini nomen: porta caeli. 7. Credis hoc? 8. Sonum tubárum annuntiántem victóriam hóminum fórtium audíre potúimus. 9. Manus istae supplicántes ad caelum elevátae sunt. 10. Ad hanc civitátem véniunt qui adjutórium nostrum implórent. 11. Dicta tua in aúribus géntium perniciosárum ne perdántur. 12. Ille vir in lacum cécidit. 13. Ipsa scribit bene. 14. Vita hóminis in paradíso pura atque ínnocens erat. 15. Panis et vinum qui in altári sunt, corpus et sanguis Christi sunt. 16. Spe et caritáte munímur, et érimus salvi. 17. Óculi nostri mala hujus mundi vidérunt. 18. Lumen ignis fácies ómnium circumstántium illuminábat. 19. Rex illíus regni bene regnávit. 20. Pedem meum

in illo loco non pósui. 21. Gentes ab légibus regnándae sunt. 22. His homínibus non díximus, qui in óstio expéctant. 23. In nocte portae civitátis ab servis muniebántur. 24. In illa die omnes hómines vocabúntur, ut domus atque famílias suas salvent. 25. Ne tímeas ora impiórum mala nuntiántia. 26. Servis beátis haec múnera a suo rege misericórde data sunt. 27. Rex ipse ópera dírigit et omnes hómines civitátem illam múniunt. 28. In óculis ejus lumen caritátis poterámus vidére. 29. Portae hujus civitátis in illo igne magno pérditae sunt. 30. Rex ille leges bonas dedit nobis. 31. Regnábant bene et istas gentes ímpias non timébant. 32. Hic servus intrat ut múnera regis vírgini ipsi det. 33. Púeri illi hunc cálicem ponébant in altári alto. 34. Prídie loca illa a viris fórtibus deleántur. 35. Óculis nostris vidémus; áuribus nostris audímus.

Unit Two

A. 1. Ex voluntáte Patris. 2. Líbera me per hoc sacrosánctum Corpus et Sánguinem tuum ab ómnibus iniquitátibus meis. 3. Ego indígnus súmere praesúmo. 4. Non mihi provéniat in judícium et condemnatiónem. 5. Dómine, non sum dignus, ut intres sub tectum meum. 6. Corpus Dómini nostri Jesu Christi custódiat ánimam meam in vitam aetérnam. 7. Laudans invocábo Dóminum, et ab inimícis meis salvus ero. 8. Sanguis Dómini nostri Jesu Christi custódiat ánimam meam in vitam aetérnam. 9. Ore súmpsimus. 10. Pura mente. 11. De múnere temporáli. 12. Pura et sancta sacraménta. 13. Deo grátias. 14. Et praesta, ut sacrifícium tibi sit acceptábile. 15. Benedícat vos omnípotens Deus, Pater et Fílius et Spíritus Sanctus. 16. In princípio erat Verbum, et Verbum erat apud Deum, et Deus erat Verbum. 17. Hoc erat in princípio apud Deum. 18. In ipso vita erat, et vita erat lux hóminum. 19. Fuit homo missus a Deo. 20. Hic venit in testimónium, ut omnes créderent per illum. 21. Non erat ille lux. 22. In mundo erat. 23. His qui credunt in nómine ejus. 24. Et habitávit in nobis. 25. Et vídimus glóriam ejus. 26. In die illa treménda. 27. Dies illa, dies irae, calamitátis et misériae. 28. Fidélium ómnium. 29. Léctio libri Apocalýpsis beáti Joánnis Apóstoli. 30. Ópera illórum. 31. Ab auditióne mala non timébit. 32. Absólve, Dómine, ánimas ómnium fidélium. 33. Ego sum panis vivus, qui de caelo descéndi. 34. Ex hoc pane. 35. Pro mundi vita. 36. Dixit ergo eis Jesus. 37. Amen, amen dico vobis. 38. Non habébitis vitam in vobis. 39. Qui bibit meum sánguinem habet vitam aetérnam, et ego resuscitábo eum in novíssimo die. 40. Pro animábus illis.

B. Give the meaning of these phrases.

1. hi viri. 2. horum lácuum. 3. hujus lúminis. 4. hos pedes. 5. hunc sonum. 6. hanc malítiam. 7. hoc sánguine. 8. horum regum. 9. has portas. 10. his áuribus. 11. hanc finem. 12. huic igni. 13. haec múnera 14. horum oculórum. 15. hoc loco.

C. Give the meaning of these phrases.

1. illíus caritátis. 2. illae leges. 3. illud vinum. 4. illa óstia. 5. illórum malórum. 6. illo ore. 7. illis diébus. 8. illíus fídei. 9. illis dictis. 10. illo lábio. 11. illo conspéctu. 12. illa delícta. 13. illa spes. 14. illíus mundi. 15. illum agnum.

UNIT THREE

A. Give the meaning of these phrases.

1. ista múnera. 2. istos reges. 3. istae portae. 4. isti lácui. 5. istas leges. 6. ista cáritas. 7. istíus lúminis. 8. istum óculum. 9. istam spem. 10. isto loco.

B. Vocabulary building.

a) **Derivations.** Find, in Units One and Two, the words that have the same derivation as the following:

1. regnum (kingdom). 2. timor (fear). 3. régere (to govern). 4. audíre (to hear). 5. ánimus (mind). 6. illumináre (to illuminate). 7. virtus (power). 8. altáre (altar). 9. bonus (good). 10. dies (day). 11. pure (purely). 12. replére (to fill). 13. purgáre (to purify). 14. scríbere (to write). 15. docére (to teach). 16. discípulus (disciple).

17. **sacer** (sacred). 18. **sacérdos** (priest). 19. **dux** (leader). 20. **spes** (hope). 21. **ígnitus** (burning). 22. **praesúmere** (to presume). 23. **deposítio** (burial).

b) Observe the relation between these Latin and English words.

Latin	English	Latin	English
timére	timidity	muníre	munitions
sonus	resonant	sanguis	sanguine
vinum	vintage	lex	legislature
pes	pedestal	ignis	ignition
locus	location	lumen·	illumination
porta	portal	vinum	vineyard
vir	virile	altus	altitude
óculus	occulist	munus	munificent

c) Observe the relation of

these verbs	to	these nouns

adjuváre (to help) — adjutórium (help)

adunáre (to unite) — únitas (unity)

aestimáre (to esteem) — aestimátor (one who esteems)

aggregáre (to add to) — grex (flock)

amáre (to love) — amátor (lover)

cogitáre (to think) — cogitátio (thought)

cóndere (to found) — cónditor (founder, creator)

connumeráre (to number amongst) — númerus (number)

discútere (to disperse) — discússio (dispersal)

donáre (to give) — donum (gift)

dormíre (to sleep) — dormítio (sleep)

LESSON XII

Sanctificétur nomen tuum. *Hallowed be Thy name.*

Vocabulary

quáerere (quaesívi, quaesítus), *to seek, to ask*
scire, *to know*
apparére, *to appear*
vívere (vixi, victus), *to live*
accéndere (accéndi, accénsus), *to kindle*
factor, factóris, m., *maker*
amor, amóris, m., *love*
vox, vocis, f., *voice*
inítium, -ii, n., *beginning*
multus, -a, -um, *many*
mirus, -a, -um, *wonderful*
unigénitus, -a, -um, *only begotten*
tértius, -a, -um, *third*
defúnctus, -a, -um, *dead*
vespertínus, -a, -um, *evening* (adj.)
totus, -a, -um (gen. totíus), *all, the whole*
si (conj.), *if*
tam (adv.), *so* (modifies adj. or adv.)
num (conj.), *whether*
quis (pron.), *who*
quid (pron.), *what;* (adv.) *why?*
ubi (adv. and conj.), *where*
quot (conj.), *how many*
cum (conj.), *when, since, although*

quantus, -a, -um (adj.), *how much, how great*
tantus, -a, -um (adj.), *so much, so great;* pl. *so many*
quando (adv. and conj.), *when*

29. Imperfect subjunctive. Its forms are as follows:

Active Voice

I	II	III	IV
laudárem	monérem	dúcerem	audírem
laudáres	monéres	dúceres	audíres
laudáret	monéret	dúceret	audíret
laudarémus	monerémus	ducerémus	audirémus
laudarétis	monerétis	ducerétis	audirétis
laudárent	monérent	dúcerent	audírent

Passive Voice

laudárer	monérer	dúcerer	audírer
laudaréris	moneréris	duceréris	audiréris
laudarétur	monerétur	ducerétur	audirétur
laudarémur	monerémur	ducerémur	audirémur
laudarémini	monerémini	ducerémini	audirémini
laudaréntur	moneréntur	duceréntur	audiréntur

30. Imperfect subjunctive of esse, posse, and ire.

(esse, *to be*)	(posse, *to be able*)	(ire, *to go*)
essem	possem	irem
esses	posses	ires
esset	posset	iret
essémus	possémus	irémus
essétis	possétis	irétis
essent	possent	irent

31. Further uses of the subjunctive.

a) Result is expressed by the subjunctive introduced by **ut** (negative ut non).

My brothers were so good that they were praised by my father.	Fratres mei tam boni erant, ut a patre meo laudaréntur.
The men's strength was so great that they were not driven from the city.	Fortitúdo hóminum tanta erat, ut non ex civitáte repelleréntur.

b) An indirect question takes its verb in the subjunctive.

I knew who was coming.	Scivi quis veníret.
He asks whether we have the book.	Quaerit num librum habeámus.
We do not know where she is.	Nescímus ubi sit ea.
He asked how many men you were sending.	Quaerébat quot hómines mitterétis.

c) Cum meaning *since* (*because*) and *although* governs the subjunctive.

Since they were not at home we could not see them.	Cum domi [1] non essent eos vidére non poterámus. (causal clause)
Although they are poor they will not seek help.	Cum paúperes sint, auxílium non quaerent. (concessive clause)

d) Cum meaning *when* regularly takes the subjunctive when the time indicated is past.

When we had given him the bread he sat down to eat it.	Cum ei panem dedissémus (pluperfect subj.), sedit ad eum manducándum.
When Christ was born, Herod was king.	Cum Christus natus esset, Heródes rex erat.

e) Conditional sentences of doubt and conditional sentences contrary to fact require the subjunctive in both clauses.

If your mother should speak we would hear her.	Si mater tua dicat, eam audiámus. (pres. subj. in both clauses to express a future doubt)

[1] Locative case of **domus.**

If he was praising them they would be good.	Si eos laudáret, boni essent. (imp. subj. in both clauses to express an idea contrary to fact at the present moment)
If he had praised them they would have been good.	Si eos laudavísset, boni fuíssent. (pluperfect subj. in both clauses to express an idea contrary to fact in the past)

EXERCISES

A. Cognates. Nouns ending in -tas in Latin have the ending -ty in English. They are all feminine in Latin. Pronounce the following and give the English equivalent.

1. calámitas. 2. cláritas. 3. dígnitas. 4. divínitas. 5. humánitas. 6. humílitas. 7. iníquitas. 8. majéstas. 9. sánctitas. 10. socíetas. 11. Trínitas. 12. únitas. 13. difficúltas. 14. opportúnitas. 15. grávitas. 16. fragílitas. 17. píetas. 18. immortálitas.

B. Verbs compounded with e- or ex- convey the idea of *out of* or *out from.*

1. exíre (to go out of, to exit). 2. edúcere (to lead out of). 3. emíttere (to send out, to emit). 4. exprímere (to press out of, to express). 5. excípere (to take out of, to except). 6. expéllere (to drive out of, to expel). 7. erúmpere (to break out of, to erupt). 8. evocáre (to call out of, to evoke). 9. ejícere (to cast out of, to eject). 10. expónere (to put out or forth, to expose).

C. Read and translate into English.

1. Prídie quaerébat, quare ad civitátem venirémus. 2. Lux in caelo tam mira erat, ut omnes de ea dícerent. 3. Nescímus num hódie domi sint. 4. Si ignem in monte accendátis, flammas videámus. 5. Cum rex in civitáte esset, perfídiam illórum hóminum malórum expósuit. 6. Hic liber non dicit quot portas cívitas hábeat. 7. Mater veniébat ut púeros admonéret. 8. Inimíci ejus tanti sunt, ut ab illis non

salvétur. 9. Hic panis tam bonus est, ut totum manducémus. 10. Cum nobis múnera dent, grátiae agéndae sunt. 11. Si inimícos suos timérent, muri civitátis muniréntur. 12. Sciebámus quid ad lacum addúceret. 13. Quaero quis ad domum Maríae tecum eat. 14. Mater nos vocábat ut vultum et manus nostras lavarémus. 15. Cum veritátem díceres, non in te credébant. 16. Ne repelléntur quoniam ópera sua bona atque pia fuérunt. 17. Óculos meos avertébam ne misérias paúperum vidérem. 18. Nesciunt quando tibi scribat. 19. Frater meus quaerit ubi eámus. 20. Lux magna in ostio domus appáruit. 21. Cum hic víveret, semper beáta erat. 22. Cum vultus suus serénus esset, cor suum conturbátum erat. 23. Si me vocent, eos áudiam. 24. Nesciebámus quantae essent calamitátes eorum. 25. Mens vírginis tam afflícta est, ut clamáre non possit.

Unit Two

A. Translate the following:

1. Credo in unum Deum, Patrem omnipoténtem, factórem caeli et terrae, visibílium ómnium et invisibílium. 2. Et in unum Dóminum Jesum Christum, Fílium Dei unigénitum. 3. Deum de Deo, lumen de lúmine, Deum verum de Deo vero. 4. Et resurréxit tertia die secúndum Scriptúras. 5. Da nobis per hujus aquae et vini mystérium. 6. Qui tecum vivit et regnat in unitáte Spíritus Sancti, Deus, per ómnia saécula saeculórum. 7. Ut in conspéctu divínae majestátis tuae, pro nostra, et totíus mundi salúte cum odóre suavitátis ascéndat. 8. Veni, sanctificátor omnípotens, aetérne Deus, et bénedic hoc sacríficium tuo sancto nómini praeparátum. 9. Incénsum istud a te benedíctum, ascéndat ad te, Dómine; et descéndat super nos misericórdia tua. 10. Dirigátur, Dómine, orátio mea, sicut incénsum in conspéctu tuo; elevátio manuum meárum sacrifícium vespertínum. 11. Accéndat in nobis Dóminus ignem sui amóris, et flammam aetérnae caritátis. 12. Lavábo inter innocéntes manus meas, et circúmdabo altáre tuum, Dómine, ut áudiam vocem laudis. 13. Ne perdas cum ímpiis, Deus, ánimam meam, et cum viris sánguinum vitam meam. 14. Déx-

tera eórum repléta est munéribus. 15. Pes meus stetit in directo; in ecclésiis benedícam te, Dómine. 16. Sursum corda. Habémus ad Dóminum. 17. Grátias agámus Dómino Deo nostro. 18. Caeli, caelorúmque virtútes, ac beata Séraphim exsultátione concélebrant. 19. Hosánna in excélsis. 20. Uti accépta hábeas, et benedícas, haec dona, haec múnera, haec sancta sacrifícia. 21. Pro Ecclésia tua sancta cathólica. 22. Hoc sacrifícium laudis. 23. Pacificáre, custodíre, adunáre, et régere. 24. Pro spe salútis. 25. Ut in ómnibus protectiónis tuae muniámur auxílio. 26. In sanctas ac venerábiles manus suas. 27. Tibi grátias agens. 28. Benedíxit, dedítque discípulis suis. 29. Manducáte ex hoc omnes. 30. Bíbite ex eo omnes.

B. Fill the blanks with the correct ending for the imperfect subjunctive active voice:

1. ego mitte——. 2. is veni——. 3. nos accende——. 4. tu da——. 5. vos appare——. 6. ea sci——. 7. ei regna——. 8. ego poss——. 9. nos i——. 10. id ess——.

C. Fill the blanks with the correct ending for the imperfect subjunctive, passive voice:

1. tu muni——. 2. nos perde——. 3. ego libera——. 4. is dirige——. 5. vos tribue——. 6. ei munda——. 7. ea doce——. 8. ego ostende——. 9. tu vide——. 10. nos muni——.

Unit Three

A. Learn from the Appendix how the future perfect indicative and the perfect subjunctive are formed.

B. Vocabulary building.

a) **Derivations.** Find, in Units One and Two, the words that have the same derivation as the following:

1. **quaésere** (to beseech). 2. **vivus** (living). 3. **fácere** (to make). 4. **amáre** (to love). 5. **vocáre** (to call). 6. **vivificáre** (to bring to life). 7. **amátor** (one who loves). 8. **multitúdo** (multitude). 9. **mirábilis** (wonderful). 10. **génitus** (begotten). 11. **quotiescúmque** (as often as). 12.

mirabília (wonders). 13. génitrix (mother). 14. quasi (as if, like). 15. mirabíliter (wonderfully). 16. quotquot (however many). 17. factum (deed). 18. sócius (together, allied). 19. unus (one). 20. sociáre (to share in). 21. clarus (clear). 22. gravis (heavy, grave). 23. difficilis (difficult). 24. praeclárus (excellent). 25. jácere (to throw).

b) Observe the relation between these Latin and English words.

Latin	English	Latin	English
apparére	apparition	vívere	revive
quaérere	question	scire	science
accéndere	incendiary	amor	amorous
vox	vocal	inítium	initiate
unigénitus	generation	tértius	tertiary
vespertínus	vespers	totus	total
quantus	quantity	mirus	admirable
factor	benefactor	sociáre	association

c) Observe the relation of

these verbs	to	these nouns
scire		sciéntia (knowledge)
vívere		vita
fácere (to make)		factor
amáre (to love)		amor
vocáre		vox

d) Observe the force of the suffix -issimus when added to adjectives.

altus (high)	altíssimus (most high)
diléctus (beloved)	dilectíssimus (most beloved)
purus (pure)	puríssimus (most pure)
clarus (clear)	claríssimus (most clear)
novus (new)	novíssimus (newest, last)
justus (just)	justíssimus (most just)
sanctus (holy)	sanctíssimus (most holy)

READING LESSON

1. Cum ergo natus esset Jesus in Bethlehem Juda in diebus Herodis regis, ecce magi ab Oriente venerunt Jerosolymam,

2. Dicentes: Ubi est qui natus est rex Judaeorum? Vidimus enim stellam ejus in Oriente, et venimus adorare eum.

3. Audiens autem Herodes rex, turbatus est, et omnis Jerosolyma cum illo.

4. Et congregans omnes principes sacerdotum, et scribas populi, sciscitabatur ab eis ubi Christus nasceretur.

5. At illi dixerunt ei: In Bethlehem Judae: Sic enim scriptum est per prophetam:

6. Et tu Bethlehem terra Juda, nequaquam minima es in principibus Juda: ex te enim exiet dux, qui regat populum meum Israel.

7. Tunc Herodes clam vocatis magis, diligenter didicit (*learned*) ab eis tempus stellae, quae apparuit eis.

8. Et mittens illos in Bethlehem, dixit: Ite, et interrogate diligenter de puero: et cum inveneritis, renuntiate mihi, ut et ego veniens adorem eum.

9. Qui cum audissent regem, abierunt. Et ecce stella, quam viderant in Oriente, antecedebat eos, usque dum veniens staret supra, ubi erat puer.

10. Videntes autem stellam gavisi sunt gaudio magno valde.

11. Et intrantes domum, invenerunt puerum cum Maria matre ejus, et procidentes adoraverunt eum: et apertis thesauris suis obtulerunt ei munera, aurum, thus, et myrrham.

12. Et responso accepto in somnis ne redirent ad Herodem, per aliam viam reversi sunt in regionem suam.

13. Qui cum recessissent, ecce angelus Domini apparuit in somnis Joseph dicens: Surge, et accipe puerum, et matrem ejus, et fuge in

Aegyptum, et esto ibi usque dum dicam tibi. Futurum est enim ut Herodes quaerat puerum ad perdendum eum.

14. Qui consurgens accepit puerum, et matrem ejus nocte, et secessit in Aegyptum.

15. Et erat ibi usque ad obitum Herodis; ut adimpleretur quod dictum est a Domino per prophetam dicentem: Ex Aegypto vocavi filium meum.

16. Tunc Herodes videns quoniam illusus esset a magis, iratus est valde, et mittens, occidit omnes pueros qui erant in Bethlehem et in omnibus finibus ejus a bimatu et infra, secundum tempus quod exquisierat a magis.

17. Tunc adimpletum est quod dictum est per Jeremiam prophetam dicentem:

18. Vox in Rama audita est, ploratus et ululatus multus: Rachel plorans filios suos, et noluit consolari, quia non sunt.

19. Defuncto autem Herode, ecce angelus Domini apparuit in somnis Joseph in Aegypto,

20. Dicens: Surge et accipe puerum et matrem ejus, et vade in terram Israel; defuncti sunt enim qui quaerebant animam pueri.

21. Qui consurgens, accepit puerum et matrem ejus, et venit in terram Israel.

22. Audiens autem quod Archelaus regnaret in Judaea pro Herode patre suo, timuit illo ire; et admonitus in somnis, accessit in partes Galilaeae.

23. Et veniens habitavit in civitate quae vocatur Nazareth; ut adimpleretur quod dictum est per prophetas: Quoniam Nazaraeus vocabitur.

(Jesu Christi Evangelium Secundum Matthaeum, caput II, 1–23.)

LESSON XIII

Unit One

Panem nostrum quotidiánum da nobis hódie.　　*Give us this day our daily bread.*

Vocabulary

suávitas, suavitátis, f., *sweetness*
sérvitus, servitútis, f., *service, servitude*
utílitas, utilitátis, f., *benefit, usefulness*
fámulus (f., -a), -i, m., *servant*
ops, opis, f., *help*
mors, mortis, f., *death*
scelus, scéleris, n., *sin, crime*
cunctus, -a, -um, *all*
univérsus, -a, -um, *all*
símilis, m. and f., símile, n., *like;* símili modo, *in like manner*
praeclárus, -a, -um, *excellent*
ínferus, -a, -um, *low;* as a noun, *hell*
quotidiánus, -a, -um, *daily*
praetéritus, -a, -um, *past*
idem, éadem, idem (decline like is, adding -dem to each form), *same*
placére, *to please, to be pleasing to*
frángere (fregi, fractus), *to break*
coenáre, *to eat supper*
effúndere (effúdi, effúsus), *to shed, to pour out*
respícere (respéxi, respéctus), (an -io verb), *to look, look upon*
relínquere (relíqui, relíctus), *to leave behind*
remanére (remánsi, remánsus), *to remain*

89

trémere, *to tremble*
enim (adverbial conj.), *for*
postquam (conj.), *after*
quoque, *also*

32. Third conjugation verbs in -io.

a) These verbs have the following peculiarities:

The indicative and subjunctive forms are like those of fourth conjugation verbs with two exceptions, namely: the second person singular of the present indicative passive and all persons of the imperfect subjunctive; these forms are those of the third conjugation. Thus: fáceris, fácerem.

The ending of the present participle is -iens; of the gerundive, -iendus.

For the complete conjugation of third conjugation -io verbs, see Appendix.

The imperative has the forms of the third conjugation. (But the imperative forms of fácere are fac, fácite.)

b) The commonest of these -io verbs are cápio, fácio, jácio, and their compounds.

cápere (cepi, captus), *to take*
accípere (accépi, accéptus), *to receive, to accept*
concípere (concépi, concéptus), *to conceive*
percípere (percépi, percéptus), *to partake, to attain*
recípere (recépi, recéptus), *to receive*
suscípere (suscépi, suscéptus), *to receive*
praecípere (praecépi, praecéptus), *to instruct*
    fácere (feci, factus), *to make*
profícere (proféci, proféctus), *to avail, to benefit*
refícere (reféci, reféctus), *to refresh*
    jácere (jeci, jactus), *to throw*
ejícere (ejéci, ejéctus), *to cast out*
projícere (projéci, projéctus), *to cast away*

A. Cognates. Many nouns are the same in both languages.

1. benefactor. 2. chorus (*also* choir). 3. clamor (cry, shout). 4. honor. 5. labor. 6. martyr. 7. odor. 8. seraph (*pl.* séraphim). 9. furor. 10. favor. 11. vigor. 12. terror. 13. error. 14. splendor. 15. cherub (*pl.* chérubim). 16. drachma.

B. Verbs with the prefix **in-** (**im-**) convey the idea of *in, into, on*, or *toward*.

1. indúcere (to lead into, to induce). 2. importáre (to bring or carry in, to import). 3. imploráre (to weep toward, to implore). 4. impónere (to put upon, to impose). 5. inveníre (to come upon, to find, to invent). 6. incípere (to take on, to begin). 7. impendére (to hang upon, to impend). 8. inscríbere (to write in, to inscribe). 9. inspícere (to look into, to inspect). 10. infúndere (to pour into, to infuse). 11. inváderе (to go into, to invade). 12. inspiráre (to breathe into, to inspire).

C. Read and give the English for the following:

1. Timémus advéntum hostium qui véniunt ut civitátes nostras perdant. 2. Puer malus est quoniam novam tubam suam fregit. 3. Quaerébant num rex servos suos relínqueret, cum ei tam fidéliter servivíssent. 4. Manus ejus tam fortes erant ut crucem magnam ab terra eleváre posset. 5. Tríbuat Deus ut ópera nostra ei pláceant. 6. Chrístus coenábat cum discípulis suis. 7. Domi remánsit ut patri suo scribat. 8. Fámula bona et fidélis dóminae suae panem facit. 9. Hac aqua lavábunt se et reficiéntur. 10. Illi hómines ímpii ex dómibus suis ejécti sunt. 11. Múnera mísimus ad eos, sed non recepérunt. 12. Cápite hunc panem ut manducétis in via. 13. Libros suos ad terram jecérunt. 14. Non scit num rex haec dona accípiat. 15. Servi vias faciébant in terra nova. 16. Cálicem in manus suas cepit. 17. Mártyres in univérsis pártibus mundi apparuérunt, ut plebi virtútem sacrifícii osténdant. 18. Tremébant quoniam scélera sua judicabántur. 19. Omnes hómines

praeclári terrae in hac civitáte congregavérunt quia rex eos convocávit.
20. Deprecatiónes nostrae defúnctis váleant. 21. Postquam ei scrípsi-
mus, venit. 22. Christus sánguinem suum pro cunctis géntibus effúdit
23. Ea quaerit quis cum patre remáneat. 24. Splendor lúminis caeléstis
tantus erat, ut laetificáret omnes qui vidébant. 25. Invenérunt púerum
et matrem suam dormiéntes.

Unit Two

A. 1. Adjutórium nostrum in nómine Dómini, qui fecit caelum et
terram. 2. Qui tollis peccáta mundi, súscipe deprecatiónem nostram.
3. Inítium sancti Evangélii secúndum Lucam. 4. Súscipe, sancte Pater
omnípotens, aetérne Deus, hanc immaculátam hostiam, ut mihi et
illis profíciat ad salútem in vitam aetérnam. 5. Pro ómnibus fidélibus
christiánis vivis atque defúnctis. 6. Cum odóre suavitátis. 7. In spíritu
humilitátis, et in ánimo contríto suscipiámur a te, Dómine. 8. Ut
pláceat tibi, Dómine Deus. 9. Incénsum istud a te benedíctum, ascéndat ad te, Dómine. 10. Súscipe, sancta Trínitas, hanc oblatiónem.
11. Ob memóriam passiónis, resurrectiónis et ascensiónis Jesu Christi
Dómini nostri. 12. Et in honórem beátae Maríae semper Vírginis, et
beáti Joánnis Baptístae, et sanctórum Apostolórum Petri et Pauli, et
istórum, et ómnium sanctórum, ut illis profíciat ad honórem, nobis
autem ad salútem. 13. Suscípiat Dóminus sacrifícium de mánibus
tuis, ad laudem, et glóriam nóminis sui, ad utilitátem quoque nostram, totiúsque Ecclésiae suae sanctae. 14. Sacrifícium laudis. 15.
Beatórum Apostolórum ac Mártyrum tuórum. 16. Per éumdem Christum Dóminum nostrum. 17. Hanc ígitur oblatiónem servitútis nostrae, sed et cunctae famíliae tuae, quaésumus, Dómine, ut placátus
accípias. 18. Accépit panem in sanctas, ac venerábiles manus suas.
19. Hoc est enim corpus meum. 20. Símili modo postquam coenátum
est, accípiens et hunc praeclárum cálicem in sanctas, ac venerábiles
manus suas: item tibi grátias agens, benedíxit, dedítque discípulis
suis, dicens: Accípite, et bíbite ex eo omnes. 21. Hic est enim calix
Sánguinis mei, novi et aetérni testaménti, mystérium fídei, qui pro

vobis et pro multis effundétur in remissiónem peccatórum. 22. Haec quotiescúmque fecéritis, in mei memóriam faciétis. 23. Praeclárae Majestáti tuae. 24. Famulórum, famularúmque tuárum. 25. Nobis quoque peccatóribus fámulis tuis, de multitúdine miseratiónum tuárum sperántibus. 26. Cum tuis sanctis Apóstolis et Martýribus. 27. Per ipsum et cum ipso et in ipso, est tibi Deo Patri omnipoténti, in unitáte Spíritus Sancti, omnis honor, et gloria, per ómnia saécula saeculórum. Amen. 28. Líbera nos, quaésumus, Dómine, ab ómnibus malis, praetéritis, praeséntibus et futúris. 29. Ope misericórdiae tuae. 30. A peccáto simus semper líberi, et omni perturbatióne secúri. 31. Pacem relínquo vobis. 32. Ne respícias peccáta mea. 33. Per mortem tuam mundum vivificásti. 34. Cum eódem Deo Patre. 35. Panem caeléstem accípiam et nomen Dómini invocábo.

B. Change the infinitive to the right form of the perfect indicative.

1. ego (fácere). 2. is (cápere). 3. nos (refícere). 4. ei (ejícere). 5. vos (profícere). 6. tu (jácere). 7. ea (percípere). 8. tu (profícere). 9. vos (recípere). 10. nos (projícere). 11. ego (praecípere). 12. eae (suscípere).

C. Conjugate.

a) cápere in the future indicative active.
b) fácere in the present indicative active.
c) jácere in the present subjunctive active.
d) concípere in the imperfect indicative active.
e) accípere in the perfect subjunctive passive.

UNIT THREE

A. Turn to the Appendix and learn how to form the pluperfect indicative and the pluperfect subjunctive of all verbs.

B. Vocabulary building.

a) **Derivations.** Find, in Units One and Two, the words that have the same derivation as the following:

1. suavis (sweet). 2. servíre (to serve). 3. família (family). 4. mórtuus (dead). 5. placátio (propitiation). 6. fragílitas (frailty). 7. despícere (to despise). 8. relíquiae (relics). 9. tremor (fear). 10. factor (maker). 11. clamáre (to shout). 12. honoráre (to honor). 13. laboriósus (toilsome). 14. portáre (to carry). 15. ploráre (to weep). 16. vádere (to go). 17. accéptus (welcome). 18. percéptio (partaking). 19. praecéptum (precept). 20. laetári (to rejoice). 21. quotídie (adv.) (daily). 22. infúndere (to pour into). 23. confúndere (to confound). 24. placátus (appeased). 25. testis (witness).

b) Observe the relation between these Latin and English words.

Latin	English	Latin	English
fámulus	familiar	mors	mortal
univérsus	university	símilis	resemble
placére	placate	frángere	fraction
relínquere	relinquish	remanére	remnant
trémere	tremulous	inscríbere	inscription

c) Observe these word families.

Noun	Verb	Adjective	Adverb
suávitas		suavis	suáviter
sérvitus	servíre	sérvilis	servíliter
utílitas	uti (to use)	útilis (useful)	utíliter
fámulus		familiáris	familiáriter
mors	mori (to die)	mortális	mortáliter

READING LESSON

1. Videns autem Jesus turbas, ascendit in montem, et cum sedisset, accesserunt ad eum discipuli ejus.

2. Et aperiens os suum docebat eos, dicens:

3. Beati pauperes spiritu: quoniam ipsorum est regnum caelorum.

4. Beati mites: quoniam ipsi possidebunt terram.

5. Beati qui lugent: quoniam ipsi consolabuntur.

6. Beati qui esuriunt et sitiunt justitiam: quoniam ipsi saturabuntur.

7. Beati misericordes: quoniam ipsi misericordiam consequentur.

8. Beati mundo corde: quoniam ipsi Deum videbunt.

9. Beati pacifici: quoniam filii Dei vocabuntur.

10. Beati qui persecutionem patiuntur propter justitiam: quoniam ipsorum est regnum caelorum.

11. Beati estis cum maledixerint vobis, et persecuti vos fuerint, et dixerint omne malum adversum vos mentientes, propter me:

12. Guadete et exultate, quoniam merces vestra copiosa est in caelis: sic enim persecuti sunt prophetas, qui fuerunt ante vos.

13. Vos estis sal terrae. Quod si sal evanuerit, in quo salietur? Ad nihilum valet ultra nisi ut mittatur foras, et conculcetur ab hominibus.

14. Vos estis lux mundi. Non potest civitas abscondi supra montem posita.

15. Neque accendunt lucernam et ponunt eam sub modio, sed super candelabrum ut luceat omnibus qui in domo sunt.

16. Sic luceat lux vestra coram hominibus: ut videant opera vestra bona, et glorificent patrem vestrum, qui in caelis est.

17. Nolite putare quoniam veni solvere legem, aut prophetas: non veni solvere, sed adimplere.

18. Amen quippe dico vobis, donec transeat caelum et terra, iota unum, aut unus apex non praeteribit a lege, donec omnia fiant.

19. Qui ergo solverit unum de mandatis istis minimis et docuerit sic homines, minimus vocabitur in regno caelorum: qui autem fecerit et docuerit, his magnus vocabitur in regno caelorum.

20. Dico enim vobis, quia nisi abundaverit justitia vestra plus quam scribarum et Pharisaeorum, non intrabitis in regnum caelorum.

21. Audistis quia dictum est antiquis: Non occides: qui autem occiderit reus erit judicio.

22. Ego autem dico vobis: quia omnis qui irascitur fratri suo, reus erit judicio. Qui autem dixerit fratri suo, raca: reus erit concilio. Qui autem dixerit, fatue: reus erit gehennae ignis.

23. Si ergo offers munus tuum ad altare, et ibi recordatus fueris quia frater tuus habet aliquid adversum te:

24. Relinque ibi munus tuum ante altare, et vade prius reconciliari fratri tuo: et tunc veniens offeres munus tuum.

(Jesu Christi Evangelium secundum Matthaeum, caput V, 1-24.)

LESSON XIV

Unit One

Agnus Dei, qui tollis peccáta *Lamb of God, who takest away the sins*
mundi, miserére nobis.   *of the world, have mercy on us.*

Vocabulary

jubére (**jussi, jussus**), *to command*
confitéri (**conféssus sum**), dep., *to confess, to praise*
cónsequi (**consecútus sum**), dep., *to obtain, to secure*
ulcísci (**ultus sum**), dep., *to avenge*
dignári, dep., *to vouchsafe, to grant, to deign*
precári, dep., *to beseech, to pray*
mori (**mórtuus sum**) (**-io** verb), dep., *to die*
nasci (**natus sum**), dep., *to be born*
pati (**passus sum**) (**-io** verb), dep., *to suffer, to permit*
oblivísci (**oblítus sum**), dep., *to forget*
pérfrui (**perfrúctus sum**) (takes its dir. obj. in the abl.) dep., *to enjoy*
íngredi (**ingréssus sum**) (**-io** verb), dep., *to walk*
loqui (**locútus sum**), dep., *to speak*
miseréri (**misértus sum**), dep., *to have mercy*
audére (**ausus sum**), semi-dep., *to dare*
fídere (**fisus sum**), semi-dep., *to trust*
gaudére (**gavísus sum**), semi-dep., *to rejoice*
solére (**sólitus sum**), semi-dep., *to be accustomed*
nunquam, *never*
dominátio, dominatiónis, f., *dominion*
tutaméntum, -i, n., *safety, safeguard*
mandátum, -i, n., *commandment, command*
caro, carnis, f., *flesh*

medéla, -ae, f., *healing remedy*
plenus, -a, -um, *full*
sócius, -a, -um, *associated with, together with*
adhuc, *yet*

33. **Deponent verbs.** These verbs have passive forms with active meanings. They should be translated by an active verb in English.

confitéri, *to praise, to confess;* confíteor, *I praise*
cónsequi, *to obtain;* cónsequor, *I obtain*
venerári, *to venerate;* véneror, *I venerate*
ulcísci, *to avenge;* ulcíscor, *I avenge* (past participle, **ultus**)

34. **Semideponent verbs.** These verbs have their perfect tenses in the passive form only. The meaning, however, is active.

audére, *to dare;* ausus sum, *I have dared*
gaudére, *to rejoice;* gavísus sum, *I have rejoiced*
solére, *to be accustomed;* sólitus sum, *I have been accustomed*
fídere, *to trust;* fisus sum, *I have trusted*

EXERCISES

A. Cognates. Many adjectives ending in -us in Latin have the ending -*al* in English. Pronounce and give the English for:

1. ánnuus. 2. aetérnus. 3. inférnus. 4. inimícus. 5. perpétuus. 6. univérsus. 7. matérnus. 8. corpóreus. 9. funéreus. 10. patérnus. 11. fratérnus.

B. Prae in composition means *before, beforehand, in advance.*

1. **praecédere** (to go before, to precede). 2. **praescríbere** (to write in advance, to prescribe). 3. **praedícere** (to say beforehand, to predict). 4. **praeférre** (to bring before, to prefer). 5. **praeparáre** (to get ready in advance, to prepare). 6. **praeclúdere** (to close beforehand, to preclude). 7. **praesidére** (to sit before, to preside). 8. **praeíre** (to go be-

fore). 9. **praesúmere** (to take beforehand, to presume). 10. **praesentíre** (to feel in advance, to have a presentiment).

C. Read and give the English for the following:

1. Timebámus quoniam fídere eis non audebámus. 2. Diébus nostris afflígitur mundus dominatióne hóminum impiórum. 3. Néscimus quis loquátur. 4. In monte ingrediebántur, cum fratrem tuum vidérent. 5. Quaesívit quid jussísses. 6. Si eis auxílium dedissémus, non mórtui essent. 7. Cum nimis passus sit, dimíttet inimícis suis. 8. Verba scripta in libro nunc oblítus sum. 9. Volúntas ejus tam fortis erat, ut honórem magnum consequerétur. 10. Mandáta tua non obliviscémur. 11. Intercéssit ob fílii sui tutaméntum. 12. Dóminus delícta contra fámulum suum ultus est. 13. Christus in stábulo natus est. 14. Gaudére solébant, cum vocem matris suae audírent. 15. Ei fisi sumus, sed fidélis non fuit. 16. Judicáre eos non ausa est. 17. Gavísus sum, quia munus consecútus est. 18. Precátur, ut rex frátribus ejus misereátur. 19. Cum ópera sua bona et justa fúerint, laude hóminum cunctórum perfrúcti sunt. 20. Nunquam loquéntur. 21. Non obliviscebántur. 22. Jussit nos remanére hodie domi, ut mater nostra nobis oratiónes docéret. 23. Ingrediebámur in via quando appáruit servus auxílium precans. 24. Oratiónum vespertinárum nunquam oblivíscor.[1] 25. Propter mandátum ecclésiae suae carnem non manducavérunt hódie.

UNIT TWO

A. 1. Confitébor tibi. 2. Spera in Deo, quóniam adhuc confitébor illi, salutáre vultus mei, et Deus meus. 3. Misereátur tui omnípotens Deus. 4. Confíteor Deo omnipoténti, beátae Maríae semper Vírgini, beáto Joánni Baptístae, sanctis apóstolis Petro et Paulo, ómnibus sanctis, et tibi, Pater, quia peccávi nimis cogitatióne, verbo, et ópere, mea culpa, mea culpa, mea máxima culpa. 5. Ídeo precor beátam Maríam semper Vírginem, beátum Michaélum Archángelum, beá-

---

[1] Verbs of remembering and forgetting take their direct object either in the accusative or in the genitive.

tum Joánnem Baptístam, sanctos apóstolos Petrum et Paulum, omnes sanctos, et te, Pater, oráre pro me ad Dóminum Deum nostrum. 6. Misereátur vestri omnípotens Deus. 7. Et plebs tua laetábitur in te. 8. Orámus te, Dómine, per mérita sanctórum tuórum, ut indulgére dignéris ómnia peccáta mea. 9. Qui tollis peccáta mundi, miserére nobis. 10. Qui sedes ad déxteram Patris, miserére nobis. 11. Ita me tua grata miseratióne dignáre mundáre, ut sanctum Evangélium tuum digne váleam nuntiáre. 12. Ex Patre natum ante ómnia saécula. 13. Sub Póntio Piláto passus. 14. Qui locútus est per Prophétas. 15. Confíteor unum baptísma in remissiónem peccatórum, et exspécto resurrectiónem mortuórum, et vitam ventúri saéculi. 16. Per intercessiónem beáti Michaélis Archángeli, stantis a dextris altáris incénsi, et ómnium electórum suórum, incénsum istud dignétur Dóminus benedícere et in odórem suavitátis accípere. 17. Déxtera eorum repléta est munéribus. 18. Ego autem in innocéntia mea ingréssus sum. 19. Miserére mei. 20. Et illi pro nobis intercédere dignéntur in caelis. 21. Laudant Ángeli, adórant Dominatiónes. 22. Caeli, caelorúmque Virtútes, ac beáta Séraphim, sócia exsultatióne concélebrant. 23. Deprecámur. 24. Pleni sunt caeli et terra glória tua. 25. Ne respícias peccáta mea, sed fidem Ecclésiae tuae; eamque secúndum voluntátem tuam pacificáre et coadunáre dignéris. 26. Percéptio córporis tui, Dómine Jesu Christe, quod ego indígnus súmere praesúmo, non mihi provéniat in judícium et condemnatiónem; sed pro tua pietáte prosit mihi ad tutaméntum mentis et córporis, et ad medélam percipiéndam. 27. Corpus tuum, Dómine, quod sumpsi. 28. Ite, Missa est. 29. Pláceat tibi, sancta Trínitas, obséquium servitútis meae. 30. Inítium sancti Evangélii secúndum Joánnem. 31. Plenum gratiae et veritátis. 32. Sancta ergo, et salúbris est cogitátio pro defúnctis exoráre, ut a peccátis solvántur. 33. Descéndi de caelo, non ut fáciam voluntátem meam, sed voluntátem ejus qui misit me. 34. Haec est autem volúntas ejus, qui misit me, Patris: ut omne, quod dedit mihi, non perdam ex eo, sed resúscitem illud in novíssimo die. 35. Haec est autem volúntas Patris mei, qui misit me: ut omnis, qui videt Fílium, et credit in eum hábeat vitam aetérnam et ego resuscitábo eum in novíssimo die. 36. Exáudi oratiónem meam, ad te omnis caro véniet.

B. Translate the following:

confitémur	confitébitur	conféssus eram	oblivíscitur
venerábimur	venerátur	venerábor	móritur
ulti sumus	ultus erat	ultus sum	loquebátur
consequámur	consequétur	cónsequor	náscitur
patiebámur	pátitur	patiébar	audent
ausi erámus	ausus est	ausus sum	patiémini
nati sumus	náscitur	nascor	conséquimur
loquámur	lóquitur	loquar	ulcíscor
moriámur	mórtuus est	móriar	venerátur
oblíti sumus	obliviscétur	oblítus sum	confiteúntur

UNIT THREE

A. Give the meanings of these forms.

1. jussérunt. 2. ulciscímini. 3. consequéntur. 4. dignétur. 5. precábitur. 6. mórtui sunt. 7. natus esset. 8. passus est. 9. oblivíscor. 10. perfruebámur. 11. ingréssus sum. 12. locútus est. 13. ausi sumus. 14. gavísa erat. 15. sóliti sumus. 16. miserére. 17. confíteor. 18. ultus est. 19. áudeo. 20. loquéntur. 21. pátitur. 22. moritúri sumus. 23. jubet. 24. consecútus est. 25. dignéris. 26. patior. 27. nati sunt. 28. confitébor. 29. nascerétur. 30. oblítus esset. 31. perfrúcti sunt. 32. júbeat. 33. fidémus. 34. misereátur. 35. solébant.

B. Vocabulary building.

a) **Derivations.** Find in Units One and Two the words that have the same derivation as the following:

1. **sequi** (to follow). 2. **últio** (vengeance). 3. **indígnus** (unworthy). 4. **deprecári** (to beseech). 5. **mórtuus** (dead). 6. **sequéntia** (continuation). 7. **pássio** (suffering). 8. **frui** (to enjoy). 9. **miserátio** (mercy).

10. fides (faith). 11. fructus (fruit). 12. dóminus (master). 13. tutus (safe). 14. fidélis (faithful). 15. mandáre (to command). 16. sociáre (to share in). 17. annus (year). 18. sempitérnus (everlasting). 19. ínferus (below). 20. amícus (friend). 21. mater (mother). 22. corpus (body). 23. pater (father). 24. frater (brother). 25. paráre (to pre-pare). 26. sentíre (to feel, to perceive). 27. inúltus (unpunished). 28. jussus (command). 29. égredi (to come out).

b) Observe the relation between these Latin and English words.

Latin	English	Latin	English
fídere	fiduciary	mandátum	mandate
caro	carnal	sócius	associate
audére	audacious	oblivísci	oblivion
miseréri	commiserate	nasci	renascent
loqui	loquacious	cónsequi	consequence
mori	mortuary	fides	fidelity

c) Observe these word families:

Noun	Adjective	Verb
ultor (avenger)	ultrix (avenging)	ulcísci (to avenge)
dígnitas (worth)	dignus (worthy)	dignári (to consider worthy)
preces (prayers)	precárius (begged for)	precári (to pray)
mors (death)	mortális (mortal)	mori (to die)
natívitas (birth)	naturális (natural)	nasci (to be born)
oblívio (forgetfulness)	obliviósus (forgetful)	oblivísci (to forget)
fructus (fruit)	fructuósus (fruitful)	frui (to enjoy)
miserátio (mercy)	miséricors (merciful)	miseréri (to have mercy)
audácia (boldness)	audax (bold)	audére (to dare)
fides (trust)	fidus (trusty)	fídere (to trust)
gaudium (joy)		gaudére (to rejoice)

READING LESSON

1. Cum autem descendisset de monte, secutae sunt eum turbae multae.

2. Et ecce leprosus veniens, adorabat eum, dicens: Domine, si vis, potes me mundare.

3. Et extendens Jesus manum, tetigit eum, dicens: Volo. Mundare. Et confestim mundata est lepra ejus.

4. Et ait illi Jesus: Vide, nemini dixeris: sed vade, ostende te sacerdoti, et offer munus quod praecepit Moyses, in testimonium illis.

5. Cum autem introisset Capharnaum, accessit ad eum centurio, rogans eum.

6. Et dicens: Domine, puer meus jacet in domo paralyticus, et male torquetur.

7. Et ait illi Jesus: Ego veniam et curabo eum.

8. Et respondens centurio, ait: Domine, non sum dignus ut intres sub tectum meum: sed tantum dic verbo, et sanabitur puer meus.

9. Nam et ego homo sum sub potestate constitutus, habens sub me milites, et dico huic: Vade, et vadit: et alii, Veni, et venit: et servo meo, Fac hoc, et facit.

10. Audiens autem Jesus miratus est, et sequentibus se dixit: Amen dico vobis, non inveni tantam fidem in Israel.

11. Dico autem vobis, quod multi ab Oriente, et Occidente venient, et recumbent cum Abraham et Isaac et Jacob in regno caelorum.

12. Filii autem regni ejicientur in tenebras exteriores: ibi erit fletus, et stridor dentium.

13. Et dixit Jesus centurioni: Vade, et sicut credidisti, fiat tibi. Et sanatus est puer in illa hora.

14. Et cum venisset Jesus in domum Petri, vidit socrum ejus jacentem et febricitantem.

15. Et tetigit manum ejus, et dimisit eam febris et surrexit, et ministrabat eis.

16. Vespere autem facto, obtulerunt ei multos daemonia habentes: et ejiciebat spiritus verbo: et omnes male habentes curavit:

17. Ut adimpleretur quod dictum est per Isaiam prophetam, dicentem: Ipse infirmitates nostras accepit: et aegrotationes nostras portavit.

18. Videns autem Jesus turbas multas circum se, jussit ire trans fretum.

19. Et accedens unus scriba, ait illi: Magister, sequar te quocumque ieris.

20. Et dicit ei Jesus: Vulpes foveas habent, et volucres caeli nidos: filius autem hominis non habet ubi caput reclinet.

21. Alius autem de discipulis ejus ait illi: Domine, permitte me primum ire, et sepelire patrem meum.

22. Jesus autem ait illi: Sequere me, et dimitte mortuos sepelire mortuos suos.

23. Et ascendente eo in naviculam, secuti sunt eum discipuli ejus.

24. Et ecce motus magnus factus est in mari, ita ut navicula operiretur fluctibus, ipse vero dormiebat.

25. Et accesserunt ad eum discipuli ejus, et suscitaverunt eum, dicentes: Domine, salva nos, perimus.

26. Et dicit eis Jesus: Quid timidi estis, modicae fidei? Tunc surgens imperavit ventis et mari, et facta est tranquillitas magna.

27. Porro homines mirati sunt, dicentes: Qualis est hic, quia venti et mare obediunt ei?

28. Et cum venisset trans fretum in regionem Gerasenorum, occurrerunt ei duo habentes daemonia, de monumentis exeuntes, saevi nimis, ita ut nemo posset transire per viam illam.

29. Et ecce clamaverunt, dicentes: Quid nobis et tibi, Jesu fili Dei? Venisti huc ante tempus torquere nos?

30. Erat autem non longe ab illis grex multorum porcorum pascens.

31. Daemones autem rogabant eum, dicentes: Si ejicis nos hinc, mitte nos in gregem porcorum.

32. Et ait illis: Ite. At illi exeuntes abierunt in porcos, et ecce impetu abiit totus grex per praeceps in mare: et mortui sunt in aquis.

33. Pastores autem fugerunt: et venientes in civitatem, nuntiaverunt omnia, et de eis qui daemonia habuerant.

34. Et ecce tota civitas exiit obviam Jesu: et viso eo rogabant ut transiret a finibus eorum.

(Jesu Christi Evangelium secundum Matthaeum, caput VIII, 1–34.)

LESSON XV

Agnus Dei, qui tollis peccáta   *Lamb of God, who takest away the sins*
mundi, dona nobis pacem.   *of the world, grant us peace.*

Vocabulary

tempus, témporis, n., *time*
tentátio, tentatiónis, f., *temptation*
débitum, -i, n., *debt, trespass*
aer, aeris, m. (*pl.* aeres or acra), *air*
tabernáculum, -i, n., *tabernacle*
obséquium, -ii, n., *homage*
sapiéntia, -ae, f., *wisdom*
potéstas, potestátis, f., *power*
lassus, -a, -um, *tired*
primus, -a, -um, *first;* in primis, *in the first place*
profúndus, -a, -um, *deep*
trádere (trádidi, tráditus), *to deliver up, to hand over*
dilígere (diléxi, diléctus), *to love*
cognóscere (cognóvi, cógnitus), *to learn* [1]
cessáre, *to cease*
inténdere (inténdi, inténtus or inténsus), *to be attentive*
mutáre, *to change*
pétere (petívi or -ii, petítus), *to beseech, to ask for*
requiéscere (requiévi, requiétus), *to rest*
sepelíre (sepelívi or -ii, sepúltus), *to bury*
tenére (ténui), *to hold*
sanáre, *to heal*
ferre (tuli, latus), *to bring*

[1] In the perfect tenses this verb means *to know.*

nemo, néminis, m. and f., *nobody*
nihil (nil), n., indecl., *nothing*
tunc, *then*
ubíque, *everywhere*

35. Qui. As a relative pronoun, **qui** means *who, which,* or *that.* As an interrogative adjective it means *what.* It is declined as follows.

Singular	Plural
Nom. qui (quae, quod)	qui (quae, quae)
Gen. cujus	quorum (quarum, quorum)
Dat. cui	quibus
Acc. quem (quam, quod)	quos (quas, quae)
Abl. quo (qua, quo)	quibus

The man who is coming is my father.	Homo qui venit pater meus est.
The servants whom they were calling have come in.	Servae quas vocábant intravérunt.
The boy to whom you gave the book is studious.	Puer cui librum dedísti studiósus est.
What reward did he send to those men?	Quod munus misit ad illos hómines?
The house which you see is mine.	Domus quam vides est mea.

36. Quis. The interrogative pronouns *who* and *what* are **quis** and **quid** in Latin.

Singular	Plural
Nom. quis (n. quid)	Like the relative qui
Gen. cujus	
Dat. cui	
Acc. quem (n. quid)	
Abl. quo	

Who drank the wine?	Quis vinum bibit?
To whom did you write?	Quibus scripsístis?

Whom did he see?   Quem vidit?
What did they have?   Quid habébant?

37. **Indefinite pronouns and adjectives.** These are compounds of quis and qui and are declined like them.

Pronouns

some one, something	aliquis (n. aliquid)
	alicujus
	alicui, *etc.*

each one, every one	quisque (n. quidque)
	cujusque
	cuique, *etc.*

a certain one	quidam (quaedam, quiddam)
	cujusdam
	cuidam, *etc.*

Adjectives

some	aliqui (aliqua, aliquod)
	alicujus
	alicui, *etc.*

| each | quisque (quaeque, quodque) |
| certain | quidam (quaedam, quoddam) |

38. **Ferre,** *to bring.* This irregular verb (as also its compounds) doubles the r in the infinitive, in the 2nd person sing. of the pres. ind. pass., and throughout the imperfect subjunctive. Elsewhere the -rr of the infinitive is not retained.

Present Indicative

Active		Passive	
fero	férimus	feror	férimur
fers	fertis	ferris (ferre)	ferímini
fert	ferunt	fertur	ferúntur

Observe that the present tense is slightly irregular.

EXERCISES

A. Cognates. Nouns ending in -tudo in Latin end in *-tude* in English. They are all feminine. Pronounce and give the English for:

1. beatitúdo. 2. fortitúdo. 3. multitúdo. 4. magnitúdo. 5. lassitúdo. 6. solitúdo. 7. amplitúdo. 8. sollicitúdo. 9. altitúdo (height). 10. latitúdo (breadth). 11. longitúdo (length).

The genitive singular of these nouns is **beatitúdinis**, etc.

B. Pro- as a prefix signifies *forth, forward, in front of, for.*

1. **propónere** (to put forth, to propose). 2. **projícere** (to throw forth, to project). 3. **procédere** (to go forth, to proceed). 4. **prodúcere** (to lead forth, to produce). 5. **prógredi** (dep., to walk forward, to progress). 6. **prósequi** (dep., to follow forth, to pursue). 7. **providére** (to see before or in advance, to provide). 8. **promíttere** (to send forth, to promise). 9. **provocáre** (to call forth, to provoke). 10. **proclamáre** (to shout forth, to proclaim). 11. **proférre** (to bring forth). 12. **proveníre** (to come forth).

C. Read and give the English for the following:

1. Puer agnum díligit, quem pater suus dedit ei. 2. Vírgines, quae lassae nimis sunt, sedérunt ut requiéscant. 3. Homo praeclárus, cui scripsi, mihi respóndit. 4. Quos libros tulit? 5. Tabernáculum in quo cálicem ponit sacérdos, supra altáre est. 6. Observámus obséquium, quod hi fílii boni paréntibus praestitérunt. 7. Débita sua dimitténda sunt. 8. Homo miser in manus inimicórum suórum tráditus est. 9. Mater pia, quam vidísti cum fámulis suis, Evangélia docet eis. 10. Ille vir, cujus domus in monte est, fílios suos ad civitátem misit. 11. Áliquis libros sústulit, quos relíqui hic. 12. Quisque discípulus lectiónem suam bene parávit hódie. 13. Quidam auxílium petens venit ad domum patris mei. 14. Alíquibus rex terrae illae múnera magna donábit. 15. Homínibus quibúsdam Dóminus multum dedit, multis nihil. 16. Quaeque mater scit num ópera filiórum suórum bona sint. 17. Aqua illíus lacus, quem vidétis, nimis profúnda est. 18. Postquam mórtuos

sepelivérunt, domus suas tristes rediérunt. 19. Cum sanáti sint, non cessant clamáre. 20. Néminem in via vídeo. 21. Condítio mutáta vitárum suárum laetificábat eos. 22. Quid tenes tu in manu déxtera? Nihil. 23. Verba et ópera illíus sancti praeclári univérsis géntibus cógnita sunt. 24. Si modum vivéndi ante mortem suam mutavísset, delícta sua indúlta essent. 25. Potéstas et sapiéntia regis nóbilis nostri terram nostram a malítia hóminum impiórum salvábunt. 26. Aer in illo monte suavis erat.

Unit Two

A. 1. Introíbo ad altáre Dei; ad Deum qui laetíficat juventútem meam. 2. Emítte lucem tuam, et veritátem tuam; ipsa me dedúxerunt, et addúxerunt in montem sanctum tuum, et in tabernácula tua. 3. Orámus te, Dómine, per mérita Sanctórum tuórum, quórum relíquiae hic sunt, et ómnium Sanctórum, ut indulgére dignéris ómnia peccáta mea. 4. Credo in unum Deum, Patrem omnipoténtem, factórem caeli et terrae, visibílium ómnium, et invisibílium. Et in unum Dóminum Jesum Christum, Fílium Dei unigénitum. Et ex Patre natum ante ómnia saécula. Deum de Deo, lumen de lúmine, Deum verum de Deo vero. Génitum, non factum, consubstantiálem Patri, per quem ómnia facta sunt. 5. Qui propter nos hómines et propter nostram salútem descéndit de caelis. Et incarnátus est de Spíritu Sancto ex María Vírgine, et homo factus est. 6. Crucifíxus étiam pro nobis, sub Póntio Piláto passus, et sepúltus est. 7. Et íterum ventúrus est cum glória judicáre vivos et mórtuos, cujus regni non erit finis. 8. Dómine, diléxi decórem domus tuae, et locum habitatiónis glóriae tuae. 9. Ne perdas cum ímpiis, Deus, ánimam meam, et cum viris sánguinum vitam meam; in quorum mánibus iniquitátes sunt, déxtera eórum repléta est munéribus. 10. Et illi pro nobis intercédere dignéntur in caelis, quorum memóriam ágimus in terris. 11. Vere dignum et justum est, aequum et salutáre, nos tibi semper, et ubíque grátias ágere. 12. Per quem majestátem tuam laudant Ángeli, adórant Dominatiónes, tremunt Potestátes. 13. Cum quibus et nostras voces, ut admítti júbeas, deprecámur, súpplici confessióne dicéntes: sanctus, sanctus, sanctus,

Dóminus Deus Sábaoth (of hosts). 14. Communicántes, et memóriam venerántes, in primis, gloriósae semper Vírginis Maríae, genitrícis Dei et Dómini nostri Jesu Christi. 15. Quorum méritis precibúsque concédas, ut in ómnibus protectiónis tuae muniámur auxílio. 16. Qui prídie quam paterétur, accépit panem in sanctas, ac venerábiles manus suas, et elevátis óculis in caelum ad te Deum Patrem suum omnipoténtem, tibi grátias agens, benedíxit, fregit, dedítque discípulis suis, dicens: Accípite, et manducáte ex hoc omnes.

B. Translate the following:

1. Quis locútus est? 2. Púerum vidi cui tubam dédisti. 3. Homo cum quo ingrediebátur frater meus erat. 4. Servus cujus dóminus mórtuus est, ad civitátem ibit. 5. Invénit crucem quam perdíderat. 6. Fámulae quas vocábant apparuérunt. 7. Verba quae dixit vera nimis sunt. 8. Fílii qui paréntibus placent ipsi beáti sunt. 9. Opus quod fecit praeclárum est. 10. Cui dábimus hos libros novos? 11. Quam lectiónem doces discípulos? 12. Aqua in qua stant non profúnda est. 13. Abjécit cornu quod in manu tenébat. 14. Misériae plebis quas vidébat, conturbábant eum. 15. Osténdit ei ómnia regna quae habitúrus erat.

C. Change the indefinite pronouns to the correct form where necessary.

1. (aliquis) introit. 2. vídeo (quisque). 3. (quidam) dixérunt. 4. (quisque) loquor. 5. invénit (aliquis). 6. verba (quidam) vera sunt. 7. (quisque) veritátem cognóscit. 8. Scripsit (aliquis). 9. míttimus (quidam) ad domum. 10. ópera (quisque) judicabúntur. 11. Incedébat cum (aliquis). 12. (quidam) munus dat.

Unit Three

A. Make the indefinite adjectives agree correctly with the nouns.

1. aquam (aliqui). 2. (quisque) ánimae. 3. (quidam) vias. 4.

(aliqui) filiórum. 5. regni (quisque). 6. sancto (quidam). 7. auxílii (aliqui). 8. (quidam) nómine. 9. (quisque) librum. 10. (aliqui) cornua. 11. (quidam) veritátibus. 12. (quisque) cruci. 13. (aliqui) panem. 14. (quidam) matris.

B. Give the present indicative active and passive of these compounds of **ferre.**

1. auférre (to take away). 2. conférre (to accompany, to confer). 3. offérre (to offer). 4. perférre (to bring up or through). 5. proférre (to bring out, to bring forth).

C. Vocabulary building.

a) **Derivations.** Find in Units One and Two the words that have the same derivation as the following:

1. débitor (debtor). 2. notus (known). 3. profúndum (depth). 4. promíssio (promise). 5. sepúlcrum (sepulcher). 6. sustinére (to sustain). 7. quiétas (quiet). 8. compétere (to be capable of). 9. réquies (rest). 10. tentáre (to tempt). 11. posse (to be able). 12. dilectíssimus (most beloved). 13. sanus (healthy). 14. beátus (happy). 15. fortis (strong). 16. lassus (tired). 17. multus (many). 18. latus (broad). 19. longus (long). 20. altus (high). 21. ámplius (yet more). 22. magnus (large). 23. solus (alone). 24. quiéscens (resting). 25. debére (owe, ought, must). 26. collátio (gathering).

b) Observe the relation between these Latin and English words.

Latin	English	Latin	English
tempus	temperature	potéstas	potentate
dilígere	delectable	cognóscere	recognize
débitum	debit	primus	primitive
cessáre	incessant	mutáre	mutations
pétere	petition	sanáre	sanitary

c) Observe these word families.

Noun	Adjective	Verb
sapiéntia (wisdom)	sápiens (wise)	
potéstas (power)	potens (powerful)	posse (to be able)
cognítio (knowledge)	cógnitus (known)	cognóscere (to know)
mutátio (a change)	mutábilis (change-able)	mutáre (to change)
réquies (rest)	requiétus (rested)	requiéscere (to rest)
sánitas (health)	sanus (healthy)	sanáre (to heal)

REVIEW LESSON NUMBER III

A. Read these statements and decide whether they are right or wrong.

1. Nomen púeri Lúcia erat. 2. Christiáni credunt in unum Deum. 3. Hómines páuperes semper iníqui sunt. 4. Aquam atque vinum bíbimus. 5. Apóstoli inimíci Christi erant. 6. Óculi in mánibus sunt. 7. Pax inter omnes gentes esse potest. 8. Scríbimus déxtera manu. 9. Agni córnua habent. 10. Omnes libri boni sunt. 11. Matres semper míserae sunt. 12. Dormímus in tecto domus. 13. Panem manducámus. 14. Rex légibus regnat. 15. Cogitatiónes in mente creántur.

B. Translate the following.

víximus	lavábimus	munivérimus	ut possímus
vixérimus	lavámus	muniámus	póssumus
vivámus	lavémus	munímus	poterámus
vívimus	lavavérimus	munívimus	potúimus
vivémus	lavávimus	muniémus	potuérimus
míttitur	crédimus	dirigétur	audítus est
mittétur	credémus	diréctus est	audiebátur
missus est	credídimus	dirigebátur	audiátur
mittebátur	credidérimus	dirigátur	audirétur
mittátur	credámus	dirígitur	audítur
	salvabátur	moveátur	
	salvétur	movebátur	
	salvátus est	motus est	
	salvábitur	movébitur	
	salvátur	movétur	

C. Give the Latin word that means the opposite of each of these words.

1. aqua. 2. ánima. 3. ex. 4. cum. 5. bonus. 6. princípium. 7. beátus. 8. virgo. 9. míttere. 10. pater. 11. tristis. 12. de. 13. ire. 14. laetificáre. 15. terra. 16. manus. 17. dies. 18. fides. 19. dignus. 20. visíbilis. 21. ascéndere. 22. respóndere. 23. bene. 24. vivus. 25. ignomínia.

D. Give the English for these verb forms.

1. despício. 2. condúcam. 3. invadébant. 4. ejécta est. 5. evocábit. 6. lava me. 7. munda me. 8. est. 9. peccávi. 10. ut justificéris. 11. justificáris. 12. manifestásti. 13. mundábor. 14. lavábis. 15. exsultábunt. 16. avérte. 17. dele. 18. crea. 19. ne projícias me. 20. docébo. 21. converténtur. 22. annuntiábit. 23. dedíssem. 24. non despícies. 25. fac. 26. suscipiéntes. 27. suscípiat. 28. impónent. 29. acceptábis. 30. dona ei. 31. exáudi. 32. véniet. 33. sperávit. 34. crédidit. 35. dormiéntibus. 36. habent. 37. resurréxit. 38. dormiérunt. 39. addúcet. 40. dícimus. 41. vívimus. 42. praeveniémus. 43. descéndet. 44. sunt. 45. relínquimur. 46. érimus. 47. erit. 48. timébit. 49. absólve. 50. est futúrus.

E. Give the English meaning of these active periphrastic forms (future active participle + esse).

1. ventúrus est. 2. remansúri erant. 3. dictúrus sum. 4. fractúri sunt. 5. perditúri erámus. 6. exitúri erátis. 7. regnatúrus fúerat. 8. quaesitúra est. 9. effusúrus eras. 10. accensúri sumus. 11. coenatúri erant. 12. munitúri estis. 13. sumptúrus est. 14. habitúrae erant. 15. statúri sunt.

F. Give the English meaning of these passive periphrastic forms (gerundive + esse).

1. dandum est. 2. audiénda sunt. 3. mitténdi erant. 4. judicándae erant. 5. vocándi erámus. 6. ponéndum erat. 7. dicéndum est. 8. docénda eram. 9. scribéndum erat. 10. dirigéndi sumus. 11. movéndus es. 12. eruéndi erátis. 13. liberándae erant. 14. serviéndus eras. 15. relinquéndi erámus. 16. ostendéndi estis.

G. Fill each blank with a suitable word.

1. Manducámus ———. 2. Bíbimus ———. 3. María ——— vir·
ginis est. 4. Lábium pars ——— est. 5. Joánnis nomen ——— est. **6.**
Mater et pater ——— famíliae sunt. 7. Pes pars ——— est. 8. Cor in
——— est. 9. Ecclésia domus ——— est. 10. Tectum super ———
est. 11. Rex ——— regnat. 12. ——— omnibus placet.

H. Give the Latin verb that tells what each of the following does
or is intended for.

1. aqua. 2. via. 3. servus. 4. orátio. 5. lux. 6. manus. 7. domus. 8.
cívitas. 9. crux. 10. liber. 11. fides. 12. indulgéntia. 13. mens. 14.
volúntas. 15. spes. 16. lábia. 17. os. 18. óstium. 19. vinum. 20. rex.
21. auris. 22. pes. 23. cáritas. 24. lumen. 25. óculus. 26. vox.

I. From the column of English words select the correct meaning
of the Latin words.

ulcísci	same	dilígere	and
nunquam	to deliver up	accéndere	upward
fratérnus	servant	mirus	to enjoy
trádere	never	quot	to enkindle
sanguis	to avenge	tutaméntum	wonderful
fámulus	help	pérfrui	how many
idem	brotherly	atque	safeguard
ops	blood	sursum	to love

frángere	safe
adhuc	voice
vox	to break
mors	full
salvus	ear
plenus	death
quoque	yet
auris	also

READING LESSON

1. Et iterum intravit Capharnaum post dies.

2. Et auditum est quod in domo esset, et convenerunt multi, ita ut non caperet neque ad januam et loquebatur eis verbum.

3. Et venerunt ad eum ferentes paralyticum, qui a quattuor portabatur.

4. Et cum non possent offerre eum illi prae turba, nudaverunt tectum ubi erat: et patefacientes submiserunt grabatum in quo paralyticus jacebat.

5. Cum autem vidisset Jesus fidem illorum, ait paralytico: Fili, dimittuntur tibi peccata tua.

6. Erant autem illic quidam de scribis sedentes, et cogitantes in cordibus suis:

7. Quid hic sic loquitur? Blasphemat. Quis potest dimittere peccata nisi solus Deus?

8. Quo statim cognito Jesus spiritu suo quia sic cogitarent intra se, dicit illis: Quid ista cogitatis in cordibus vestris?

9. Quid est facilius dicere paralytico: Dimittuntur tibi peccata: an dicere: Surge, tolle grabatum tuum, et ambula?

10. Ut autem sciatis quia Filius hominis habet potestatem in terra dimittendi peccata (ait paralytico):

11. Tibi dico: Surge, tolle grabatum tuum et vade in domum tuam.

12. Et statim surrexit ille: et, sublato grabato, abiit coram omnibus, ita ut mirarentur omnes et honorificarent Deum, dicentes: Quia numquam sic vidimus.

13. Et egressus est rursus ad mare: omnisque turba veniebat ad eum, et docebat eos.

14. Et cum praeteriret, vidit Levi Alphaei sedentem ad telonium, et ait illi: Sequere me. Et surgens secutus est eum.

15. Et factum est, cum accumberet in domo illius, multi publicani et peccatores simul discumbebant cum Jesu et discipulis ejus: erant enim multi, qui et sequebantur eum.

16. Et scribae et Pharisaei videntes quia manducaret cum publicanis et peccatoribus, dicebant discipulis ejus: Quare cum publicanis et peccatoribus manducat et bibit Magister vester?

17. Hoc audito, Jesus ait illis: Non necesse habent sani medico, sed qui male habent: non enim veni vocare justos, sed peccatores.

18. Et erant discipuli Joannis, et Pharisaei jejunantes. Et veniunt, et dicunt illi: Quare discipuli Joannis et Pharisaeorum jejunant, tui autem discipuli non jejunant?

19. Et ait Jesus: Numquid possunt filii nuptiarum, quamdiu sponsus cum illis est, jejunare? Quanto tempore habent sponsum, non possunt jejunare.

20. Venient autem dies cum auferetur ab eis sponsus: et tunc jejunabunt in illis diebus.

21. Nemo assumentum panni rudis assuit vestimento veteri: alioquin aufert supplementum novum a veteri, et major scissura fit.

22. Et nemo mittit vinum novum in utres veteres: alioquin dirumpet vinum utres, et vinum effundetur, et utres peribunt. Sed vinum novum in utres novos mitti debet.

23. Et factum est iterum cum Dominus sabbatis ambularet per sata, et discipuli ejus coeperunt progredi, et vellere spicas.

24. Pharisaei autem dicebant ei: Ecce, quid faciunt sabbatis quod non licet?

25. Et ait illis: Numquam legistis quid fecerit David, quando necessitatem habuit, et esuriit ipse, et qui cum eo erant?

26. Quomodo introivit in domum Dei sub Abiathar principe sacerdotum, et panes propositionis manducavit, quos non licebat manducare, nisi sacerdotibus, et dedit eis, qui cum eo erant?

27. Et dicebat eis: Sabbatum propter hominem factum est, et non homo propter sabbatum.

28. Itaque Dominus est filius hominis, etiam sabbati.

(Jesu Christi Evangelium secundum Marcum, caput II, 1–28.)

LESSON XVI

Dona eis réquiem sempitérnam.   *Grant them eternal rest.*

Vocabulary

cálculus, -i, m., *coal, pebble, stone*
orbis, orbis (gen. pl., orbium), m., *world, orbit*
antístes, antístitis, m., *bishop*
Papa, -ae, m., *Pope*
cultor, cultóris, m., *worshipper, one who professes*
incolúmitas, incolumitátis, f., *safety*
votum, -i, n., *vow*
vénia, -ae, f., *pardon*
commíxtio, commixtiónis, f., *mingling, mixing*
víscera, -um, n. pl., *bowels, innermost parts*
ténebrae, -arum, f. pl., *darkness*
consors (gen. consórtis), adj., *partaking*
illibátus, -a, -um, *unblemished*
ratus, -a, -um, *ratified, settled*
rationábilis (m. and f.), rationábile (n.), *reasonable, acceptable*
summus, -a, -um, *high, highest*
próprius, -a, -um, *one's own*
meréri (dep.), *to deserve, to be worthy*
cóndere (cóndidi, cónditus), *to create, to found*
enarráre, *to tell, to relate*
réddere (réddidi, rédditus), *to restore, return, to pay*
erípere (erípui, eréptus), *to rescue*
aestimáre, *to esteem*
largíri (dep.), *to grant*
potáre, *to drink*

lucére (luxi), *to shine*
perhibére, *to bring forward, to report*
rogáre, *to beseech*
vel, *or*
quotquot, *however many, as many as, all who*

39. **Ablative absolute.** This construction consists of a phrase in the ablative case made up of a noun or adjective and a participle, a noun and an adjective, or two nouns. As its name implies, it is grammatically independent of the sentence in which it occurs, that is, it does not refer to the same person or thing as the subject or object of the main verb. It is best translated by a clause introduced by *although, when, since,* or the like.

Defúnctis sepúltis, abiérunt milites domus suas.	*When the dead were buried, the soldiers went home.* (Literally, *with the dead buried*).
Multis convocátis, intravérunt in civitátem.	*After many had been called together, they entered the city.*
Heróde rege, Christus natus est.	*At the time that Herod was king, Christ was born.*

40. **Fíeri,** *to be made, to become.* The verb fácere, *to make,* is irregular in the simple tenses of the passive voice. The irregular tenses (besides the passive infinitive **fíeri**) are as follows:

Indicative		Subjunctive	
Present		Present	
fio	fimus	fiam	fiámus
fis	fitis	fias	fiátis
fit	fiunt	fiat	fiant
Imperfect		Imperfect	
fiébam, *etc.*		fíerem, *etc.*	

Future

fiam	fiémus
fies	fiétis
fiet	fient

EXERCISES

A. Suffixes. The suffix -tor (*f.* -trix) is added to verb stems to denote the agent or doer of an action.

1. mercátor, merchant (from mercári, to trade). 2. explorátor, scout (from exploráre, to seek out). 3. victor, victor (from víncere, to conquer). 4. imperátor, emperor (from imperáre, to command). 5. gubernátor, pilot, governor (from gubernáre, to steer, to govern). 6. pastor, shepherd (from páscere, to lead to pasture). 7. largítor, a liberal giver (from largíri, to give abundantly). 8. scriptor, writer (from scríbere, to write). 9. génitor, father (from generáre, to beget). 10. ultor, avenger (from ulcísci, to avenge). 11. invéntor, inventor (from veníre, to find). 12. venátrix, huntress (from venári, to hunt). 13. génetrix, mother (from generáre, to beget). 14. nutrix, nurse (from nutríre, to nourish). 15. cultor, cultivator (from cólere, to cultivate).

B. Re- as a verb prefix means *back* or *again*.

1. recípere (to take back, to receive). 2. revérti (to turn back, to revert). 3. repéllere (to drive back, to repel). 4. retinére (to hold back, to retain, to detain). 5. redímere (to buy back, to redeem). 6. rejícere (to throw back, to reject). 7. redíre (to go back, to return). 8. réddere (to give back, to restore). 9. reprímere (to press back, to repress). 10. recreáre (to create again, to recreate). 11. revocáre (to call back, to revoke). 12. renásci (to be born again). 13. renováre (to make new again, to renew). 14. remíttere (to send back, to remit). 15. reférre (to bring back, to refer).

Unit Two

A. Read and translate into English.

1. Coram rege stabant et véniam delictórum suórum petébant.
2. Apóstoli plebi enarrábant ómnia quae Dóminus díxerat fecerátque. 3. Homo tam bonus erat, ut largirétur paupéribus omne quod possidébat. 4. Quis réddere potest, id quod pérditum est? 5. Omne vinum non potavérunt; aliquid relíctum est. 6. Quaero num eas hódie ad civitátem vel remáneas hic. 7. Cum lucéret lux, ténebrae non erant. 8. Quotquot bene servivérunt ei, pater eis múnera dedit. 9. Illis diébus condidérunt civitátem, cujus nomen Roma vocátum est. 10. Si púeri ex aqua ab hómine forti erépti non essent, mórtui essent. 11. Propter ténebras inveníre non póterant montem quem eis osténdi. 12. Non merémur dona et favóres quos illi hómines generósi nobis largíti sunt. 13. Non se aestimábant dignos ad accipiéndam laudem ejus. 14. Quot púeri sciunt Papam antístidem Románum esse? 15. In cálice commíxtio aquae et vini est. 16. Testimónium perhíbuit de conditiónibus malis in quibus vivébant omnes páuperes illíus civitátis. 17. Dixítque Deus: Fiat lux. Et facta est lux. 18. Fácio hoc, ut fiam cultor fidélis religiónis meae. 19. Quaedam vota ab quoque sacerdóte faciénda sunt. 20. In illa die treménda totus orbis terrae in flammis futúrus est. 21. Agno pérdito, púeri tristes erant. 22. Lotis mánibus suis, vírgines sedébant qui manducárent. 23. Luce visa, hómines ad montem rediérunt. 24. Auxílium oblátum, accépimus. 25. Pane manducáto, discípuli vinum bibérunt.

B. 1. Misereátur tui omnípotens Deus, et dimíssis peccátis tuis, perdúcat te ad vitam aetérnam. 2. Aufer a nobis, quaésumus, Dómine, iniquitátes nostras, ut ad Sancta sanctórum puris mereámur méntibus introíre. 3. Munda cor meum, ac lábia mea, omnípotens Deus, qui lábia Isaíae prophétae cálculo mundasti igníto, ita me tua grata miseratióne dignáre mundáre, ut sanctum Evangélium tuum digne váleam nuntiáre. 4. Súscipe, sancte Pater omnípotens, aetérne Deus, hanc immaculátam hostiam, quam ego indígnus fámulus tuus óffero tibi, Deo meo vivo et vero, pro innumerabílibus peccátis, et offensiónibus, et negligéntiis meis, et pro ómnibus circumstántibus, sed et pro ómnibus fidélibus christiánis vivis atque defúnctis, ut mihi, et illis profíciat ad salútem in vitam aetérnam. 5. Deus, qui humánae substántiae dignitátem mirabíliter condidísti, et mirabílius reformásti, da nobis per hujus aquae et vini mystérium, ejus divinitátis esse consórtes, qui humanitátis nostrae fíeri dignátus est párticeps, Jesus Christus, Fílius tuus, Dóminus noster. 6. In spíritu humilitátis, et in ánimo contríto suscipiámur a te, Dómine, et sic fiat sacrifícium nostrum in conspéctu tuo hódie, ut pláceat tibi, Dómine Deus. 7. Lavábo inter innocéntes, manus meas, et circúmdabo altáre tuum, Dómine, ut áudiam vocem laudis, et enárrem univérsa mirabília tua. 8. Oráte fratres, ut meum ac vestrum sacrifícium acceptábile fiat apud Deum Patrem omnipoténtem. 9. Te ígitur, clementíssime Pater, per Jesum Christum Fílium tuum Dóminum nostrum, súpplices rogámus, ac pétimus, uti accépta hábeas, et benedícas, haec dona, haec múnera, haec sancta sacrifícia illibáta. 10. In primis, quae tibi offérimus pro Ecclésia tua sancta cathólica, quam pacificáre, custodíre, adunáre, et régere dignéris toto orbe terrárum; una cum fámulo tuo Papa nostro, et Antístite nostro, et ómnibus orthodóxis atque cathólicae, et apóstolicae fídei cultóribus. 11. Pro spe salútis, et incolumitátis suae. 12. Tibíque reddunt vota sua aetérno Deo, vivo et vero. 13. Quam oblatiónem tu, Deus, in ómnibus, quaésumus, benedíctam, adscríptam, ratam, rationábilem, acceptabilémque fácere dignéris, ut nobis Corpus, et Sanguis fiat dilectíssimi Fílii tui Dómini nostri Jesu Christi. 14. Supra quae propítio ac seréno vultu respícere dignéris, et accépta habére, sícuti accépta habére dignátus es múnera púeri tui justi Abel, et sacrifícium Patriárchae nostri Abrahae, et quod tibi óbtulit summus sacérdos tuus Melchísedech, sanctum sacrifícium, immaculátam hóstiam. 15. Fiat volúntas tua, sicut in caelo, et in terra. 16. Haec commíxtio, et consecrátio Córporis et Sánguinis Dómini nostri Jesu Christi, fiat accipiéntibus nobis in vitam aetérnam. 17. Corpus tuum, Dómine, quod sumpsi, et Sanguis quem potávi, adhaéreat viscéribus meis. 18. Lux in ténebris lucet, et ténebrae eam non comprehendérunt. 19. In mundo erat, et mundus per ipsum factus est, et mundus eum non cognóvit. 20. In própria venit, et sui eum non recepérunt.

UNIT THREE

A. Translate these ablative absolutes with a clause in English.

1. óculis elevátis. 2. dimíssis peccátis vestris. 3. viso eo. 4. viris jussis. 5. plebe docta. 6. mátribus conturbátis. 7. tubis audítis. 8. adjutório rogáto. 9. servis vocátis. 10. salváto mundo. 11. aqua bíbita. 12. vocátis nomínibus suis. 13. via osténta. 14. sanctis justificátis. 15. munéribus datis. 16. pacificáta mente sua. 17. fácie avérsa.

B. Give the English for the following:

1. Fiat lux. 2. Homo factus est. 3. Sic fiat sacrifícium nostrum in conspectu tuo hodie, ut pláceat tibi. 4. Oráte fratres, ut meum ac vestrum sacrifícium acceptábile fiat apud Deum Patrem omnipoténtem. 5. Fiat volúntas tua. 6. Haec commíxtio et consecrátio Córporis et Sánquinis Dómini nostri Jesu Christi, fiat accipiéntibus nobis in vitam aetérnam. 7. Fiat nobis remédium sempitérnum. 8. Mundus per ipsum factus est. 9. Fáciam vos fíeri piscatóres hóminum. 10. Ántequam terra fíeret. 11. Fortes facti sunt in bello. 12. Clamor factus est.

C. Vocabulary building.

a) Derivations. Find in Units One and Two the words that have the same derivation as the following:

1. cólere (to cultivate). 2. incólumis (unharmed). 3. tenebrósus (dark). 4. rátio (reckoning). 5. propríetas (peculiarity, distinction). 6. aestimátor (one who esteems). 7. cónditor (creator). 8. consórtium (company). 9. largítor (generous giver). 10. lux (light). 11. méritum (merit). 12. rogátio (request, question). 13. suscípere (to receive). 14. tenére (to hold). 15. émere (to buy). 16. jácere (to throw). 17.

invocáre (to call upon). 18. **novus** (new). 19. **offérre** (to offer). 20. **nasci** (to be born).

b) Observe the relation between these Latin and English words.

Latin	English	Latin	English
cálculus	calculate	cultor	culture
votum	votary	vénia	venial
commíxtio	mixture	consors	consort
rationábilis	rational	próprius	property
meréri	meritorious	aestimáre	estimation
largíri	largesse	potáre	potable
lucére	translucent	rogáre	interrogatory
enarráre	narrative	mercátor	mercantile

c) Observe these word families.

Noun	Adjective	Verb
nóvitas (new-ness)	novus (new)	renováre (to renew)
ultrix (avenging woman)	inúltus (unpunished)	ulcísci (to avenge)
génitor (father)	unigénitus (only begotten)	generáre (to beget)
largítor (giver)	largus (abundant)	largíri (to give abundantly)
pastor (shepherd)	pastorális (pastoral)	páscere (to feed)
victor (victor)	invíctus (unconquered)	víncere (to conquer)
lux (light)	lúcidus (bright)	lucére (to shine)

READING LESSON

1. In diebus illis iterum cum turba multa esset, nec haberent, quod manducarent, convocatis discipulis, ait illis:

2. Misereor super turbam: quia ecce jam triduo sustinent me, nec habent quod manducent:

3. Et si dimisero eos jejunos in domum suam, deficient in via: quidam enim ex eis de longe venerunt.

4. Et responderunt ei discipuli sui: Unde illos quis poterit hic saturare panibus in solitudine?

5. Et interrogavit eos: Quot panes habetis? Qui dixerunt: Septem.

6. Et praecepit turbae discumbere super terram. Et accipiens septem panes, gratias agens fregit, et dabat discipulis suis ut apponerent, et apposuerunt turbae.

7. Et habebant pisciculos paucos: et ipsos benedixit, et jussit apponi.

8. Et manducaverunt, et saturati sunt, et sustulerunt quod superaverat de fragmentis, septem sportas.

9. Erant autem qui manducaverunt, quasi quattuor millia: et dimisit eos.

10. Et statim ascendens navim cum discipulis suis, venit in partes Dalmanutha.

11. Et exierunt Pharisaei, coeperunt conquirere cum eo, quaerentes ab illo signum de caelo, tentantes eum.

12. Et ingemiscens spiritu, ait: Quid generatio ista signum quaerit? Amen dico vobis, si dabitur generationi isti signum.

13. Et dimittens eos, ascendit iterum navim, et abiit trans fretum.

14. Et obliti sunt panes sumere: et nisi unum panem habebant secum in navis.

15. Et praecipiebat eis, dicens: Videte, et cavete a fermento Pharisaeorum, et fermento Herodis.

16. Et cogitabant ad alterutrum, dicentes: Quia panes non habemus.

17. Quo cognito, ait illis Jesus: Quid cogitatis, quia panes non habetis? Nondum cognoscitis nec intelligitis? Adhuc caecatum habetis cor vestrum?

18. Oculos habentes non videtis? et aures habentes non auditis? Nec recordamini.

19. Quando quinque panes fregi in quinque millia: quot cophinos fragmentorum plenos sustulistis? Dicunt ei: Duodecim.

20. Quando et septem panes in quattuor millia: quot sportas fragmentorum tulistis? Et dicunt ei: Septem.

21. Et dicebat eis: Quomodo nondum intelligitis?

22. Et veniunt Bethsaidam, et adducunt ei caecum, et rogabant eum ut illum tangeret.

23. Et apprehensa manu caeci, eduxit eum extra vicum: et expuens in oculos ejus impositis manibus suis, interrogavit eum si quid videret.

24. Et aspiciens, ait: Video homines velut arbores ambulantes.

25. Deinde iterum imposuit manus super oculos ejus: et coepit videre: et restitutus est ita ut clare videret omnia.

26. Et misit illum in domum suam, dicens: Vade in domum tuam: et si in vicum introieris, nemini dixeris.

27. Et egressus est Jesus, et discipuli ejus in castella Caesareae Philippi: et in via interrogabat discipulos suos, dicens eis: Quem me dicunt esse homines?

28. Qui responderunt illi, dicentes: Joannem Baptistam, alii Eliam, alii vero quasi unum de prophetis.

29. Tunc dicit illis: Vos vero quem me esse dicitis? Respondens Petrus, ait ei: Tu es Christus.

30. Et comminatus est eis, ne cui dicerent de illo.

31. Et coepit docere eos quoniam oportet filium hominis pati multa, et reprobari a senioribus, et a summis sacerdotibus, et Scribis, et occidi: et post tres dies resurgere.

32. Et palam verbum loquebatur. Et apprehendens eum Petrus, coepit increpare eum.

33. Qui conversus, et videns discipulos suos, comminatus est Petro, dicens: Vade retro me satana, quoniam non sapis quae Dei sunt, sed quae sunt hominum.

34. Et convocata turba cum discipulis suis, dixit eis: Si quis vult me sequi, deneget semetipsum: et tollat crucem suam, et sequatur me.

35. Qui enim voluerit animam suam salvam facere, perdet eam: qui autem perdiderit animam suam propter me, et Evangelium, salvam faciet eam.

36. Quid enim proderit homini, si lucretur mundum totum: et detrimentum animae suae faciat?

37. Aut quid dabit homo commutationis pro anima sua?

38. Qui enim me confusus fuerit, et verba mea in generatione ista adultera et peccatrice: et filius hominis confundetur eum, cum venerit in gloria patris sui cum angelis sanctis.

39. Et dicebat illis: Amen dico vobis, quia sunt quidam de hic stantibus, qui non gustabunt mortem donec videant regnum Dei veniens in virtute.

(Jesu Christi Evangelium secundum Marcum, caput VIII, 1–39.)

LESSON XVII

Unit One

Ecce Agnus Dei; ecce qui tollit peccáta mundi.   *Behold the Lamb of God; behold Him who taketh away the sins of the world.*

Vocabulary

aedificáre, *to build*
aperíre (apérui, apértus), *to open*
aspérgere (aspérsi, aspérsus), *to sprinkle*
cánere (cécini, cantus), *to sing*
cógere (coégi, coáctus), *to lead* or *bring together, to assemble*
effulgére (effúlsi), *to shine*
sentíre (sensi, sensus), *to feel*
deínde (adv.), *then*
ita (adv.), *so, even*
quasi (adv.), *as if, like*
tantum (adv.), *but, only*
argentum, -i, n., *silver*
cinis, cíneris, m., *ashes*
epíscopus, -i, m., *bishop*
epístola, -ae, f., *epistle, letter*
lingua, -ae, f., *tongue*
sinus, sinus, m., *breast, bosom*
semen, séminis, n., *seed, descendant*
leo, leónis, m., *lion*
milítia, -ae, f., *army*
exércitus, exércitus, m., *army, host*
ovis, ovis (gen. pl., **ovium**), f., *sheep*
amárus, -a, -um, *bitter*

125

benígnus, -a, -um, *favorable*
certus, -a, -um, *certain*
céterus, -a, -um, *the other*
praetéritus, -a, -um, *past*

41. Indirect discourse. An indirect quotation occurring after a verb meaning *to say, to think,* or *to know* is expressed by an infinitive with the subject in the accusative case. All subordinate clauses occurring in an indirect quotation are put in the subjunctive.

They say that their sons are coming.	Dicunt fílios suos veníre (pres. inf.).
They say that their sons have come.	Dicunt fílios suos venísse (perf. inf.).
They say that their sons will come.	Dicunt fílios suos ventúros esse (fut. inf.).
They said that their sons were coming.	Dixérunt fílios suos veníre (pres. inf.).
They said that their sons had come.	Dixérunt fílios suos venísse (perf. inf.).
They said that their sons would come.	Dixérunt fílios suos ventúros esse (fut. inf.).
She knew that he was sleeping because he was tired.	Sciébat eum dormíre quod lassus esset.
He said that they had asked where he would be.	Dixit eos quaesivísse ubi futúrus esset.

Note the following:

1) An introductory word for *that* is not needed in an indirect quotation in Latin.

2) The present infinitive is used when the time is the same as that of the principal verb.

3) The perfect infinitive is used when the time precedes that of the main verb.

4) The future infinitive is used when the time follows that of the main verb.

5) A frequent substitute for the construction given above is a subordinate clause introduced by *quod* or *quia*. The verb is in the indicative mood.

I know that he shall rise again in the resurrection on the last day.
Scio quia resúrget in resurrectióne in novíssimo die.

Study in the Appendix the infinitives of the four conjugations.

EXERCISES

A. Suffixes. The suffix -or is added to verb stems to form nouns signifying *activity, condition,* or *state.*

1. dolor, pain (from dolére, to suffer). 2. amor, love (from amáre, to love). 3. timor, fear (from timére, to fear). 4. labor, labor (from laboráre, to labor). 5. clamor, cry (from clamáre, to cry out). 6. error, error (from erráre, to wander). 7. splendor, brightness (from splendére, to glitter). 8. decor, beauty (from decoráre, to adorn). 9. calor, heat (from calére, to be warm). 10. sudor, sweat (from sudáre, to sweat). 11. sopor, sleep (from sopíre, to put to sleep). 12. stridor, grating, gnashing (from stridére, to make a harsh noise).

B. Compounded with verbs, **sub- (sus-, suc-, sup-, suf-)** means *under, up, close to, to the aid of.*

1. suscípere (to take up, to receive). 2. subíre (to go under or close to). 3. sustinére (to hold up, to succeed to). 4. succéndo (to set on fire from beneath, to kindle, to inflame). 5. subésse (to be under). 6. subjícere (to throw or put under, to subjugate). 7. submíttere (to put under, to let down or lower). 8. subveníre (to come up to, to assist). 9. succúrrere (to run under or up to, to hasten to help, to succor). 10. sufférre (to carry under, to endure, to suffer). 11. submérgere (to plunge under, to submerge). 12. suppónere (to put under).

C. Read and give the English for the following:

1. Dicit eos ecclésiam novam in civitáte sua aedificavísse. 2. Sacérdos dixit verba epíscopi ad missas cunctas annuntiátum iri. 3. Púeri sciébant se non meréri ut ab patre suo sibi indulgerétur. 4. Si leo atque ovis in loco eódem simul poneréntur, leo ovem manducáret. 5. Aquam benedícent et turbam ea aspérgent. 6. Cálicem frángere non potes, quia argénto factus est. 7. Apóstoli epístolas scribébant discípulis suis, ut eos docérent veritátes quas ex ore Christi audíverant. 8. Dixit se in terram illam itúrum esse, ut magnum exércitum cógeret. 9. Scimus hunc hóminem multa mala passum esse. 10. Cógitat patrem vestrum jussisse hic nos remanére. 11. Dixit nobis servos vidísse lumen in monte lucens. 12. Dixi me non recepísse libros quos míseris ad me. 13. Crédimus hóminem primum in paradíso creátum esse. 14. Dicit fidem scriptúras apostolórum inspiravísse. 15. Nesciébant lacum tam profúndum esse, ita ut tota cívitas in illum submérgi posset. 16. Cultor terram bonam colit et sémina mittit in illam. 17. Dicit omnes nómina sua in librum inscríbere. 18. Dicti sumus nos non salvátum iri, si vitas nostras in malítiis perdámus. 19. Sciunt delícta inimicórum suórum non inúlta futúra esse. 20. Dixérunt servos christiános multo argénto redémptos esse. 21. Ne apériant ora sua, quóniam verba eorum non audiéntur.

Unit Two

1. Súpplices te rogámus, omnípotens Deus, jube haec perférri per manus sancti Angeli tui in sublíme altáre tuum, in conspéctu divínae majestátis tuae, ut quotquot, ex hac altáris participatióne sacrosánctum Fílii tui, Corpus et Sánguinem sumpsérimus, omni benedictióne caelésti et grátia repleámur. 2. Nobis quoque peccatóribus fámulis tuis, de multitúdine miseratiónum tuárum sperántibus, partem áliquam, et societátem donáre dignéris, cum tuis sanctis Apóstolis, et Martýribus, et ómnibus Sanctis tuis, intra quorum nos consórtium, non aestimátor mériti, sed véniae, quaésumus, largítor admítte. 3. Et dimítte nobis débita nostra, sicut et nos dimíttimus debitóribus

nostris. 4. Quid retríbuam Dómino pro ómnibus quae retríbuit mihi? 5. Dómine, non sum dignus ut intres sub tectum meum; sed tantum dic verbo et sanábitur ánima mea. 6. Et vídimus glóriam ejus, glóriam quasi Unigéniti a Patre, plenum grátiae et veritátis. 7. Aspérges me hyssópo, et mundábor. 8. Líbera me de sanguínibus, Deus, Deus salútis meae, et exultábit língua mea justítiam tuam. 9. Dómine, lábia mea apéries. 10. Benígne fac, Dómine, in bona voluntáte tua Sion, ut aedificéntur muri Jerúsalem. 11. Exáudi oratiónem meam, ad te omnis caro véniet. 12. Tuba coget omnes ante thronum. 13. Inter oves locum praesta. 14. Scio quia resúrget in resurrectióne in novíssimo die. 15. Líbera eas de ore leónis. 16. Quam Ábrahae promisísti, et sémini ejus. 17. Lux aetérna lúceat eis, Dómine. 18. Líbera me, Dómine, de morte aetérna, in die illa treménda, quando caeli movéndi sunt et terra. 19. Tremens factus sum ego, et tímeo. 20. Dies illa, dies irae, calamitátis et misériae, dies magna et amára. 21. Omnis qui vivit et credit in me, non moriétur in aetérnum. 22. In diebus illis: Audívi vocem de caelo, dicéntem mihi: Scribe, Beáti mórtui, qui in Dómino moriúntur. 23. Líbera nos, quaésumus, Dómine, ab ómnibus malis, praetéritis, praeséntibus et futúris. 24. In quo nobis spes beátae resurrectiónis effúlsit, ut quos contrístat certa moriéndi condítio, eósdem consolétur futúrae immortalitátis promíssio. 25. Et ídeo cum Ángelis et Archángelis, cum Thronis et Dominatiónibus, cumque omni milítia caeléstis exércitus, hymnum glóriae tuae cánimus, sine fine dicéntes: Sanctus, sanctus, sanctus.

UNIT THREE

A. Change each of these sentences to indirect discourse by placing a verb of saying, thinking, or knowing before each one.

1. Cum lassae sint, non ventúrae sunt. 2. Ea vivet sola in domo illa magna super montem. 3. Abiérunt postquam opus fecérunt. 4. Eos vidit dum hic erant. 5. Multum paupéribus donat, quia bonus et clemens est. 6. Liber a patre ejus scribebátur. 7. Agnus, quem mater sua dedit ei, mórtuus est. 8. Non ei ostendébant, ubi sessúrus erat. 9. Non crede-

bámus in verba ejus, quóniam sciebámus ea vera non esse. 10. Púeri laetántur, cum patres sui eos laudant.

B. Vocabulary building.

a) **Derivations.** Find in Units One and Two the words that have the same derivation as the following:

1. spárgere (to scatter). 2. incértus (uncertain). 3. miles (soldier). 4. benígne (favorably). 5. incértum (uncertainty). 6. aedifícium (building). 7. cantus (song). 8. semináre (to sow). 9. amátor (lover). 10. occúrrere (to meet). 11. cantor (singer). 12. dolorósus (sorrowful). 13. cúrrere (to run).

b) Observe the relation between these Latin and English words.

Latin	English	Latin	English
cánere	incantation	cógere	cogent
effulgére	effulgent	sentíre	sentiment
cinis	incinerator	epíscopus	episcopal
lingua	linguist	semen	disseminate
leo	leonine	milítia	military

c) Note these masculine nouns with their feminine equivalents.

Males	Females
pater (father)	mater (mother)
frater (brother)	soror (sister)
puer (boy)	virgo, puella (maiden, girl)
fílius (son)	fília (daughter)
servus (man servant)	serva (maid servant)
fámulus (man servant)	fámula (maid servant)
sanctus (man saint)	sancta (woman saint)
deus (god)	dea (goddess)
génitor (father)	génetrix (mother)
cantor (singer)	cantrix (woman singer)
venátor (hunter)	venátrix (huntress)

READING LESSON

1. Jesus autem plenus Spiritu sancto regressus est a Jordane: et agebatur a Spiritu in desertum,

2. Diebus quadraginta, et tentabatur a diabolo. Et nihil manducavit in diebus illis: et consummatis illis esuriit.

3. Dixit autem illi diabolus: Si filius Dei es, dic lapidi huic ut panis fiat.

4. Et respondit ad illum Jesus: Scriptum est: Quia non in solo pane vivit homo, sed in omni verbo Dei.

5. Et duxit illum diabolus in montem excelsum, et ostendit illi omnia regna orbis terrae in momento temporis.

6. Et ait illi: Tibi dabo potestatem hanc universam, et gloriam illorum: quia mihi tradita sunt: et cui volo do illa.

7. Tu ergo si adoraveris coram me, erunt tua omnia.

8. Et respondens Jesus, dixit illi: Scriptum est: Dominum Deum tuum adorabis et illi soli servies.

9. Et duxit illum in Jerusalem, et statuit eum super pinnam templi et dixit illi: Si filius Dei es, mitte te hinc deorsum.

10. Scriptum est enim quod Angelis suis mandavit de te, ut conservent te.

11. Et quia in manibus tollent te, ne forte offendas ad lapidem pedem tuum.

12. Et respondens Jesus, ait illi: Dictum est: Non tentabis Dominum Deum tuum.

13. Et consummata omni tentatione, diabolus recessit ab illo usque ad tempus.

14. Et regressus est Jesus in virtute Spiritus in Galilaeam, et fama exiit per universam regionem de illo.

15. Et ipse docebat in synagogis eorum, et magnificabatur ab omnibus.

16. Et venit Nazareth, ubi erat nutritus, et intravit secundum consuetudinem suam die sabbati in synagogam, et surrexit legere.

17. Et traditus est illi Liber Isaiae prophetae. Et ut revolvit librum, invenit locum ubi scriptum erat:

18. Spiritus Domini super me: propter quod unxit me, evangelizare pauperibus misit me, sanare contritos corde.

19. Praedicare captivis remissionem, et caecis visum, dimittere confractos in remissionem, praedicare annum Domini acceptum, et diem retributionis.

20. Et cum plicuisset librum, reddidit ministro, et sedit. Et omnium in synagoga oculi erant intendentes in eum.

21. Coepit autem dicere ad illos: Quia hodie impleta est haec scriptura in auribus vestris.

22. Et omnes testimonium illi dabant: et mirabantur in verbis gratiae, quae procedebant de ore ipsius, et dicebant: Nonne hic est filius Joseph?

23. Et ait illis: Utique dicetis mihi hanc similitudinem: Medice, cura teipsum: quanta audivimus facta in Capharnaum fac et hic in patria tua.

24. Ait autem: Amen dico vobis, quia nemo propheta acceptus est in patria sua.

25. In veritate dico vobis, multae viduae erant in diebus Eliae in Israel, quando clausum est caelum annis tribus, et mensibus sex; cum facta esset fames magna in omni terra.

26. Et ad nullam illarum missus est Elias, nisi in Sarepta Sidoniae, ad mulierem viduam.

27. Et multi leprosi erant in Israel, sub Elisaeo propheta: et nemo eorum mundatus est nisi Naaman Syrus.

28. Et repleti sunt omnes in synagoga ira, haec audientes.

29. Et surrexerunt, et ejecerunt illum extra civitatem: et duxerunt illum usque ad supercilium montis, super quem civitas illorum erat aedificata, ut praecipitarent eum.

30. Ipse autem transiens per medium illorum, ibat.

31. Et descendit in Capharnaum civitatem Galilaeae, ibique docebat illos sabbatis.

32. Et stupebant in doctrina ejus, quia in potestate erat sermo ipsius.

33. Et in synagoga erat homo habens daemonium immundum, et exclamavit voce magna,

34. Dicens: Sine, quid nobis, et tibi Jesu Nazarene? venisti perdere nos? scio te quis sis, Sanctus Dei.

35. Et increpavit illum Jesus, dicens: Obmutesce, et exi ab eo. Et cum projecisset illum daemonium in medium, exiit ab illo, nihilque illum nocuit.

36. Et factus est pavor in omnibus, et colloquebantur ad invicem, dicentes: Quod est hoc verbum, quia in potestate et virtute imperat immundis spiritibus, et exeunt?

37. Et divulgabatur fama de illo in omnem locum regionis.

(Jesu Christi Evangelium secundum Lucam, caput IV, 1–37.)

LESSON XVIII

Unit One

Corpus Dómini nostri Jesu
Christi custódiat ánimam
tuam in vitam aetérnam.

*May the body of our Lord Jesus
Christ preserve thy soul to life
everlasting.*

Vocabulary

vínculum, -i, n., *bond, chain*
Judaéi, Judaeórum, m., *Jews*
poena, -ae, f., *pain, punishment, penalty*
tártarus, -i, m., *hell*
praémium, -ii, n., *gift, reward*
ros, roris, m., *dew*
os, ossis, n., *bone*
umbra, -ae, f., *shadow*
vicis (gen.) (nom. missing), f., *punishment, change*
turma, -ae, f., *squadron, troop, throng*
túmulus, -i, m., *mound, grave*
vanus, -a, -um, *empty, vain*
perénnis (m. and f.), perénne (n.), *eternal*
optáre, *to desire*
litigáre, *to quarrel, to dispute, to strive*
absorbére, *to absorb, to swallow*
repraesentáre, *to lead; to show, to represent*
purgáre, *to cleanse*
juráre, *to swear*
júngere (junxi, junctus), *to join, to bind, to unite*
párcere (pepérci, párcitus), *to spare*

migráre, *to depart*
expedíre, *to deliver from*
jam (adv.), *now, already*
ínvicem, *one another, each other*
ad ínvicem, *among themselves, reciprocally*
quómodo (interr. adv.), *how*
olim (adv.), *formerly, once*
foras (adv.), *out of doors, outside*
páriter (adv.), *at the same time*
illic (adv.), *there*
quondam (adv.), *formerly, once*
nisi, ni (conj.), *if not, unless, except*

42. **Impersonal verbs.** An impersonal verb is one that is used in the third person singular only, its subject being the impersonal pronoun *it*.

licére, *to be permitted, to be lawful*

I am permitted to do this.	Hoc mihi fácere licet (It is permitted to me).
They were permitted to enter the building.	Intráre in aedifícium eis licébat (It was permitted to them).

decére, *to fit, suit, to be becoming*

It is suitable to offer gifts to the king.	Múnera regi offérre decet.

Verbs not ordinarily impersonal are frequently used impersonally in the passive voice.

He (they, etc.) came.	Ventum est (It was come).
They ate.	Coenátum est (It was eaten).
It happened, it came to pass.	Factum est (It was made).

43. **Adjectives of special declension.** The following adjectives have -ius in the genitive singular and -i in the dative singular of all genders. Otherwise they are declined like **bonus.**

alius (*n.* aliud), other	neuter (neutrı́us) neither (of
alter, the other (of two)	two)
ullus, any	solus, alone
nullus, no, not any	totus, whole
uter (utrı́us), which (of two)	unus, one

of the other man	alı́us hóminis
to any mother	ulli matri
to which boy	utri púero
of neither book	neutrı́us libri
of the whole world	totı́us mundi

44. Uses of the dative.

a) As indirect object.

He gave me the trumpet.	Tubam mihi dedit.

b) With verbs compounded with ab, ad, ante, circum, con, in, inter, post, prae, pro, sub, super.

He was in command of the army.	Exercı́tui praéerat.
She laid the bread before us.	Panem nobis antepósuit.
We promised him a reward.	Munus ei promı́simus.
They will help the boy.	Púero subvénient.

c) With intransitive verbs meaning *benefit* or *injure, please* or *displease, command* or *obey, serve* or *resist, believe* or *distrust, persuade, pardon, spare, envy, threaten, be angry,* and the like.

She has served you.	Ea tibi servı́vit.
This book will please them.	Hic liber eis placébit.
They do not believe me.	Mihi non credunt.
He persuaded the servants.	Servis persuásit.

d) To express the agent with the passive periphrastic.

You must open the gate.	Porta tibi aperiénda est. (The gate must be opened by you.)

e) To express possession with **esse**, the possessor being in the dative case.

The boy has a book.   **Púero liber est.** (The book is to the boy.)

f) To denote purpose.

They will send some men as an aid to the city.   **Hómines áliquos civitáti auxílio mittent.** (**Auxílio** is dative of purpose.)

EXERCISES

A. Suffixes. The endings **-io**, **-tio**, and **-tus** are added to verb stems to form verbal nouns which denote an act or the result of an act.

1. **conjurátio**, conspiracy (from **conjuráre**, to conspire). 2. **orátio**, prayer (from **oráre**, to pray). 3. **suspício**, suspicion (from **suspícere**, to suspect). 4. **dubitátio**, doubt (from **dubitáre**, to doubt). 5. **offénsio**, offense (from **offéndere**, to offend). 6. **dedítio**, surrender (from **dédere**, to surrender). 7. **conspéctus**, sight (from **conspícere**, to look at). 8. **fructus**, fruit (from **frui**, to enjoy). 9. **luctus**, mourning (from **lugére**, to mourn). 10. **fletus**, weeping (from **flere**, to weep). 11. **cantus**, song (from **cánere**, to sing). 12. **conátus**, an attempt (from **conári**, to attempt).

B. Trans- as a prefix means *through* or *across*.

1. **transíre** (to go through). 2. **trádere** (to give or hand across). 3. **tradúcere** (to lead across). 4. **transfígere** (to pierce through, to transfix). 5. **transportáre** (to carry across, to transport). 6. **transférre** (to bring through, to transfer). 7. **transmíttere** (to send across, to transmit). 8. **tranáre** (to swim across).

C. Read the Latin and translate into English.

1. Litigábant ad ínvicem, quóniam non credébant quod eis díxerat dóminus eórum. 2. Si nos júngimus turmis inimicórum, nobis non

parcétur. 3. Quómodo túmulos mórtuis olim faciébant? 4. Juravé-
runt, nisi migrárent ex civitáte, ipsos eos ejectúros esse foras. 5. Púeri
non in domo erant, dum ego illic eram. 6. Ossa multórum sanctórum
et mártyrum in illis túmulis invénta sunt. 7. Virum alium non vidi,
quia in umbra stabat. 8. Dicta hujus hóminis vera sunt, sed dicta alíus
vana et dolósa sunt. 9. Nullus homo per ignem transíre potest incólumis. 10. Decébat praémia offérre eis qui multum sacrificáverant pro
pátria sua. 11. Quondam eos convértere ab malítiis suis conátus erat,
sed conátus sui vani erant. 12. Vita ullíus hóminis sine mácula esse
debet, ut álios in vias rectas addúcat. 13. Libros neutri púero dabo.
14. Nobis non licébat remanére in civitáte illa die. 15. Multae ecclésiae discípulis in terris novis aedificándae erant. 16. Cum fámuli sui
ei bene servivíssent, servitútis fidélis eórum oblítus est. 17. Ópera
bona vestra vobis profícient, diebus quibus adjutórium aliórum
necessárium erit. 18. Factum est, cum ad ínvicem conjuravíssent, rex
per illam viam ibat. 19. Virgínibus auxílio veniébant. 20. Illa domus
meo fratri est.

UNIT TWO

A. 1. Tibi soli peccávi, et malum coram te feci. 2. Dómine Jesu
Christi, Rex glóriae, líbera ánimas ómnium fidélium defunctórum de
poenis inférni et de profúndo lacu. 3. Líbera eos de ore leónis, ne
absórbeat eas tártarus, ne cadant in obscúrum, sed sígnifer sanctus
Míchaël repraeséntet eas in lucem sanctam, quam olim Ábrahae
promisísti, et sémini ejus. 4. Fac eas, Dómine, de morte transíre ad
vitam. 5. Praesta, quaésumus, omnípotens Deus, ut ánima fámuli tui,
quae hódie de hoc saéculo migrávit, his sacrifíciis purgáta, et a peccátis expedíta, indulgéntiam páriter et réquiem cápiat sempitérnam.
6. Non intres in judícium cum servo tuo, Dómine, quia nullus apud
te justificábitur homo, nisi per te ómnium peccatórum ei tribuátur
remíssio. 7. Deus, cui próprium est miseréri semper et párcere, te
súpplices exorámus pro ánima fámulae tuae, quam hódie de hoc

saéculo migráre jussísti, ut non tradas eam in manus inimíci, neque
obliviscáris in finem, sed júbeas eam a sanctis Angelis súscipi, et ad
pátriam paradísi perdúci; ut, quia in te sperávit et crédidit, non poenas inférni sustíneat, sed gáudia aetérna possídeat. 8. In illo témpore,
dixit Jesus turbis Judaeórum: Omne, quod dat mihi Pater, ad me
véniet: et, eum, qui venit ad me, non ejíciam foras, quia descéndi de
caelo, non ut fáciam voluntátem meam, sed voluntátem ejus, qui misit
me. 9. Fidélium, Deus, omnium Cónditor et Redémptor, animábus
famulórum, famularúmque tuárum remissiónem cunctórum tríbue
peccatórum; ut indulgéntiam quam semper optavérunt, piis suppli-
catiónibus consequántur. 10. Litigábant ergo Judaéi ad ínvicem, dicentes: Quómodo potest hic nobis carnem suam dare ad manducán-
dum? 11. Illumináre his, qui in ténebris et in umbra mortis sedent;
ad dirigéndos pedes nostros in viam pacis. 12. Fac, quaésumus, Dómine, hanc cum servo tuo defúncto misericórdiam, ut factórum
suórum, in poenis non recípiat vicem, qui tuam in votis tenuit voluntátem; ut sicut hic eum vera fides junxit fidélium turmis ita illic eum
tua miserátio sóciet angélicis choris.

B. Form as many sentences as possible with the following combina-
tions and translate each into English.

	aqua in lacu profúnda nimis erat.
Decet	veritátem omnes hómines docére.
Licébat	nobis, ópera Dei judicáre.
Decébat	plebi intráre in ecclésias suas.
Licébit	laudáre eos qui nobis sérviunt bene.
Licet	peccáta dimíttere eórum qui conféssi sunt.
Factum est:	terra nimis tremébat.
Décuit	repéllere inimícos qui nos afflígunt.
Non licébat	honoráre viros ímpios et dolósos.
Non decet	sonum tubárum et córnuum in nocte audiébant.
Non licet	viris in illa regióne vinum bíbere.
	paupéribus múnera donáre.

C. Change the adjective in parentheses to the right form to agree with the noun.

1. (*alius*) vínculi. 2. (*nullus*) poenae. 3. (*totus*) mundi. 4. (*solus*) praémio. 5. (*unus*) Dei. 6. (*ullus*) óssibus. 7. (*alter*) túmuli. 8. (*uter*) virum. 9. (*neuter*) leónis. 10. (*ullus*) roris. 11. (*totus*) tártaro. 12. (*unus*) exercítui. 13. (*alius*) Judaéos. 14. (*alter*) ovi. 15. (*solus*) linguae. 16. (*ullus*) epíscopo. 17. (*nullus*) cíneris. 18. (*uter*) antístiti. 19. (*alius*) cálculo. 20. (*neuter*) diei.

UNIT THREE

A. Explain the use of the dative in each of these sentences.

1. Nobis panem dedérunt. 2. Adhaéreat viscéribus meis. 3. Tectum domui superpónunt. 4. Prosit mihi ad tutaméntum mentis et córporis. 5. Nemo tibi nocébit. 6. Cívitas plebi condénda est. 7. Púeri virgínibus anteíbunt. 8. Paupéribus succúrrit. 9. Praémia eis non placébant. 10. Domus illa fratri meo est. 11. Dona nobis pacem. 12. Muros civitáti circumdábant. 13. Fac me tuis semper inhaerére mandátis. 14. Non mihi próveniat in judícium et condemnatiónem. 15. Fuit homo missus a Deo, cui nomen erat Joánnes. 16. Pláceat tibi. 17. Miserére nobis. 18. Carthágo Románis delénda est. 19. Confíteor Deo omnipoténti. 20. Ei mandávit, ut némini id díceret. 21. Fámula dómino servit. 22. Venérunt auxílio patri suo. 23. Offérimus praeclárae majestáti tuae. 24. Mátribus et fíliis pepercérunt. 25. Grátias ágimus tibi.

B. Vocabulary building.

a) Derivations. Find in Units One and Two the words that have the same derivation as the following:

1. jusjurándum (oath). 2. parce (sparingly). 3. vincíre (to bind). 4. umbrósus (shady). 5. expedítio (expedition). 6. par (equal). 7. annus (year). 8. vánitas (emptiness). 9. sorbére (to suck). 10. purus (pure). 11. juráre (to swear). 12. pérfrui (to enjoy). 13. ire (to go). 14. portáre (to carry). 15. ferre (to bring). 16. nare (to swim).

b) Observe the relation between these Latin and English words.

Latin	English	Latin	English
vicis	vicissitude	perénnis	perennial
absorbére	absorbent	vanus	vanity
litigáre	litigant	purgáre	purgatory
júngere	conjunction	migráre	immigrant
expedíre	expeditious	os	ossify
juráre	jury	optáre	optional
tranáre	natatorium		

c) Observe the relation of

these adjectives	to	these verbs
dúbius (doubtful)		dubitáre (to doubt)
cálidus (warm)		calére (to be warm)
tímidus (timid)		timére (to fear)
purus (pure)		purgáre (to cleanse)
fidélis (faithful)		fídere (to trust)
amábilis (loveable)		amáre (to love)
dolorósus (sorrowful)		dolére (to suffer)
sanus (healthy)		sanáre (to heal)
mutábilis (changeable)		mutáre (to change)
salvus (safe)		salváre (to save)
vivus (living)		vívere (to live)
miséricors (merciful)		miseréri (to have mercy)

READING LESSON

1. Et factum est cum esset in quodam loco orans, ut cessavit, dixit unus ex discipulis ejus ad eum: Domine, doce nos orare, sicut docuit et Joannes discipulos suos.

2. Et ait illis: Cum oratis, dicite: Pater, sanctificetur nomen tuum. Adveniat regnum tuum.

3. Panem nostrum quotidianum da nobis hodie.

4. Et dimitte nobis peccata nostra, siquidem et ipsi dimittimus omni debenti nobis. Et ne nos inducas in tentationem.

5. Et ait ad illos: Quis vestrum habebit amicum, et ibit ad illum media nocta, et dicet illi: Amice, commoda mihi tres panes.

6. Quoniam amicus meus venit de via ad me, et non habeo quod ponam ante illum,

7. Et ille deintus respondens dicat: Noli mihi molestus esse, jam ostium clausum est, et pueri mei mecum sunt in cubili: non possum surgere, et dare tibi.

8. Et si ille perseveraverit pulsans, dico vobis: et si non dabit illi surgens eo quod amicus ejus sit, propter improbitatem tamen ejus surget, et dabit illi quotquot habet necessarios.

9. Et ego dico vobis: Petite, et dabitur vobis: quaerite, et invenietis: pulsate, et aperietur vobis.

10. Omnis enim qui petit, accipit: et qui quaerit, invenit: et pulsanti aperietur.

11. Quis autem ex vobis patrem petit panem, numquid lapidem dabit illi? Aut piscem: numquid pro pisce serpentem dabit illi?

12. Aut si petierit ovum: numquid porriget illi scorpionem?

13. Si ergo vos cum sitis mali, nostis bona data dare filiis vestris: quanto magis Pater vester de caelo dabit spiritum bonum petentibus se?

14. Et erat ejiciens daemonium, et illud erat mutum. Et cum ejecisset daemonium, locutus est mutus, et admiratae sunt turbae.

15. Quidam autem ex eis dixerunt: In Beelzebub principe daemoniorum ejicit daemonia.

16. Et alii tentantes, signum de caelo quaerebant ab eo.

17. Ipse autem ut videt cogitationes eorum, dixit eis: Omne regnum in seipsum divisum desolabitur, et domus supra domum cadet.

18. Si autem et Satanas in seipsum divisus est, quomodo stabit regnum ejus? quia dicitis in Beelzebub me ejicere daemonia.

19. Si autem ego in Beelzebub ejicio daemonia: filii vestri in quo ejicient? Ideo ipsi judices vestri erunt.

20. Porro si in digito Dei ejicio daemonia: profecto pervenit in vos regnum Dei.

21. Cum fortis armatus custodit atrium suum, in pace sunt ea quae possidet.

22. Si autem fortior eo superveniens vicerit eum, universa arma ejus auferet, in quibus confidebat, et spolia ejus distribuet.

23. Qui non est mecum, contra me est: et qui non colligit mecum, dispergit.

24. Cum immundus spiritus exierit de homine, ambulat per loca inaquosa, quaerens requiem: et non inveniens dicit: Revertar in domum meam unde exivi.

25. Et cum venerit, invenit eam scopis mundatam et ornatam.

26. Tunc vadit, et assumit septem alios spiritus secum, nequiores se, et ingressi habitant ibi. Et fiunt novissima hominis illius pejora prioribus.

(Jesu Christi Evangelium secundum Lucam, caput XI, 1–26.)

LESSON XIX

Ite, Missa est.   *Go, the Mass is finished.*

Vocabulary

relaxáre, *to loosen*
annúere (ánnui), *to assent, to nod to, to hear*
constitúere (constítui, constitútus), *to constitute, to decree*
contráhere (contráxi, contráctus), *to contract*
coronáre, *to crown*
dealbáre, *to make white*
delectáre, *to be delighted*
discútere (-io verb) (discússi, discússus), *to disperse, to judge*
gérere (gessi, gestus), *to carry, to manage*
ignoráre, *to be ignorant of, not to know*
sequestráre, *to separate*
latére, *to lie hidden*
útique, *indeed, certainly*
certámen, certáminis, n., *strife*
cíthara, -ae, f., *harp*
cura, -ae, f., *care*
favílla, -ae, f., *ashes*
haedus, -i, m., *goat*
nix, nivis, f., *snow*
reus, rei, m., *criminal, sinner;* as adj., **guilty**
incolátus, incolátus, m., *sojourn, residence*
cassus, -a, -um, *vain, worthless*
contribulátus, -a, -um, *troubled*

horréndus, -a, -um, *dreadful*
lacrimósus, -a, -um, *tearful*
quisquis (decline both parts like quis), *whoever*

45. Comparison of adjectives and adverbs. The comparative of adjectives is formed by adding -ior (neuter, -ius) to the base of the positive, the comparative of adverbs being, for the most part, the same as the neuter comparative of the adjective. The superlative is usually formed by adding to the base of the positive -issimus for adjectives ending in -s or -x (adverbs -íssime), -rimus for adjectives ending in -r (adverbs -rime), and -limus for adjectives ending in -ilis (adverbs -lime).

Positive	Comparative	Superlative
altus, high	áltior, higher	altíssimus, highest
fortis, strong	fórtior, stronger	fortíssimus, strongest
velox, swift	velócior, swifter	velocíssimus, swiftest
miser, wretched	misérior, more wretched	misérrimus, most wretched
acer, sharp	ácrior, sharper	acérrimus, sharpest
fácilis, easy	facílior, easier	facíllimus, easiest
difficilis, difficult	difficílior, more difficult	difficíllimus, most difficult
húmilis, humble	humílior, humbler	humíllimus, humblest
fórtiter, bravely	fórtius, more bravely	fortíssime, most bravely
mísere, wretchedly	misérius, more wretchedly	misérrime, most wretchedly
fácile, easily	facílius, more easily	facíllime, most easily
ácriter, sharply	ácrius, more sharply	acérrime, most sharply

46. Irregular comparisons. Some common adjectives and adverbs are compared irregularly.

Positive	Comparative	Superlative
bonus, good	mélior, better	óptimus, best
malus, bad	pejor, worse	péssimus, worst
magnus, great	major, greater	máximus, greatest
parvus, small	minor, smaller	mínimus, smallest
bene, well	mélius, better	óptime, best
male, badly	pejus, worse	péssime, worst
magnópere, greatly	magis, more	máxime, most
multum, much	plus, more	plúrimum, most
parum, little	minus, less	mínime, least

47. Velle, *to wish, to be willing;* nolle, *to be unwilling.* These partly irregular verbs double the l only in the infinitive and in the imperfect subjunctive. Elsewhere they have but one l. The present indicative only presents special difficulty.

Present Indicative

(velle, *to wish, to be willing*)		(nolle, *to be unwilling*)	
volo	vólumus	nolo	nólumus
vis	vultis	non vis	non vultis
vult	volunt	non vult	nolunt

The imperative of nolle is often used with an infinitive to express a command: Noli dícere, *Do not say.*

See Appendix for the remaining tenses.

48. Uses of the ablative.

a) Ablative absolute.

When they had received the king's commands they returned to the city.	Mandátis regis accéptis, ad civitátem redivérunt.

b) Accompaniment with cum.

The boys went to church with their father.	Púeri cum patre suo ad ecclésiam iérunt.

c) After a comparative when **quam** (*than*) is omitted.

The boy is taller than his father.
{ Fílius major est quam pater.
{ Fílius major patre est.

d) To express the agent or doer of an action with the passive voice and the preposition **ab (a)**.

The kingdom was saved by its faithful men.
Regnum ab homínibus suis fidélibus salvabátur.

e) To express cause without a preposition.

They all shouted with joy.
Omnes gáudio clamábant.

f) To express degree of difference in a sentence involving **a** comparison.

This house is ten feet higher than that one.
Haec domus decem pédibus áltior est quam illa.

g) To express manner with or without the preposition **cum**.

They entered the city with loud shouts.
Magnis clamóribus introíbant in civitátem.

h) To express means or instrument without a preposition.

They have been saved by the grace of God.
Grátia Dei salváti sunt.

i) To express place *in, on,* or *from which* with the prepositions **in, ab, de,** and **ex**.

They are standing in the shade.	Stant in umbra.
We live on the earth.	In terra vívimus.
They come from Rome.	Roma véniunt.
He descended from heaven.	Descéndit de caelis.
They went out of the house.	Ex domo iérunt.

j) To express quality or description without a preposition, the noun being modified by an adjective.

He was a king of great power.
Rex magna potestáte erat.

k) To express specification without a preposition.

He was ever diligent in the cause of peace.	Causa pacis semper díligens erat.

l) To express separation with or without a preposition.

They will be delivered from their miseries.	Misériis suis eruéntur.
From all evil, O Lord, deliver us.	Ab omni malo, líbera nos, Dómine.

m) To express time when, with or without a preposition.

In one day many buildings were burned.	Una die multa aedifícia cremáta sunt.
Mercifully grant peace in our days.	Da propítius pacem in diébus nostris.

n) Certain prepositions, ab, de, cum, ex, sine, pro, and prae regularly govern the ablative.

We cannot do this without help.	Non póssumus hoc fácere sine auxílio.
They will speak in our behalf.	Loquéntur pro nobis.
The men walked ahead of the boys.	Viri prae púeris ingréssi sunt.

o) The deponent verbs uti (*to use*), frui (*to enjoy*), fungi (*to perform*), potíri (*to take possession of*), vesci (*to eat*) and their compounds take their direct objective in the ablative case.

He will use our books.	Nostris libris utétur.
They are enjoying their new freedom.	Nova libertáte sua fruúntur.
He has performed his tasks well.	Opéribus suis bene functus est.
The army got possession of all the hills around the city.	Milítia potíta est ómnibus móntibus circum civitátem.
They eat meat and bread.	Carne atque pane vescunt.

EXERCISES

A. Suffixes. The suffixes -men, -mentum, -bulum, -culum, -crum, -trum are added to verb stems to denote means or instrument.

1. nomen, name (from **nóscere,** to know; that is, a means of knowing). 2. **vínculum,** bond (from **vincíre,** to bind; that is, a means of binding). 3. **flúmen,** river (from **flúere,** to flow). 4. **certámen,** strife (from **certáre,** to contend). 5. **semen,** seed (from **sérere,** to sow). 6. lumen, light (from **lucére,** to shine). 7. **testaméntum,** testament (from **testári,** to bear witness). 8. **firmaméntum,** firmament, prop (from **firmáre,** to make firm). 9. **sepúlcrum,** sepulcher (from **sepelíre,** to bury). 10. **tutaméntum,** safeguard (from **tutáre,** to protect). 11. **monstrum,** portent (from **monére,** to warn). 12. **stábulum,** stable (from **stare,** to stand).

B. The prefix in- with adjectives has a negative force.

1. **inimícus,** enemy (in + **amícus** = not friendly). 2. **incredíbilis,** incredible (in + **credíbilis** = not credible). 3. **immortális,** immortal (in (im) + **mortális** = not mortal). 4. **incógnitus,** unknown (in + **cógnitus** = not known). 5. **ínsciens,** unaware (in + **sciens** = not knowing). 6. **iníquus,** uneven, unjust (in + **aequus** = not even). 7. **inútilis,** useless (in + **útilis** = not useful). 8. **indígnus,** unworthy (in + **dignus** = not worthy). 9. **inúltus,** unavenged (in + **ultus** = not avenged). 10. **incértus,** uncertain (in + **certus** = not certain). 11. **immúndus,** unclean (in + **mundus** = not clean). 12. **immaculátus,** immaculate (in + **maculátus** = not stained). 13. **ínnocens,** innocent (in + **nocens** = not harmful). 14. **infórmis,** shapeless (in + **forma** = not having a form).

UNIT TWO

A. Read and translate into English.

1. In nómine Patris, et Fílii et Spíritus Sancti. 2. Discérne causam meam de gente non sancta. 3. Ab hómine iníquo et dolóso érue me. 4. Confitébor tibi in cíthara, Deus, Deus meus. 5. Sicut erat in prin-

cípio et nunc et semper. 6. Dimíssis peccátis tuis. 7. Quia peccávi nimis cogitatióne, verbo, et ópere. 8. Mea culpa, mea culpa, mea máxima culpa. 9. Dóminus vobíscum. Et cum spíritu tuo. 10. Aufer a nobis iniquitátes nostras, ut ad Sancta sanctórum puris mereámur méntibus introíre. 11. Glória in excélsis Deo, et in terra pax homínibus bonae voluntátis. 12. Munda cor meum, ac lábia mea, omnípotens Deus, qui lábia Isaíae prophétae cálculo mundásti igníto. 13. Dóminus sit in corde tuo. 14. Deum de Deo, lumen de lúmine, Deum verum de Deo vero. 15. Crucifíxus étiam pro nobis, sub Póntio Piláto passus, et sepúltus est. 16. Et íterum ventúrus est cum glória. 17. Qui cum Patre, et Fílio simul adorátur. 18. Offérimus tibi, Dómine, cálicem salutáris, tuam deprecántes cleméntiam, ut in conspéctu divínae majestátis tuae, pro nostra, et totíus mundi salúte cum odóre suavitátis ascéndat. 19. In spíritu humilitátis, et in ánimo contríto suscipiámur a te, Dómine. 20. Ne perdas cum ímpiis, Deus, ánimam meam, et cum viris sánguinum vitam meam. 21. In quorum mánibus iniquitátes sunt, déxtera eórum repléta est munéribus. 22. In ecclésiis benedícam te, Dómine. 23. Pleni sunt caeli et terra glória tua. 24. Elevátis óculis. 25. Símili modo. 26. Supra quae propítio ac seréno vultu respícere dignéris. 27. Omni benedictióne caelésti et grátia repleámur. 28. Qui nos praecessérunt cum signo fídei et dórmiunt in somno pacis. 29. Praecéptis salutáribus móniti, et divína institutióne formáti, audémus dícere. 30. Sed líbera nos a malo. 31. Líbera nos, quaésumus, Dómine, ab ómnibus malis, praetéritis, praeséntibus et futúris, et intercedénte beáta, et gloriósa semper Vírgine Dei Genitríce María, cum beátis Apóstolis Petro et Paulo, atque Andréa, et ómnibus Sanctis, da propítius pacem in diébus nostris; ut ope misericórdiae tuae adjúti, et a peccáto simus semper líberi, et ab omni perturbatióne secúri. 32. Sed tantum dic verbo. 33. Quod ore súmpsimus, Dómine, pura mente capiámus. 34. Requiéscant in pace. 35. Sine ipso factum est nihil, quod factum est. 36. Lux in ténebris lucet. 37. Aspérges me hyssópo, et mundábor; lavábis me, et super nivem dealbábor. 38. Holocáustis non delectáberis. 39. Sacrifícium Deo spíritus contribulátus. 40. Fratres: Nólumus vos ignoráre de dormiéntibus, ut non contristémini, sicut et céteri qui spem non hábent. 41. Dies irae, dies illa, solvet saeclum (saéculum) in favílla. 42. Tantus labor non sit cassus. 43. Quantus tremor est futúrus, quando judex est ventúrus, cuncta stricte discussúrus. 44. Quidquid latet, apparébit. 45. Inter oves locum praesta, et ab haedis me sequéstra. 46. Oro supplex et acclínis, cor contrítum quasi cinis, gere curam mei finis. 47. Ánnue nobis, quaésumus, Dómine, ut ánimae fámuli tui haec prosit oblátio, quam immolándo totíus mundi tribuísti relaxári delícta. 48. Quóniam, si voluísses sacrifícium, dedíssem útique; holocáustis non delectáberis. 49. Lacrimósa dies illa, qua resúrget ex favílla judicándus homo reus; huic ergo parce Deus. 50. Tuis enim fidélibus, Dómine, vita mutátur, non tóllitur, et dissolúta hujus incolátus domo, aetérna in caelis habi-tátio comparátur. 51. Da nobis, Dómine, ut ánimam fámuli tui Epís-copi, quam de hujus saéculi eduxísti laborióso certámine, sanctórum tuórum tríbuas esse consórtem. 52. Caeléstis participátio sacraménti, quaésumus, Dómine, animábus patris et matris meae réquiem et lu-cem obtíneat perpétuam; meque cum illis grátia tua corónet aetérna. 53. Pro animábus famulórum, famularúmque tuárum, et ómnium catholicórum hic et ubíque in Christo dormiéntium, hóstiam, Dómine, súscipe benígnus oblátam; ut hoc sacrifício singulári, vínculis horrén-dae mortis exúti, vitam mereántur aetérnam. 54. Súpplices, Dómine, pro animábus famulórum, famularúmque tuárum preces effúndimus; obsecrántes, ut quidquid conversatióne contraxérunt humána, et cle-ménter indúlgeas, et in tuórum sede laetántium constítuas redemp-tórum.

B. Give the comparative and superlative forms of each of these ad-jectives and adverbs.

1. potens. 2. altus. 3. diléctus. 4. magnópere. 5. fortis. 6. nova. 7. sancti. 8. beátum. 9. clemens. 10. fácile. 11. velox. 12. bene. 13. fórtiter. 14. mísera. 15. acris. 16. malus. 17. bonus. 18. male. 19. multum. 20. mag-nus. 21. parva. 22. parum. 23. excélsus. 24. nóbilis. 25. certus.

A. Give the forms of velle and nolle as indicated.

velle

ego {
present indicative
imperfect subjunctive
future
pluperfect subjunctive
imperfect indicative
}

vos {
future perfect indicative
present indicative
perfect subjunctive
imperfect subjunctive
pluperfect indicative
}

nolle

nos {
present subjunctive
future
imperfect indicative
perfect subjunctive
present indicative
}

ei {
imperfect indicative
future perfect indicative
present indicative
present subjunctive
imperfect subjunctive
}

B. Write ten short sentences in Latin, each one to illustrate a different use of the ablative.

C. Vocabulary building.

a) Derivations. Find in Units One and Two the words that have the same derivation as the following:

1. coróna (wreath). 2. albus (white). 3. discússio (dispersal). 4. certáre (to contend). 5. latro (robber). 6. nivósus (snowy). 7. reátus (criminal condition). 8. lácrima (tear). 9. curáre (to care for). 10. testis (witness). 11. laetári (to rejoice). 12. monstruósus (monstrous).

b) Observe the relation between these Latin and English words.

Latin	English	Latin	English
relaxáre	relaxation	coronáre	coronet
delectáre	delectable	latére	latent
cura	curate	contribulátus	tribulation
nomen	nominate	lumen	luminous

c) Observe these word families.

Noun	Adjective	Verb
ignorántia (ignorance)	ignótus (unknown)	ignoráre (to be ignorant of)
nix (snow)	nivósus (snowy)	níngere (to snow)
horror (horror)	horréndus (dreadful)	horrére (of hair, to stand on end)
lácrima (tear)	lacrimósus (tearful)	lacrimáre (to weep)
cura (care)	curiósus (careful)	curáre (to care for)

READING LESSON

1. Haec cum dixisset Jesus, egressus est cum discipulis suis trans Torrentem Cedron, ubi erat hortus in quem introivit ipse, et discipuli ejus.

2. Sciebat autem et Judas, qui tradebat eum, locum: quia frequenter Jesus convenerat illuc cum discipulis suis.

3. Judas ergo cum accepisset cohortem, et a pontificibus et pharisaeis ministros, venit illuc cum laternis et facibus, et armis.

4. Jesus itaque sciens omnia quae ventura erant super eum, processit, et dixit eis: Quem quaeritis?

5. Responderunt ei: Jesum Nazarenum. Dicit eis Jesus: Ego sum. Stabat autem et Judas qui tradebat eum, cum ipsis.

6. Ut ergo dixit eis, Ego sum, abierunt retrorsum et ceciderunt in terram.

7. Iterum ergo interrogavit eos: Quem quaeritis? Illi autem dixerunt: Jesum Nazarenum.

8. Respondit Jesus: Dixi vobis quia ego sum: si ergo me quaeritis, sinite hos abire.

9. Ut impleretur sermo quem dixit: Quia quos dedisti mihi, non perdidi ex eis quemquam.

10. Simon ergo Petrus habens gladium eduxit eum: et percussit pontificis servum: et abscidit auriculam ejus dexteram. Erat autem nomen servo Malchus.

11. Dixit ergo Jesus Petro: Mitte gladium tuum in vaginam. Calicem quem dedit mihi Pater, non bibam illum?

12. Cohors ergo, et tribunus, et ministri Judaeorum comprehenderunt Jesum, et ligaverunt eum:

13. Et adduxerunt eum ad Annam primum; erat enim socer Caiphae, qui erat pontifex anni illius.

14. Erat autem Caiphas, qui consilium dederat Judaeis: Quia expedit, unum hominem mori pro populo.

15. Sequebatur autem Jesum Simon Petrus, et alius discipulus. Discipulus autem ille erat notus pontifici, et introivit cum Jesu in atrium pontificis.

16. Petrus autem stabat ad ostium foris. Exivit ergo discipulus alius qui erat notus pontifici, et dixit ostiariae: et introduxit Petrum.

17. Dicit ergo Petro ancilla ostiaria: Numquid et tu ex discipulis es hominis istius? Dicit ille: Non sum.

18. Stabant autem servi et ministri ad prunas, quia frigus erat, et calefaciebant se: erat autem cum eis et Petrus stans, et calefaciens se.

19. Pontifex ergo interrogavit Jesum de discipulis suis, et de doctrina ejus.

20. Respondit ei Jesus: Ego palam locutus sum mundo: ego semper docui in synagoga, et in templo, quo omnes Judaei conveniunt: et in occulto locutus sum nihil.

21. Quid me interrogas? Interroga eos qui audierunt quid locutus sim ipsis: ecce hi sciunt quae dixerim ego.

22. Haec autem cum dixisset, unus assistens ministrorum dedit alapam Jesu, dicens: Sic respondens pontifici?

23. Respondit ei Jesus: Si male locutus sum, testimonium perhibe de malo: si autem bene, quid me caedis?

24. Et misit eum Annas ligatum ad Caipham pontificem.

25. Erat autem Simon Petrus stans, et calefaciens se. Dixerunt ergo ei: Numquid et tu ex discipulis ejus es? Negavit ille, et dixit: Non sum.

26. Dicit ei unus ex servis pontificis, cognatus ejus, cujus abscidit Petrus auriculam: Nonne ego te vidi in horto cum illo?

27. Iterum ergo negavit Petrus: et statim gallus cantavit.

28. Adducunt ergo Jesum a Caipha in praetorium. Erat autem mane: et ipsi non introierunt in praetorium, ut non contaminarentur sed ut manducarent pascha.

29. Exivit ergo Pilatus ad eos foras, et dixit: Quam accusationem affertis adversus hominem hunc?

30. Responderunt, et dixerunt ei: Si non esset hic malefactor, **non** tibi tradidissemus eum.

31. Dixit ergo eis Pilatus: Accipite eum vos, et secundum legem vestram judicate eum. Dixerunt ergo ei Judaei: Nobis non licet interficere quemquam.

32. Ut sermo Jesu impleretur, quem dixit, significans qua morte esset moriturus.

33. Introivit ergo iterum in praetorium Pilatus, et vocavit Jesum, et dixit ei: Tu es rex Judaeorum?

34. Respondit Jesus: A temetipso hoc dicis, an alii dixerunt tibi de me?

35. Respondit Pilatus: Numquid ergo Judaeus sum? Gens tua et pontifices tradiderunt te mihi: quid fecisti?

36. Respondit Jesus: Regnum meum non est de hoc mundo: si **ex** hoc mundo esset regnum meum, ministri mei utique decertarent ut non traderer Judaeis; nunc autem regnum meum non est hinc.

37. Dixit itaque ei Pilatus: ergo rex es tu? Respondit Jesus: Tu dicis quia rex sum ego. Ego in hoc natus sum, et ad hoc veni in mundum, ut testimonium perhibeam veritati: omnis qui est ex veritate, audit vocem meam.

38. Dicit ei Pilatus: Quid est veritas? Et cum hoc dixisset, iterum exivit ad Judaeos, et dicit eis: Ego nullam invenio in eo causam.

39. Est autem consuetudo vobis, ut unum dimittam vobis in pascha: vultis ego dimittam vobis regem Judaeorum?

40. Clamaverunt ergo rursum omnes dicentes: Non hunc, sed Barabbam. Erat autem Barabbas latro.

(Jesu Christi Evangelium secundum Joannem, caput XVIII, 1–40.)

LESSON XX

Benedícat vos omnípotens Deus, Pater et Fílius et Spíritus Sanctus.	*May almighty God bless you, the Father, the Son, and the Holy Ghost.*

Vocabulary

exsultáre, *to exult*

vigére, *to thrive, to be active*

ingemíscere (ingémui), *to sigh, to groan*

obsecráre, *to implore*

possidére (possédi, posséssus), *to possess*

prémere (pressi, pressus), *to press (upon)*

rápere (rápui, raptus) (-io verb), *to snatch, to seize*

recordári, dep., *to remember*

respiráre, *to breathe*

reveláre, *to reveal, to unveil*

rubére, *to be red, to blush*

stupére, *to be amazed*

póscere (popósci), *to demand*

unde (adv.), *therefore, thence, whence*

usque (adv.), *all the way;* ad usque, *even until*

valde (adv.), *exceedingly*

vix (adv.), *scarcely, with difficulty*

neque (adv. and conj.), *and not, neither, nor*

nec non (adv.), *and also, nor less*

óbviam (adv.), *on the way*

tamquam (adv.), *like*

fons, fontis, m., *fountain, source*
vítulus, -i, m., *calf*
nubes, nubis (g. pl., núbium), f., *cloud*
refrigérium, -ii, n., *refreshment*
sermo, sermónis, m., *word, discourse*
occúltus, -a, -um, *hidden*
propínquus, -a, -um, *near;* as a noun, *a near relative*
singuláris, m. and f., singuláre, n., *remarkable, excellent*
memor, m., f., and n.; gen. mémoris, *mindful*

49. Questions.

a) A question that may be answered by *"yes"* or *"no"* may merely be a matter of vocal inflection.

You believe this.	**Credis hoc.**
Do you believe this?	**Credis hoc?**

Or the syllable **-ne** may be attached to the most emphatic word, usually the first.

Was he carrying the cross?   **Portabátne crucem?**

b) When the answer *"yes"* is expected, the question is introduced by **nonne.**

Do they not please you?   **Nonne tibi placent?**

c) When the answer *"no"* is expected, the question is introduced by **num** or, frequently, **numquid.**

Can we all be saints?   **Numquid omnes póssumus esse sancti?**

d) Double questions are introduced by **utrum ... an; -ne ... an,** or just **an** before the alternative part of the question.

Is he a friend or an enemy?
- **Utrum amícus est an inimícus?**
- **Amícusne est an inimícus?**
- **Amícus est an inimícus?**

e) Latin has no single word that is equivalent to our word *"yes,"* although various adverbs, such as **etiam**, *even so,* are used as a substitute or the important part of the question is repeated as a statement.

Do you believe this? Yes.   Credis hoc? Credo or Etiam.

"No" may be expressed by the simple word **non** or the verb of the question may be repeated with **non**.

Can you do these things? No.   Potestísne haec fácere? Non or
                                      Non póssumus.

50. **Defective verbs.** These are verbs that have lost certain of their tenses.

a) **coepísse**, *to have begun;* **odísse**, *to hate;* **meminísse**, *to remember*. These verbs occur only in the perfect tenses.

PERFECT INFINITIVE: **coepísse**, *to have begun;* **odísse**, *to hate;* **meminísse**, *to remember*.
PERFECT INDICATIVE: **coépi**, *I began;* **odi**, *I hate;*[1] **mémini**, *I remember*.
PAST PARTICIPLE: **coeptus**, *begun;* **osus**, *hated*.

OBSERVE. The perfect, pluperfect, and future perfect of **odísse** and **meminísse** have the meanings of a present, imperfect and future respectively.

odi, *I hate;* **óderam**, *I hated;* **ódero**, *I shall hate.*

mémini, *I remember;* **memíneram**, *I remembered;* **memínero**, *I shall remember.*

b) Other verbs have lost their perfect tenses and are partly defective in other tenses.

áio, *I say.* The commonest forms of this verb are the third person singular and plural of the present indicative: **áit**, *he says (saith)*, **aiunt**, *they say.*

---

[1] Also, sometimes, *I hated*.

51. Uses of the accusative.

a) As the direct object of a verb.

We saw your brother. **Vidimus fratrem tuum.**

b) After certain prepositions, the commonest being **ad, ante, apud, circum, contra, inter, per,** and **trans.**

They sent aid to the city. **Adjutórium ad civitátem misérunt.**

He stood in the presence of the king. **Stabat apud regem.**

We built a wall around our house. **Aedificávimus murum circum domum nostram.**

c) As subject of the infinitive in indirect discourse.

He said that his mother had come. **Dixit matrem suam venísse.**

d) To express duration of time and extent of space.

They will stay here for one day. **Unam diem [1] hic remanébunt.**
The wall extended for many feet. **Murus multos pedes exténdit.**

EXERCISES

A. Suffixes. The suffix **-ax** is added to verb stems to form adjectives denoting a tendency, usually an extreme tendency.

1. **audax,** bold (from **audére,** to dare). 2. **ferax,** fertile (from **ferre,** to bear). 3. **sagax,** clever (from **sagíre,** to perceive quickly). 4. **mendax,** lying (from **mentíri,** to lie). 5. **edax,** greedy (from **édere,** to eat). 6. **tenax,** tenacious (from **tenére,** to hold).

B. The suffix **-idus** is added to verb stems to form adjectives denoting a state or settled condition.

1. **tímidus,** timid (from **timére,** to fear). 2. **cúpidus,** desirous (from

---

[1] The ablative may also be used.

cúpere, to desire). 3. lánguidus, weak (from languére, to be weak). 4. frígidus, cold (from frigére, to be cold). 5. áridus, dry (from arére, to be dry). 6. rápidus, rapid (from rápere, to snatch). 7. válidus, strong, well (from valére, to be strong, to be well). 8. nítidus, bright (from nitére, to shine). 9. cándidus, shining white (from candére, to glitter). 10. pállidus, pale (from palére, to be pale).

Unit Two

A. Read and translate into English.

1. Te ígitur, clementíssime Pater, per Jesum Christum Fílium tuum Dóminum nostrum, súpplices rogámus, ac pétimus, uti accépta hábeas, et benedícas, haec dona, haec múnera, haec sancta sacrifícia illibáta. 2. In primis, quae tibi offérimus pro Ecclésia tua sancta cathólica; quam pacificáre, custodíre, adunáre, et régere dignéris toto orbe terrárum; una cum fámulo tuo Papa nostro Pío, et Antístite nostro Paulo, et ómnibus orthodóxis atque cathólicae, et apostólicae fídei cultóribus. 3. Meménto (*imperative*), Dómine, famulórum famularúmque N. et N. et ómnium circumstántium, quorum tibi fides cógnita est, et nota devótio, pro quibus tibi offérimus; vel qui tibi ófferunt hoc sacrifícium laudis, pro se, suisque ómnibus; pro redemptióne animárum suárum, pro spe salútis, et incolumitátis suae; tibíque reddunt vota sua aetérno Deo, vivo et vero. 4. Unde et mémores, Dómine, nos servi tui, sed et plebs tua sancta, ejúsdem Christi Fílii tui Dómini nostri tam beátae Passiónis, nec non et ab ínferis Resurrectiónis, sed et in caelos gloriósae Ascensiónis; offérimus praeclárae Majestati tuae, de tuis donis, ac datis, hóstiam puram, hóstiam sanctam, hóstiam immaculátam, Panem sanctum vitae aetérnae et Cálicem salútis perpétuae. 5. Meménto, etiam, Dómine, famulórum, famularúmque tuárum N. et N. qui nos praecessérunt cum signo fídei et dórmiunt in somno pacis. 6. Ipsis, Dómine, et ómnibus in Christo quiescéntibus, locum refrigérii, lucis et pacis, ut indúlgeas, deprecámur. 7. Quotquot autem recepérunt eum, dedit eis potestátem fílios Dei fíeri, his, qui credunt in nómine ejus; qui non ex sanguínibus,

neque ex voluntáte carnis, neque ex voluntáte viri, sed ex Deo nati sunt. 8. Tibi soli peccávi, et malum coram te feci; ut justificéris in sermónibus tuis, et vincas cum judicáris. 9. Ecce enim veritátem dilexísti; incérta et occúlta sapiéntiae tuae manifestásti mihi. 10. Deínde nos, qui vívimus, qui relínquimur, simul rapiémur cum illis in núbibus óbviam Christo in áëra et sic semper cum Dómino érimus. 11. Mors stupébit et natúra, cum resúrget creatúra, judicánti responsúra. 12. Quid sum miser tunc dictúrus? Quem patrónum rogatúrus, cum vix justus sit secúrus? 13. Rex treméndae Majestátis, qui salvándos salvas gratis, salva me, fons pietátis. 14. Recordáre, Jesu pie, quod sum causa tuae viae; ne me perdas illa die. 15. Ingemísco, tamquam reus; culpa rubet vultus meus; supplicánti parce, Deus. 16. Dixit Martha ad Jesum: Dómine, si fuísses hic, frater meus non fuísset mórtuus; sed et nunc scio, quia quaecúmque popósceris a Deo, dabit tibi Deus. 17. Ait illi: Útique, Dómine, ego crédidi, quia tu es Christus Fílius Dei vivi, qui in hunc mundum venísti. 18. Non ergo eum, quaésumus, tua judiciális senténtia premat, quem tibi vera supplicátio fídei Christiánae comméndat; sed grátia tua illi succurrénte mereátur evádere judícium ultiónis, qui dum víveret, insignítus est signáculo sanctae Trinitátis. 19. Dies illa, dies irae, calamitátis et misériae, dies magna et amára valde. 20. Salus ex inimícis nostris, et de manu ómnium qui odérunt nos. 21. Absólve, quaésumus, Dómine, ánimam fámuli tui ab omni vínculo delictórum; ut in resurrectiónis glória inter sanctos et eléctos tuos resuscitátus respíret. 22. Deus, véniae largítor, et humánae salútis amátor; quaésumus cleméntiam tuam; ut nostrae congregatiónis fratres, propínquos, et benefactóres, qui ex hoc saéculo transiérunt, beáta María semper Vírgine intercedénte cum ómnibus sanctis tuis, ad perpétuae beatitúdinis consórtium perveníre concédas. 23. Pro animábus famulórum, famularúmque tuárum, et ómnium catholicórum hic et ubíque in Christo dormiéntium, hóstiam, Dómine, súscipe benígnus oblátam; ut hoc sacrifício singulári, vínculis horréndae mortis exúti, vitam mereántur aetérnam. 24. Súpplices, Dómine pro animábus famulórum, famularúmque tuárum preces effúndimus; obsecrántes, ut quidquid conversatióne contraxérunt humána, et cleménter indúlgeas, et in tuórum sede laetántium constítuas redemptórum. 25. Tunc acceptábis sacrifícium justítiae, oblatiónes et holocáusta; tunc impónent super altáre tuum vítulos. 26. Deus, cui proprium est miseréri semper et párcere, te súpplices exorámus pro ánima fámuli tui N., quam hódie de hoc saéculo migráre jussísti; ut non tradas eam in manus inimíci; neque obliviscáris in finem, sed júbeas eam a sanctis Angelis súscipi, et ad pátriam paradísi perdúci; ut, quia in te sperávit et crédidit, non poenas inférni sustíneat, sed gáudia aetérna possídeat. 27. Vere dignum et justum est, aequum et salutáre, nos tibi semper, et ubíque grátias ágere; Dómine sancte, Pater omnípotens aetérne Deus; qui cum unigénito Fílio tuo, et Spíritu Sancto, unus es Deus, unus es Dóminus; non in uníus singularitáte personae, sed in uníus Trinitáte substántiae. 28. Quod enim de tua glória, revelánte te, crédimus, hoc de Fílio tuo, hoc de Spíritu Sancto, sine differéntia discretiónis sentímus. 29. Quaésumus, Dómine, ut ánimae fámuli tui N., cujus depositiónis diem tértium commemorámus, sanctórum atque electórum tuórum largíri dignéris consórtium; et rorem misericórdiae tuae perénnem infúndas. 30. Deus, qui inter apostólicos Sacerdótes, fámulum tuum N. pontificáli fecísti dignitáte vigére; praesta, quaésumus, ut eórum quoque perpétuo aggregétur consórtio.

Unit Three

A. *a*) Explain the use of **-ne, nonne, num, numquid** in asking questions.

b) How are double questions expressed?

B. *a*) Name four defective verbs.

b) Which ones are conjugated only in the perfect tenses?

c) Which one has no perfect tenses?

d) What is unusual about the meaning of the perfect forms of **odísse** and **meminísse**?

C. Give four uses of the accusative case and illustrate each with a short sentence in Latin.

D. **Vocabulary building.**

a) **Derivations.** Find in Units One and Two the words that have the same derivation as the following:

1. occúltum (hidden thing). 2. singuláritas (oneness). 3. velum (curtain, veil). 4. ruber (red). 5. stúpidus (stupid). 6. via (road). 7. núbilus (cloudy). 8. frígidus (cold). 9. occúlte (secretly). 10. prope (near). 11. memorári (to remember). 12. horríbilis (horrible).

b) Observe the relation between these Latin and English words.

Latin	English	Latin	English
rápere	rapture	recordári	recorder
respiráre	respiratory	reveláre	revelation
rubére	rubrics	stupére	stupefy
fons	font	refrigérium	refrigerator
propínquus	propinquity	memor	memorable
sagax	sagacious	mendax	mendacious

c) **Diminutives.** Endings such as -lus, -ulus, -culus, -ellus in any gender are frequently added to nouns or adjectives to give the word a special significance, such as endearment, pity or contempt, or merely smallness.

1. navícula, a little ship, a skiff (from navis, ship). 2. castéllum, castle, fortress (from castrum, fort). 3. tabernáculum, tent, a small hut (from taberna, a hut). 4. léctulus, a small bed (from lectus, a bed). 5. ósculum, a little mouth, a kiss (from os, mouth). 6. muliércula, a disgraceful woman (from múlier, woman). 7. párvulus, very small (from parvus, small). 8. libéllus, note-book (from liber, book). 9. flagéllum, a small whip (from flagrum, a scourge, a whip). 10. círculus, a small circle (from circus, circle). 11. malléolus, a little hammer (from málleus, a hammer, a mallet). 12. tabélla, a tablet (from tábula, a board).

REVIEW LESSON NUMBER IV

A. Give a noun in Latin suggested by each of the following adjectives.

1. gloriósus. 2. beátus. 3. sanctus. 4. humánus. 5. corpóreus. 6. magnus. 7. aetérnus. 8. clemens. 9. iníquus. 10. miséricors. 11. fortis. 12. fratérnus. 13. matérnus. 14. miser. 15. fidélis. 16. dignus. 17. potens. 18. evangélicus. 19. temporális. 20. apostólicus. 21. sacerdotális. 22. terríbilis. 23. memorábilis. 24. pius. 25. laboriósus. 26. ínnocens. 27. prudens. 28. verus. 29. vivus. 30. salvus. 31. altus. 32. multus. 33. unigénitus. 34. suavis. 35. sócius. 36. lassus. 37. largus. 38. própius. 39. divínus. 40. voluntárius.

B. Write six short sentences in Latin involving indirect discourse, two after a verb of saying, two after a verb of knowing, and two after a verb of thinking.

C. Give a noun in Latin suggested by each of the following verbs.

1. posse. 2. vocáre. 3. salváre. 4. laudáre. 5. dúcere. 6. dícere. 7. servíre. 8. clamáre. 9. oráre. 10. judicáre. 11. speráre. 12. dormíre. 13. scríbere. 14. docére. 15. peccáre. 16. conturbáre. 17. salutáre. 18. cogitáre. 19. deprecári. 20. sequi. 21. dilígere. 22. ascéndere. 23. offérre. 24. redímere. 25. timére. 26. scire. 27. vívere. 28. fácere. 29. mori. 30. fídere.

D. Give an adjective that describes correctly each of the following nouns.

1. vultus. 2. óvibus. 3. voluntátis. 4. die. 5. spem. 6. somno. 7. pace. 8. panes. 9. córporum. 10. cordis. 11. verbis. 12. muri. 13. púerum. 14. monti. 15. lábia.

E. Compose four Latin questions and answers illustrating the use of -ne, nonne, num, and numquid.

F. Indicate whether these statements are right or wrong.

1. Pius nomen Papae est. 2. Non vidémus quod invisíbile est. 3. Pes pars vultus est. 4. Homo potens, sed Deus omnípotens est. 5. Ecclésia cathólica semper crucem habet. 6. Fílii boni non credunt id quod dicunt patres sui. 7. Ópera sanctórum mirabília erant. 8. Quando ego sum cum fratre meo, non solus sum. 9. Púeri diligéntes labórem díligunt. 10. In pátria nostra multae civitátes sunt. 11. Oves pastórem sequúntur. 12. Nocte mundus in ténebris est. 13. Quando lassi sumus, dormímus. 14. Homo qui multum paupéribus dat, laudis dignus est. 15. Inimíci nostri semper repélli possunt. 16. In novíssimo die innocéntes recípient munus suum in regno caelórum. 17. Multae veritátes tam difíciles sunt, ut non comprehendántur ab ómnibus. 18. Áliquae natiónes magnos exércitus sústinent. 19. Omnes púeri canunt bene. 20. Per óstium in domum introímus.

G. Give the meaning of each of these words.

1. princípium. 2. posse. 3. culpa. 4. cor. 5. acer. 6. nunc. 7. pónere. 8. nomen. 9. gens. 10. audére. 11. juvéntus. 12. quare. 13. erúere. 14. sicut. 15. pars. 16. ígitur. 17. fácies. 18. somnus. 19. ecce. 20. item. 21. vultus. 22. spes. 23. dexter. 24. valére. 25. lábium. 26. amárus. 27. céterus. 28. foras. 29. óstium. 30. atque. 31. sanguis. 32. auris. 33. pes. 34. ignis. 35. lumen. 36. autem. 37. prídie. 38. accéndere. 39. vox. 40. tértius. 41. vespertínus. 42. num. 43. quot. 44. scelus. 45. quotidiánus. 46. frángere. 47. dignári. 48. íngredi. 49. pétere. 50. ténebrae.

H. Write ten short sentences in Latin, each one to illustrate a different use of the ablative.

I. Write complete Latin sentences using the following words or expressions.

1. lumen. 2. illumináre. 3. salvátio. 4. ímpius. 5. non movére. 6. deprecátio. 7. vultus. 8. mundáre. 9. non beátus. 10. tenére. 11. loqui.

12. vir. 13. dare laudem. 14. vocáre alta voce. 15. ovis júvenis. 16. milí-tia. 17. non certus. 18. servus. 19. spem habére. 20. condítio. 21. sólvere. 22. ejícere foras. 23. dimíttere. 24. indulgéntia. 25. quondam. 26. be-nígnus. 27. praémium. 28. saéculum. 29. parens famíliae. 30. aetérnus. 31. domus Dei. 32. bíbere. 33. manducáre. 34. valére. 35. fidem habére. 36. spíritus. 37. omnis. 38. quia. 39. liberáre. 40. magnus nimis. 41. amáre multum. 42. quod offértur. 43. intráre. 44. discípulus Christi. 45. partes córporis quibus ingrédimur. 46. requiéscere in somno. 47. non abíre. 48. non vivus. 49. non dignus. 50. pétere.

J. Use each of the following in a question and compose a suitable answer to each question.

1. quisquis. 2. póscere. 3. nubes. 4. certámen. 5. gérere. 6. útique. 7. quondam. 8. ad ínvicem. 9. párcere. 10. túmulus. 11. céterus. 12. amárus. 13. ovis. 14. exércitus. 15. conspéctus. 16. dirígere. 17. nimis. 18. dexter. 19. spes. 20. adjutórium. 21. vultus. 22. verbum. 23. opus. 24. osténdere. 25. novus. 26. docére. 27. somnus. 28. tectum. 29. panis. 30. missa. 31. fides. 32. ergo. 33. crédere. 34. pauper. 35. miseréri. 36. gaudére. 37. tutaméntum. 38. caro. 39. aperíre. 40. íngredi. 41. loqui. 42. lassus. 43. quaérere. 44. cinis. 45. argéntum. 46. effulgére. 47. téne-brae. 48. meréri. 49. antístes. 50. dilígere.

READING LESSON

1. Una autem sabbati, Maria Magdalene venit mane, cum adhuc tenebrae essent, ad monumentum et vidit lapidem sublatum a monumento.

2. Cucurrit ergo, et venit ad Simonem Petrum, et ad alium discipulum quem amabat Jesus, et dicit illis: Tulerunt Dominum de monumento, et nescimus ubi posuerunt eum.

3. Exiit ergo Petrus, et ille alius discipulus, et venerunt ad monumentum.

4. Currebant autem duo simul, et ille alius discipulus praecucurrit citius Petro, et venit primus ad monumentum.

5. Et cum se inclinasset, vidit posita linteamina, non tamen introivit.

6. Venit ergo Simon Petrus sequens eum, et introivit in monumentum, et vidit linteamina posita.

7. Et sudarium quod fuerat super caput ejus, non cum linteaminibus positum, sed separatim involutum in unum locum.

8. Tunc ergo introivit et ille discipulus qui venerat primus ad monumentum, et vidit, et credidit:

9. Nondum enim sciebant Scripturam, quia oportebat eum a mortuis resurgere.

10. Abierunt ergo iterum discipuli ad semetipsos.

11. Maria autem stabat ad monumentum foris, plorans. Dum ergo fleret, inclinavit se, et prospexit in monumentum:

12. Et vidit duos angelos in albis, sedentes, unum ad caput, et unum ad pedes, ubi postum fuerat corpus Jesu.

13. Dicunt ei illi: Mulier, quid ploras? Dicit eis: Quia tulerunt Dominum meum; et nescio ubi posuerunt eum.

14. Haec cum dixisset, conversa est retrorsum, et vidit Jesum stantem: et non sciebat quia Jesus est.

15. Dicit ei Jesus: Mulier, quid ploras? quem quaeris? Illa existi-

mans quia hortulanus esset, dicit ei: Domine, si tu sustulisti eum, dicito mihi ubi posuisti eum; et ego eum tollam.

16. Dicit ei Jesus: Maria. Conversa illa, dicit ei: Rabboni (quod dicitur magister).

17. Dicit ei Jesus: Noli me tangere, nundum enim ascendi ad Patrem meum: vade autem ad fratres meos, et dic eis: Ascendo ad Patrem meum, et Patrem vestrum, Deum meum, et Deum vestrum.

18. Venit Maria Magdalene annuntians discipulis: Quia vidi Dominum, et haec dixit mihi.

19. Cum ergo sero esset die illo, una sabbatorum, et fores essent clausae, ubi erant discipuli congregati propter metum Judaeorum; venit Jesus, et stetit in medio, et dixit eis: Pax vobis.

20. Et cum hoc dixisset, ostendit eis manus et latus. Gavisi sunt ergo discipuli, viso Domino.

21. Dixit ergo eis iterum: Pax vobis. Sicut misit me Pater, et ego mitto vos.

22. Haec cum dixisset, insufflavit, et dixit eis: Accipite Spiritum Sanctum.

23. Quorum remiseritis peccata, remittuntur eis: et quorum retinueritis, retenta sunt.

24. Thomas autem unus ex duodecim, qui dicitur Didymus, non erat cum eis quando venit Jesus.

25. Dixerunt ergo ei alii discipuli: Vidimus Dominum. Ille autem dixit eis: Nisi videro in manibus ejus fixuram clavorum, et mittam digitum meum in locum clavorum, et mittam manum meam in latus ejus, non credam.

26. Et post dies octo, iterum erant discipuli ejus intus: et Thomas cum eis. Venit Jesus, januis clausis, et stetit in medio, et dixit: Pax vobis.

27. Deinde dicit Thomae: Infer digitum tuum huc, et affer manum tuam, et mitte in latus meum: et noli esse incredulus, sed fidelis.

28. Respondit Thomas, et dixit ei: Dominus meus et Deus meus.

29. Dixit ei Jesus: Quia vidisti me, Thoma, credidisti: beati qui non viderunt et crediderunt.

30. Multa quidem et alia signa fecit Jesus in conspectu discipulorum suorum, quae non sunt scripta in libro hoc.

31. Haec autem scripta sunt ut credatis quia Jesus est Christus Filius Dei: et ut credentes, vitam habeatis in nomine ejus.

(Jesu Christi Evangelium secundum Joannem, caput XX, 1–31.)

APPENDIX

52. Irregular declensions.

deus, m., God	dea, f., goddess	domus, f., house	vis, f., force, strength

Singular

	deus	dea	domus	vis
Nom.	deus	dea	domus	vis
Gen.	dei	deae	domus, -i	
Dat.	deo	deae	dómui, -o	
Acc.	deum	deam	domum	vim
Abl.	deo	dea	domu, -o	vi

Plural

	dei, dii, di	deae	domus	vires
Nom.	dei, dii, di	deae	domus	vires
Gen.	deórum, deum	deárum	dómuum, -órum	vírium
Dat.	deis, diis, dis	deábus	dómibus	víribus
Acc.	deos	deas	domus, -os	viris, -es
Abl.	deis, diis, dis	deábus	dómibus	víribus

53. Numerals.

Cardinal	Ordinal
1. unus, -a, -um	primus, -a, -um
2. duo, duae, duo	secúndus
3. tres, tria	tértius
4. quáttuor	quartus
5. quinque	quintus
6. sex	sextus
7. septem	séptimus
8. octo	octávus

9. novem	nonus
10. decem	décimus
11. úndecim	undécimus
12. duódecim	duodécimus
13. trédecim	tértius décimus
14. quattuórdecim	quartus décimus
15. quíndecim	quintus décimus
16. sédecim	sextus décimus
17. septéndecim	séptimus décimus
18. duodevigínti	duodevicésimus
19. undevigínti	undevicésimus
20. vigínti	vicésimus
21. vigínti unus	vicésimus primus
(unus et vigínti)	
29. undetrigínta	undetricésimus
30. trigínta	tricésimus
40. quadragínta	quadragésimus
50. quinquagínta	quinquagésimus
60. sexagínta	sexagésimus
70. septuagínta	septuagésimus
80. octogínta	octogésimus
90. nonagínta	nonagésimus
100. centum	centésimus
200. ducénti, -ae, -a	ducentésimus
300. trecénti	trecentésimus
400. quadringénti	quadringentésimus
500. quingénti	quingentésimus
600. sescénti	sescentésimus
700. septingénti	septingentésimus
800. octingénti	octingentésimus
900. nongénti	nongentésimus
1000. mille	millésimus
2000. duo mília	bis millésimus

VERBS

54. First conjugation

laudáre, *to praise*

Indicative

Present

Active Voice		Passive Voice	
laudo	laudámus	laudor	laudámur
laudas	laudátis	laudáris [1]	laudámini
laudat	laudant	laudátur	laudántur

Imperfect

laudábam	laudabámus	laudábar	laudabámur
laudábas	laudabátis	laudabáris	laudabámini
laudábat	laudábant	laudabátur	laudabántur

Future

laudábo	laudábimus	laudábor	laudábimur
laudábis	laudábitis	laudáberis	laudabímini
laudábit	laudábunt	laudábitur	laudabúntur

Perfect

laudávi	laudávimus	laudátus sum	laudáti sumus
laudavísti	laudavístis	laudátus es	laudáti estis
laudávit	laudavérunt	laudátus est	laudáti sunt
	(laudavére)		

Pluperfect

laudáveram	laudaverámus	laudátus eram	laudáti erámus
laudáveris	laudaverátis	laudátus eras	laudáti erátis
laudáverat	laudáverant	laudátus erat	laudáti erant

[1] In the present, imperfect, and future of the passive voice, the second person singular has also a form in -re. Thus laudáre, laudabáre, laudábere.

Future Perfect

laudávero	laudavérimus	laudátus ero	laudáti érimus
laudáveris	laudavéritis	laudátus eris	laudáti éritis
laudáverit	laudáverint	laudátus erit	laudáti erunt

Subjunctive

Present

laudem	laudémus	lauder	laudémur
laudes	laudétis	laudéris	laudémini
laudet	laudent	laudétur	laudéntur

Imperfect

laudárem	laudarémus	laudárer	laudarémur
laudáres	laudarétis	laudaréris	laudarémini
laudáret	laudárent	laudarétur	laudaréntur

Perfect

laudáverim	laudavérimus	laudátus sim	laudáti simus
laudáveris	laudavéritis	laudátus sis	laudáti sitis
laudáverit	laudáverint	laudátus sit	laudáti sint

Pluperfect

laudavíssem	laudavissémus	laudátus essem	laudáti essémus
laudavísses	laudavissétis	laudátus esses	laudáti essétis
laudavísset	laudavíssent	laudátus esset	laudáti essent

Imperative

Sing., lauda   *Plur.*, laudáte   *Sing.*, laudáre   *Plur.*, laudámini

Infinitive

Pres. laudáre, *to praise*   laudári, *to be praised*

Perf. laudavísse, *to have praised*   laudátus esse, *to have been praised*

Fut. laudatúrus esse, *to be about to praise*   laudátum iri, *to be about to be praised*

Participles

Pres. laudans, -antis, *praising*	Perf. laudátus, -a, -um, *having*
Fut. laudatúrus, -a, -um, *about*	*been praised*
to praise	

Gerund	Gerundive
Gen. laudándi, *of praising*	laudándus, -a, -um, *to be praised,*
Dat. laudándo, *for praising*	etc.
Acc. laudándum, *praising*	
Abl. laudándo, *by praising*	

Supine

Acc. laudátum, *to praise*
Abl. laudátu, *to praise*

55. Second conjugation.

monére, *to advise, warn*

Indicative

Present

Active Voice		Passive Voice	
móneo	monémus	móneor	monémur
mones	monétis	monéris	monémini
monet	monent	monétur	monéntur

Imperfect

monébam	monebámus	monébar	monebámur
monébas	monebátis	monebáris	monebámini
monébat	monébant	monebátur	monebántur

Future

monébo	monébimus	monébor	monébimur
monébis	monébitis	monéberis	monebímini
monébit	monébunt	monébitur	monebúntur

Perfect

mónui	monúimus	mónitus sum	móniti sumus
monuísti	monuístis	mónitus es	móniti estis
mónuit	monuérunt	mónitus est	móniti sunt
	(monuére)		

Pluperfect

monúeram	monuerámus	mónitus eram	móniti erámus
monúeras	monuerátis	mónitus eras	móniti erátis
monúerat	monúerant	mónitus erat	móniti erant

Future Perfect

monúero	monuérimus	mónitus ero	móniti érimus
monúeris	monuéritis	mónitus eris	móniti éritis
monúerit	monúerint	mónitus erit	móniti erunt

Subjunctive

móneam	moneámus	mónear	moneámur
móneas	moneátis	moneáris	moneámini
móneat	móneant	moneátur	moneántur

Imperfect

monérem	monerémus	monérer	monerémur
monéres	monerétis	moneréris	monerémini
monéret	monérent	monerétur	moneréntur

Perfect

monúerim	monuérimus	mónitus sim	móniti simus
monúeris	monuéritis	mónitus sis	móniti sitis
monúerit	monúerint	mónitus sit	móniti sint

Pluperfect

monuíssem	monuissémus	mónitus essem	móniti essémus
monuísses	monuissétis	mónitus esses	móniti essétis
monuísset	monuíssent	mónitus esset	móniti essent

Imperative
Present

Sing. mone   *Plur.* monéte   *Sing.* monére   *Plur.* monémini

Infinitive

Pres. monére, *to advise*   monéri, *to be advised*

Perf. monuísse, *to have advised*   mónitus esse, *to have been advised*

Fut. monitúrus esse, *to be about to advise*   mónitum iri, *to be about to be advised*

Participles

Pres. monens, -entis, *advising*   Perf. mónitus, -a, -um, *having been advised*

Fut. monitúrus, -a, -um, *about to advise*

Gerund   Gerundive

Gen. monéndi, *of advising*   monéndus, -a, -um, *to be advised*

Dat. monéndo, *for advising*

Acc. monéndum, *advising*

Abl. monéndo, *by advising*

Supine

Acc. mónitum, *to advise*

Abl. mónitu, *to advise*

56. Third conjugation.

dúcere, *to lead*

Indicative
Present

Active Voice		Passive Voice	
duco	dúcimus	ducor	dúcimur
ducis	dúcitis	dúceris	ducímini
ducit	ducunt	dúcitur	ducúntur

Imperfect

ducébam	ducebámus	ducébar	ducebámur
ducébas	ducebátis	ducebáris	ducebámini
ducébat	ducébant	ducebátur	ducebántur

Future

ducam	ducémus	ducar	ducémur
duces	ducétis	ducéris	ducémini
ducet	ducent	ducétur	ducéntur

Perfect

duxi	dúximus	ductus sum	ducti sumus
duxísti	duxístis	ductus es	ducti estis
duxit	duxérunt	ductus est	ducti sunt
	(duxére)		

Pluperfect

dúxeram	duxerámus	ductus eram	ducti erámus
dúxeras	duxerátis	ductus eras	ducti erátis
dúxerat	dúxerant	ductus erat	ducti erant

Future Perfect

dúxero	duxérimus	ductus ero	ducti érimus
dúxeris	duxéritis	ductus eris	ducti éritis
dúxerit	dúxerint	ductus erit	ducti erunt

Subjunctive
Present

ducam	ducámus	ducar	ducámur
ducas	ducátis	ducáris	ducámini
ducat	ducant	ducátur	ducántur

Imperfect

dúcerem	ducerémus	dúcerer	ducerémur
dúceres	ducerétis	ducceréris	ducerémini
dúceret	dúcerent	ducerétur	duceréntur

Perfect

dúxerim	duxérimus	ductus sim	ducti simus
dúxeris	duxéritis	ductus sis	ducti sitis
dúxerit	dúxerint	ductus sit	ducti sint

Pluperfect

duxíssem	duxissémus	ductus essem	ducti essémus
duxísses	duxissétis	ductus esses	ducti essétis
duxísset	duxíssent	ductus esset	ducti essent

Imperative

Present

Sing. duc(e) Plur. dúcite   Sing. dúcere Plur. ducímini

Infinitive

Pres. dúcere, *to lead*   duci, *to be led*
Perf. duxísse, *to have led*   ductus esse, *to have been led*
Fut. ductúrus esse, *to be about* ductum iri, *to be about to be led*
    to lead

Participles

Pres. ducens, -entis, *leading*   Perf. ductus, -a, -um, *having*
Fut. ductúrus, -a, -um, *about to*   *been led*
    lead

Gerund   Gerundive

Gen. ducéndi, *of leading*   ducéndus, -a, -um, *to be led*
Dat. ducéndo, *for leading*
Acc. ducéndum, *leading*
Abl. ducéndo, *by leading*

Supine

Acc. ductum, *to lead*

Abl. ductu, *to lead*

57. Fourth conjugation.

audíre, *to hear*

Indicative

Present

Active Voice		Passive Voice	
áudio	audímus	áudior	audímur
audis	audítis	audíris	audímini
audit	áudiunt	audítur	audiúntur

Imperfect

audiébam	audiebámus	audiébar	audiebámur
audiébas	audiebátis	audiebáris	audiebámini
audiébat	audiébant	audiebátur	audiebántur

Future

áudiam	audiémus	áudiar	audiémur
áudies	audiétis	audiéris	audiémini
áudiet	áudient	audiétur	audiéntur

Perfect

audívi	audívimus	audítus sum	audíti sumus
audivísti	audivístis	audítus es	audíti estis
audívit	audivérunt	audítus est	audíti sunt

Pluperfect

audíveram	audiverámus	audítus eram	audíti erámus
audíveras	audiverátis	audítus eras	audíti erátis
audíverat	audíverant	audítus erat	audíti erant

Future Perfect

audívero	audivérimus	audítus ero	audíti érimus
audíveris	audivéritis	audítus eris	audíti éritis
audíverit	audíverint	audítus erit	audíti erunt

Subjunctive

Present

áudiam	audiámus	áudiar	audiámur
áudias	audiátis	audiáris	audiámini
áudiat	áudiant	audiátur	audiántur

Imperfect

audírem	audirémus	audírer	audirémur
audíres	audirétis	audiréris	audirémini
audíret	audírent	audirétur	audiréntur

Perfect

audíverim	audivérimus	audítus sim	audíti simus
audíveris	audivéritis	audítus sis	audíti sitis
audíverit	audíverint	audítus sit	audíti sint

Pluperfect

audivíssem	audivissémus	audítus essem	audíti essémus
audivísses	audivissétis	audítus esses	audíti essétis
audivísset	audivíssent	audítus esset	audíti essent

Imperative

Present

Sing. audi   Plur. audíte   Sing. audíre   Plur. audímini

Infinitive

Pres. audíre, *to hear*   audíri, *to be heard*
Perf. audivísse, *to have heard*   audítus esse, *to have been heard*
Fut. auditúrus esse, *to be about* auditum iri, *to be about to be*
     to hear   *heard*

Participles

Pres. áudiens, -entis, *hearing*

Fut. auditúrus, -a, -um, *about to hear*

audítus, -a, -um, *heard, having been heard*

Gerund	Gerundive
Gen. audiéndi, *of hearing*	audiéndus, -a, -um, *to be heard*
Dat. audiéndo, *for hearing*	
Acc. audiéndum, *hearing*	
Abl. audiéndo, *by hearing*	

Supine

Acc. audítum, *to hear*

Abl. audítu, *to hear*

58. Third conjugation verbs in -io.

cápere, *to take*

Indicative

Present

Active Voice		Passive Voice	
cápio	cápimus	cápior	cápimur
capis	cápitis	cáperis	capímini
capit	cápiunt	cápitur	capiúntur

Imperfect

capiébam, etc.   capiébar, etc.

Future

cápiam	capiémus	cápiar	capiémur
cápies	capiétis	capiéris	capiémini
cápiet	cápient	capiétur	capiéntur

Perfect

cepi, etc.   captus sum, etc.

Pluperfect

céperam, etc.   captus eram, etc.

Future Perfect

cépero, etc.   captus ero, etc.

Subjunctive

Present

cápiam	capiámus	cápiar	capiámur
cápias	capiátis	capiáris	capiámini
cápiat	cápiant	capiátur	capiántur

Imperfect

cáperem, etc.   cáperer, etc.

Perfect

céperim, etc.   captus sim, etc.

Pluperfect

cepíssem, etc.   captus essem, etc.

Imperative

Present

Sing. cape   *Plur.* cápite   *Sing.* cápere   *Plur.* capímini

Infinitive

Pres. cápere, *to take*   capi, *to be taken*
Perf. cepísse, *to have taken*   captus esse, *to have been taken*
Fut. captúrus esse, *to be about to*   captum iri, *to be about to be*
    take   taken

Participles

Pres. cápiens, -ientis, *taking*   Perf. captus, -a, -um, *taken, hav-*
Fut. captúrus, -a, -um, *about to*   *ing been taken*
    take

Gerund	Gerundive
Gen. capiéndi, *of taking*	capiéndus, -a, -um, *to be taken*
Dat. capiéndo, *for taking*	
Acc. capiéndum, *taking*	
Abl. capiéndo, *by taking*	

Supine

Acc. captum, *to take*

Abl. captu, *to take*

IRREGULAR VERBS

59. esse, *to be*   posse, *to be able*

Indicative

Present

sum	sumus	possum	póssumus
es	estis	potes	potéstis
est	sunt	potest	possunt

Imperfect

eram	erámus	póteram	poterámus
eras	erátis	póteras	poterátis
erat	erant	póterat	póterant

Future

ero	érimus	pótero	potérimus
eris	éritis	póteris	potéritis
erit	erunt	póterit	póterunt

Perfect

fui	fúimus	pótui	potúimus
fuísti	fuístis	potuísti	potuístis
fuit	fuérunt	pótuit	potuérunt

Pluperfect

fúeram	fuerámus	potúeram	potuerámus
fúeras	fuerátis	potúeras	potuerátis
fúerat	fúerant	potúerat	potúerant

Future Perfect

fúero	fuérimus	potúero	potuérimus
fúeris	fuéritis	potúeris	potuéritis
fúerit	fúerint	potúerit	potúerint

Subjunctive

Present

sim	simus	possim	possímus
sis	sitis	possis	possítis
sit	sint	possit	possint

Imperfect

essem	essémus	possem	possémus
esses	essétis	posses	possétis
esset	essent	posset	possent

Perfect

fúerim	fuérimus	potúerim	potuérimus
fúeris	fuéritis	potúeris	potuéritis
fúerit	fúerint	potúerit	potúerint

Pluperfect

fuíssem	fuissémus	potuíssem	potuissémus
fuísses	fuissétis	potuísses	potuissétis
fuísset	fuíssent	potuísset	potuíssent

Imperative

Sing. es   *Plur.* este   ——   ——

Infinitive

Pres. esse, *to be*   posse, *to be able*

Perf. fuísse, *to have been*   potuísse, *to have been able*

Fut. futúrus esse, $\left.\begin{array}{l} \\ \text{or} \\ \text{fore} \end{array}\right\}$ *to be about to be*

Participles

Future	Present
futúrus, -a, -um, *about to be*	potens, -éntis (*used as an adjective*), *powerful*

60. **velle**, *to wish*   **nolle**, *to be unwilling*   **malle**, *to prefer*

Indicative

Present

volo	vólumus	nolo	nólumus	malo	málumus
vis	vultis	non vis	non vultis	mavis	mavúltis
vult	volunt	non vult	nolunt	mavult	malunt

Imperfect

volébam	nolébam	malébam

Future

volam	nolam	malam

Perfect

vólui	nólui	málui

Pluperfect

volúeram	nolúeram	malúeram

Future Perfect

volúero	nolúero	malúero

Subjunctive

Present

velim	velímus	nolim	nolímus	malim	malímus
velis	velítis	nolis	nolítis	malis	malítis
velit	velint	nolit	nolint	malit	malint

Imperfect

vellem   nollem   mallem

Perfect

volúerim   nolúerim   malúerim

Pluperfect

voluíssem   noluíssem   maluíssem

Imperative

Present

Sing. noli   *Plur.* nolíte

Infinitive

Pres. velle	nolle	malle
Perf. voluísse	noluísse	maluísse

Participles

Pres. volens   nolens   ———

61. ferre, *to bear, carry*

Present

Active Voice		Passive Voice	
fero	férimus	feror	férimur
fers	fertis	ferris	ferímini
fert	ferunt	fertur	ferúntur

Imperfect

ferébam ferébar

Future

feram ferar

Perfect

tuli latus sum

Pluperfect

túleram latus eram

Future Perfect

túlero latus ero

Subjunctive

Present

feram ferar

Imperfect

ferrem ferrer

Perfect

túlerim latus sim

Pluperfect

tulíssem latus essem

Imperative

Sing. fer   *Plur.* ferte   *Sing.* ferre   *Plur.* ferímini

Infinitive

Pres. ferre   ferri
Perf. tulísse   latus esse
Fut. latúrus esse latum iri

Participles

Pres. **ferens** —
Perf. —— **latus**
Fut. **latúrus** —

Gerund	Gerundive
Gen. **feréndi**	**feréndus**
Dat. **feréndo**	
Acc. **feréndum**	
Abl. **feréndo**	

Supine

Acc. **latum**
Abl. **latu**

62. ire, *to go*

Indicative

Present	Imperfect	Future	Perfect	Pluperfect
eo imus	**ibam**	**ibo**	**ii**	**ieram**
is itis				
it eunt				

Future Perfect

iero

Subjunctive

Present	Imperfect	Perfect	Pluperfect
eam	**irem**	**ierim**	**issem**

Imperative

Present

Sing. **i**   *Plur.* **ite**

Infinitive

Pres. ire
Perf. isse (iisse)
Fut. itúrus esse

Participles

Pres. iéns, eúntis
Fut. itúrus

Gerund

Gen. eúndi
Dat. eúndo
Acc. eúndum
Abl. eúndo

Supine

Acc. itum
Abl. itu

63. fíeri, *to be made, become*

Indicative

Present		Imperfect	Future
fio	fímus	fiébam	fiam
fis	fitis		
fit	fiunt		

Perfect	Pluperfect	Future Perfect
factus sum	factus eram	factus ero

Subjunctive

Present	Imperfect	Perfect	Pluperfect
fiam	fíerem	factus sim	factus essem

Imperative

Sing. fi   *Plur.* fite

Infinitive

Pres. fíeri
Perf. factus esse
Fut. factum iri

Participles

Pres. ——
Perf. factus

Gerundive

faciéndus

VOCABULARY

EXPLANATION

1. All proper nouns that are the same in both languages have been omitted from this vocabulary.
2. Numbers following verbs refer to conjugations.
3. After some verbs, eo is added to indicate that the verb is a compound of ire.
4. After some verbs, io is added to indicate that the verb is an -io verb of the third conjugation.
5. The following abbreviations are used:

c., common gender
defect., defective
f., feminine
impers., impersonal
m., masculine
n., neuter
voc., vocative

VOCABULARY

A

a, by, from
a (*interj.*), ah
ab, by, from
abalienári, *dep.,* to be estranged, go away
abba, abba, Father
abbas, -atis, *m.,* abbot
abbátia, -ae, *f.,* abbacy, abbey
abbreviáre, to shorten
ábdere, -didi, -ditus, to secrete, hide
abdicáre, to abandon, give up
ábditum, -i, *n.,* hidden place, secret
aberráre, to go astray
abésse, abfui or afui, afutúrus, to be away; absit, God forbid! Far from it!
abhorrére, to shrink away from

Abías, -ae, *m.,* Abia
abiégnus, -a, -um, of fir, of the fir tree
ábies, -etis, *f.,* fir tree
abígere, -egi, -actus, to rid, banish, drive away
abíre, -ivi and -ii, -itus, (eo), to go away
abjéctio, -onis, *f.,* outcast
abjícere, -jeci, -jectus, to cast off or away, refuse
abjurátio, -onis, *f.,* abjuration
ablactáre, to wean
ablúere, -lui, -lutus, to wash away
ablútio, -onis, *f.,* a washing away
abnegáre, to deny
abolére, -evi, -itus, to abolish, destroy
abominábilis, -e, hateful
abomINári, *dep.,* to abhor
abominátio, -onis, *f.,* abomination

abortívus, -a, -um, born prematurely

abra, -ae, *f.*, maid

Abrahámus, -i, *m.*, Abraham

abrenuntiáre, to renounce

abrípere, -rípui, -reptus, to drag away

abs, *prep.*, from, by

Absalómus, -i, *m.*, Absalom

abscédere, -cessi, -cessus, to depart

abscíndere, -scidi, -scissus, to cut off, take away

abscóndere, -condi, -cónditus, to hide, shield

abscóndite, secretly

abscónditum, -i, *n.*, hidden thing; in abscóndito, in secret, in the secret part

abscónsio, -onis, *f.*, shelter

abscónsus, -a, -um, hidden, secret

absis, -idis, *f.*, apse

absístere, -stiti, -stitus, to be banished, cease

absolúte, absolutely, completely, alone

absolútio, -onis, *f.*, absolution

absólvere, -solvi, -solútus, to absolve, complete

absorbére, to swallow up

absque, without, except, besides

abstémius, -a, -um, temperate

abstergére, -tersi, -tersus, to wipe away, blot out

abstinéntia, -ae, *f.*, abstinence

abstinére, -tínui, -tentus, to refrain, abstain

abstráhere, -traxi, -tractus, to draw away, bring forth

absúmere, -sumpsi, -sumptus, to consume, take away

absúrde, absurdly

absýnthium, -ii, *n.*, wormwood

Ábula, -ae, *f.*, Avila

abundánter, abundantly, fully

abundántia, -ae, *f.*, abundance, prosperity

abundántius, more frequently

abundáre, to abound

abúnde, abundantly

abúsio, -onis, *f.*, scorn, contempt

abúti, -usus sum, *dep. 3*, to destroy

abýssus, -i, *f.*, the deep, depths, abyss

ac, and

académia, -ae, *f.*, academy

Accaronítae, -arum, *m.*, Accaronites; people of Accaron or Ekron

accédere, -cessi, -cessus, to come, approach

acceleráre, to hasten

accelerátio, -onis, *f.*, hastening

accéndere, -cendi, -census, to kindle

acceptábilis, -e, acceptable

acceptáre, to accept, receive with pleasure

accéptio, -onis, *f.*, respect

accéptus, -a, -um, agreeable, welcome, worthy

accérsere, -ivi, -itus, to send for, summon

accéssus, -us, *m.*, access

accidéntia, -orum, *n.*, accidents, appearances

accídere, -cidi, to happen

accíngere, -cinxi, -cinctus, to gird about

accípere, -cepi, -ceptus, to take, receive, accept

acclínis, -e, leaning, bowing

áccola, -ae, *c.*, sojourner

accomodáre, to adjust, incline

accréscere, -crevi, -cretus, to grow

accubáre, to lie down

accúbitus, -us, *m.*, repose; seat

accúmbere, -cúbui, -cúbitus, to sit at table

accuráte, accurately

accurátus, -a, -um, careful, accurate

accúrrere, -curri and -cucúrri, -cursus, to run to

accusáre, to accuse

accusátio, -onis, *f.*, accusation

accusátor, -oris, *m.*, accuser

acer, acris, acre, sharp, bitter, ardent

acérbitas, -atis, *f.*, bitterness, evil, wickedness

acérbus, -a, -um, sour

acérra, -ae, *f.*, casket for incense

acérvus, -i, *m.*, heap

acétum, -i, *n.*, vinegar

Achíllas, -ae, *m.*, Achilles

ácies, -ei, *f.*, edge, keenness; line of battle; pupil of the eye or the eye itself

ácinus, -i, *m.*, berry, grape

acólythus, -i, *m.*, acolyte

acquiéscere, -quiévi, -quiétus, to follow, agree

acquírere, -quisívi, -quisítus, to acquire, procure

acquisítio, -onis, *f.*, purchase, acquisition

áctio, -onis, *f.*, action, deed; gratiárum áctio, thanksgiving

actor, -oris, *m.*, governor

actuósus, -a, -um, active

actus, -us, *m.*, act, office, work, celebration, deed

acúere, -ui, -utus, to sharpen

acúleus, -i, *m.*, sting, sharp point, prick

acus, -us, *f.*, pin

acútus, -a, -um, sharp; bis acútus, two-edged

ad, to, toward, unto, at, against, near

adamántinus, -a, -um, adamantine, unconquered

adamáre, to love

ádamas, -antis, *m.*, adamant

Adamíti, -orum, *m.*, Adamites

Adámus, -i, *m.*, Adam

adaperíre, -pérui, -pertus, to open

adaquáre, to water, to give to drink

adaugére, -auxi, -auctus, to increase

áddere, -didi, -ditus, to give, to add

addícere, -dixi, -dictus, to doom, adjudge, condemn

addúcere, -duxi, -ductus, to bring, provoke

ádeo, even, so much, to that point

adeps, -ipis, *m.* and *f.*, fat, marrow, the best, finest

adésse, áffui (ádfui), to attend, be present, relieve, be mindful of

adhaerére, -haesi, -haesus, to adhere to, cleave to

adhibére, to add to, apply, take

adhuc, yet, still, now, as

adimplére, -plevi, -pletus, to fill

adinveníre, -veni, -ventus, to find

adinvéntio, -onis, *f.*, plan, device, deed, work

adipísci, adéptus sum, *dep. 3,* to gain, obtain

adíre, -ivi and -ii, -itus, (eo), to approach

áditus, -us, *m.*, approach, gate

adjícere, -jeci, -jectus, (io), to add, grant, to direct one's thoughts toward

adjudicáre, to give sentence

adjumentum, -i, *n.*, help

adjúngere, -junxi, -junctus, to join

adjuráre, to adjure

adjútor, -oris, *m.*, helper, coadjutor

adjutórium, -ii, *n.*, help

adjútrix, -icis, *f.*, helper

adjuváre, -juvi, jutus, to help

adlaboráre, to toil

adléctus, -i, *m.*, member elected into a collegium

adminículum, -i, *n.*, support, prop

adminíster, -tri, *m.*, assistant

administráre, to minister, adminster

administratórius, -a, -um, ministering

admirábilis, -e, wonderful, admirable

admirári, *dep.*, to wonder, be in admiration

admíttere, -misi, -missus, to join, admit

admíxtio, -onis, *f.*, mixture

admonére, to warn

adníti, -nisus or -nixus sum, *dep.* 3, to strive

adnotáre, to note

adolére, to burn, smell

adoléscens, -entis, *m.*, young man

adolescéntia, -ae, *f.*, youth

adolescéntior, -oris, younger; *as a noun*, young man

adolescéntula, -ae, *f.*, young maiden

adolescéntulus, -i, *m.*, young man

adóptio, -onis, *f.*, adoption

adorándus, -a, -um, adorable

adoráre, to adore, worship

adorátor, -oris, *m.*, adorer, worshiper

adoríri, -ortus sum, *dep.* 4, to undertake

adornáre, to adorn

adscíscere, -scivi, -scitus, to admit, receive

adscríptus, -a, -um, approved

adspícere, -spexi, -spectus, to look on

adspiráre, to inspire, to breathe upon

adstáre, -stiti, to stand by

adstipulári, *dep.*, to assent to, strengthen

adsum; *see* adesse

adulátio, -onis, *f.*, flattery

adúlter, -i, *m.*, adulterer

adúltera, -ae, *f.*, adulteress

adulteráre, to commit adultery

adulterínus, -a, -um, not genuine, bastard

adultérium, -ii, *n.*, adultery

adúlterus, -a, -um, adulterous

adúltus, -a, -um, adult, grown

adunáre, to unite

adúrere, -ussi, -ustus, to kindle, set fire to, burn

ádvena, -ae, *c.*, stranger

adveníre, -veni, -ventus, to come

adventáre, to come

advéntus, -us, *m.*, coming, arrival, advent

advérsa, -orum, *n.*, adverse things, adversity

adversári, *dep.*, to oppose, resist

adversárius, -ii, *m.*, adversary, foe

advérsitas, -atis, *f.*, adversity, harm

advérsum, -i, *n.*, harm

advérsum, against; ex advérso, opposite, over against, in the front

advérsus, against, in comparison with

advértere, -verti, -versus, to perceive, remark

advesperáscit, -avit, *imperson.* 3, to be toward evening

advocáre, to call to

advocátus, -i, *m.*, advocate

advoláre, to fly, hasten

advólvere, -volvi, -volútus, to roll

aedes, -is, *f.*, temple

aedícula, -ae, *f.*, little house or building

aedíficans, -antis, *m.*, builder

aedificáre, to build

aedificátio, -onis, *f.*, building, edifying

aedificátor, -oris, *m.*, repairer

aedítuus, -i, *m.*, keeper or warden of a temple

Aegéa, -ae, *f.*, Aegae

aeger, -gra, -grum, sick

Aegídius, -ii, *m.*, Giles

aegre, badly, ill

aegritúdo, -inis, *f.*, sickness

aegrotáre, to be sick, fall sick

aegrotátio, -onis, *f.*, illness

aegrótus, -a, -um, sick

Aegyptíacus, -a, -um, Egyptian

Aegýptii, -orum, *m.*, Egyptians

Aegyptius, -a, -um, Egyptian

Aegýptus, -i, *f.*, Egypt

Aelamítae, -arum, *m.*, Elamites

Aemília, -ae, *f.*, Emilia

Aemiliánus, -i, *m.*, Aemilian

aémula, -ae, *f.*, rival

aemulári, *dep.*, to envy

aemulátio, -onis, *f.*, emulation, envy

aemulátor, -oris, *m.*, zealous imitator

aéneus, -a, -um, brazen

aenígma, -atis, *n.*, riddle, hard question, obscurity; in aenígmate, in a dark manner

aequális, -e, equal

aequálitas, -atis, *f.*, equality

aequanímiter, calmly

aequáre, to equal

aequiparáre, to compare

aéquitas, -atis, *f.*, justice, righteousness

aéquor, -oris, *n.*, sea

aéquus, equal, right; aéquo ánimo, cheerful in mind

aër, aëris (*pl.*, aëres, aëra), *m.*, air

aerárium, -ii, *n.*, treasury

aëreus, -a, -um, airy, windy, raging

aéreus, -a, -um, of brass, bronze, or copper

aerúgo, -inis, *f.*, rust, blight, mildew

aerúmna, -ae, *f.*, hardship, affliction

aerumnosus, -a, -um, sorrowing

aes, aeris, *n.*, brass, copper, money; aes aliénum, debt

aestas, -atis, *f.*, summer

aestimáre, to esteem, consider, suppose, account

aestimátio, -onis, *f.*, evaluation, appraisement; count

aestimátor, -oris, *m.*, one who esteems

aestívus, -a, -um, of the summer

aestuáre, to be hot; scorch; kindle

aestus, -us, *m.*, heat

aetas, -atis, *f.*, age; aetátem habére, to be of age

aeternális, -e, eternal

aetérnitas, -atis, *f.*, eternity

aetérnus, -a, -um, eternal, everlasting; in aetérnum, forever

aether, -eris (acc., aethera), *m.*, upper air, sky

aethéreus, -a, -um, airy, ethereal; of heaven

Aethiópia, -ae, *f.*, Ethiopia

Aéthiops, -opis, *m.*, Ethiopian

aevum, -i, *n.*, eternity

Afer, -fra, -frum, African

affári, *dep.*, to speak, say

áffatim, sufficiently, earnestly

afféctus, -us, *m.*, devotion, love, affection; sense

afférre, attúli, allátus, to bring forth, give; bring to

afficere, -feci, -fectus, (io), to affect, cause a change in; to treat

affirmáre, to affirm

affíxio, -onis, *f.*, fastening, nailing

affláre, to inspire, teach

afflátus, -us, *m.*, a blowing upon; breath, inspiration, spirit

afflictátio, -onis, *f.*, suffering, misery, chastisement

afflíctio, -onis, *f.*, affliction

afflígere, -flixi, -flictus, to afflict, mortify, punish

afflúere, -fluxi, -fluxus, to abound, flow to

Áfricus, -i, *m.*, south, south wind

Agaréni, -orum, *m.*, Agarites

Ágatha Gothórum, -ae, *f.*, Agata dei Goti (church)

ager, -gri, *m.*, field; county, country, district

ágere, egi, actus, to do, drive, put in motion, deal, practice; grátias ágere, to give thanks

Aggaéus, -i, *m.*, Aggeus

agger, aggeris, *m.*, mound

aggraváre, to be heavy

ággredi, -gressus sum, (io), *dep. 3*, to approach

aggregáre, to add to, to join with

agitáre, to shake

agmen, -inis, *n.*, throng, host

agnéllus, -i, *m.*, little lamb

agnítio, -onis, *f.*, knowledge

Agnoítae, -arum, *m. pl.*, Agnoites

agnómen, -inis, *n.*, surname

Agnónus, -i, f., Agnone

agnóscere, -novi, -notus, to know, understand, acknowledge, recognize

agnus, -i, m., lamb

agon, -onis, m., a contest in the public games; agony; in agóne, for the mastery

agonía, -ae, f., agony

agonizáre, to die

agréstis, -e, wild

agrícola, -ae, m., farmer, husbandman

agricultúra, -ae, f., farming

ait. def. verb, he says

aiunt, they say

ajébat = aiébat, he said

ajunt = aiunt

ala, -ae, f., wing

alabástrum, -i, n., alabaster box

álacer (álacris), -cris, -cre, quick, active, cheerful

alácritas, -atis, f., eagerness

alácriter, eagerly

álapa, -ae, f., blow, box on the ear, slap

alátus, -a, -um, winged

Alba, -ae, f., Alva

Albanénsis, -e, of Albano

Albertus, -i, m., Albert

albéscere, to grow white or bright

Albigénses, -ium, m., Albigensians

album, -i, n., tablet; list

albus, -a, -um, white

aleph, the first letter of the Hebrew alphabet

álere, álui, altus and álitus, to feed, nourish

Ales, Hales

ales, -itis, winged

Alexándria, -ae, f., Alexandria; Alessandria

Alexandríni, -orum, m., Alexandrians

Alexandrínus, -a, -um, of Alexandria

Aléxius, -ii, m., Alexius, Alexis

alga, -ae, f., sea weed

álgidus, -a, -um, cold

álias, elsewhere

álibi, elsewhere

alienáre, to estrange

alienátus, -a, -um, strange

alienígena, -ae, m., foreigner, stranger

aliénus, -a, -um, strange

aliméntum, -i, n., food, refreshment

alimónium, -ii, n., nourishment

alióquin, otherwise

aliquámdiu, for a while

aliquándo, at any time, heretofore, at last

aliquantísper, for a while

aliquántulum, a little, somewhat

aliquátenus, to a certain degree

áliqui, -quae, -quod, some

áliquis, -qua, -quid, someone, something, anyone, anything

áliquot, some, several

aliquóties, several times

áliter, otherwise

aliúnde, another way

álius, -a, -ud, other, another; álius . . . álius, one another; álii . . . álii, some . . . others

allaboráre, to labor

allegoría, -ae, f., allegory, figure

allelúia, alleluia (Hebrew, praise ye the Lord)

alleváre, to lift up

alleviáre, to raise up

allícere, -lexi, -lectus, (io), to allure, charm, attract

allídere, -lisi, -lisus, to strike against, cast down

alligáre, to bind

allocútio, -onis, f., address, speech; encouragement, comfort

álloqui, -locútus sum, 3, dep., to converse with

allóquium, -ii, n., conversation, exhortation

almus, -a, -um, gracious, kind; — Spíritus, Holy Ghost

áloe, -es, *f.*, aloe
Aloísius, -ii, *m.*, Aloysius
alpha, alpha (the first letter of the Greek alphabet)
Alphaéus, -i, *m.*, Alpheus
altáre, -is, *n.*, altar
alter, -tera, -terum, the other of two; alter . . . alter, the one . . . the other; alter . . . ab áltero, one from the other; — altérius, of one another; in áltero . . . in áltero, on the one hand . . . on the other hand
altercári, to dispute
alternáre, to change
alternátim, alternately
altérnus, -a, -um, one after the other, by turns, alternate
altéruter, -tra, -trum, one of two, one toward another; ad altérutrum, one to another
áltilis, -e, fatted; altília, fatlings
altitúdo, -inis, *f.*, height, high place; depth
altum, -i, *n.*, the deep
altus, -a, -um, high; deep; exalted
alúmnus, -i, *m.*, student
alvéolus, -i, *m.*, bowl
Alvérnia, -ae, *f.*, Alverno; Mons Alvérniae, Mount Alverno
Alvérnus, -a, -um, Alverno
álveus, -i, *m.*, channel, bed (of a river)
alvus, -i, *f.*, womb
Amálphis, -is, *f.*, Amalfi
amánter, lovingly
amáre, to love
amáre (*adv.*), bitterly
amaréscere, to become bitter
Amarías, -ae, *m.*, Amarias
amaritúdo, -inis, *f.*, bitterness, anguish
amárus, -a, -um, bitter; amára, *n. pl.*, bitterness
amátor, -oris, *m.*, lover

amátrix, -icis, *f.*, lover
Ambiánum, -i, *n.*, Amiens
ambígere, to doubt, hesitate
ambíre, to strive for
ambitiósus, -a, -um, ambitious
ámbitus, -us, *m.*, circle; cope
ambo, -ae, -o, both
Ambrosiánus, -a, -um, Ambrosian, of St. Ambrose
Ambrósius, -ii, *m.*, Ambrose
ambuláre, to walk
amen, amen (*Hebrew*, so be it)
améntia, -ae, *f.*, madness, insanity
amethýstus, -i, *f.*, amethyst
amicítia, -ae, *f.*, friendship, friends; league
amíctus, -a, -um, clothed
amíctus, -us, *m.*, vesture
amícus, -i, *m.*, friend
Amidéus de Amidéis, -i, *m.*, Amadeo de' Amidei
amíttere, -misi, -missus, to disperse, to send away
Ammonítes, -is, *m.*, Ammonite
Ammonítidae, -arum, *f.*, women of Ammon
ámodo, henceforth, hereafter
amoénus, -a, -um, pleasant
amor, -oris, *m.*, love
Amorrhaéus, -a, -um, Amorrhite
amovére, -movi, -motus, to put aside, turn away, remove
amphiteátrum, -i, *n.*, amphitheater
ámphora, -ae, *f.*, bottle, pitcher
amplécti, -plexus sum, *dep. 3*, to embrace
amplificáre, to increase
amplificátor, -oris, *m.*, one who extends or increases
ámplior, ámplius, greater
ámplius (*adv.*), yet more, any more
ampúlla, -ae, *f.*, bottle, phial
amputáre, to cut off, remove, take away

an, *conj.*, or
anachoréticus, -a, -um, eremitical
anachoríta, -ae, *m.*, hermit, anchorite
anáthema, anathema
anathematizáre, to curse
anceps, -cípitis, two-edged
ánchora, -ae, *f.*, anchor
ancílla, -ae, *f.*, handmaid, maidservant, bondwoman
anfráctus, -us, *m.*, bending, winding
Andréas, -ae, *m.*, Andrew
Ángela Merícia, -ae, *f.*, Angela Merici
Angélicae, -arum, *f.*, Angelicals
angélicus, -a, -um, angelic
ángelus, -i, *m.*, angel
ángere, to trouble
Angli, -orum, *m.*, English
Anglia, -ae, *f.*, England
ánglice (*adv.*), into English
Ánglicus, -i, *m.*, Englishman
angor, -oris, *m.*, distress
angoriáre, to force
anguis, -is, *c.*, snake
anguláris, -e, angular, corner
ángulus, -i, *m.*, corner; bastion, stay
angústia, -ae, *f.*, straitness; want
angústiae, -arum, *f.*, distresses, necessities, tribulations
angustiátus, -a, -um, distressed
angústus, -a, -um, narrow
Aniánus, -i, *m.*, Annianus
Anícium, -ii, *n.*, Le Puy
ánima, -ae, *f.*, soul, life
animadvérsio, -onis, *f.*, punishment
animadvértere, verti, -versus, to mark, take notice of
ánimal, -is, *n.*, animal, living creature, beast
ánimans, -antis, living; *as a noun*, living creature
animátus, -a, -um, living
animósitas, -atis, *f.*, high spirits
ánimus, -i, *m.*, heart, mind, spirit; **ex** ánimo, from the heart

Annésium, -ii, *n.*, Annecy
annículus, -a, -um, of one year, one year old
anniversárius, -a, -um, anniversary
annóna, -ae, *f.*, crop, grain; means of subsistence, rations
annúere, -nui, to nod, beckon, wink; assent, grant
ánnulus, -i, *m.*, ring
annumeráre, to number
annuntiáre, to announce, declare, show forth, relate
annuntiátio, -onis, *f.*, declaration, annunciation
annuntiátor, -oris, *m.*, announcer, herald
annus, -i, *m.*, year
ánnuus, -a, -um, annual, yearly, by the year
ansa, -ae, *f.*, handle; opportunity
Ansélmus, -i, *m.*, Anselm
ante, before; (before an expression of time), ago
ántea, before, formerly
anteáctus, -a, -um, past
antecédere, -cessi, -cessus, to go before, to surpass
antecéllere, to excel
antecéssor, -oris, *m.*, predecessor
anteíre, -ivi and -ii, -itus, (eo), to go before
antelucánum, -i, *n.*, dawn
antelucánus, -a, -um, before daybreak
antemurále, -is, *n.*, bulwark
ántequam, before
antérior, -oris, previous, before
antevértere, -verti, -versus, to come before, precede
anticipáre, to prevent, to anticipate
Antiochéni, -orum, *m.*, Antiochians
Antiochénsis, -e, of Antioch
Antiochénus, -a, -um, of Antioch
Antióchia, -ae, *f.*, Antioch
antíphona, -ae, *f.*, antiphon

antiquárius, -ii, *m.*, antiquary, old scribe

antíquus, -a, -um, former, of old

Antissiodorénsis, -e, of Auxerre

antístes, -stitis, *m.*, bishop

Antónius, -ii, *m.*, Anthony

antrum, -i, *n.*, cave, den

Antvérpia, -ae, *f.*, Antwerp

anus, -us, *f.*, old woman

anxiári, *dep.*, to be in anguish

anxíetas, -atis, *f.*, anxiety

aper, apri, *m.*, boar

aperíre, -pérui, -pertus, to open

aperítio, -onis, f., opening

apernári, *dep.*, to scorn

apérte, openly, clearly, plainly

apex, -icis, *m.*, top or summit, point

apis, apis, *f.*, bee

Apocalýpsis, -is, *f.*, revelation, Apocalypse

apócrypha, -orum, *n.*, apocryphal gospels

apócryphus, -a, -um, apocryphal

apología, -ae, *f.*, defense, justification

apoplécticus, -a, -um, apoplectic

apopléxia, -ae, *f.*, apoplexy

aporiári, *dep.*, to be in need, be straitened, be perplexed

apostásia, -ae, *f.*, apostasy

apóstata, -ae, *m.*, apostate

apostatáre, to fall off or away from

apostáticus, -a, -um, rebel, apostate

apostátrix, -icis, rebellious, apostate

apostolátus, -us, *m.*, apostleship

apostólicus, -a, -um, apostolic

apóstolus, -i, *m.*, apostle

apothéca, -ae, *f.*, storeroom

apparére, to appear, show oneself, shine forth

apparítio, -onis, f., manifestation, apparition

appáritor, -oris, *m.*, servant

appelláre, to call

appellátio, -onis, f., appellation

appéllere, -puli, -pulsus, to bring or drive to

appéndere, -pendi, -pensus, to weigh, weigh out, balance

appétere, -ivi and -ii, -itus, to hunger after, reach to, pursue, seize on

appetítor, -oris, *m.*, coveter

appetítus, -us, *m.*, hunger, appetite, passion

Áppius, -a, -um, Appian

applicáre, -avi, -atus and -ui, -itus, to bring, add to; to set to shore

appónere, -pósui, -pósitus, to add to, put to, do unto, proceed

appósitus, -a, -um, placed near; appropriate

apprehéndere, -prehéndi, -prehénsus, to take hold of, lay hands on, seize, embrace, apprehend

appretiáre, to prize, value, put a price on

appríme, exceedingly, above all

approbátio, -onis, *f.*, sanction, approbation

appropiáre, to come near

appropinquáre, to approach, be at hand

approximáre, to approach

Aprílis, -is, *m.*, April

Aprútius, -ii, *m.*, the Abruzzi

aptáre, to fit to, adapt to, prepare

aptus, -a, um, fitting

apud, to, with, near, in the presence of, at the house of

aqua, -ae, *f.*, water

aquadúctus, -us, *m.*, water course, conduit, aqueduct

Aquae Tarbéllae, -arum, *f.*, Dax

Aquénsis, -e, of Aix

áquila, -ae, *f.*, eagle

Aquilánus, -a, -um, of Aquila

Aquilejénsis, -e, of Aquileia

áquilo, -onis, *m.*, north

Aquinas, -atis, of Aquin

Aquínus, -i, *m.,* Aquinas

Aquisgranénsis, -e, of Aachen

Aquitánia, -ae, *f.,* Aquitaine

Aquitánus, -a, -um, of Aquitaine

ara, -ae, *f.,* altar

Arabéllae, -arum, *f.,* Arabella (Arbella, Arbela)

Árabes, -um, *m.,* Arabs, Arabians

Aragónia, -ae, *f.,* Aragon

Aragónius, -a, -um, Aragonian

aránea, -ae, *f.,* spider

aráre, to plow; devise

arátor, -oris, *m.,* plowman

arátrum, -i, *n.,* plow

árbiter, -tri, *m.,* judge

arbitrári, *dep.,* to think

arbitrátus, -us, *m.,* choice, will

arbítrium, -ii, *n.,* free choice, free will

arbor, -oris, *f.,* tree

arbústum, -i, *n.,* orchard; arbústa, *n. pl.,* branches

arca, -ae, *f.,* ark

Arcádius, -a, -um, Arcadian

arcánum, -i, *n.,* secret place

arcánus, -a, -um, secret; arcána, *n.,* hidden or secret things

arcére, -ui, to prevent

arcéssere, -ivi, -itus, to summon, call

archángelus, -i, *m.,* archangel

archibasílica, -ae, *f.,* basilica, cathedral church

archiconfratérnitas, -atis, *f.,* archconfraternity

archiepiscopátus, -us, *m.,* archbishopric

archimandríta, -ae, *m.,* archimandrite

archipraésul, -is, *m.,* archbishop

archisodálitas, -atis, *f.,* archsodality

archisynagógus, -i, *m.,* ruler of the synagogue

architéctus, -us, *m.,* architect

architriclínus, -i, *m.,* chief steward

árctius, more closely, more firmly

arctus, -a, -um, narrow, tight

arcus, -us, *m.,* bow; rainbow

Ardeatínus, -a, -um, of Ardea, Ardeatine

ardens, -entis, flaming, burning

ardénter, ardently

ardére, arsi, arsus, to burn

Ardferténsis, -e, of Ardfert

ardor, -oris, *m.,* burning

árduus, -a, -um, steadfast

área, -ae, *f.,* floor, threshing floor

arefácere, -feci, -factus, (io), to parch

Areláte, *n.,* and Árelas, -atis, *f.,* Arles

Arelaténsis, -e, of Arles

aréna, -ae, *f.,* sand

arenária, -ae, *f.,* sand pit

aréola, -ae, *f.,* small plot, garden-bed

Areopagíta, -ae, *m.,* Areopagite

arére, arui, to wither, dry up

aréscere, árui, to become dry, wither away; to pine away

Argentárius: Mons ——, Mount Argentaro

argénteus, -a, -um, of silver

argénteus, -i, *m.,* piece of silver

Argentorátum, -i, *n.,* Strasbourg

argéntum, -i, *n.,* silver; money

argúere, -ui, -utus, to rebuke, reprove, accuse, convince

argumentátio, -onis, *f.,* argument, debate

argumentósus, -a, -um, busy

arguméntum, -i, *m.,* proof

Ari, *vocative of* Arius

Ariáni, -orum, *m.,* Arians

Arianísmus, -i, *m.,* Arianism

árida, -ae, *f.,* dryness, dry land

áridus, -a, -um, dry, withered

áries, -etis, *m.,* ram

Arimathaéa, -ae, *f.,* Arimathea

Ariminénsis, -e, of Rimini

aríolus, -i, *m.,* cunning man, soothsayer

arma, -orum, *n.,* arms, weapons, armor

Armachána, -ae, *f.*, Armagh
armatúra, -ae, *f.*, armor
armátus, -a, -um, armed
Arméni, -orum, *m.*, Armenians
arméntum, -i, *n.*, cattle; a herd
ármiger, -gera, -gerum, bearing arms
  or armor
armílla, -ae, *f.*, bracelet
armus, -i, *m.*, shoulder
aróma, -atis, *n.*, spice; perfume, aroma
aromatízans, -antis, aromatic
Arrétium, -ii, *n.*, Arezzo
arridére, -risi, -risus, to smile, laugh
arrípere, rípui, réptus, (io), to lay
  hold on, seize, take
ars, artis, *f.*, art, artifice, scheme,
  knowledge; trade
arthrítis, -idis, *f.*, gout
artículus, -i, *m.*, finger; moment; in
  artículo diéi illíus, in the same day
ártifex, -icis, *m.*, artificer
artifícium, -ii, *n.*, handicraft, art, skill
artus, -us, *m.*, joint, limb
arundinétum, -i, *n.*, reeds; a growth of
  reeds
arúndo, -inis, *f.*, reed
áruspex, -icis, *m.*, soothsayer
arvum, -i, *n.*, field
arx, arcis, *f.*, fortress, castle; throne
as, assis, *m.* (a small bronze coin), far-
  thing
ascéndere, -scendi, -scensus, to ascend,
  grow up, climb up
ascénsio, -onis, *f.*, Ascension; ascent,
  going up
ascénsor, -oris, *m.*, rider
ascénsus, -us, *m.*, ascent, means of ascent; chariot
ascéta, -ae, *m.*, ascetic, hermit
ascetérium, -ii, *n.*, monastery
áscia, -ae, *f.*, hatchet
ascíre, to take, get
ascíscere, -scivi, -scitus, to receive
Asculánus, -a, -um, of Ascoli

Ásculum, -i, *n.*, Ascoli
aséllus, -i, *m.*, a young ass, donkey
Asiánus, -a, -um, of Asia, Asian
ásina, -ae, *f.*, a she-ass
asinárius, -a, -um, pertaining to an
  ass; mola asinária, millstone
ásinus, -i, *m.*, ass
Asmodaéus, -i, *m.*, Asmodeus
aspéctus, -us, *m.*, vision; sightliness;
  countenance
ásper, -a, -um, sharp, rough, difficult
asperáre, to make rough
aspérgere, -spersi, -spersus, to sprinkle
aspernári, *dep.*, to despise
aspernátor, -oris, *m.*, contemner
aspérsio, -onis, *f.*, sprinkling
aspersus, -a, -um, sprinkled, spattered
aspícere, -spexi, -spectus, (io), to regard, behold
aspiráre, to assist, be favorable to
aspis, -idis, *f.*, asp, adder
asportáre, to bring
ássecla, -ae, *m.*, follower
assentíri, -sensus sum, *dep. 4*, to agree
ássequi, -secútus sum, *dep. 3*, to follow
asser, -eris, *m.*, board, plank, lath
assérere, -sérui, -sértus, to declare, justify, assert; remark
assértor, -oris, *m.*, champion, defender
asseveránter, absolutely, emphatically
Assidaéi, -orum, *m.*, Assideans
assidúitas, -atis, *f.*, custom
assíduus, -a, -um, continual
assignáre, to assign, designate
assimiláre, to make like to, compare
assimilári, *dep.*, to become like, be
  compared
Assísinas, -atis, of Assisi
Assísium, -ii, *n.*, Assisi
assístere, ástiti, to be present, stand
  around; to have come
assístrix, -icis, *f.*, helper
assolére, to be accustomed, be usual

assúmere, -sumpsi, -sumptus, to take, receive, take up, take unto oneself

assúmptio, -onis, *f.*, Assumption; protection

Assur, Assyria

assus, -a, -um, roasted, broiled

Assýrii, -orum, *m.*, Assyrians

ast (at), but

astáre (adstare), ástiti, to stand by or near

asteríscus, -i, *m.*, asterisk

astríngere, -strinxi, -strictus, to bind, fetter; draw closer; se —, to be guilty of

astrúere, -struxi, -structus, to establish, add, form, build; teach

astrum, -i, *n.*, star

astus, -us, *m.*, cunning, cleverness

astútia, -ae, *f.*, craftiness, subtlety

at, but

ater, atra, atrum, dark, black

Athanasiánus, -a, -um, of Athanasius

Athénae, -arum, *f.*, Athens

Atheniénsis, -e, of Athens, Athenian

athléta, -ae, *m.*, wrestler, athlete, champion

Atlánticus, -a, -um, Atlantic

atque, and

atraméntum, -i, *n.*, ink

Atrébas, -batis, *m.*, Arras

átrium, -ii, *n.*, court, hall

atrox, -cis, terrible, fierce, horrible

áttamen, nevertheless

atténdere, -tendi, -tentus, attend, take heed, hearken, to beware

atténte, attentively

atténtius, more attentively

attenuáre, to weaken

attérere, -trivi, -tritus, to bruise; destroy

attestátio, -onis, *f.*, act of attesting; proof, evidence

attéxere, -téxui, -tectus, to add

attinére, -tínui, -tentus, to pertain to

attíngere, -tigi, -tactus, to manage

attóllere, to support, lift up

attónitus, -a, -um, astonished

attráhere, -traxi, -tractus, to draw to

attrectáre, to feel, touch, lay hands on

attribútio, -onis, *f.*, giving

attrítus, -a, -um, hard

auctor, -oris, *m.*, author, creator, founder

auctóritas, -atis, *f.*, authority

auctrix, -icis, *f.*, authoress, mother, forebear

audácter, boldly

audére, ausus sum, *semidep.* 2, to dare

audíre, to hear

audítio, -onis, *f.*, hearing, report

audítor, -oris, *m.*, hearer, listener

audítus, -us, *m.*, hearing

auférre, ábstuli, ablátus, to take away

aufúgere, -fugi (io), to flee

augére, auxi, auctus, to increase

augéscere, áuxi, to increase

augméntum, -i, *n.*, increase, advancement

augur, -uris, *c.*, soothsayer

Augústa Praetória, -ae, -ae, *f.*, Aosta

Augustínus, -i, *m.*, Augustine

Augustodunénsis, -e, of Autun

Augustodúnum, -i, *n.*, Autun

Augústus, -i, *m.*, Augustus; August

aula, -ae, *f.*, dwelling, temple; court; — transvérsa, transept

aura, -ae, *f.*, air, breath, breeze

Áurea, -ae, *f.*, Aurea, Aure

Aureliánus, -i, *m.*, Aurelian

Aurélius, -a, -um, Aurelian

áureus, -a, -um, of gold, golden

áureus, -i, *m.*, piece of gold

aurichálcum, -i, *n.*, fine brass

aurícula, -ae, *f.*, ear

auríga, -ae, *c.*, charioteer

auris, -is, *f.*, ear

auróra, -ae, *f.*, morning

áurum, -i, *n.*, gold

LATIN GRAMMAR

auscultáre, to listen to
auspicári, *dep.*, to begin
auspicátus, -a, -um, happy, auspicious
auspícium, -ii, *n.*, divination, omen
auster, -tri, *m.*, south; south wind
austéritas, -atis, *f.*, rigor
austérus, -a, -um, austere
austrális, -e, south
Austríacus, -a, -um, of Austria
aut, or
autem, but, however; and, and also; whereupon
autumnális, -e, autumn, autumnal; withered
autúmnus, -i, *m.*, autumn
auxiliári, *dep.*, to help
auxiliátor, -oris, *m.*, helper
auxiliátrix, icis, *f.*, helper
auxílium, -ii, *n.*, help, aid
Auximánus, -i, *n.*, of Ossimo
Áuximum, -i, *n.*, Ossimo
avarítia, -ae, *f.*, covetousness
avárus, -a, -um, covetous
avárus, -i, *m.*, miser
ave, hail
Avellanénsis, -e, of Avellano
Avellanítae, -arum, *m.*, inhabitants or inmates of Font-Avellano
avéllere, -velli and -vulsi, -vulsus, to withdraw, tear away, separate
Avénio, -onis, *f.*, Avignon
avérnus, -i, *m.*, the infernal regions
aversáre, to turn away from
avérsio, -onis, *f.*, apostasy
avértere, -verti, -versus, to turn away; pervert
ávia, -ae, *f.*, grandmother
ávide, eagerly
avídius, more eagerly
avis, avis, *f.*, bird
avítus, -a, -um, ancestral
avocáre, to withdraw oneself
avúnculus, -i, *m.*, uncle
avus, -i, *m.*, grandfather

Azarías, -ae, *m.*, Azarias
Azótii, -orum, *m.*, Azotians
ázyma, -orum, *n.*, unleavened bread; azyme
ázymus, -a, -um, unleavened

B

Babylónii, -orum, *m.*, Babylonians
bacca, -ae, *f.* (berry), fruit of the olive
bacíllum, -i, *n.*, staff
Bactri, -orum, *m.*, Bactrians
báculus, -i, *m.*, staff
bajuláre, to bear, carry
baláre, to bleat
balbutíre, to babble
Baleáres, -ium, *f.*, Balearic Islands
Baleáris Major, -is, *f.*, Majorca
Balneorégium, -ii, *n.*, Bagnorea
bálneum, -i, *n.*, bath
bálsamum, -i, *n.*, balm
bálteus, -i, *m.*, belt
Baltimorénsis, -e, of Baltimore
Bambérga, -ae, *f.*, Bamberg
Bambergénsis, -e, of Bamberg
baptísma, -atis, *n.*, baptism
baptísmus, -i, *m.*, baptism
Baptísta, -ae, *m.*, Baptist
baptistérium, -ii, *n.*, baptistery
baptizáre, to baptize
bárathrum, -i, *n.*, bottomless pit, the lower world
barba, -ae, *f.*, beard
Bárbari, -orum, *m.*, natives of Barbary
bárbarus, -a, -um, of Barbary; foreign, strange
Barbatiánus, -i, *m.*, Barbatian
Bárcino, -onis, *f.*, Barcelona
Barcinonénsis, -e, of Barcelona
Barénsis, -e, of Bari
Bárium, -ii, *n.*, Bari
Bartholomaéus, -i, *m.*, Bartholomew
basílica, -ae, *f.*, church
basilíscus, -i, *m.*, basilisk

Basílius, -ii, *m.*, Basil
basis, -is, *f.*, base, foundation, pedestal; bases, feet
Baváricus, -a, -um, of Bavaria
beáre, to bless
beatitúdo, -inis, *f.*, happiness
Béatrix, -icis, *f.*, Beatrice
beátus, -a, -um, happy, blessed
Beccénsis, -e, of Bec
Beda, -ae, *m.*, Bede
Belgae, -arum, *m.*, Belgians
belláre, to fight against, make war
bellátor, -oris, *m.*, warrior
bellicósus, -a, um, of war, warlike
béllicus, -a, -um, warlike; vasa béllica, arms
belligeráre, to war, wage war
béllua, -ae, *f.*, monster, savage beast
bellum, -i, *n.*, war, battle
Benácus (Lacus), -i, *m.*, Lake Garda
bene, well
benedícere, -dixi, -dictus, to bless
benedíctio, -onis, *f.*, blessing, benediction
Benedíctus, -i, *m.*, Benedict
benefácere, -feci, -factus, (io), to do good, do well
benefáctor, -oris, m., benefactor
benefáctum, -i, *n.*, good deed; benefit, favor
beneficéntia, -ae, *f.*, liberality
benefícium, -ii, *n.*, benefit
benéficus, -a, -um, beneficent
beneplácens, -entis, acceptable
beneplácitum, -i, *n.*, good pleasure, favor; pleasure, lust
beneplácitus, -a, -um, acceptable
benesónans, -antis, loud; sweet-sounding
Benevéntum, -i, *n.*, Benevento
benévolus, -a, -um, kind
benígne, favorably
benígnitas, -atis, *f.*, goodness, benignity, favor

benígnus, -a, -um, merciful, favorable, good, benign, loving
Benítii, -orum, *m.*, Benizzi
Berengária, -ae, *f.*, Berenguela
Berengárius, -ii, *m.*, Berenger
Bergoménsis, -e, of Bergamo
Bérgomum, -i, *n.*, Bergamo
Bernardínus, -i, *m.*, Bernardine
Bernárdus, -i, *m.*, Bernard
Berothíta, -ae, *m.*, Berothite
Berthóldus, -i, *m.*, Berthold
berýllus, -i, *c.*, beryl
béstia, -ae, *f.*, beast
beth, second letter of the Hebrew alphabet corresponding to English *b*
Bethlehemítis, -is, *m.*, Bethlehemite
Bethsamítae, -arum, *m.*, Bethsamites
bíbere, bibi, bíbitus, to drink
biceps, -cípitis, two-headed, two-edged
bícolor, -oris, of two colors
bidens, -entis, *f.*, animal for sacrifice, sheep
bíduum, -i, *n.*, space of two days
biénnium, -ii, *n.*, space of two years
bilínguis, -e, double-tongued, treacherous
bilocátio, -onis, *f.*, the ability to be in more than one place at the same time
bimátus, -us, *m.*, the age of two years
bini, -ae, -a, two, two apiece, two of a sort
bipertítus, -a, -um, having two parts, double
Birgítta, -ae, *f.*, Bridget
bis, twice
Biscópius, -ii, *m.*, Biscop
Biterrénsis, -e, of Beziers
bitúmen, -inis, *n.*, pitch, slime, cement
Blancha, -ae, *f.*, Blanche
blandiméntum, -i, *n.*, allurement
blandíri, *dep. 4*, to caress
blandítia, -ae, *f.*, flattery
blandus, -a, -um, soft, soothing

Blásius, -ii, *m.*, Blaise

blasphémia, -ae, *f.*, blasphemy

blasphémus, -i, *m.*, blasphemer

Blésium, -ii, *n.*, Blois

Boéticus, -a, -um, Andalusian

Boétis, -is, *f.*, Andalusia

Bogoténsis, -e, of Bogota

Bohémi, -orum, *m.*, Bohemians

Bolesláus, -i, *m.*, Boleslav

Boleslávia, -ae, *f.*, Mlada Boleslav

Bonajúncta Manéttus, -ae, -i, *m.*, Bonajuncta Manetti

Bonaventúra, -ae, *m.*, Bonaventure

Bonfílius Monáldius, -i, -i, *m.*, Bonfiglio Monaldi

Bonifátius, -ii, *m.*, Boniface

bónitas, -atis, *f.*, goodness

Bonónia, -ae, *f.*, Bologna

bonus, -a, -um, good; in bonum, for good

bonum, -i, *n.*, good, advantage; bona, *n.*, goods, possessions

boreális, -e, northern; boreália, *n.*, northern parts

borith (*indecl.*), borith; possibly the soapwort used formerly for cleaning

Borna, -ae, *f.*, Born

Borromaéi, -orum, *m.*, the Borromeos

bos, bovis, *m.* and *f.*, ox

Boschum, -i, *n.*, Bosco

botrus, -i, *m.*, bunch, cluster of grapes

brácca, -ae, *f.*, coat

bráchium, -ii, *n.*, arm

bránchia, -ae, *f.*, gill

Bráulius, -ii, *m.*, Braulio

bravíum, -ii, *n.*, prize

breve, -is, *n.*, brief

breviáre, to shorten

breviárium, -ii, breviary

brevículus, -a, -um, somewhat short; in brevículo, after a little while

brevis, -e, short; in brevi, in a short space

Brígida, -ae, *f.*, Brigid

Británni, -orum, *m.*, Britons

Británnia, -ae, *f.*, England; Brittany

Brithuáldus, -i, *m.*, Brithwald

Britónes, -um, *m.*, Britons

Bríxia, -ae, *f.*, Brescia

Brixiánus, -a, -um, of Brescia

brúchus, -i, *m.*, bruchus, locust

bruma, -ae, *f.*, winter

brumális, -e, of winter, wintry

búbalus, -i, *m.*, buffalo

buccélla, -ae, *f.*, morsel, sop, fragment

búccina, -ae, *f.*, trumpet

buccináre, to sound a trumpet

Bucclánicum, -i, *n.*, Bacchianico

Bulgári, -orum, *m.*, Bulgarians

Burdígala, -ae, *f.*, Bordeaux

Burdigalénsis, -e, of Bordeaux

Burgénsis, -e, of Burgos

Burgúndia, -ae, *f.*, Burgundy

bútyrum, -i, *n.*, butter

býssinus, -a, -um, of silk or fine linen

byssus, -i, *m.*, fine linen

Byténius, -ii, *m.*, Byten

Byzantínus, -a, -um, Byzantine

C

cabus, -i, *m.*, a corn measure, cabe

cácabus, -i, *m.*, earthen pot

cacúmen, -inis, *n.*, top, summit, highest point

cadáver, -eris, *n.*, corpse, carcass

cádere, cécidi, cassus, to fall, fall down

cadúcitas, -atis, *f.*, frailty, perishableness

cadúcus, -a, -um, perishable, transitory

cadus, -i, *m.*, a large vessel, a jug

caecátus, -a, -um, blinded

Caecília, -ae, *f.*, Cecilia

caécitas, -atis, *f.*, blindness, darkness

caecus, -a, -um, blind

caecus, -i, *m.*, blind man

caédere, cecídi, caesus, to strike, beat; cut, hew

caedes, -is, *f.*, slaughter

caeles, -itis, heavenly

Caelestínus, -i, *m.*, Celestine

caeléstis, -e, heavenly, divine; caeléstia, *n.*, heavenly things, high places

caelícola, -ae, *m.*, inhabitant of heaven

caélicus, -a, -um, heavenly, angelic

caélitus, divinely, by heavenly direction

Caélius, -a, -um, Caelian

caelum, -i, *n.*, heaven

caeméntum, -i, *n.*, mortar

caéperis = coéperis (coepi, *etc.*), began

caerúleus, -a, -um, blue

caesar, -aris, *m.*, emperor

Caesaraéa, -ae, *f.*, Caesarea

Caesaraugústa, -ae, *f.*, Saragossa

Caesariénsis (Caesareénsis), -e, of Caesarea

caesáries, -ei, *f.*, head of hair

caetus (coetus), -us, *m.*, assemblage

Caínus, -i, *m.*, Cain

Cajetánus, -i, *m.*, Cajetan

Calamína, -ae, *f.*, Coromandel Coast

calámitas, -atis, *f.*, calamity, distress

cálamus, -i, *m.*, reed; fishing rod; pen

Calaróga, -ae, *f.*, Calaruega

calcábilis, -e, that can be trod upon

calcáneum, -i, *n.*, heel

calcar, -aris, *n.*, spur

calcáre, to tread upon, trample

calcátor, -oris, *m.*, treader

calceaméntum, -i, *n.*, shoe

calceáre, to put on (shoes)

calceátus, -a, -um, shod, with shoes on

calcitráre, to kick

cálculus, -i, *m.*, pebble, stone

caldária, -ae, *f.*, cauldron

calefácere, -feci, -factus, (io), to warm

calefíeri, -factus sum, to grow warm

caléndae, -arum, *f. pl.*, the first day of the month

cáliga, -ae, *f.*, sandal

caligáre, to be misty, be in darkness

caliginósus, -a, -um, misty, dark

cáligo, -inis, *f.*, mist, cloud, dark cloud; darkness

cálipha, -ae, *m.*, caliph

calix, -icis, *m.*, chalice, cup

cállide, craftily

callíditas, -atis, *f.*, craftiness

cállidus, -a, -um, subtle

callis, -is, *m.* and *f.*, footpath

callus, -i, *m.*, hard skin

calor, -oris, *m.*, heat

calúmnia, -ae, *f.*, false accusation; oppression

calumniáre (-ari), to calumniate; oppress

calumniátor, -oris, *m.*, oppressor

Calvária, -ae, *f.*, Calvary

calvária, -ae, *f.*, skull

Calviniánus, -a, -um, Calvinist, of Calvin

Calvinísta, -ae, *m.*, Calvinist

calx, -cis, *f.*, heel; lime; viva calce, in quick lime

Camaldulénsis, -e, of Camaldoli, Camaldolese

Camaldulénsis, -is, *m.*, Camaldolese hermit

camélus, -i, *m.* and *f.*, camel

cámera, -ae, *f.*, vault

Cameracénsis, -e, of Cambrai

Camerínum, -i, *n.*, Camerino

Camiénsis, -e, of Camien

Camiliánum, -i, *n.*, Camiliano

camínus, -i, *m.*, furnace

Campánia, -ae, *f.*, Champagne, Campagna

Campánus, -a, -um, of Campagna

campéster, -tris, -tre, pertaining to a plain, flat

campus, -i, *m.*, field, plain

camus, -i, *m.*, bit, curb

Canadénsis, -e, of Canada

Canáriae ínsulae, -arum, -arum, *f.*, Canary Islands

cancellátus, -a, -um, crossed

cancéllus, -i, *m.*, lattice, enclosure; grating

candéla, -ae, *f.*, candle

candelábrum, -i, *n.*, candlestick

Candacénsis, -e, of Candé

candens, -entis, glowing hot

candidátio, -onis, *f.*, glistening whiteness

candidátus, -a, -um, white robed

candor, -oris, *m.*, brightness

cánere, cécini, cantus, to sing; blow; prophesy

canis, -is, *m.* and *f.*, dog

canístrum, -i, *n.*, basket

caníties (-em, -e; other cases are lacking), *f.*, gray, old age

canon, -onis, *m.*, canon

canonicátus, -us, *m.*, office of a canon, canonry

canónicus, -i, *m.*, canon

canonizátio, -onis, *f.*, canonization

canor, -oris, *m.*, song

canórus, -a, -um, melodious

cantábilis, -e, worthy of song

Cantabrígia, -ae, *f.*, Cambridge

cantáre, to sing; crow

cantátio, -onis, *f.*, song

cánticum, -i, *n.*, canticle, song

cántio, -onis, *f.*, song

Cántium, -ii, *n.*, Kent

Cántius, -ii, *m.*, Kenty or Kanty (St. John), Cantius

Cantuária, -ae, *f.*, Canterbury

Cantuariénsis, -e, of Canterbury

cantus, -us, *m.*, crowing

Canútus, -i, *m.*, Canute

capax, -acis, capable, fit for

capella, -ae, *f.*, chapel; sancta —, Sainte Chapelle

capellánus, -i, *m.*, chaplain

cápere, cepi, captus, (io), to receive, take, obtain; to hold, contain; to understand

capéssere, -ivi and -ii, -itus, to seize; gain

caph, the eleventh letter of the Hebrew alphabet corresponding to English *k*

capíllus, -i, *m.*, hair

Capistránum, -i, *n.*, Capistrano

capitális, -e, capital

Capitolínus, -a, -um, Capitoline

capítulum, -i, *n.*, little chapter

Cáppadox, -ocis, Cappadocian

cáprea, -ae, *f.*, roe

caprínus, -a, -um, relating to a goat

capsélla, -ae, *f.*, coffer, little box

captáre, to strive after; desire; seize, win

cáptio, -onis, *f.*, prey; net, trap

captívitas, -atis, *f.*, captivity

captívus, -a, -um, captive

captúra, -ae, *f.*, catch (of fish)

captus, -us, *m.*, catching, capture

Capuccíni, -orum, *m.*, Capuchins

Capuccínus, -a, -um, Capuchin

caput, -itis, *n.*, head; chapter

carbasínus, -a, -um, green

carbo, -onis, *m.*, coal

carbúnculus, -i, *m.*, carbuncle

Carcasóna, -ae, *f.*, Carcassonne

carcer, -eris, *m.*, prison

cardinalátus, -us, *m.*, office of cardinal

cardinális, -is, *m.*, cardinal

cardo, -inis, *m.*, pole of the earth; hinge; door

carduus, -i, *m.*, thistle

cáritas, -atis, *f.*, charity, love

Carmelítae, -arum, *m.* and *f.*, Carmelites

Carmélus, -i, *m.*, Carmel

carmen, -inis, *n.*, song, lay, canticle

carnális, -e, bodily, carnal

carnálitas, -atis, *f.*, carnality, sensuality

carnáliter, carnally

cárneus, -a, -um, of flesh, fleshly

cárnifex, -icis, *m.*, executioner

carníficus, -a, -um, of the flesh, corporal

caro, carnis, *f.*, flesh, meat

Cárolus Borromaéus, -i, -i, *m.*, Charles Borromeo

Cárolus, -i, *m.*, Charles

Cárolus Martéllus, -i, -i, *m.*, Charles Martel

cárpere, -psi, -ptus, to pluck, seize

cartállus, -i, *m.*, basket

Carthaginiénsis, -e, of Carthage

Carthágo, -inis, *f.*, Carthage; Nova —, Cartagena

Carthusiáni, -orum, *m.*, Carthusians, charterhouse monks

carus, -a, -um, dear, beloved; caríssimi, dearly beloved

cáseum, -i, *n.*, cheese

cásia, -ae, *f.*, cassia

Casimírus, -i, *m.*, Casimir

Cássia, -ae, *f.*, Cascia

Cassiánus, -i, *m.*, Cassian

Cassínas, -atis, of Monte Cassino

Cassinénsis, -e, of Monte Cassino

Cassínum, -i, *n.*, Cassino

cassis, -idis, *f.*, helmet

cassus, -a, -um, vain, useless

Castélla, -ae, *f.*, Castile; — Nova, New Castile

Castellátium, -ii, *n.*, Castellazzo

Castéllio, -onis, *f.*, Châtillon

Castéllio Stivórum, -onis, *f.*, Castiglione delle Stiviere

castéllum, -i, *n.*, town, village

castigáre, to chastise, punish, chasten

castigátio, -onis, *f.*, chastisement

castimónia, -ae, *f.*, chastity

cástitas, -atis, *f.*, chastity

castramentári, *dep.*, to pitch camp, encamp

castráre, to castrate

castrum, -i, *n.*, fortress, castle; castra, *n. pl.*, camp, army

Castrum novum, -i, *n.*, Castelnuovo

castus, -a, -um, chaste

cásula, -ae, *f.*, cottage

casus, -us, *m.*, case; peril, misfortune

catábulum, -i, *n.*, menagerie

catacúmba, -ae, *f.*, catacomb

Cataláunia, -ae, *f.*, Catalonia

catálogus, -i, *m.*, list, catalogue

Cátana, -ae, *f.*, Catania

Catanénsis, -e, of Catania; Catanénses, people of Catania

catarácta, -ae, *f.*, cataract, floodgate

catásta, -ae, *f.*, block, scaffold, rack

catástrophe, -es, *f.*, disaster, catastrophe

catechésis, -is, *f.*, catachesis; oral instruction to catachumens

catechísmus, -i, *m.*, catechism

catechizáre, to instruct, teach

catechúmena, -ae, *f.*, catechumen

catechúmenus, -i, *m.*, catechumen

catéllus, -i, *m.*, whelp

caténa, -ae, *f.*, chain

caténula, -ae, *f.*, chain

catérva, -ae, *f.*, crowd, congregation

catervátim, *adv.*, in troops

Catharína, -ae, *f.* (Senénsis), Catharine (of Siena)

Catharína Flisca, -ae, -ae, *f.*, Caterina Fieschi

cáthedra, -ae, *f.*, chair; professorship

cathedrális, -e, cathedral

Cathólicus, -a, -um, Catholic

catínum, -i, *n.*, and catínus, -i, *m.*, dish

cátulus, -i, *m.*, cub, whelp

cauda, -ae, *f.*, tail

caula, -ae, *f.*, fold, sheepfold

causa, -ae, *f.*, cause; means; matter; sine —, in vain

caute, carefully, circumspectly

cáutio, -onis, *f.*, caution, warning; guilt; bill

cávea, -ae, *f.*, cage

cavére, cavi, cautus, to take heed, beware

cavérna, -ae, f., hollow place, cave

cédere, cessi, cessus, to yield

cédrinus, -a, -um, of cedar

cedrus, -i, f., cedar

celáre, to hide

céleber, -bris, -bre, solemn

celebráre, to celebrate

celébritas, -atis, f., celebration, feast

cella, -ae, f., cellar

cellárium, -ii, n., chamber

céllula, -ae, f., hut

celsitúdo, -inis, f., height, exaltation

celsus, -a, -um, high, sublime

celtis, -is, m., instrument, tool, chisel

cenodóxia, -ae, f., vainglory

censére, -sui, -sum, to call; approve

census, -us, m., tribute; cost, expense

centenárius, -a, -um, hundredfold

centésimus, -a, -um, hundredth

centrum, -i, n., center

centum, one hundred

Centum Cellae, -arum, f., Civita Vecchia

céntuplum, a hundredfold

centúrio, -onis, m., captain over a hundred men, centurion

cera, -ae, f., wax

cérebrum, -i, n., brain

ceremónia, -ae, f., ceremony

céreus, -i, m., wax taper, candle

cérnere, crevi, cretus, to see, discern

cérnuus, -a, -um, falling down, prostrate

certámen, -inis, n., strife, fight

certáre, to fight

certátim, eagerly

certe, surely

certus, -a, -um, certain, fixed, determined; cértior fíeri, to be informed

cervix, -icis, f., neck

cervus, -i, m., deer, stag, hart

Cervus Frígidus, -i, -i, m., Cerfroid

cespes, -itis, m., turf, grassy sward

cessáre, to cease

céterus, -a, -um, the other; de cétero, finally

Cethaétus, -a, -um, Cethite

cetus, -i, m. (pl., cete, n.), whale

ceu, as, like, as when

Chaballicénsis, -e, of Chablais

Chalcedonénsis, -e, of Chalcedon

chalcedónius, -ii, f., chalcedony

Chaldaei, -órum, m., Chaldees

Chaldaéus, -a, -um, Chaldean

Chaldáicus, -a, -um, Chaldaic

chameúnia, -ae, f., sleeping on the floor or ground

Chananaéus, -a, -um, Canaanite

chaos, n., chaos, the lower world

charácter, -eris, m., character

charísma, -ae, m., spiritual gift

charta, -ae, f., paper

chártula, -ae, f., a small piece of paper

Chazári, -orum, m., Khazars

Chersona, -ae, f., Cherson, Gallipoli

cherub (indecl.), pl., chérubim, m., cherub

Chicagiénsis, -e, of Chicago

chirógraphum, -i, n., handwriting

chlamys, -ydis, f., cloak

Chloës, Chloe

chorda, -ae, f., string, stringed instrument

choréa, -ae, f., choir

chorus, -i, m., choir; dancing

chrisma, -atis, n., chrism

Christíades, -um, m., Christians

Christíadum, -i, n., Christendom

Christiánitas, -atis, f., Christianity

Christiánus, -a, -um, Christian

Chrístifer, -fera, -ferum, Christ-bearing

Christifidélis, -e, faithful to Christ, Christian

Christóphorus, -i, m., Christopher

Christus, -i, m., Christ

christus, -a, -um, anointed

chrysólithus, -i, m. and f., chrysolite, topaz

chrysóprasus, -i, *f.,* chrysoprasus

Chrysóstomus, -i, *m.,* Chrysostom

cibáre, to feed, to give to eat

cibária, -orum, *n. pl.,* food, victuals

cibus, -i, *m.,* food, meat; fuel

cicátrix, -icis, *f.,* scar, wound

cicónia, -ae, *f.,* stork, crane

cicúta, -ae, *f.,* hemlock

ciére, civi, citus, to call by name, invoke

cilícium, -ii, *n.,* sackcloth, haircloth, hair shirt

cimélium, -ii, *m.,* treasure

Cinaéus, -i, *m.,* Cinite

Cincinnaténsis, -e, of Cincinnati

cinctórium, -ii, *n.,* girdle

cinctus, -us, *m.,* girding, girdle

cíngulum, -i, *n.,* girdle

cíngulus, -i, *m.,* girdle

cínifes, -um, *m.,* gnats

cinis, -eris, *m.,* ashes, embers; **Feria IV**
Cínerum, Ash Wednesday

cinnamómum, -i, *n.,* cinnamon

cínyrum, -i, *n.,* lute

circa, *adv.,* about; *prep.,* with

círciter, *adv.,* about

circuíre, -ivi and -ii, -itus, (eo), to go about; compass

circúitus, -us, *m.,* circuit; in circúitu, round about

círculus, -i, *m.,* circle

circumamíctus, -a, -um, clothed about

circumcídere, -cidi, -cisus, to circumcize

circumcíngere, -cinxi, -cinctus, to gird about

circumcísio, -onis, *f.,* circumcision

circumcursátio, -onis, *f.,* attention

circumdáre, -dedi, -datus, to encompass

circumdoláre, to hew about with an axe

circumdúcere, -duxi, -ductus, to lead about

circumférre, -tuli, -latus, to carry about

circumfódere, -fodi, -fossus, (io), to dig a ditch around

circumfúlgere, -fulsi, -fulsus, to shine round about

circumligáre, to bind up

circumornátus, -a, -um, adorned round about

circumplécti, -plexus sum, *dep. 3,* to compass about

circumpónere, -pósui, -pósitus, to put upon

circumquáque, *adv.,* all around

circumséptus, -a, -um, covered on all sides

circumspéctor, -oris, *m.,* one who sees all

circumspícere, -spexi, -spectus, to look about

circumstántia, -ae, *f.,* fortification; details, circumstances

circumstáre, -steti, to stand around, to be present

circumtéctus, -a, -um, covered about

circumveníre, -veni, -ventus, to circumvent, overreach

circumvéntio, -onis, *f.,* a surrounding

circumvoláre, to fly about

Cisterciénsis, -e, of Citeaux, Cistercian

cistérna, -ae, *f.,* pit

citátus, -a, -um, swift

citérior, -ius, hither

cíthara, -ae, *f.,* harp

citháraedus, -i, *m.,* harper

citharizáre, to play on a harp

cito, *adv.,* speedily, easily

citra, *prep.,* beyond

cítrinus, -a, -um, citrous; **malum cítrinum,** lime

cívicus, -a, -um, civic

civis, -is, *m.* and *f.,* citizen

cívitas, -atis, *f.,* city

clades, -is, *f.,* disaster, defeat

clam, privately

clamáre, to cry out, proclaim
clamitáre, to shout loudly
clamor, -oris, *m.*, cry
clangor, -oris, *m.*, sound
Clara, -ae, *f.*, Clare
Claravallénsis, -e, of Clairvaux
claréscere, clárui, to shine forth
clarificáre, to glorify
clarificátio, -onis, *f.*, glorification
cláritas, -atis, *f.*, light, clarity, brightness; renown, glory
clarus, -a, -um, clear; well-known
classis, -is, *f.*, class; navy, fleet
cláudere, clausi, clausus, to shut, close
claudicáre, to limp
claudus, -a, -um, lame
claustrális, -e, of the cloister, cloistral
clava, -ae, *f.*, cudgel, maul
claviculárius, -ii, *m.*, key bearer
clavis, -is, *f.*, key
clavus, -i, *m.*, nail
Clemens, -entis, *m.*, Clement
clemens, -entis, merciful
cleménter, mercifully, graciously
cleméntia, -ae, *f.*, clemency
clericális, -e, priestly
cléricus, -i, *m.*, cleric, clerk, priest
clerus, -i, *m.*, clergy; something assigned by lot, spoil
clíbanus, -i, *m.*, oven
Clippiácum, -i, *n.*, Clichy
clivus, -i, *m.*, hill
cloáca, -ae, *f.*, sewer
Clodoáldus, -i, *m.*, Clodoald, (St.) Cloud
Clodovéus, -i, *m.*, Clovis
Clonardiénsis, -e, of Clonard
Clonferténsis, -e, of Clonfert
Cluniacénsis, -e, of Cluny
Cluníacum, -i, *n.*, Cluny
clusor, -oris, *m.*, smith
clýpeus, -i, *m.*, buckler
coacerváre, to heap up
coácte, *adv.*, by constraint

coadjútor, -oris, *m.*, coadjutor
coadunáre, to unite
coaedificáre, to build together
coaequális, -e, coequal
coaequáre, to rank with, make equal; fill up
coaetáneus, -a, -um, equal
coaetérnus, -a, -um, coeternal
coaévus, -i, *m.*, one equal in age
coagitáre, to shake together
coagmentáre, to join together
coaguláre, to curdle
coagulátus, -a, -um, curdled; craggy
coaléscere, -álui, -álitus, to grow together, take firm root
coangustáre, to straiten, hem in
coapóstolus, -i, *m.*, fellow apostle
coarctáre, to straiten
coccíneus, -a, -um, scarlet
cóccinum, -i, *n.*, scarlet
cocus, -i, *m.*, cook
codex, -icis, *m.*, document, scroll; book
Coelesýria, -ae, *f.*, Celesyria
coelibátus, -us, *m.*, celibacy
coelum, -i, *n.*, heaven
coemetérium, -ii, *n.*, cemetery
coena, -ae, *f.*, supper, dinner, feast
coenáculum, -i, *n.*, dining room
coenáre, to sup, have supper
coenobíta, -ae, *m.*, monk
coenobíticus, -a, -um, monastic
coenóbium, -ii, *n.*, convent
coenomyía, -ae, *f.*, dog fly
coepíscopus, -i, *m.*, fellow bishop
coepisse, coeptus (*defect.*), to begin
coërcére, -cui, -citus, to restrain
coetus, -us, *m.*, assembly, host
cógere, coégi, coáctus, to lead, bring, assemble; constrain
cogitáre, to think; purpose; take counsel together
cogitátio, -onis, *f.*, thought
cogitátum, -i, *n.*, care

cogitátus, -us, *m.*, counsel
cognáta, -ae, *f.*, cousin
cognátio, -onis, *f.*, kindred
cognátus, -i, *m.*, kinsman
cógnitor, -oris, *m.*, knower, witness
cognoméntum, -i, *n.*, name
cognomináre, to name
cognominári, *dep.*, to be surnamed
cognóscere, -novi, -nitus, to know
cognoscibíliter, recognizably
cohaerére, -haesi, -haesus, to cleave to
cohéres, -edis, *m.*, coheir
cohibére, to hinder, restrain
cohors, -tis, *f.*, band, guard, cohort
cohortátio, -onis, *f.*, exhortation
coinquináre, to defile
colaphizáre, to box one's ears
cólaphus, -i, *m.*, a box on the ear
coláre, to refine
cólere, cólui, cultus, to till; worship,
    adore, revere; celebrate
collábi, -lapsus sum, *dep. 3*, to fall,
    collapse
collactáneus, -i, *m.*, foster brother
collaetári, *dep.*, to rejoice together
collátio, -onis, *f.*, gathering, meeting
collaudáre, to praise together
collaudátio, -onis, *f.*, praise
collécta, -ae, *f.*, collection or contribu-
    tion in money; collect
colléctus, -a, -um, shut
colléga, -ae, *m.*, companion, fellow
collégium, -ii, *n.*, company, society;
    school
collídere, -lisi, -lisus, to dash together,
    bruise, crush; cast down
colligáre, to bind
colligátio, -onis, *f.*, band
collígere, -legi, -lectus, to gather up,
    take in
collineáre, to direct in a straight line
colliquefácere, -feci, -factus, (io), to
    melt
colliquéscere, to melt

collis, -is, *m.*, hill
collocáre, to place
collóqui, -cutus or -quutus sum, *dep.
    3*, to converse together
collucére, to shine, burn
colluctátio, -onis, *f.*, wrestling
collum, -i, *n.*, neck
collustráre, to illuminate
collýrium, -i, *n.*, salve
colónia, -ae, *f.*, city
Colónia Agrippína, -ae, -ae, *f.*, Cologne
Coloniénses, -e, of Cologne
colónus, -i, *m.*, inhabitant, dweller
color, -oris, *m.*, color
Colossénses, -ium, *m.*, Colossians
colúmba, -ae, *f.*, dove, pigeon
Columbénsis, -e, of Columbus
cólumen, -inis, *n.*, pillar, support
colúmna, -ae, *f.*, pillar
coma, -ae, *f.*, hair, lock of hair; comam
    nutríre, to allow hair or beard to
    grow freely
combúrere, -bussi, -bustus, to burn
combústio, -onis, *f.*, burning
comédere, -edi, -esus or -estus, to eat,
    devour; comedétis vescentes, you
    shall eat in plenty
comes, -itis, *m.*, companion; count,
    earl
comessátio, -onis, *f.*, revel, feasting,
    riotous feasting
coméstio, -onis, *f.*, eating
cóminus, *adv.*, in close combat
comitári, *dep.*, to accompany, follow,
    be together
comitátus, -us, *m.*, company, train
commártyr, -is, *c.*, fellow martyr
commemoráre, to commemorate
commemorátio, -onis, *f.*, commemora-
    tion
commendáre, to commend
commendátio, -onis, *f.*, recommenda-
    tion
commensális, -is, *m.*, table companion

commentárius, -ii, *m.*, commentary

comméntum, -i, *n.*, fiction, invention

commércium, -ii, *n.*, intercourse, fellowship; work; rite

commigráre, to go, travel

commílito, -onis, *m.*, comrade in war, fellow soldier

comminári, *dep.*, to threaten

comminúere, -ui, -utus, to break into small pieces

commiscére, -míscui, -mixtus or -mistus, to mingle, to lie with

commissárius, -ii, *m.*, commissary

committere, -misi, -missus, to bring together, unite; to begin, set forth; commit

commíxtio, -onis, *f.*, mingling

commodáre, to lend

cómmodum, -i, *n.*, favor, blessing

commonére, to admonish, remind, warn

commonítio, -onis, *f.*, reminder, warning

commorári, *dep.*, to stay, tarry, abide

commorátio, -onis, *f.*, dwelling, habitation

cómmori, -mortuus sum, (io), to die together with

commótio, -onis, *f.*, movement, commotion, disturbance

commovére, -movi, -motus, to move

commúne, -is, *n.*, common

communicáre, to communicate; receive Communion; partake of; associate with

communicátor, -oris, *m.*, partaker

commúnio, -onis, *f.*, communion

communíre, to strengthen

commúnitas, -atis, *f.*, commonwealth

commúniter, together

commutáre, to change

commutátio, -onis, *f.*, change, barter, sale; price

compáctus, -a, -um, compacted

compáges, -is, *f.*, a joining together; joint

compagináre, to join together

compágo, -inis, *f.*, joining together; bodily structure

compar, -aris, *c.*, companion

compar, -aris, *adj.*, like, similar, equal

comparáre, to prepare; buy; compare

comparátio, -onis, *f.*, comparison; preparation

compárticeps, cipis, sharing jointly

compáti, -passus sum, *dep. 3*, (io), to suffer with

compátiens, -entis, having compassion

compedítus, -i, *m.*, prisoner, captive

compéllere, -puli, -pulsus, to subdue, constrain, oblige, compel

comperíre, -peri, -pertus, to find

compes, -edis, *f.*, a fetter for the feet

compéscere, -péscui, to withhold, restrain

competénter, fitly

compétere, -ivi and -ii, -itus, to be capable of

compíngere, -pegi, -pactus, to construct; furnish with

cómpitum, -i, *n.*, crossroad

complacére, -cui or -citus sum, to please, be acceptable to

complanáre, to make plain; to level, plane

complantáre, to plant together

complécti, -plexus sum, *dep. 3*, to encircle

complére, -plevi, -pletus, to fill, fulfill, accomplish, end

completórium, -ii, *n.*, compline

complexáre, to embrace

complicáre, to fold together

complódere, -plosi, -plosus, to beat or strike together

Complútum, -i, *n.*, Alcalá de Henares

compónere, -pósui, -pósitus, to place, order, compose; reconcile; forge comportáre, to lay up, to collect, to bring together

compos, -otis, possessed of, sharing in; compos voti, one whose wish is fulfilled

compositio, -onis, *f.*, composing, arrangement

compósitus, -a, -um, comely, decked out

Compostellánus, -a, -um, of Compostela

comprehéndere, -prehéndi, -prehénsus, to comprehend; obtain; take; overtake, apprehend; seize

comprímere, -pressi, -pressus, to suppress, restrain

comprobáre, to approve

compúnctio, -onis, *f.*, compunction, sorrow

compúngere, -punxi, -punctus, to prick, wound; feel remorse

computáre, to reckon, count

Comum, -i, *n.*, Como

conári, *dep.*, to strive

concaléscere, -cálui, to grow hot, burn, glow

concaptívus, -i, *m.*, fellow captive

cóncava, -ae, *f.*, glen

concédere, -cessi, -cessus, to grant

concelebráre, to celebrate together

concéntus, -us, *m.*, harmony, concord

concéptio, -onis, *f.*, idea, conception

concéptus, -us, *m.*, conception

concertáre, to strive eagerly

concéssio, -onis, *f.*, concession

Conchéssa, -ae, *f.*, Conchessa

concídere, -cidi, to fall down; be disheartened

concídere, -cidi, -cisus, to cut, slice

conciliábulum, -i, *n.*, market place

conciliáre, to procure, obtain

conciliátrix, -icis, *f.*, ambassadress

concílium, -ii, *n.*, council

concínere, -cínui, -centus, to sing

concinnáre, to arrange; frame, weave, forge

concínnus, -a, -um, elegant, polished

cóncio, -onis, *f.*, sermon

concionári, *dep.*, to preach

concionátor, -oris, *m.*, preacher

concípere, -cepi, -ceptus, (io), to conceive

concitáre, to stir up, arouse, move, raise

concívis, -is, *c.*, fellow citizen

concláve, -is, *n.*, a room that may be locked

conclúdere, -clusi, -clusus, to conclude; enclose; to shut up

conclúsio, -onis, *f.*, conclusion

concordáre, to be of one mind, agree

concórdia, -ae, *f.*, union, peace

concórditer, with one accord

concorporátus, -a, -um, united in one body

concorpóreus, -a, -um, of one body with

concors, -cordis, of one mind, harmonious

concremáre, to kindle, burn up

concrepáre, -ui, to rattle, resound

concréscere, -crevi, -cretus, to grow together; increase

concrétus, -a, -um, thickened, dried up

concubína, -ae, *f.*, concubine

concubinárius, -ii, *m.*, keeper of concubines

concúbitor, -oris, *m.*, one who lives or sleeps with another

concúbitus, -us, *m.*, cohabitation

conculcáre, to tread on, trample under foot

concúmbere, -cúbui, -cúbitus, to lie with

concupiscéntia, -ae, *f.*, lust; love

concupíscere, -pivi, -pitus, to long for, covet

concupiscíbilis, -e, very desirable

concútere, -cussi, -cussus, (io), to strike, cause to tremble

condecoráre, to decorate

condelectári, *dep.*, to be delighted with

condemnáre, to condemn

condénsus, -a, um, thickly covered; condénsa, *n. pl.*, leafy boughs; thick woods

cóndere, -didi, -ditus, to found, create; put in; lay up

condescéndere, -scendi, -scensus, to condescend; descend

condícere, -dixi, -dictus, to appoint

condígnus, -a, -um, worthy to be compared with

condiméntum, -i, *n.*, spice, seasoning

condíre, to season; embalm

condiscípulus, -i, *m.*, fellow disciple

condítio, -onis, *f.*, condition, nature

cónditor, -oris, *m.*, founder, creator

condolére, -dólui, to have compassion

condúcere, -duxi, -ductus, to hire

confabulári, *dep.*, to talk

conférre, -tuli, collátus, to accompany; grant, confer; ponder; gain; press down; se —, to betake oneself to

confessárius, -ii, *m.*, confessor

conféssio, -onis, *f.*, confession; praise

conféssor, -oris, *m.*, confessor

conféstim, immediately, forthwith

confíctus, -a, -um, forged

confidéntia, -ae, *f.*, confidence

confídere, -fisus sum (*semidep.*), to trust, confide, hope, be of good heart

confígere, -fixi, -fixus, to nail, fasten or fix in

configuráre, to fashion

configurátus, -a, -um, made like or conformable

confirmáre, to strengthen, uphold

confitéri, -fessus sum, *dep.* 2, to confess, acknowledge, praise; give thanks, give glory

conflans, -antis, refining

confláre, to weld, forge, refine, melt

conflátilis, -e, molten

conflictáre, to contend with

conflíctus, -us, *m.*, conflict

conflígere, -flixi, -flictus, to strive

conflúere, -fluxi, to stream together; resort

confódere, -fodi, -fossus, (io), to stab

confoederáre, to bind together

confoederátio, -onis, *f.*, confederation, union

conformáre, to conform

confortáre, to strengthen

confortári, *dep.*, to take courage, wax strong

confortátio, -onis, *f.*, solace

confráctio, -onis, *f.*, breaking; gap, breach

confrátres, -um, *m. pl.*, guild brothers

confrígere, -frixi, -frictus, to burn up

confríngere, -fregi, -fractus, to break in pieces, burst, shatter, destroy

confúgere, -fugi, (io), to flee

confúsio, -onis, *f.*, confusion, shame

confúsus, -a, -um, confused, disordered

confutáre, to confute

confúndere, -fudi, -fusus, to confound; put to shame

congaudére, -gavísus sum, *semidep.*, to rejoice with

congelátus, -a, -um, frozen

congéner, -eris, of the same kind, kindred

congérere, -gessi, -gestus, to heap

conglorificáre, to glorify

conglutináre, to bind together

conglutinári, *dep.*, to cleave to

congratulári, *dep.*, to rejoice with

congregáre, to gather together, collect, assemble

congregátio, -onis, *f.*, company, gathering, assembly, congregation

congréssio, -onis, *f.*, meeting

cóngruens, -entis, proper, suitable, seasonable

congruénter, suitably, becomingly

congrúere, -ui, to correspond with

cóngruus, -a, -um, fitting, becoming

Conímbria, -ae, *f.*, Coimbra

Conimbricénsis, -e, of Coimbra

conjícere, -jeci, -jectus, (io), to cast; conjecture, guess

conjugális, -e, conjugal

conjúnctio, -onis, *f.*, joining together, union, conjunction

conjúngere, -junxi, -junctus, to join, have affinity with

conjux, -jugis, *c.*, husband, wife, spouse

Connáchti, -orum, *m.*, Connaught

connéctere, -néxui, -nexus, to fasten together, unite; cause

connéxus, -a, -um, joined together

connúbium, -ii, *n.*, matrimony

connumeráre, to number among

conopéum, -i, *n.*, canopy

conquadráre, to cut square

conquassáre, to crush

cónqueri, -questus sum, *dep. 3,* to complain

conquiéscere, -quiévi, -quiétus, to rest

conquisítio, -onis, *f.*, dispute

conquisítor, -oris, *m.*, disputer

conregnáre, to reign with

consalutáre, to salute one another

consanguíneus, -a, -um, of one blood with

consanguíneus, -i, *m.*, cousin

conscéndere, -scendi, -scensus, to ascend

consciéntia, -ae, *f.*, consciousness; conscience; acknowledgment

conscíndere, -scidi, -scissus, to rend

cónscius, -a, -um, conscious, knowing

conscriptus, -a, -um, written

consecráre, to consecrate, sanctify, hallow

consecrátio, -onis, *f.*, consecration

consénior, -oris, *m.*, ancient, elder

consénsus, -us, *m.*, concord, harmony

consentáneus, -a, -um, consonant with, fit, suitable

consentíre, -sensi, -sensus, to consent

consepelíre, -sepelívi and -ii, -sepúltus, to bury with

consequénter, consequently

cónsequi, -secútus sum, *dep. 3,* to follow; obtain

consérere, -sevi, -situs, to sow

conserváre, to keep, preserve

conservátus, -a, -um, inviolate

consérvus, -i, *m.*, fellow servant or slave

conséssus, -us, *m.*, seat, place; primi conséssus, foremost places, precedence

consideráre, to look, consider

consignáre, to sign with

consiliári, *dep.*, to meditate

consiliárius, -ii, *m.*, counselor, adviser, judge

consílium, -ii, *n.*, counsel; assembly

consímilis, -e, like

consístere, -stiti, to stand together, continue

consociáre, to associate with, share

consolári, *dep.*, to comfort

consolátio, -onis, *f.*, consolation, comfort

consolátor, -oris, *m.*, comforter

consolidáre, to strengthen

cónsonus, -a, -um, in harmony with, harmonious

consors, -sortis, having a common lot, partaking

consors, -sortis, *c.*, sharer, fellow

consórtium, -ii, *n.*, consort, company

conspéctor, -oris, *m.*, beholder

conspéctus, -us, *m.*, sight, presence

conspérgere, -spersi, -spersus, to sprinkle, strew

conspérsio, -onis, *f.*, paste, dough

conspícere, -spexi, -spectus, (io), to see, consider, look at, stare upon

conspiráre, to unite, agree

conspirátio, -onis, *f.*, one common opinion; agreement

conspúere, -spui, -sputus, to spit upon

constánter, earnestly

Constantiniánus, -a, -um, of Constantine

Constantinópolis, -is, *f.*, Constantinople

Constantinopolitánus, -a, -um, of Constantinople

Constantínus, i, *m.*, Constantine

constáre, -steti, -statúrus, to consist; exist

consternátus, -a, -um, in consternation

constitúere, -ui, -utus, to constitute, decree, appoint, set, ordain; stand

constitútio, -onis, *f.*, constitution; order, foundation

constríngere, -strinxi, -strictus, to bind fast

construére, -struxi, -structus, to build; frame together

constupráre, to corrupt

consubstantiális, -e, consubstantial

consudáre, to sweat

consúere, -sui, -sutus, to sew together

consuéscere, -suevi, -suetus, to be accustomed

consuetúdo, -inis, *f.*, custom, intercourse, intimacy

consuétus, -a, -um, wonted, accustomed

consul, -sulis, *m.*, consul

consúltum, -i, *n.*, resolution

consúltus, -a, -um, wise; consúltius, more wisely

consúmere, -sumpsi, -sumptus, to consume, bring to an end

consummáre, to consummate, accomplish, fulfill, consume, spend, finish

consummátio, -onis, *f.*, perfecting; consummation; end of the world

consúmptio, -onis, *f.*, utter destruction; a wasting

consúrgere, -surréxi, -surréctus, to rise up or with, stand up

contabéscere, -tábui, to pine away

contáctus, -us, *m.*, contact, touch, approach

contágio, -onis, *f.*, contagion

contagiósus, -a, -um, contagious

contágium, -ii, *n.*, touch, contagion; temptation

contamináre, to defile

contégere, -texi, -tectus, to cover, envelop

contemnáre, to despise

contémnere, -tempsi, -temptus, to despise, slight

contemperáre, to mix, infuse

contempláre, to behold, contemplate

contemplátor, -oris, *m.*, contemplator

contemptíbilis, -e, contemptible

contémptio, -onis, *f.*, contempt

contémptor, -oris, *m.*, despiser

contémptus, -us, *m.*, contempt

conténdere, -tendi, -tentus, to maintain, assert; strive

conténtio, -onis, *f.*, contention, strife, obstinacy

contentióse, contentiously, rebelliously

conténtus, -a, -um, content

contérere, -trivi, -tritus, to break in pieces, grind to powder, crush, destroy; bruise

contérritus, -a, -um, frightened

contestári, *dep.*, to testify

contéxtus, -a, -um, woven

conticéscere, -tícui, to be silent

contignátio, -onis, *f.*, woodwork

cóntinens, -entis, *f.*, continent, mainland

continéntia, -ae, *f.*, self-denial, restraint, abstinence

continére, -tínui, -tentus, to uphold; stop; keep silence; possess, hold fast; contain; keep back

contíngere, -tigi, -tactus, to touch; happen to, fall to; belong to

continuátus, -a, -um, continual

contínuo, immediately

contínuus, -a, -um, continual, infinite

contorquére, -torsi, -torsus, to wind about

contra, *prep.* and *adv.*, against, before; the opposite, on the contrary; **e contra**, coming toward him

contradícere, -dixi, -dictus, to contradict; resist, contend with

contradíctio, -onis, *f.*, contradiction; strife

contráhere, -traxi, -tractus, to contract, draw in; commit

contraíre, -ivi and -ii, -itus, (eo), to go against, brave

contrárius, -a, -um, against, contrary; **e contrário**, on the contrary

contrectáre, to handle

contrémere, -trémui, to tremble

contremíscere, -trémui, to tremble

contribuláre, to crush

contribulátus, -a, -um, troubled

contríbulis, -is, *m.*, countryman

contristáre, to sadden

contrítio, -onis, *f.*, grief, contrition

contrítus, -a, -um, contrite

controvérsia, -ae, *f.*, controversy

contubérnium, -ii, *n.*, a common dwelling; comradeship, intimacy

contuéri, -túitus sum, *dep.* 2, to consider

contumácia, -ae, *f.*, insolence

contumélia, -ae, *f.*, outrage

contumeliáre, to outrage

contumeliósus, -a, -um, contumelious

contúndere, -tudi, -tusus, to bruise, crush

conturbáre, to disquiet, trouble

conturbátio, -onis, *f.*, trouble, vexation

contutári, *dep.*, to keep safe; to communicate with

convalére, -válui, to recover strength, to regain health

convaléscere, -válui, to gain strength

convállis, -is, *f.*, valley

convéniens, -entis, agreeing

conveniénter, duly

conveníre, -veni, -ventus, to come together, agree; resort

conventículum, -i, *n.*, meeting, gathering

convéntio, -onis, *f.*, agreement, concord

conventuális, -e, pertaining to a convent; **Minóres Conventuáles**, Friars Minor Conventuals

convéntus, -us, *m.*, assembly, — **Laudántium**, Guild of Praise

conversáre, to turn around

conversári, *dep.*, to converse

conversátio, -onis, *f.*, intercourse, conversation; manner of living, conduct

convérsio, -onis, *f.*, conversion

convérsus, -a, -um, turned toward

convértere, -verti, -versus, to convert, change

convésci, *dep. 3*, to eat with

convícium, -ii, *n.*, reproach, insult

convíncere, -vici, -victus, to convict

convitiári, *dep.*, to revile

convivántes, -ium, *m. pl.*, banqueters

conviári, *dep.*, to feast with

convivificáre, to quicken together with

convívium, -ii, *n.*, banquet

convólvere, -volvi, -volútus, to roll up

cooperáre, to cooperate

cooperátor, -oris, *m.*, fellow helper

cooperíre, -pérui, -pertus. to cover

coopértus, -a, -um, clothed, arrayed

cooptáre, to elect

cóphinus, -i, *m.*, basket, hod
cópia, -ae, *f.*, abundance, store
copiósitas, -atis, *f.*, abundance
copiósius, *adv.*, in greater numbers
copiósus, -a, -um, plentiful, great
cópula, -ae, *f.*, union
copuláre, to join together
copulári, *dep.*, to be united with; to embrace
cóquere, coxi, coctus, to cook, boil, bake
cor, cordis, *n.*, heart
coram, *prep.*, in the presence of, before
corbóna, -ae, *f.*, treasury
Corcyrénsis, -e, of Corfu
Córduba, -ae, *f.*, Córdoba
Cordubénsis, -e, of Cordoba
coriárius, -ii, *m.*, tanner
Corínthii, -orum, *m. pl.*, Corinthians
Corínthus, -i, *f.*, Corinth
córium, -ii, *n.*, hide
Corneliénsis, -e, of Imola
Cornélius, -a, -um, Cornelian
córneus, -a, -um, made of horn
corniculárius, -ii, *m.*, trumpeter
cornu, -us, *n.*, horn; mountain top
coróna, -ae, *f.*, wreath, crown
coronáre, to crown
coronátor, -oris, *m.*, crowner, bestower
corporáliter, with one body; bodily
corpóreus, -a, -um, bodily, corporeal
corpus, -oris, *n.*, body; carcass
corpúsculum, -i, *n.*, small body
corréctio, -onis, *f.*, correction; prop, support
corréptio, -onis, *f.*, correction, chastising
corrígere, -rexi, -rectus, to correct; establish
corrígia, -ae, f., shoe lace
corrípere, -rípui, -reptus, (io), to rebuke, admonish, chastise, smite
corrobáre, to strengthen
corrogátio, -onis, *f.*, contribution

corrósio, -onis, *f.*, gnawing
corrúere, -rui, to fall (to the ground)
corrúmpens, -entis, baleful
corrúmpere, -rupi, -ruptus, corrupt, pervert
corruptéla, -ae, *f.*, bribery, corruption
corruptíbilis, -e, corruptible
corruptíbilitas, -atis, *f.*, corruptibility
corrúptio, -onis, *f.*, corruption
corrúptus, -a, -um, corrupted
corus, -i, *m.*, quarter, measure
coruscáre, to glitter, shine, gleam
coruscátio, -onis, *f.*, lightning
corúscus, -i, *m.*, lightning
corvus, -i, *m.*, raven
Cósmedin, Cosmedine
costa, -ae, *f.*, side; rib
cóstula, -ae, *f.*, rib
Cottiénsis, -e, of Cotyaeus
cotúrnix, -icis, *f.*, quail
couti, -usus sum, *dep. 3*, to communicate with
Cracóvia, -ae, *f.*, Cracow
Cracoviénsis, -e, of Cracow
crápula, -ae, f., surfeiting, drunkenness
crapulátus, -a, -um, surfeited
cras, *adv.*, tomorrow
crassíties, -ei, *f.*, grossness, coarseness
crassitúdo, -inis, *f.*, thickness, fatness; a clod
crassus, -a, -um, thick, fat
crastínus, -a, -um, relating to tomorrow crastína die, tomorrow; dies crastína, the following day; in crastínum, on the next day
crater, -eris, *m.*, a large bowl in which wine was mixed with water; chalice
cratícula, -ae, *f.*, gridiron, grating
cratis, -is, *f.*, grating, gridiron
creáre, to create
creátio, -onis, *f.*, creation
creátor, -oris, *m.*, creator
creatúra, -ae, *f.*, creature
crebro, *adv.*, frequently

crédere, -didi, -ditus, to believe, trust; to be faithful (in the passive)

credíbilis, -e, trustworthy

créditor, -oris, *m.*, creditor

créditus, -a, -um, entrusted, committed to the care of

credúlitas, -atis, *f.*, faith, belief

cremáre, to burn

crémium, -ii, *n.*, fuel

crepáre, -ui, -itus, to crack, burst asunder

crepído. -inis, *f.*, base, foot

crépitus, -us, *m.*, explosion

crepúsculum, -i, *n.*, twilight

créscere, crevi, cretus, to increase, grow; spring up

Creta, -ae, *f.*, Crete

Creténses, -ium, *m. pl.*, Cretans

Cretes, -um, *m. pl.*, Cretans

cribráre, to sift

crimen, -inis, *n.*, guilt, sin

crimináre, to accuse

crimínari, *dep.*, to accuse

criminátor, -oris, *m.*, detractor

criminátrix, -icis, *f.*, false accuser

cróceus, -a, -um, scarlet

crocus, -i, *m.*, saffron

cruciáre, to torture, torment

cruciátio, -onis, *f.*, punishment

crucifígere, -fixi, -fixus, to crucify

crudélis, -e, cruel

crudus, -a, -um, raw

cruentáre, to torture, lash

cruentátus, -a, -um, bleeding

cruéntus, -a, -um, bloody

cruor, -oris, *m.*, gore, blood

crus, cruris, *n.*, leg

crux, crucis, *f.*, cross

crypta, -ae, *f.*, crypt, catacomb

Crýptula, -ae, *f.*, La Grotella

crystállus, -i, *f.*, crystal; ice

cubáre, -ui, -itus, to lie down

cubiculárius, -ii, *m.*, cubicular, chamberlain

cubículum, -i, *n.*, chamber, bedroom

cubíle, -is, *n.*, bed, couch; lair, den

cúbitum, -i, *n.*, cubit

cúbitus, -us, *m.*, cubit

cucúlla, -ae, *f.*, cowl

cucumerárium, -ii, *n.*, garden of cucumbers

cúdere, to stamp, coin

cujus (cuius), genitive of qui and quis, whose, of whom

cúlcitra, -ae, *f.*, mattress, bed

culex, -icis, *m.*, gnat

culmen, -inis, *n.*, top, summit, height

culpa, -ae, *f.*, fault, guilt, sin

cultor, -oris, *m.*, cultivator; dresser; professor; worshiper; dweller, inhabitant

cultrix, -icis, *f.*, worshiper

cultúra, -ae, *f.*, worship

cultus, -us, *m.*, cultivation, care; worship

cum, *prep.*, with

cum, *conj.*, when, while; whereas; although; since

cumuláre, to heap up, increase

cumulátius, *adv.*, more fully

cúmulus, -i, *m.*, heap, pile

cunae, -arum, *f. pl.*, cradle

cunctári, *dep.*, to delay

cunctus, -a, -um, all

Cunegúnda, -ae, *f.*, Cunigundis

cúpere, -ivi and -ii, -itus, (io), to desire, long for

cúpide, gladly

cupíditas, -atis, *f.*, desire, greed

cúpido, -inis, *f.*, desire

cúpidus, -a, -um, desirous

cúpiens, -entis, desirous

cur, why?

cura, -ae, *f.*, care

curáre, to cure, heal

curátio, -onis, *f.*, healing, cure

curátrix, -icis, *f.*, guardian, warden

cúria, -ae, *f.*, senate house

Cúria, -ae, f., Coire
Curiménsis, -e, of Gurina
currens, -entis, current
cúrrere, cucúrri, cursus, to run, hasten
cúrrilis, -e, pertaining to a chariot
currus, -us, m., chariot
cursitáre, to run up and down or hither and thither
cursus, -us, m., course; voyage
curváre, to bend; humble
curvéscere, to bend over
cuspis, -idis, f., point (of a spear)
custódia, -ae, f., watch; prison, ward, cell
custódiens, -entis, m., keeper
custodíre, to protect, preserve, keep; watch over
custos, -odis, m. and f., guard, watchman
Cuthbértus, -i, m., Cuthbert
cutis, -is, f., skin
cyclas, -adis, f., robe
cýmbalum, -i, n., cymbal
cýnicus, -i, m., cynic
Cydónia, -ae, f., Canea (in Crete)
cypréssinus. -a, -um, of cypress
cypréssus, -i, f., cypress tree
Cypriánus, -i, m., Cyprian
Cýprius, -a, -um, Cyprian
cyprus, -i, f., cypress
Cyrenaéus, -a, -um, of Cyrene, Cyrenian
Cyrenénsis, -e, of Cyrene, Cyrenian
Cyríllus, -i, m., Cyril

D

Daciánus, -i, m., Dacian
daemon, -onis, m., devil
daemoníacus, -i, m., possessed person
daemónium, -ii, n., devil
daleth, fourth letter of the Hebrew alphabet corresponding to English *d*

Dálmatae, -arum, m. pl., Dalmatians
dalmática, -ae, f., dalmatic
Damascéni, -orum, m. pl., Damascenes
Damascénus, -a, -um, Damascene
Damiánus, -i, m., Damian
damnáre, to condemn
damnátio, -onis, f., damnation, condemnation
damnósus, -a, -um, mistaken, harmful
damnum, -i, n., damage, loss, evil, injury, punishment
Dani, -orum, m. pl., Danes
Danúbius, -ii, m., the Danube
Daphníticus, -a, -um, of Daphne
daps, dapis, f., meal, banquet, food
dare, dedi, datus, to give, grant, yield
dator, -oris, m., giver
datum, -i, n., gift
Davídicus, -a, -um, Davidical
de, from, down from, out of; concerning
dea, -ae, f., goddess
dealbáre, to make white
deambuláre, to walk about
deargentáre, to plate with silver
deaurátus, -a, -um, gilded
debelláre, to wage war
debére, to owe; ought
débilis, -e, feeble; maimed
debílitas, -atis, f., weakness
débitor, -oris, m., debtor
débitrix, -icis, f., debtor
débitum, -i, n., debt
débitus, -a, -um, due
decachórdus, -a, -um, ten stringed
decálogus, -i, m., decalogue, the Ten Commandments
decantáre, to sing
decantátio, -onis, f., singing
decas, -adis, f., decade, set of ten
decem, ten
decem et octo, eighteen
decénni, -ae, -a, ten years; decénnis, at the age of ten

decénter, fittingly

Decentiánum, -i, *n.*, Desenzano

decéptor, -oris, *m.*, deceiver, enemy

decérnere, -crevi, -cretus, to intend, ordain, determine

decérpere, -cerpsi, -cerptus, to take away

decertáre, to strive

decéssor, -oris, *m.*, predecessor

decet, -uit, *impers.* 2, it is becoming

décidens, -entis, fading

decídere, -cidi, to fall down, die, wither

décima, -ae, *f.*, tenth, tithe

decimátio, -onis, *f.*, tithe

décimus, -a, -um, tenth

décimus (-a, -um) nonus (-a -um), nineteenth

décimus (-a, -um) octávus (-a, -um), eighteenth

décimus (-a, -um) quartus (-a, um), fourteenth

décimus (-a, -um) sextus (-a, -um), sixteenth

decípere, -cepi, -ceptus, (io), to deceive

declaráre, to signify

declarátio, -onis, *f.*, declaration

declináre, to incline; go aside, turn away, step aside, lean to one side

decolláre, to behead

decollátio, -onis, *f.*, beheading

decoloráre, to discolor

decóquere, -coxi, -coctus, to cook, boil, roast

decor, -oris, *m.*, beauty, comeliness

decoráre, to adorn; honor; endow

decorticáre, to tear off the bark, to strip bare

decórus, -a, -um, beauteous, comely

decrépitus, -a, -um, infirm

decréscere, -crevi, -cretus, to decrease, wane

decretália, -orum, *n. pl.*, decretals

decretórius, -a, -um, decreeing, embodying a decree

decrétum, -i, *n.*, decree

decúrio, -onis, *m.*, counselor; captain over ten men

decúrrere, -curri and -cucúrri, -cursus, trickle down; run through

decúrsus, -us, *m.*, completion; maneuver, attack; a running down

decus, -oris, *n.*, grace, beauty; honor, glory

dédecens, -entis, unbecoming

dédecus, -oris, *n.*, dishonor, shame

dedicáre, to dedicate

dedicátio, -onis, *f.*, dedication

dedignári, *dep.*, to scorn, disdain, reject as unworthy

dedignátio, -onis, *f.*, scorn, indignation

déditus, -a, -um, devoted

dedúcere, -duxi, -ductus, to lead, conduct, bring down

deésse, -fui, to be wanting, be lacking

defaecátus, -a, -um, purified, refined

deféctio, -onis, *f.*, fainting

deféctus, -us, *m.*, failing, defect

deféndere, -fendi, -fensus, to defend, revenge

defénsio, -onis, *f.*, defense, protection

deférre, -tuli, -latus, to offer, bring

defícere, -feci, -fectus, (io), to fail, faint; waste; vanish

definíre, to determine, define, solve

defíxus, -a, -um, fixed

defléctere, -flexi, -flexus, to turn aside

deflére, -flevi, -fletus, to weep

deflúere, -fluxi, to pass away, fall, wither

defóret (for deésset), another form of the imperfect subjunctive of deésse

deformáre, to engrave

defúnctus, -a, -um, dead

dégener, -eris, unworthy, ignoble

dégere, degi, to live, spend time

deglutíre, to swallow up

degustáre, to taste, partake of

déifer, -fera, -ferum, God-bearing

dein, thereupon, then

deínceps, henceforth, again, any more, any longer; successively, in order of succession

deínde, then

deíntus, from within

Deípara, -ae, *f.*, Mother of God, the Blessed Virgin

Déitas, -atis, *f.*, Deity, Godhead, Divinity

dejéctus, -a, -um, fallen

dejícere, -jeci, -jectus, (io), to break down; cast down

delectábilis, -e, delightful

delectaméntum, -i, *n.*, delight, sweetness; sweetness and delight

delectáre, to be delighted, rejoice

delectátio, -onis, *f.*, pleasure, delight

delegáre, to entrust, assign

delére, -evi, -etus, to blot out, wash away, destroy

delibáre, to sacrifice

delibúere, -ui, -utus, to besmear, anoint

delicátus, -a, -um, delightful

delícia, -ae, *f.*, delight

delíctum, -i, *n.*, crime, sin, dishonor

delineáre, to outline; prophesy

delínquere, -liqui, -lictus, to fail, offend, sin

delitéscere, -tui, to lie hidden

delúbrum, -i, *n.*, temple, shrine

demandáre, to entrust

démere, dempsi, demptus, to take away

demeréri, *dep.* 2, to deserve

demérgere, -mersi, -mersus, to sink, plunge into, drown; swallow

demirári, *dep.*, to be amazed, wonder at

demísse, humbly

demíssio, -onis, *f.*, lowliness

demíssus, -a, -um, lowly, humble

demolíri, *dep.* 4, to consume, demolish, destroy

demonstráre, to show, discover

demorári, *dep.*, to abide, dwell

démori, -mórtuus sum, *dep.* 3 (io), to die

demulcére, -mulsi, -mulsus or -mulctus, to soften, persuade

demum, at length, at last

denárius, -ii, *m.*, denarius (a coin worth about twenty cents)

denegáre, to deny

deni, -ae, -a, by tens; ter denis, thirtyfold

denotáre, to denote

dens, dentis, *m.*, tooth

densus, -a, -um, thick

denudáre, to lay bare

denuntiáre, to threaten

dénuo, again, a second time

deórsum, down, beneath, lower

deosculári, *dep.*, to kiss

depáscere, -pavi, -pastus, to feed upon

depéllere, -puli, -pulsus, to keep from, drive away, dispel

depíngere, -pinxi, -pictus, to paint

deploráre, to grieve over, deplore

depónere, -pósui, -pósitus, to lay; bring down, take down; remove; cast headlong

depopulári, *dep.*, to ravage

deportáre, to bring; banish

depóscere, -popósci, to beseech; demand; appoint

deposítio, -onis, *f.*, laying aside, putting away; burial

depraedáre, to rob

depraváre, to pervert, corrupt

deprecábilis, -e, merciful, gracious

deprecári, *dep.*, to beseech

deprecátio, -onis, *f.*, prayer, supplication

deprecátor, -oris, *m.*, intercessor, pleader

deprehéndere, -prehéndi, -prehénsus, to find, take, seize; perceive deprímere, -pressi, -pressus, to press down, weigh down; oppress, afflict

deprómere, -prompsi, -promptus, to bring forth, fetch out, pour out, produce

depurgáre, to wash

deputáre, to appoint, depute; condemn; reckon, count; prune, cut off

derelínquere, -liqui, -lictus, to leave, forsake

derepente, suddenly

deridére, -risi, -risus, to laugh at, deride

derísus, -us, m., derision

deriváre, to divert; convey abroad

desaevíre, to rage violently

descéndere, -scendi, -scensus, to come down, run down, descend

descríbere, -scripsi, -scriptus, to enroll; describe

descríptio, -onis, f., enrolling; description

desérere, -sérui, -sertus, to forsake, neglect; fail to appear

desértio, -onis, f., desertion, treason

desértor, -oris, m., rebel

desértum, -i, n., desert, wilderness

desértus, -a, -um, deserted, desolate, arid

deservíre, to serve

deses, -idis, idle, lazy, slothful

desiderábilis, -e, desirable

desideráre, to desire

desidérium, -ii, n., desire; lust

desídia, -ae, f., sloth

designáre, to appoint; signify

desilíre, -sílui, -sultus, to leap

desínere, -sivi or -sii, -situs, to cease

desoláre, to bring to desolation, lay waste

desolátio, -onis, f., desolation

desolatórius, -a, -um, destroying; carbónibus desolatóriis, with hot burning coals

desolatórius, -ii, m., destroyer

desolátus, -a, -um, desolate

despéctio, -onis, f., contempt, a looking down upon

desperáre, to despair

despicábilis, -e, unworthy

despícere, -spexi, -spectus, (io), to slight, despise, abhor

despoliáre, to strip

despondére, -spondi, -sponsus, to promise in marriage, espouse, betroth

desponsátus, -a, -um, espoused

destitúere, -stítui, -stitútus, to abandon; to be lacking (in the passive)

destrúctor, -oris, m., destroyer

destrúere, struxi, -structus, to pull or tear down, ruin, destroy; overcome

desuéscere, -suevi, -suetus, to lay aside a custom

desúmere, -sumpsi, -sumptus, to choose, select

désuper, from above, from the top; thereon

desúrsum, from above

detégere, -texi, -tectus, to uncover, lay bare, disclose

deténtio, -onis, f., abode

detergére, -tersi, -tersus, to cancel, wipe away

detérior, -ius, worse

determináre, to determine

deterrére, -térrui, -térritus, to deter by fear

detestári, dep., to curse

detinére, -tínui, -tentus, to hold back, withhold, detain

detráhere, -traxi, -tractus, to take away; bring down; slander

detrectáre, to speak against, disparage; refuse

detriméntum, -i, n., loss

detrúdere, -trusi, -trusus, to thrust down

Deus, -i, *m.,* God

deuteronómium, -ii, *n.,* Deuteronomy

deveníre, -veni, -ventus, to come to

deviáre, to wander away from

devíncere, -vici, -victus, to conquer, overcome

devitáre, to shun, avoid

dévius, -a, -um, wandering from the way

devoráre, to devour

devorátio, -onis, *f.,* devouring; prey

devóte, devoutly

devótio, -onis, *f.,* devotion

devótus, -a, -um, devout, devoted

devovére, -vovi, -votus, to devote, consecrate

dexter, -a, -um, or -tra, -trum, right; ad déxteram, at the right hand

déxtera (dextra), -ae, *f.,* the right hand

dextéritas, -atis, *f.,* skill

dextralíolum, -i, *n.,* bracelet

diabólicus, -a, -um, diabolic, of the devil

diábolus, -i, *m.,* devil

diaconía, -ae, *f.,* hospice, chapel

diaconátus, -us, *m.,* diaconate

diáconus, -i, *m.,* deacon

diadéma, -atis, *n.,* diadem

diálogus, -i, *m.,* dialogue, conversation

dicáre, to dedicate, devote

dicátus, -a, -um, hallowed

dícere, dixi, dictus, to say, tell, call; dícitur, is called

dício (dítio), -onis, *f.,* dominion

díctio, -onis, *f.,* language

dictum, -i, *n.,* word

dictus, -us, *m.,* word, saying, command

dies, -ei, *m.* and *f.,* day; de die in diem, from day to day

diétim, day by day, daily

diffamáre, to spread abroad; accuse

dífferens, -entis, different

differéntia, -ae, *f.,* difference

differéntior, -ius, more different, more excellent

différre, dístuli, dilátus, to cast off; defer; differ

dífficultas, -atis, *f.,* difficulty; obstinacy

diffidéntia, -ae, *f.,* suspicion, unbelief

diffídere, -fisus sum, *semidep. 3,* to mistrust

diffitéri, *dep. 2,* to deny, disavow

diffluere, -fluxi, -fluxus, to fall or flow out; flow freely

diffúgere, -fugi, -fúgitus, (io), to flee

diffúndere, -fudi, -fusus, to pour abroad, pour forth, spread throughout

digérere, -gessi, -gestus, to digest

digéstus, -a, -um, set in order

dígitus, -i, *m.,* finger; toe

dignánter, worthily

dignári, *dep.,* to grant, vouchsafe

dignátio, -onis, *f.,* condescension, graciousness

digne, worthily, rightly

dígnitas, -atis, *f.,* worth, merit, dignity

dignóscere, -novi, to discern, distinguish

dignus, -a, -um, worthy, becoming, deserved

dígredi, -gressus sum, *dep. 3,* (io), to depart; digress

dijudicáre, to discern, examine, judge

dilaceráre, to tear to pieces

dilaniáre, to tear in pieces, rend

dilargíre, to give liberally

dilatáre, to make broad, extend, enlarge, spread; increase, multiply

dilátio, -onis, *f.,* delay

diléctio, -onis, *f.,* love

diléctus, -a, -um, beloved; lovely

diligénter, diligently

diligéntius, more diligently, more carefully

dilígere, -lexi, -lectus, to love

dilúcide, clearly

dilúculum, -i, *n.,* dawn, daybreak, morning light; dilúculo, early

dilúere, -lui, -lutus, to wash, efface

dilúvium, -ii, *n.,* flood

dimanáre, to flow in different directions

dimetíri, -mensus sum, *dep. 4,* to measure, mete out

dimicáre, to fight, struggle

dimidiáre, to divide into halves

dimidiátus, -a, -um, half

dimídius, -a, -um, half

dimídium, -ii, *n.,* the half

diminúere, -ui, -utus, to lessen, diminish

dimíttere, -misi, -missus, to put or send away; dismiss, release; leave; forgive; let down

dinumeráre, to number

Diocletiánus, -i, *m.,* Diocletian

dioecesánus, -a, -um, diocesan

dioecésis, -is, or -eos, *f.,* diocese

Dionýsius, -ii, *m.,* Dionysius; Denis

dióryx, -ygis, *f.,* channel, canal

Dióscorus, -i, *m.,* Dioscorus

díplois. -idis, *f.,* a double cloak, mantle

diplóma, -atis, *n.,* privilege conferred by the government

dipóndium, -ii, *n.,* two farthings

diréctio, -onis, *f.,* direction; uprightness

diréctus, -a, -um, direct; in dirécto, in the direct way

dirémptio, -onis, *f.,* separation

dirígere, -rexi, -rectus, to direct; straighten; prosper (in the passive)

dirípere, -ripui, -reptus, (io), to plunder

dirúmpere, -rupi, -ruptus, to break asunder, to cleave

dirus, -a, -um, cruel

discédere, -cessi, -cessus, to pass away, depart

disceptáre, to dispute with, discuss, determine

disceptátio, -onis, *f.,* dispute

díscere, dídici, to learn

discérnere, -crevi, -cretus, to discern, distinguish

discérpere, -cerpsi, -cerptus, to tear, to rend

discéssio, -onis, *f.,* revolt

discéssus, -us, *m.,* removal

disciplína, -ae, *f.,* study, instruction; chastisement, discipline

discipulátus, -us, *m.,* discipleship

discípulus, -i, *m.,* disciple

discíssus, -a, -um, torn, rent

díscolor, -oris, of different colors, speckled

díscolus, -a, -um, deformed

discórdia, -ae, *f.,* dissension

discrepáre, to disagree with, be different from; depart from

discrétio, -onis, *f.,* discernment; separation

discrétor, -oris, *m.,* discerner

discrímen, -inis, *n.,* danger, peril, hazard

discrimináre, to plait, braid

discruciáre, to torture

discúmbens, -entis, *m.,* guest

discúmbere, -cúbui, -cúbitus, to sit down

discúrrere, -cucúrri and -curri, -cursus, to run to and fro

discus, -i, *m.,* dish

discússio, -onis, *f.,* dispersal

discútere, -cussi, -cussus, to disperse

disérte, eloquently

disértus, -a, -um, eloquent

disgregáre, to rend asunder

disjúngere, -junxi, -junctus, to put asunder

dispar, -is, unlike, different, unequal

dispéndere, -pensus sum, *semidep. 3,* to weigh out, dispense dispensáre, to distribute

dispensátio, -onis, *f.,* dispensation, administration

dispensátor, -oris, *m.,* dispenser, steward

dispensatórius, -a, -um, dispensing, administering

dispérdere, -didi, -ditus, to cut off, destroy

dispérgere, -spersi, -spersus, to scatter

disperíre, -ii, (eo), to perish

dispérsio, -onis, *f.,* dispersal

dispertíre, to distribute; separate, part, divide

displicére, -plícui, -plícitus, to displease

dispónere, -pósui, -pósitus, to dispose, order

dispositio, -onis, *f.,* disposition, providence, decree

dispósitor, -oris, *m.,* disposer

disputáre, to treat about, dispute

disputátio, -onis, *f.,* argumentation

disrúmpere, -rupi, -ruptus, to break asunder

dissecáre, to dry up

dissecáre, -sécui, -sectus, to cut

dissénsio, -onis, *f.,* quarrel

dissérere, -sérui, -sertus, to discuss, converse, discourse

díssidens, -entis, being at variance, dissenting

dissidére, -sedi, -sessus, to disagree

dissídium, -ii, *n.,* quarrel; disunion

dissimilitúdo, -inis, *f.,* difference

dissimuláre, to dissemble, conceal

dissipáre, to destroy, abolish; scatter; waste; lay waste

dissipátio, -onis, *f.,* desolation

díssitus, -a, -um, widely scattered

dissolútus, -a, -um, loose; feeble

dissólvere, -solvi, -solútus, to loose, dissolve, destroy; scatter

dissonántia, -orum, *n. pl.,* differences

distans, -antis, separate, distant

distántia, -ae, *f.,* distance

distáre, to be different, distinct or distant from

disténdere, -tendi, -tentus, to stretch apart, rack

disténtus, -a, -um, busy, occupied

distilláre, to drip or drop

distillátio, -onis, *f.,* bodily fluid

distíncte, distinctly

distínctio, -onis, *f.,* distinction

distínctus, -a, -um, adorned

distínguere, -stinxi, -stinctus, to discriminate; speak distinctly

distórtus, -a, -um, misshapen

distribúere, -bui, -butus, to distribute

distribútio, -onis, *f.,* allotment, distribution

distribútor, -oris, *m.,* giver

distrícte, severely

distríctio, -onis, *f.,* strictness, severity

ditáre, to enrich, endow

dítio, -onis, *f.,* power, dominion, jurisdiction, authority, sovereignty

dítius, more abundantly

dittáre, to declare, repeat

diu, *adv.,* long

diúrnus, -a, -um, a day, per day; lasting for a day

diutúrnus, -a, -um, of long duration; chronic

divéllere, -velli, -vulsus, to tear asunder

divéndere, -véndidi, -vénditus, to sell

divérsitas, -atis, *f.,* diversity

diversórium, -ii, *n.,* inn; lodging; guest chamber

divérsus, -a, -um, different; in divérsum, back

divértere, -verti, to turn aside

dives, dívitis, rich

divexáre, to plunder; tear asunder

divídere, -visi, -visus, to divide, part, put asunder

divinátio, -onis, *f.,* divination

divínitas, -atis, *f.*, divinity
divínitus, divinely, by divine influence
divínus, -a, -um, divine
Dívio, -onis, *f.*, Dijon
divísio, -onis, *f.*, diversity; part
divítia, -ae, *f.*, wealth; divítiae, riches
divórtium, -ii, *n.*, divorce
divus, -a, -um, divine
Divus, -i, *m.*, saint
docére, -ui, doctus, to teach
docíbilis, -e, apt, teachable
doctor, -oris, *m.*, doctor, teacher
doctrína, -ae, *f.*, instruction, learning, doctrine
documéntum, i, *n.*, example
dogma, -atis, *n.*, dogma; edict
dogmáticus, -a, -um, dogmatic
doláre, to hew with an axe
dolére, to suffer, grieve, be sorrowful
dolíolum, -i, *n.*, small keg or cask
dólium, -ii, *m.*, earthenware cask
dolor, -oris, *m.*, sorrow, pain
dolorósus, -a, -um, sorrowful
dolóse, deceitfully
dolósus, -a, -um, deceitful, false
dolus, -i, *m.*, fraud, subtlety, deceit
doma, -atis, *n.*, roof; house, dwelling
domáre, -ui, -itus, to conquer
doméstícus, -a, -um, domestic, home; of the household
doméstícus, -i, *m.*, domestic; doméstici, those of the household
domicílium, -ii, *n.*, dwelling, home, house
dómina, -ae, *f.*, mistress
dominári, *dep.*, to rule, have dominion over
dominátio, -onis, *f.*, dominion
dominátor, -oris, *m.*, ruler, lord, Lord
dómine, *voc.*, Sir; Dómine, Lord
Domínica, -ae, *f.*, Sunday
dominicális, -e, pertaining to Sunday
Domínicus, -i, *m.*, Dominic
Dóminus, -i, *m.*, Lord

dóminus, -i, *m.*, lord, master
Domitiánus, -i, *m.*, Domitian
domne (*voc.* of dóminus), Sir
domúncula, -ae, *f.*, little dwelling
domus, -i or -us, *f.*, house; de domo in domum, from house to house
donáre, to give, grant; forgive; remit a debt
donárium, -ii, *n.*, shrine
donátio, -onis, *f.*, giving; gift
Donatístae, -arum, *m. pl.*, Donatists
donátus, -us, *m.*, gift
donec, until; while
donum, -i, *n.*, gift, present
Dorestádium, -ii, *n.*, Dorestadt
dormíre, to sleep, lie down to rest
dormitare, to slumber
dormitátio, -onis, *f.*, slumber
dormítio, -onis, *f.*, sleep, repose
Doróthea, -ae, *f.*, Dorothy
dorsum, -i, *n.*, back
dos, dotis, *f.*, gift
dotáre, to endow
drachma, -ae, *f.*, drachma
draco, -onis, *m.*, dragon
dromedárius, -ii, *m.*, dromedary
dubíetas, -atis, *f.*, doubt
dubitánter, hesitantly
dubitáre, to hesitate, waver, doubt; non —, to firmly believe
ducátus, -us, *m.*, leadership, guidance; rank
ducentésimus, -a, -um, two hundredth
ducénti, -ae, -a, two hundred
dúcere, duxi, ductus, to lead, bring; marry; launch out; hold, consider; derive
dúctilis, -e, beaten out (of metal), drawn
ductor, -oris, *m.*, leader
dudum, *adv.*, a little while ago, even now
duéllum, -i, *n.*, conflict
dulcédo, -inis, *f.*, sweetness, goodness

dulcéscere (dulcéssit), to become sweet

dulcis, -e, sweet, fresh; kind

dulcísonus, -a, -um, sweet sounding, harmonious

dúlciter, sweetly

dulcor, -oris, *m.*, sweetness

dum, while

dúmmodo, provided that

dumtáxat, *adv.*, in so far as, only

Dunclínum, -i, *n.*, Durham

duo, -ae, -o, two

duódecim, twelve

duodécimus, -a, -um, twelfth

duodenárius, -a, -um, twelve

duodéni, -ae, -a, twelve

duodevigínti, eighteen

duplex, -icis, double, twofold; **duplícibus,** with double garments

duplicáre, to double

duplicátus, -a, -um, double

duplícitas, -atis, *f.*, deceit

duplum, -i, *n.*, the double

durítia, -ae, *f.*, hardness

duríties, -ei, *f.*, hardness

durus, -a, -um, stiff, hard; obstinate; **dura,** *n. pl.*, hardships

dux, ducis, *m.* and *f.*, leader, captain, guide; duke, earl

dýscolus, -a, -um, bold, impudent

E

e, ex, *prep.*, from, out of, of

eátenus, *adv.*, so far

ebíbere, -bibi, -bitus, to drink up, drink in

Ebionítae, -arum, *m. pl.*, Ebionites

Eborácum, -i, *n.*, York

ebríetas, -atis, *f.*, drunkenness

ebriósus, -i, *m.*, drunkard

ébrius, -a, -um, drunk, drunken; *as a noun*, drunken man

ebullíre, to break forth; bubble

ebur, -oris, *n.*, ivory

ebúrneus, -a, -um, of ivory

ecce, *interj.*, behold

ecclésia, -ae, *f.*, church; assembly

ecclesiásticus, -a, -um, of or for the church

Echínadae, *f. pl.* (Echínades, -um, *f. pl.*), the Urchin Islands (Lepanto)

écstasis, -is, *f.*, ecstasy, trance

édere, -didi, -ditus, to bring forth, produce, publish

édere, edi, esus, to eat

Edessénus, -a, -um, of Edessa

edíctum, -i, *n.*, decree

edíscere, -dídici, to learn thoroughly

edissérere, -sérui, -sertus, to expound, explain, set forth

edítio, -onis, *f.*, birth, a bringing forth; a statement

edocére, -ui, -doctus, to teach completely

edoláre, to hew, plane

edomáre, -dómui, -dómitus, to tame thoroughly, subdue entirely

Eduárdus, -i, *m.*, Edward

educáre, to bring up, nourish

educátor, -oris, *m.*, tutor

edúcere, -duxi, -ductus, to bring forth, produce; take away

édulis, -e, edible; edúlia, *n. pl.*, food

effári, -fatus sum, *dep. 1*, to utter

effátu (*supine*), to express

efféctor, -oris, *m.*, maker

efféctus, -us, *m.*, effect, work; reward; answer

effeminátus, -a, -um, effeminate

efferátus, -a, -um, wild, raging

effére, éxtuli, elátus, to bring or carry out; bear, lift up

effervéscere, -férbui and -fervi, to boil up, rage

efficácia, -ae, *f.*, accomplishment

efficáciter, effectually

éfficax -acis, powerful, effectual; zealous

effícere, -feci, -fectus, (io), to make, render; make ready; become (in the passive)

effígies, -ei, f., figure, image

efflagitáre, to entreat

effláre, to breathè out, give forth

efflorére, -ui, to flourish

efflúere, -fluxi, to flow forth

effódere, -fodi, -fossus, (io), to break through

efformáre, to form, shape

effrons, -tis, bold, brazen, shameless, insulting

effugáre, to drive away from

effugátio, -onis, f., driving away

effúgere, -fugi, -fúgitus, (io), to escape

effulgére, -fulsi, -fulsus, 2, to shine upon

effúndere, fudi, -fusus, to shed, pour out or forth; bring out; slip

effúsus, -a, -um, pouring, excessive

egens, -entis, needy

egénus, -a, -um, needy, poor

egére, -ui, to be in want, have need of

egéstas, -atis, f., want, poverty, need

ego, I

égredi, -gressus sum, dep. 3, (io), to come out, go out or forth

egrégius, -a, -um, illustrious

egréssio, -onis, f., going forth, departure

egréssus, -us, m., going forth

eheu, interj., ah

eia (eja), interj., quick! come then! well!

ejéctio, -onis, f., banishment

ejéctus, -us, m., casting out; exile

ejícere, -jeci, -jectus, (io), to cast out; bring forth

ejulátus, -us, m., lamenting, cry

ejuráre, to refuse; abandon; deny

ejus, genitive of is, of him, his

Elamítae, -arum, m. pl., Elamites

elánguens, -entis, growing weak

elápsus, -us, m., lapse

eláta, -ae, f., spray

elátio, -onis, f., elevation; breaker, billow

Elcesaéus, -i, m., Elcesite

Eleázarus, -i, m., Eleazar

eléctio, -onis, f., election

eléctrum, -i, n., amber

eléctus, -a, um, chosen, elect; bright; elécta, n. pl., chosen bits, dainties

eleemósyna, -ae, f., alms

élegans, -antis, elegant

eléison (Greek), have mercy on us

eleméntum, -i, n., element; the letters of the alphabet

eleváre, to lift up, elevate

elevátio, -onis, f., lifting up, elevation

elícere, -lícui, -lícitus, (io), to bring forth, produce, elicit

Elíci, -orum, m. pl., Elicians

elídere, -lisi, -lisus, to throw down

elígere, -legi, -lectus, to choose, elect

elimináre, to eradicate

Elisabeth, Elizabeth, Isabel

Eliséus, -i, m., Eliseus

elongáre, to be or go or remove far off

eloquéntia, -ae, f., eloquence, oratory

elóquium, -ii, n., word

Elpediánum, -i, n., Heldelfs

Elpidiénsis, -e, of Helfta

Elpídius, -ii, m., Elpidius

elucidáre, to explain

eluscéscere, to begin to be light

emanáre, to flow out

emarcére, to wither, decay

emendáre, to amend; chastise

emendicáre, to beg

emendátio, -onis, f., correction

ementíri, dep. 4, to falsify, pretend

émere, emi, emptus, to buy

Eméricus, -i, m., Emeric

eméritus, -a, -um, deserving; veteran

eméritus, -i, m., one who has served his time

emicáre, -mícui, -micátus, *1*, to shine forth; pour forth

Emígdius (Emýgdius), -ii, *m.*, Emidius

emigráre, to depart

éminens, -entis, excellent

eminére, -mínui, to be above, stand out, project

éminus, *adv.*, at a distance

emíssio, -onis, *f.*, perfume

emíttere, -misi, -missus, to send out, emit; yield up; cast out

empórium, -ii, *n.*, market

émptio, -onis, *f.*, buying, purchase

emundáre, to cleanse

emundátio, -onis, *f.*, cleansing

emoluméntum, -i, *n.*, gain, advantage

en, *interj.*, lo, behold

enarráre, to tell, relate, show forth

enavigáre, to sail away; swim

Encaénia, -orum, *n. pl.*, Feast of the Dedication

encaeniáre, to put on something new, to consecrate

enchirídium, -ii, *n.*, handbook, manual

enérviter, weakly

enim, *conj.*, for

enímvero, *adv.*, to be sure, certainly

eníti, -nisus or -nixus sum, *dep. 3*, to bring forth

enodáre, to make clear

ensis, -is, *m.*, sword

enucleáte, plainly

enumerátio, -onis, *f.*, enumeration

enuntiáre, to announce, declare

enutríre, to sustain, nourish

Eóbanus, -i, *m.*, Eoban

Eóus, -a, -um, eastern, from the East; morning

eoúsque, *adv.*, to that point

ephébia, -orum, *n. pl.*, place for youth, youth center

ephébus, -i, *m.*, page

Ephésii, -orum, *m. pl.*, Ephesians

Ephesínus, -a, -um, of Ephesus

ephod, *indecl.*, ephod, amice

Ephrathaéus, -i, *m.*, Ephrathite

Epiphánia, -ae, *f.*, Epiphany, appearance

episcopális, -e, episcopal

episcopátus, -us, *m.*, episcopacy, bishopric; office of bishop

epíscopus, -i, *m.*, bishop; patriarch

epístola, -ae, *f.*, epistle, letter

epistólium, -ii, *n.*, letter

epithalámium, -ii, *n.*, marriage song

épulae, -arum, *f. pl.*, feast, feasts

epulári (*dep.*), to feast

eques, -itis, *m.*, horseman

equéster, -tris, -tre, equestrian

équidem, *adv.*, truly

equúleus, -i, *m.*, rack

équus, -i, *m.*, horse

erádere, -rasi, -rasus, to strike or cut off, destroy

eradicáre, to root up

Ercus, -i, *m.*, Erc

eréctio, -onis, *f.*, lifting up

eréctus, -a, -um, attentive

eremíta, -ae, *m.*, hermit

eremíticus, -a, -um, eremitical

erémus, -i, *m.* and *f.*, desert, wilderness

erga, *prep.*, toward; with

ergástulum, -i, *n.*, house of correction for slaves; prison

ergo, therefore, then

erígere, -rexi, -rectus, to raise up, lift up, erect

erípere, -rípui, -reptus, (io), to rescue, deliver from

Ermembérga, -ae, *f.*, Ermenburga

erogáre, to distribute, disperse abroad

erráre, to wander, go astray, err

erro, -onis, *m.*, wanderer, nightprowler

error, -oris, *m.*, error

erubéscere, -rúbui, to be ashamed

erúca, -ae, *f.*, palmer worm

eructáre, to utter, publish; overflow

erudíre, to teach, instruct; discipline
erudítio, -onis, *f.*, learning
erúere, -ui, -utus, to deliver
erúmpere, -rupi, -ruptus, to break, break forth, break up, crush
esca, -ae, *f.*, food, meat
esse (sum), fui, futúrus, to be
esséntia, -ae, *f.*, essence
esuríre, to be hungry
esus, -us, *m.*, food, bread; eating
et, and, also
Etchénus, -i, *m.*, Etchen
étenim, *conj.*, for, but
Ethelbértus, -i, *m.*, Ethelbert
éthnici, -orum, *m. pl.*, heathen
étiam, *adv.*, also; certainly; yes
etiámnum, *adv.*, still, yet
Etrúria, -ae, *f.*, Tuscany
Etrúscus, -a, -um, Tuscan
etsi, *adv.*, yet
etymológiae, -arum, *f. pl.*, Etymológiae (of St. Isidore)
euge, *interj.*, well done!
Eugénius, -ii, *m.*, Eugene
Eugubínus, -a, -um, of Gubbio
Eugúbium, -ii, *n.*, Gubbio
eunúchus, -i, *m.*, eunuch
Európa, -ae, *f.*, Europe
Eustáchius, -ii, *m.*, Eustace
Euthychiánus, -a, -um, of Eutyches
Eva, -ae, *f.*, Eve
evacuáre, to make void; do away with; put away
evádere, -vasi, -vasus, to escape, evade
evagáre, to wander, stray away
evagináre, to unsheathe
evanéscere, -vánui, to vanish
evangélicus, -a, um, of the Gospel
evangelista, -ae, *m.*, evangelist
Evangélium, -ii, *n.*, Gospel
evangelizáre, to preach the Gospel, evangelize
evéhere, -vexi, -vectus, to raise
evéllere, -velli, -vulsus, to pluck

eveníre, -veni, -ventus, to come forth
evéntus, -us, *m.*, occurrence
everrere, -verri, -versus, to sweep out
evérsio, -onis, *f.*, overthrow, destruction
evértere, -verti, -versus, to turn away, pervert; overturn, overthrow
evidénter, manifestly
evidéntia, -ae, *f.*, evidence
evigiláre, to awaken
evíncere, -vici, -victus, to bring it about that
evocáre, to call forth
evoláre, to take flight
evulgáre, to make known, publish
ex, of, from, out of
exacerbáre, to provoke, embitter
exacerbátio, -onis, *f.*, bitterness, exasperation
exáctio, -onis, *f.*, exaction or levying of tribute
exáctor, -oris, *m.*, one who demands, oppressor, tax collector
exacúere, -ui, -utus, to sharpen
exacútus, -a, -um, sharpened
exaedificáre, to build
exaequáre, to equal, make equal
exaestuáre, to burn; surge or boil up
exaggeráre, to increase, grow worse
exagitáre, to drive out; attack
exaltáre, to lift up, exalt, extol
exaltátio, -onis, *f.*, exaltation; high praise
examináre, to try, test
exantláre, to suffer, endure; exhaust
exaráre, to write on wax tablets
exárchus, -i, *m.*, exarch
exardére, -arsi, -arus, to kindle
exardéscere, -arsi, -arsus, to take fire, flame out, be inflamed
exarmáre, to disarm
exasperáre, to provoke
exasperátrix, -icis, provoking
exaudíre, to hear favorably

exaudítor, -oris, *m.*, one who listens favorably to a prayer

excaecáre, to blind

excalceátus, -a, -um, discalced, barefooted

excandéscere, -cándui, to become hot; become violently angry

excarnificáre, to tear to pieces

excédere, -cessi, -cessus, to exceed

excéllens, -entis, excellent, distinguished

excéllere, -céllui, to excel

excélsitas, -atis, *f.*, pre-eminence

excélsus, -a, -um, high, lofty; most high; excélsa, *n. pl.*, high places; in excélso, on high; in excélsis, in the highest

exceptus, -a, -um, except, only

excéssus, -us, *m.*, excess; ecstasy

excídere, -cidi, to fall away

excídere, -cedi, -cisus, to cut down, hew out

excídium, -ii, *n.*, destruction

excípere, -cepi, -ceptus, (io), to take out, except

excísus, -us, *m.*, piece, cut; slip

excitáre, to stir up, raise up, awaken

excitátor, -oris, *m.*, awakener

exclamáre, to cry out, exclaim

exclúdere, -clusi, -clusus, to keep from, drive away

excogitátio, -onis, *f.*, invention, devising

excólere, -cólui, -cultus, to tend carefully; work for; cultivate

excommunicáre, to excommunicate

excommunicátio, -onis, *f.*, excommunication

excóquere, -coxi, -coctus, to boil down, refine

excréscere, -crevi, -cretus, to grow

excubáre, -ui, -itus, to keep watch

excúbiae, -arum, *f. pl.*, a keeping watch or guard

excusáre, to excuse; ad excusándas excusatiónes, to seek excuses

excusátio, -onis, *f.*, excuse

excússus, -a, um, cast out

excútere, -cussi, -cussus, (io), to shake, shake off, drive out

exémplar, -aris, *n.*, model

exémplum, -i, *n.*, example

exenterare, to disembowel

extenteratus, -a, -um, disemboweled

exercére, to exercise; use, employ

exercitare, to occupy; to ponder (in the passive)

exercitátio, -onis, *f.*, exercise

exércitus, -us, *m.*, army, host

exfornicátus, -a, -um, given to fornication

exháustus, -a, -um, exhausted

exhibére, to present, exhibit; return

exhibítio, -onis, *f.*, example; display; performance

exhiláre, to gladden, make cheerful

exhonoráre, to disgrace, dishonor

exhonorátio, -onis, *f.*, shame

exhorrére, to shrink, shudder

exhorréscere, -hórrui, to shudder

exhortáre (-ari), to exhort

exhortátio, -onis, *f.*, exhortation, an encouraging

exíguus, -a, -um, little

exílitas, -atis, *f.*, shrillness

exímere, -emi, -emptus, to take or draw out

exímius, -a, -um, priceless; wonderful

exinaníre, to empty, pour forth

exinanítio, -onis, *f.*, emptiness

exínde, *adv.*, henceforth

exíre, -ivi and -ii, -itus, (eo), to go out; come forth or from

existimáre, to deem, reckon, think, take account of

existimátio, -onis *f.*, esteem, estimation

exitiális, -e, destructive

exítium, -ii, *n.*, destruction

éxitus, -us, *m.*, departure end, result; éxitus viárum, highways

exoptáre, to hope or desire eagerly

exoráre, to plead, beseech, pray

exorcísta, -ae, *m.*, exorcist

exorcístus, -i, *m.*, exorcist

exorcísmus, -i, *m.*, exorcism

exorcizáre, to exorcize

exórdium, -ii, *n.*, beginning, institution

exoríri, -ortus sum, *dep. 3* and *4*, to rise or spring up

exornáre, to provide with, adorn

exornátus, -a, -um, embellished

exosculáre, to kiss

exósus, -a, -um, hated

expándere, -pansi, -pansus and -passus, to spread, stretch out

expavéscere, -pavi, to be terrified, be affrighted; tremble

expedíre, to deliver; detach; be expedient

expedítus, -a, -um, well appointed, light armed

expéllere, -puli, -pulsus, to drive away, expel

expéndere, -pendi, -pensus, to weigh

expergísci, -perrectus sum, *dep. 3*, to awake

experíri, -pertus sum, *dep. 4*, to experience

expers, -ertis, destitute of, lacking

expértus, -a, -um, tested, experienced

expétere, -ivi, -itus, to desire

expiáre, to cleanse, purify; atone, expiate

expiátio, -onis, *f.*, atonement, expiation

explanáre, to expound, explain

explanátio, -onis, *f.*, explanation

explantáre, to cast out

explére, -plevi, -pletus, to fill, fulfill

explétio, -onis, *f.*, expiration

explicáre, to unfold, extend; explain

exploráre, to implore; investigate

expolíre, to polish; redecorate

expónere, -pósui, -pósitus, to set before, make manifest

exporrígere, -rexi, -rectus, to expand, stretch out

expóscere, -póposci, to plead

exprímere, -pressi, -pressus, to represent, express

exprobráre, to reproach, upbraid

expugnáre, to fight against; overthrow

expurgátus, -a, -um, expurgated

Exquíliae, -arum, *f. pl.*, the Esquiline Hill

Exquilínus, -a, -um, Esquiline

exquírere, -sivi, -situs, to seek after, inquire diligently

exquísitor, -oris, *m.*, searcher

exquisítus, -a, -um, exquisite; painful

exsánguis, -e, bloodless

exsaturáre, to satisfy, satiate

exsaturátus, -a, -um, filled, having enough

exsecrábilis, -e, abhorrent

exsecrári, *dep.*, to curse

exsecrátio, -onis, *f.*, abomination; curse

éxsequi, -secútus sum, *dep. 3*, to perform; follow; secure

exsérere, -serui, -sertus, to thrust forth, exert

exsiccáre, to dry up

exsilíre, -sílui, -sultus, *4*, to leap, leap out

exsílium, -ii, *n.*, exile

exsístere, -stiti, -stitus, to come forth, appear

exsólvere, -solvi, -solútus, to present; pay back

exsors, -sortis, deprived of

expectáre, to look for, wait for, long for, expect

exspectátio, -onis, *f.*, hope, expectation

exspiráre, to die, expire

exspoliáre, to despoil, rob

exspúere, -spui, -sputus, to spit

exstáre, -stiti, to stand forth, come forth, appear

exstinctio, -onis, *f.*, annihilation, dissolution; slaughter

exstínguere, -stinxi, -stinctus, to extinguish

exstrúere, -struix, -structus, to build

exsuffláre, to blow away

exsul, -sulis, banished; (as a noun), an exile

exsuláre, to be banished

exsultábilis, -e, joyful

exsultáre, to rejoice, exult

exsultátio, -onis, *f.*, joy, gladness, exultation

exsuperáre, to excel, surpass

exsúrgere, -surréxi, -surréctus, to arise, awaken

éxtasis, -is, *f.*, amazement

exténdere, -tendi, -tensus or -tentus, to stretch out, spread, extend

extenuáre, to weaken, reduce; chasten, punish

extergére, -tersi, -tersus, to wipe

extérior, -ius, outward, exterior

extermináre, to cut off; disfigure; lay waste

exterminátor, -oris, *m.*, destroyer

extermínium, -ii, *n.*, utter destruction

extérnus, -a, -um, belonging to another

exterrére, -térrui, -térritus, to frighten

éxterus, -a, -um, foreign

éxterus, -i, *m.*, foreigner

extiméscere, -tímui, to fear

extolléntia, -ae, *f.*, insolence, haughtiness

extóllere, -tuli, to lift up, raise up, exalt; be insolent (in the passive)

extorquére, -torsi, -tortus, to wring forth

extórris, -e, exiled

extra, *prep.*, beside, beyond, except, outside of, without, out of

extráhere, -traxi, -tractus, to draw out

extráneus, -i, *m.*, stranger, foreigner

extrémum, -i, *n.*, end, tip; farthest part

extrémus, -a, -um, last; latter

extricáre, to extricate

extrínsecus, *adv.*, without, on the outside, outwardly

extrúdere, -trusi, -trusus, to thrust out

exturbáre, to drive away

exuberáre, to abound

exúere, -ui, -utus, to take off, strip; free from, deliver

exundáre, to abound, overflow

exúrere, -ussi, -ustus, to burn up, consume

exúviae, -arum, *f. pl.*, remains

Ezecías, -ae, *m.*, Ezechias

F

faber, -bri, *m.*, worker, artificer; carpenter

Fabiánus, -i, *m.*, Fabian

fabrefácere, -feci, -factus, (io), to make, manufacture

Fabriánum, -i, *n.*, Fabriano

fábrica, -ae, *f.*, building

fabricáre, to make, build; work

fabricátor, -oris, *m.*, creator; forger

fabrílis, -e, of a carpenter; fabrília, *n. pl.*, carpenter work

fábula, -ae, *f.*, byword

fabuláre, to talk

fabulátio, -onis, *f.*, fable; lie

fabulátor, -oris, *m.*, a teller of fables

fácere, feci, factus, (io), to make, cause; grant; yield or bring forth (fruit); commit

facéssere, -cessi, to depart

fácies, -ei, *f.*, face, appearance; presence; a fácie, because of; from before; fácie ad fáciem, face to face

facílius, more easily

fácinus, -oris, *n.*, sin, crime

fáctio, -onis, *f.*, faction

factiósus, -a, -um, quarrelsome

factor, -oris, *m.*, doer, maker

factum, -i, *n.*, deed, act, fact

factúra, -ae, *f.*, creation

facúltas, -atis, *f.*, ability; strength; authority; means, goods, possessions, resources (usually in plural)

faeculéntus, -a, -um, pertaining to dregs; worthless

faeneráre, to lend money at interest

faenerátor, -oris, *m.*, creditor

faex, faecis, *f.*, dregs; mire, ooze

Falco, -onis, *m.*, Faucon

fallácia, -ae, *f.*, deceit, falsehood

falláciter, falsely

fallax, -acis, deceitful; unreliable

fállere, féfelli, falsus; to deceive; make a slip, make ineffective; be mistaken (in the passive)

falsus, -a, -um, false

falx, -falcis, *f.*, sickle

fama, -ae, *f.*, fame, good report

famélicus, -a, -um, hungry, famished

fames, -is, *f.*, hunger, famine

família, -ae, *f.*, family, household

familiáris, -e, intimate, friendly

familiáritas, -atis, *f.*, intimacy

famósus, -a, -um, renowned

fámula, -ae, *f.*, servant

famulári, *dep.*, to serve

famulátus, -us, *m.*, service, obedience

fámulus, -i, *m.*, servant

fanum, -i, *n.*, temple

Fanum, -i, *n.*, Fano

farína, -ae, *f.*, meal

farínula, -ae, *f.*, meal

fáscia, -ae, *f.*, band, bandage

fascículus, -i, *m.*, bundle, little bundle; sheaf

fascinátio, -onis, *f.*, bewitching, fascination

fastidiósus, -a, -um, fastidious, disdainful

fastídium, -ii, *n.*, weariness

fastígium, -ii, *n.*, summit, height; dignity

fastus, -us, *m.*, pride, arrogance

fatéri, fessus sum, *dep.* 2, to admit, confess, avow

fatigátio, -onis, *f.*, toil

fatigátus, -a, -um, wearied

fatíscere, to crack

fátue, foolishly

fatúitas, -atis, *f.*, folly

fátuus, -a, -um, foolish

fátuus, -i, *m.*, a fool

fauces, -ium, *f. pl.*, jaws, throat, palate

fáustitas, -atis, *f.*, prosperity

fautor, -oris, *m.*, adviser, patron, protector, favorer

favílla, -ae, *f.*, ashes

Favéntia, -ae, *f.*, Faenza

Faventíni, -orum, *m. pl.*, citizens of Faenza

favor, -oris, *m.*, favor, approval; care

favus, -i, *m.*, honey comb

fax, facis, *f.*, torch; flame

febris, -is, *f.*, fever

Februárius, -ii, *m.*, February

fecundus, -a, -um, fruitful

fel, fellis, *n.*, gall

Feliciánus, -i, *m.*, Felician

felícitas, -atis, *f.*, felicity

felíciter, happily

felix, -icis, happy, blessed

fémina, -ae, *f.*, woman, female

feminínus, -a, -um, female

femorália, -orum, *n. pl.*, breeches

femur, -oris, *n.*, thigh

fenéstra, -ae, *f.*, window

fera, -ae, *f.*, beast

ferális, -e, deadly

férculum, -i, *n.*, tray, dish; course, food, bread

Ferdinándus, -i, *m.*, Ferdinand

fere, *adv.*, almost

féretrum, -i, *n.*, bier

féria, -ae, f., day of the week; — secunda, Monday, — tértia, Tuesday; — quarta, Wednesday; — quinta, Thursday; — sexta, Friday

feriális, -e, week day, ferial

feríre, to strike, slay; make; make a treaty

féritas, -atis, f., fierceness, savagery

ferme, adv., almost

fermentáre, to leaven

ferméntum, -i, n., leaven

ferrátus, -a, -um, sharp

ferre, tuli, latus, to carry; bring; prae se ferre, to display

Ferrérius, -ii, m., Ferrer

férreus, -a, -um, of iron, iron

ferrum, -i, n., iron; sword

fertilis, -e, fertile

ferus, -i, m., wild beast

fervens, -entis, hot; fervent; fervénte die, in the heat of the day

fervéntius, more fervently

fervére, -vui, to glow

fervor, -oris, m., fervor

fessus, -a, -um, weary

festinánter, adv., in haste

festináre, to be quick, hasten

festinátio, -onis, f., haste, hurry

festináto, adv., speedily

festívitas, -atis, f., festival, festivity

festúca, -ae, f., stalk; rod; mote

festus, -a, -um, festal, festival

festum, -i, n., feast, festival; festa, n. pl., festival

Fesulánus, -a, -um, of Fiesole

fibra, -ae, f., fiber, filament; vocal chord, voice

ficte, adv., falsely, with pretense

fíctilis, -e, made of clay, earthen

fíctio, -onis, f., guile

fictor, -oris, m., maker

fictus, -a, -um, feigned, deceitful

ficúlnea, -ae, f., fig tree

ficus, -i and -us, f., fig, fig tree

fidélis, -e, faithful, believing

fidéliter, faithfully, confidently

fidénter, confidently, courageously

fides, -ei, f., faith, faithfulness

fidúcia, -ae, f., confidence; cum fidúcia, boldly

fiduciáliter, boldly, with confidence

fiduciálius, more confidently

fíeri, factus sum, to become, be made; happen, fulfill; factum est, it came to pass

fígere, fixi, fixus, to pierce; make firm

figméntum, -i, n., creation; formation; frame; workmanship; pillar

fígulus, -i, m., potter

figúra, -ae, f., figure, fashion

figuráliter, figuratively

figuráre, to symbolize

fília, -ae, f., daughter

filiális, -e, filial

filiátio, -onis, f., sonship

filíolus, -i, m., little child

fílius, -ii, m., son, child; foal

fímbria, -ae, f., hem, fringe

fimus, -i, m., dung

finális, -e, final

fíngere, fixi, fictus, to feign; make

Finiánus, -i, m., Finnian

finíre, to end, make an end of

finis, -is, m. and f. end, boundary; fines, pl., territory, country; sine fine, continually

finítimus, -a, -um, neighboring

firmaméntum, -i, n., firmament; strength

firmáre, to make strong, strengthen; fix, establish

fírmitas, -atis, f., steadfastness

fírmiter, firmly, strongly

firmus, -a, -um, firm

fístula, -ae, f., reed, sweet cane, flute; ulcer, hemorrhoids

fixúra, -ae, f., print

fláccidus, -a, -um, weak, drooping

flagelláre, to scourge
flagellátio, -onis, *f.*, scourging
flagéllum, -i, *n.*, scourge
flagitáre, to beseech
flagitiósus, -a, -um, disgraceful
flagítium, -ii, *n.*, shameful crime
flagráre, to burn; be eager or zealous
flamen, -inis, *n.*, a blowing; wind; breath
flamen, -inis, *m.*, divine breath or spirit; Holy Ghost
flamma, -ae, *f.*, flame
flammans, -antis, flaming
flamméscere, to become inflamed
flámmeus, -a, -um, fiery, flaming
flámmifer, -fera, -ferum, flaming
fláre, to blow
flatus, -us, *m.*, blowing; breath
flébilis, -e, weeping, sorrowing, wretched
fléctere, flexi, flexus, to bend, bow; move
flére, flevi, fletus, to weep, lament
fletus, -us, *m.*, weeping
flexíbilis, -e, supple
flexus, -a, -um, bent; genu flexo, kneeling
florens, -entis, in flower
Floréntia, -ae, *f.*, Florence
Florentínus, -a, -um, of Florence
florére, -ui, to flower, bloom; flourish, prosper
flóridus, -a, -um, flourishing, plentiful
flos, floris, *m.*, flower
flósculus, -i, *m.*, little flower
fluctuáre, to toss about; be tossed to and fro; vacillate
fluctuátio, -onis, *f.*, a being tossed to and fro; insecurity
fluctus, -us, *m.*, wave
fluéntum, -i, *n.*, stream, river
flúere, fluxi, fluxus, to flow
flumen, -inis, *n.*, river
flúvius, -ii, *m.*, stream, river

fluxus, -a, -um, transitory
fluxus, -us, *m.*, flowing, issue
focária, -ae, *f.*, cook
fódere, fodi, fossus, (io), to dig; pierce
foecundáre, to make fruitful
foecundus, -a, -um, fruitful, abundant
foedáre, to disfigure
foederátus, -a, -um, united
foedus, -eris, *n.*, covenant
foedus, -a, -um, detestable
foéditas, -atis, *f.*, filth
foenerátor, -oris, *m.*, money lender
foenum, -i, *n.*, grass; dry herb
foenus (faenus), -eris, *n.*, loan
foetans, -antis, *f.*, milch-ewe
foetére, to stink
foétidus, -a, -um, stinking
foetósus, -a, -um, prolific
foetus, -us, *m.*, offspring, increase
fólium, -ii, *n.*, leaf, foliage
foméntum, -i, *n.*, poultice
fomes, -itis, *m.*, tinder; fire; nourishment
fons, fontis, *m.*, fount, fountain; well, spring; source; baptistery
Fons Avellána (Fontis Avellánae), *f.*, Font-Avellano
Fonscoopértus, -i, *m.*, Fontcouverte
Fonsíberus, -i, *m.*, Fontibere, Fuenterravia
Fontáni, -orum, *m. pl.*, Fontaines
Fontisplánus, -i, *m.*, Fuenlana
forámen, -inis, *n.*, hole, cleft
foras, *adv.*, out, forth, out of doors
forceps, -ipis, *m.* and *f.*, tongs
Forénsis, -e, of Forez
forénsis, -e, forensic; legal
forent, a form of the imperf. subj. of esse, for essent
forínsecus, *adv.*, from without
foris, *adv.*, outwardly, without, outside
foris, foris, *f.*, door
forma, -ae, *f.*, pattern; form
formáre, to form, train, guide, fashion

Fórmiae, -arum, *f. pl.*, Mola di Gaëta

formidáre, to be afraid, be in awe

formído, -inis, *f.*, dread, terror

formidolósus, -a, -um, fearful

formósus, -a, -um, beautiful

fornax, -acis, *f.*, furnace, oven

fornicári (*dep.*), to commit fornication

fornicária, -ae, *f.*, fornicatress

fornicátio, -onis, *f.*, fornication

fornicátor, -oris, *m.*, fornicator

fórsitan, *adv.*, perhaps

fortásse (fortássis), *adv.*, perhaps

forte, *adv.*, perhaps

fortis, -e, strong, mighty, valiant; grievous

fórtiter, mightily, valiantly, firmly

fortitúdo, -inis, *f.*, strength, power

fortúito (fortúitu), by chance

forum, -i, *n.*, open space, market place, forum

Forum Cornélii, -i, *n.*, Imola

fossa, -ae, *f.*, ditch

Fossa Nova, -ae -ae, *f.*, Fossa-Nuova

fóvea, -ae, *f.*, pit, ditch

fovére, fovi, fotus, to warm, keep warm; foment; cherish

fráctio, -onis, *f.*, breaking

fractúra, -ae, *f.*, breaking

fraenáre, to bridle, restrain

frágilis, -e, frail, weak, poor

fragílitas, -atis, *f.*, frailty

fragmen, -inis, *n.*, piece

fragméntum, -i, *n.*, fragment

fragrántia, -ae, *f.*, fragrant smell

frámea, -ae, *f.*, sword

Franci, -orum, *m. pl.*, Franks

Francísca, -ae, *f.*, Frances

Francísca de Nigro, -ae, *f.*, Francesca di Negro

Franciscánus, -a, -um, Franciscan

Francíscus, -i, *m.*, Francis

Francíscus Bórgia, -i, -ae, *m.*, Francis Borgia

Francíscus Salésius, -i, -ii, *m.*, Francis de Sales

frángere, fregi, fractus, to break; deal

frater, -tris, *m.*, brother; friar

fratérnitas, -atis, *f.*, brotherhood

fraudáre, to defraud; withhold

fraudulénter, falsely, deceitfully

fraus, fraudis, *f.*, wile; error

frémere, -ui, -itus, to murmur; groan; rage, roar

frémitus, -us, *m.*, fury, anger

frendére, -ui, fresus, or fressus, to gnash

frenum, -i, *n.*, bridle, curb

frequens, -entis, frequent; much

frequentáre, to frequent; have recourse to; celebrate

frequentátio, -onis, *f.*, frequentation

frequénter, often

frequéntia, -ae, *f.*, number, frequency

fretum, -i, *n.*, the sea

fretus, -a, -um, strengthened; relying on

Fribúrgus, -i, *m.*, Freiburg

Friderícus, -i, *m.*, Frederick

frigéscere, frixi, to become cold

frigus, -oris, *n.*, cold

Frisácum, -i, *n.*, Friesach

Frísia, -ae, *f.*, Friesland

Frisónes, -um, *m. pl.*, Frieslanders

frixórium, -ii, *n.*, frying pan

frondére, to be leafy; flourish

frondéscere, -ui, to blossom, to become leafy

frons, frondis, *f.*, leaf; leafy branch or twig

frons, frontis, *f.*, forehead; van, front line in battle

frúctifer, -fera, -ferum, fruitful

fructificáre, to be fruitful

fructificátio, -onis, *f.*, production of fruit

fructuósus, -a, -um, fruitful

fructus, -us, *m.*, fruit

frugálitas, -atis, *f.*, frugality, simplicity
frúgifer, -fera, -ferum, fruitful
fruítio, -onis, *f.*, enjoyment
fruméntum, -i, *n.*, corn
frustra, *adv.*, in vain
frustrári, *dep.*, to make void
frutétum, -i, *n.*, branch
frutex, -icis, *m.*, shrub, plant; shoot
frux, -gis, *f.*, fruit
fucáre, to paint, disguise
fucus, -i, red or purple color; rouge
fuga, -ae, *f.*, refuge; flight
fugáre, to put to flight
Fugátius, -ii, *m.*, Ffagan
fúgere, fugi, fúgitus, (io), to flee
fulciméntum, -i, *n.*, prop
fulcíre, fulsi, fultus, *4*, to prop up, stay, support, strengthen
Fuldénsis, -e, of Fulda
fulgére, fulsi, to shine, glow
fúlgidus, -a, -um, shining
fulgor, -oris, *m.*, brightness
fulgur, -uris, *n.*, lightning
fuguráre, to flash forth
fullo, -onis, *m.*, fuller
fulmen, -inis, *n.*, lightning, thunderbolt
fultus, -a, -um, supported by, charged with
fulvus, -a, -um, gold colored
fumáre, to smoke
fumigabúndus, -a, -um, smoking
fumigáre, to smoke
fumus, -i, *m.*, smoke
funda, -ae, *f.*, sling
fundaméntum, -i, *n.*, foundation
fundáre, to found, establish
fundátor, -oris, *m.*, founder
fúndere, fudi, fusus, to shed, pour out, pour forth
Fundi, -orum, *m. pl.*, Fondi
fundibulárius, -ii, *m.*, slinger
fúnditus, *adv.*, completely
fundus, -i, *m.*, base, foundation

fungi, functus sum, *dep. 3*, to perform, exercise
funículus, -i, *m.*, little cord; inheritance
funis, -is, *m.*, line, cord, rope, band
funus, -eris, *n.*, funeral, interment
fur, furis, *m.* and *f.*, thief
furári, *dep.*, to steal
fúria, -ae, *f.*, fury
furor, -oris, *m.*, wrath, indignation
furtum, -i, *n.*, theft; — fácere, to steal
fuscáre, to darken
fuscínula, -ae, *f.*, flesh hook, fork
fuscus, -a, -um, black
fúsius, *adv.*, more fully
fustis, -is, *m.*, club
fusus, -i, *m.*, spindle
futúrus, -a, -um, future; — esse, to be about to be

G

Galaadítis, -is, *m.*, Galaadite
Gálatae, -arum, *m. pl.*, Galatians
gálbanum, -i, *n.*, galbanum
gálea, -ae, *f.*, helmet
galeátus, -i, *m.*, man wearing a helmet
gáleo, -onis, *m.*, galleon
Gálgala, -ae, *f.*, Galgal
Galilaéa, -ae, *f.*, Galilee
Galilaéus, -a, -um, Galilean
Gállia, -ae, *f.*, Gaul; France
Gallicánus, -a, -um, Gallican, French
gallína, -ae, *f.*, hen
gallus, -i, *m.*, cock, rooster
Gallus, -i, *m.*, Frenchman
Gargánus, -i, *m.*, Monte di San Angelo
gaudére, gavísus sum, *semidep. 2*, to rejoice, be glad
gáudium, -ii, *n.*, joy
Gavus, -i, *m.*, Gave
gaza, -ae, *f.*, treasure, riches
gazophylácium, -ii, *n.*, treasure-house; treasury; treasure

gehénna, -ae, f., hell

gelu, -us, n., frost

gemebúndus, -a, -um, groaning

gémere, -ui, -itus, to groan; sigh; mourn

geminátus, -a, -um, twofold; doubled

géminus, -a, -um, double, twin

gémitus, -us, m., moan, groan; sighing; sorrow

gemma, -ae, f., jewel

gémmula, -ae, f., gem

gena, -ae, f., cheek

genealogía, -ae, f., genealogy

generális, -is, m., general

generálitas, -atis, f., generality

generáre, to engender

generátio, -onis, f., generation; pedigree; fruit

generátor, -oris, m., first author

génere, -ui, -itus, to beget, bear

Genestánum, -i, n., Genazzano

Genestanus, -a, -um, of Genazzano

Genevénsis, -e, of Geneva

génimen, -inis, n., fruit, offspring

genitále, -is, n., womb

genitális, -e, pertaining to birth

génitor, -oris, m., father

génitrix, -icis, f., mother

génitus, -a, -um, begotten; new born

Genovéfa, -ae, f., Guinevere

gens, gentis, f., nation, family, gens; gentes, Gentiles

Genséricus, -i, m., Genseric

gentílis, -e, gentile, heathen

gentílitas, -atis, f., the gentile or heathen world, paganism, heathendom

genu, -us, n., knee; flectáre génua, to kneel; genu flexo, kneeling

Genuénsis, -e, of Genoa

genufléctere, -flexi, -flexus, to genuflect

genus, -eris, n., kind, race; nation; ex génere, from my own nation

Geórgius, -ii, m., George

Geraséni, -orum, m. pl., Gergesenes

gérere, gessi, gestus, to bear; reign; do; celebrate

Germánia, -ae, f., Germany

Germánicus, -a, -um, German

germánitas, -atis, f., relationship between brothers and sisters

germánus, -i, m., brother

Germánus, -i, m., German

germen, -inis, n., bud, sprout

germináre, to bud forth, blossom; bring forth; to spring (of seed)

Gertrúdis, -is, f., Gertrude

Gervásius, -ii, m., Gervase

gestáre, to carry, wear

gestatórium, -ii, n., litter

gestátus, -us, m., bearing

gestíre, to desire passionately, long for

Gethaéi, -orum, m. pl., Gethites, people of Gath

Gethsémani, Gethsemane

ghimel, the third letter of the Hebrew alphabet, corresponding to English g (hard)

Ghisélla, -ae, f., Gisela

Ghislérii, -orum, m. pl., Ghisleri

Giennénsis, -e, of Jaen

Giénnium, -ii, n., Jaen

gigas, -antis, m., giant, strong man; hero

gígnere, génui, génitus, to bring forth, beget

Girvénsis, -e, of Jarrow

Girvum, -i, n., Jarrow

glácies, -ei, f., ice

gládius, -ii, m., sword

gleba, -ae, f., clod or lump of earth

glíscere, to swell; blaze up, rage

glóbulus, -i, m., ball, shot

globus, -i, m., ball

gloria, -ae, f., glory; boasting

gloriánter, exultingly

gloriári, dep., to glory in, boast of

gloriátio, -onis, f., glory; boasting

glorificáre, to glorify

glorificátio, -onis, *f.*, glory
glorióse, gloriously
gloriósus, -a, -um, glorious
gluten, -inis, *n.*, glue
glutíre, to swallow
gnárus, -a, -um, knowing
Gordiánus, -ii, *m.*, Gordian
Gothi, -orum, *m. pl.*, Goths
grabátus, -i, *m.*, bed, cot
Gradénsis, -e, of Grado
gradi, gressus sum, (io), *dep. 3*, to walk; follow
graduále, -is, *n.*, gradual
gradus, -us, *m.*, step; degree; place, position
graece, *adv.*, in Greek
Graeci, -orum, *m. pl.*, Greeks
Graécia, -ae, *f.*, Greece
Graecus, -a, -um, Greek
gramen, -inis, *n.*, grass
grammática, -ae, *f.*, grammar
Granaténsis, -e, of Granada
grandaévus, -a, -um, of great age
grandilóquus, -a, -um, eloquent
grandis, -e, great
grandiúsculus, -a, -um, somewhat grown up, a little older
grando, -inis, *f.*, hail, hail storm
Granérius, -ii, *m.*, Granier
gránulum, -i, *n.*, pip, seed
granum, -i, *n.*, grain
grassári, *dep.*, to proceed violently, rage
grates, *f. pl.*, thanks
grátia, -ae, *f.*, grace; thankfulness, thanks; sake; grátias ágere, to give thanks; gratis, free, without recompense; verbi grátia, for example
Gratianopolitánus, -a, -um, of Grenoble
Gratiánus, -i, *m.*, Gratian
gratificáre, to grace
gratificári, *dep.*, to oblige, gratify
gratiósus, -a, -um, favored

gratúitus, -a, -um, free, voluntary
gratulabúndus, -a, -um, joyful
gratulári, *dep.*, to rejoice
gratus, -a, -um, gracious; thankful, agreeable
graváre, to burden, grieve, be burdensome to, be chargeable to; be heavy
gravátus, -a, -um, heavy
gravidári, *dep.*, to grow heavy; become pregnant
grávidus, -a, -um, heavy
gravis, -e, heavy; grievous
gráviter, seriously
Gregórius, -i, *m.*, Gregory
Gregórius Nazianzénus, -i, -i, *m.*, Gregory of Nazianzus
gressus, -us, *m.*, step; going
grex, gregis, *m.*, flock
grossus, -i, *m.*, green fig
Guadalupénsis, -e, of Guadalupe
Gualbértus, -i, *m.*, Gualbert
gubernáculum, -i, *n.*, helm; government
gubernáre, to govern
gubernátio, -onis, *f.*, government
Guiscárdus, -i, *m.*, Guiscard
gula, -ae, *f.*, gullet; gluttony
Guliélmus, -i, *m.*, William
Gundúlphus, -i, *m.*, Gundulf
gurges, -itis, *m.*, eddy; stream; waters; sea; raging abyss
gustáre, to taste
gustátus, -us, *m.*, taste; tasting
gustus, -us, *m.*, taste; tasting, partaking
gutta, -ae, *f.*, drop; myrrh oil, aloes
guttur, -uris, *n.*, throat; palate; taste; mouth
gymnásium, -ii, *n.*, place of exercise, gymnasium
gyrus, -i, *m.*, circle; compass

H

habére, to have, hold, consider; bene —, to be well, recover; (se) male —, to be ill

habitáculum, -i, *n.*, dwelling, house; apartment

hábitans, -antis, *m.*, dweller

habitáre, to dwell

habitátio, -onis, *f.*, dwelling, habitation

habitátor, -oris, *m.*, dweller, inhabitant

hábitus, -us, *m.*, dress, habit, clothing, garments

hac illac, *adv.*, here and there

háctenus, *adv.*, so far, up to this point

Hadriánus, -i, *m.*, Hadrian; Adrian

haéccine (haec + ci + ne), is this? are these the things?

haedus, -i, *m.*, young goat, kid

haemorrhoíssus, -a, -um, having a flow of blood

haerére, haesi, haesus, to stick fast

haeresiárcha, -ae, *m.*, arch heretic

haéresis, -is, *f.*, heresy

haeréticus, -i, *m.*, heretic

haeréticus, -a, -um, heretical

haesitáre, to waver, hesitate; stagger

haesitátio, -onis, *f.*, hesitation

Hagulstadénsis, -e, of Hexham

hálitus, -us, *m.*, breath

hamus, -i, *m.*, fish hook

haríolus, -i, *m.*, soothsayer

Hassi, -orum, *m. pl.*, Hessians

Hássia, -ae, *f.*, Hesse

hasta, -ae, *f.*, spear

hastíle, -is, *n.*, shaft; staff

haud, *adv.*, not at all, by no means

haudquáquam, *adv.*, not at all

hauríre, hausi, haustus, to draw out; drink up

haustus, -us, *m.*, draught, drink

he, the fifth letter of the Hebrew alphabet, corresponding to English *h*

hebdómada, -ae, *f.*, week

hebdomadárius, -ii, *m.*, hebdomadary

hébdomas, -adis, *f.*, week

hebes, -itis, stupefied

hebetáre, to blunt

hebetúdo, -inis, *f.*, dulness, confusion

Hebraéus, -i, *m.*, Hebrew

hebráice, *adv.*, in Hebrew

Hebráicis, -e, Hebrew

hebráicus, -a, -um, Hebrew

hédera, -ae, *f.*, ivy

Hedwígis, -is, *f.*, Hedwig

hei! *interj.*, woe! alas!

Heléna, -ae, *f.*, Helen

Helvétii, -orum, *m. pl.*, the Swiss

Hélvii, -orum, *m. pl.*, Helvii, ancient inhabitants of Vivarais

Henrícus, -i, *m.*, Henry

herba, -ae, *f.*, grass; herb; blade (of wheat)

hereditáre, to inherit, to cause to inherit

hereditárius, -a, -um, hereditary; original

heréditas, -atis, *f.*, generation; inheritance

heres, -edis, *m. and f.*, heir

heri, *adv.*, yesterday

herinácius, -ii, *m.*, hedgehog

Herluinus, -i, *m.*, Herluin

Hermenegíldus, -i, *m.*, Hermenegild

Hermoniim, *plural* of Hermon, mountain range in Palestine

Heródes, -is, *m.*, Herod

Herodiáni, -orum, *m. pl.*, Herodians

Herodiánus, -a, -um, of Herod

heródius, -ii, *m.*, heron

hestérnus, -a, -um, of or relating to yesterday; dies hestérna, yesterday

heth, the eighth letter of the Hebrew alphabet, corresponding to German *ch*.

Hethaéus, -i, *m.*, Hethite

heu! *interj.*, oh! alas! woe!

Heva, -ae, *f.*, Eve

Hevaéus, -i, *m.*, Hevite

hiáre, to gape

Hibérni, -orum, *m. pl.*, the Irish

Hibérnia, -ae, *f.*, Ireland

Hiberniénsis -e, of Ireland

hic, haec, hoc, this; he, she, it

hic, *adv.*, here

hiemális, -e, pertaining to winter; wintry

hiems, -emis, *f.*, winter

hierarchía, -ae, *f.*, hierarchy

Hierónymus, -i, *m.*, Jerome

Hierosólyma, -orum, *n. pl.*, Jerusalem

hiláréscere, to become joyful

Hilário, -onis, *m.*, Hilarion

hílaris, -e, cheerful, smiling

hiláritas, -atis, *f.*, cheerfulness

Hilárius, -ii, *m.*, Hilary

Hildebrándus, -i, *m.*, Hildebrand

hinc, *adv.*, fro, hence, away from here; hinc et hinc, one on each side

hinníre, to neigh; make a joyful noise

hínnulus, -i, *m.*, young hart

Hipponénsis, -e, of Hippo

hircus, -i, *m.*, goat

hirúndo, -inis, *f.*, a swallow

Hispális, -is, *f.*, Seville

Hispalénsis, -e, of Seville

Hispánia, -ae, *f.*, Spain

Hispánia Baética, -ae, -ae, *f.*, Andalusia

Hispánia citérior, -ae, -is, *f.*, Granada

Hispánus, -i, *m.*, Spaniard

Hispánus, -i, *m.*, river in Spain; probably the Guadalquivir

híspidus, -a, -um, rough, coarse

história, -ae, *f.*, history

hódie, *adv.*, today, this day

hodiérnus, -a, -um, relating to today; this day's; hodiérna die, on this day

hoedínus, -a, -um, of a young goat

hoedus (haedus), -i, *m.*, kid, young goat

holocáustum, -i, *n.*, holocaust, burnt offering

holoséricum, -i, *n.*, silk

homicídium, -ii, *n.*, murder

homilía, -ae, *f.*, homily

homo, -inis, *m.*, man; husband

honestáre, to make honorable

honéstas, -atis, *f.*, honor, riches

honéste, honorably

honéstus, -a, -um, honest

honor, -oris, *m.*, honor

honorábilis, -e, honorable

honoráre, to honor

honorárius, -a, -um, of honor

honorátus, -a, -um, honorable

honorificáre, to honor, glorify

honorificátus, -a, -um, honorable

honorificéntia, -ae, *f.*, honor

honos, -oris, *m.*, honor

hora, -ae, *f.*, hour

hordeáceus, -a, -um, of barley

hórdeum, -i, *n.*, barley

horológium, -ii, *n.*, dial

horréndus, -a, -um, dreadful

horrére, -ii, to abhor

horréscere, -ui, to spurn

hórreum, -i, *n.*, barn

horríbilis, -e, dreadful

hórridus, -a, -um, dreadful

horror, -oris, *m.*, horror

hortaméntum, -i, *n.*, exhortation

hortári, *dep.*, to exhort

hortátor, -oris, *m.*, encourager, comforter

hortulánus, -i, *m.*, gardener

hortus, -i, *m.*, garden

Hosánna, Hosanna, a Hebrew exclamation of praise to the Lord, or an invocation of blessings

hospes, -itis, *m.* and *f.*, host, guest

hospitále, -is, *n.*, guest-house, hospital

hospitális, -e, relating to a guest; hospitable; hospitáli domo, in a guest-house or hospital hospitálitas, -atis, *f.*, hospitality; fratres Hospitalitátis, Hospital brethren, Hospitallers

hospítium, -ii, *n.*, hospice, asylum; hospitality

hóstia, -ae, *f.*, host, sacrifice, victim, offering

hósticus, -a, -um, hostile

hostílis, -e, hostile

hostílitas, -atis, *f.*, enmity; enemy

hostis, -is, *m.* and *f.*, enemy

huc, *adv.*, hither; — et illuc, to and fro

húccine, *adv.*, so far? as far as this?

Hugo, -onis, *m.*, Hugh

hujuscémodi, (of) any such

hujusmódi, of such, such a one, such a kind

humánitas, -atis, *f.*, humanity, kindness; human nature; culture, good breeding

humánus, -a, -um, human

húmerus, -i, *m.*, shoulder

humicubátio, -onis, *f.*, lying on the ground

humiliáre, to bring low, humble, humiliate; afflict; bow down

humiliátio, -onis, *f.*, humiliation

húmilis, -e, humble, lowly

humílitas, -atis, *f.*, humility, abjection, lowness, misery

humíliter, humbly, lowly

humor, -oris, *m.*, moisture; fluid; desire

humus, -i, *f.*, soil, earth, land

Hungária, -ae, *f.*, Hungary

Hunni, -orum, *m. pl.*, Huns

Hussíti, -orum, *m. pl.*, Hussites

hyacínthinus, -a, -um, violet

hyacínthus, -i, *f.*, jacinth

Hyacínthus, -i, *m.*, Hyacinth

Hyblaéus, -a, -um, Hyblaean

hydria, -ae, *f.*, water jar or pot

hydrópisis, -is, *f.*, dropsy

hydrópsicus, -a, -um, afflicted with dropsy, dropsical

hyems (hiems), -emis, *f.*, winter

hýetos, Greek word meaning rain

hymnódia, -ae, *f.*, singing of hymns

hymnus, -i, *m.*, hymn

hyperbólice, *adv.*, hyperbolically, with exaggeration

hypócrisis, -is, *f.*, hypocrisy

hypócrita, -ae, *m.*, hypocrite

Hyrcáni, -orum, *m. pl.*, Hyrcanians

hyssópus, -i, *f.*, hyssop

I

ibi, *adv.*, there

ibídem, *adv.*, in the same place

Iconómachi, -orum, *m. pl.*, Iconoclasts

ictus, -us, *m.*, blow; stream; twinkling

idcírco, *adv.*, therefore

idem, eadem, idem, same

idéntidem, *adv.*, repeatedly

ídeo, *adv.*, therefore

idióma, -matis, *n.*, language

idípsum, together; forthwith

idolólatra, -ae, *m.*, idolater

idololatría, -ae, *f.*, idolatry

idólum, -i, *n.*, idol

idóneus, -a, -um, fit, suitable

Idumaéa, -ae, *f.*, Edom

Idumaéus, -a, -um, of Edom; Edomite

idus, -uum, *f. pl.*, Ides, the middle of the Roman month

ígitur, *adv.*, therefore, accordingly

ignárus, -a, -um, ignorant of

ignávus, -a, -um, idle, slothful

ignéscere, to burn

ígneus, -a, -um, fiery

ignis, -is, *m.*, fire

ignítus, -a, -um, burning, fiery; refined

ignóbilis, -e, base

ignobílitas, -atis, *f.*, dishonor

ignomínia, -ae, *f.*, shame

ignoránter, *adv.*, through ignorance

ignorántia, -ae, *f.*, ignorance
ignoráre, to be ignorant
ignóscere, -novi, -notus, not to take notice of; forgive
ilex, -icis, *f.*, holm oak
Ilkusiénsis, -e, of Olkusz
íllabi, -lapsus sum, *dep. 3*, to fall, sink down, descend
illaésus, -a, -um, unharmed
illamentátus, -a, -um, unlamented
ille, illa, illud, that; illum et illum locum, such and such a place
illécebra, -ae, *f.*, allurement, blandishment
illibátus, -a, -um, unblemished
illic, *adv.*, there
illícere, -lexi, -lectus, (io), to allure
illícite, *adv.*, illegally
illícitus, -a, -um, forbidden
íllico, *adv.*, on the spot, immediately
illigáre, to fetter
illínere, -levi, -litus, to smear, bedaub
illo, *adv.*, thither
illuc, *adv.*, there, thither
illucéscere, -luxi, to shine upon
illúdere, -lusi, -lusus, to mock, delude, deceive; play
illumináre, to make or cause to shine, illuminate; enlighten
illuminátio, -onis, *f.*, light
illúsio, -onis, *f.*, mockery, illusion
illustráre, to illuminate; enlighten; make illustrious
illustrátio, -onis, *f.*, brightness
imaginátio, -onis, *f.*, imagination
imágo, -inis, *f.*, image, picture
imbecíllitas, -atis, *f.*, weakness
imbecíllus, -a, -um, weak, feeble
imbéllis, -e, unwarlike, cowardly
imber, -bris, *m.*, rain, shower
imbúere, -ui, -utus, to fill; nourish; instruct
imitári, *dep.*, to imitate
imitátio, -onis, *f.*, example

imitátor, -oris, *m.*, follower
imitátrix, -icis, *f.*, follower, imitator
immaculátus, -a, -um, spotless, undefiled, immaculate
immánis, -e, brutal, savage
immánitas, -atis, *f.*, fierceness
immániter, cruelly
immarcescíbilis, -e, that cannot fade or wither, unwithering, imperishable
immediáte, immediately
immedicábilis, -e, incurable
ímmemor, -oris, unmindful
imménsitas, -atis, *f.*, infinity
imménsus, -a, -um, immense, infinite
immérito, *adv.*, undeservedly; unfitly
imméritus, -a, -um, unworthy
ímminens, -entis, threatening
imminúere, -ui, -utus, to diminish, abate
immiséricors, -dis, unmerciful, merciless
immísio, -onis, *f.*, a letting loose, sending forth; infusion
immítis, -e, harsh; immítia, *n. pl.*, harsh things, cruel sights
immíttere, -misi, -missus, send; put into; encamp
immóbilis, -e, immovable
immoderántia, -ae, *f.*, excess
immoderátus, -a, -um, excessive, immoderate
immódicus, -a, -um, excessive, immoderate
immoláre, to sacrifice, immolate
immolátio, -onis, *f.*, offering
immorári, *dep.*, to stay
immortális, -e, immortal
immortálitas, -atis, *f.*, immortality
immótus, -a, -um, unmoved, steadfast
immundítia, -ae, *f.*, uncleanness
immúndus, -a, -um, unclean
immúnitas, -atis, *f.*, immunity
immúnis, -e, free from, preserved, immune

immutáre, to change, alter; do something new or different

immutári, *dep.*, to change

imparílitas, -atis, *f.*, inequality

impartíre, to impart

impassíbilis, -e, not susceptible to pain

impediméntum, -i, *m.*, impediment

impedíre, to bring low, prostrate

impéllere, -puli, -pulsus, to push

impéndere, -pendi, -pensus, to spend, expend; grant, extend; ensure

impéndium, -ii, *n.*, charge, expense

impénse, *adv.*, urgently; at great cost

imperáre, to command

imperátor, -oris, *m.*, emperor

imperféctio, -onis, *f.*, imperfection

imperfectum, -i, *n.*, something imperfect

imperítia, -ae, *f.*, ignorance

impérium, -ii, *n.*, reign, dominion, empire; precept, command; pride

impertíre, to bestow

impérvius, -a, -um, impassable

impétere, to attack

impetráre, to gain, obtain

ímpetus, -us, *m.*, force, violence; impulse, rapid motion

ímpie, wickedly

impíetas, -atis, *f.*, wickedness, ungodliness, transgression

ímpiger, -gra, -grum, diligent

impíngere, -pegi, -pactus, to put or push back; strike

impinguáre, to grow fat or thick; anoint

ímpius, -a, -um, wicked, godless

implére, -plevi, -pletus, to fill, accomplish; celebrate

implicáre, to entangle

imploráre, to implore

impollútus, -a, -um, undefiled

impónere, -pósui, -pósitus, to lay or put upon

importábilis, -e, insupportable

importúne, *adv.*, out of season

impositio, -onis, *f.*, a laying on; imposition

impossíbilis, -e, impossible

impréssio, -onis, *f.*, impression

imprímere, -pressi, -pressus, to print, imprint; press or thrust into

improbáre, to blame

impróbitas, -atis, *f.*, importunity

ímprobus, -a, -um, troublesome

improperáre, to reproach

impropérium, -ii, *n.*, reproach

imprúdens, -entis, foolish

impudéntia, -ae, *f.*, shamelessness

impudicítia, -ae, *f.*, immodesty, impurity

impugnáre, to beset, fight against

impugnátio, -onis, *f.*, assault

impugnátor, -oris, *m.*, enemy

imputáre, to impute

imus, -a, -um, lowest

in, in, into, unto, upon, for, at, to, against, among, toward

inaccesíbilis, -e, inaccessible

inaccéssus, -a, -um, inaccessible

inacúere, -ui, -utus, to sharpen; inflame

inaestimábilis, -e, inestimable, priceless

inambuláre, to walk

inamissíbilis, -e, unable to be lost

inánis, -e, vain, empty, void; inánia, *n. pl.*, vain things

inánitas, -atis, *f.*, emptiness

inániter, vainly

inaquósum, -i, *n.*, desert

inaquósus, -a, -um, without water, dry

inarátus, -a, -um, unplowed

ináuris, -is, *f.*, earring

incaléscere, -cálui, to grow warm

incanéscere, -cánui, to be gray-headed

incantáre, to charm

incarnáre, to make incarnate

incarnátio, -onis, *f.*, incarnation

incarnátus, -a, -um, incarnate

incédere, -cessi, -cessus, to go, walk

incéndere, -cendi, -census, to heat, burn; kindle, set fire to

incéndium, -ii, *n.*, fire, flame

incénsum, -i, *n.*, incense

incénsus, -a, -um, incensed

incentívum, -i, *n.*, incentive

incéntor, -oris, *m.*, promoter

incértum, -i, *n.*, uncertainty; uncertain thing

incertus, -a, -um, hidden, uncertain

incessábilis, -e, unceasing

incessánter, continually

inchoáre, to begin

inchoátio, -onis, *f.*, beginning

incídere, -cidi, to fall into

incípere, -cepi, -ceptus, (io), to begin

incircumcísus, -a, -um, uncircumcised

incircumscríptus, -a, -um, incomprehensible

incísus, -a, -um, not cut

incitáre, to provoke, blaspheme

incitátor, -oris, *m.*, instigator

inclamáre, to cry out loudly

inclináre, to bow, bend, incline

inclúdere, -clusi, -clusus, to include

inclusíve, *adv.*, inclusive

ínclytus, -a, -um, renowned, glorious

incoenátus, -a, -um, without supper

íncola, -ae, *m.* and *f.*, stranger, sojourner, exile; dweller

incolátus, -us, *m.*, sojourn, residence

incolúmitas, -atis, *f.*, safety

incombústus, -a, -um, not burnt

incommutábilis, -e, unchanging, unchangeable, immutable

incomparábilis, -e, incomparable

incomprehensíbilis, -e, incomprehensible

inconcúbius, -a, -um, relating to the dead of night

incóngruus, -a, -um, unfitting, incongruous

inconstántia, -ae, *f.*, wandering

inconsútilis, -e, not sewed together, made in one piece; without a seam

incontaminátus, -a, -um, undefiled

incorporári, *dep.*, to enter into a body, be incorporated

incorpóreus, -a, -um, without a body, incorporeal

incorruptíbilis, -e, incorruptible

incorrúptio, -onis, *f.*, incorruption

incorrúptus, -a, -um, incorruptible

incrassáre, to grow fat

increátus, -a, -um, uncreated

incredíbilis, -e, incredulous

incredúlitas, -atis, *f.*, unbelief, incredulity

incrédulus, -a, -um, faithless, incredulous

increméntum, -i, *n.*, increase

increpáre, to reprove, rebuke

increpátio, -onis, *f.*, rebuke

increpatórius, -a, -um, rebuking

incubáre, -cúbui, -cúbitus, to lie upon

incúmbere, -cúbui, -cúbitus, to lie upon

incunábula, -orum, *n. pl.*, swaddling clothes; beginning

incunctánter, not slowly, readily

incurábilis, -e, incurable

incúria, -ae, *f.*, indifference

incúrrere, -curri (cucúrri), -cursus, to come into

incúrsio, -onis, *f.*, attack

incúrsus, -us, *m.*, assault

incurváre, to bend

incurvári, *dep.*, to bow down

incútere, -cussi, -cussus, (io), to strike

indagáre, to investigate, inquire into

inde, *adv.*, hence; thereafter

indeclinábilis, -e, unwavering

indeféssus, -a, -um, unwearied

indefíciens, -entis, unfailing, never failing

índere, -didi, -ditus, to give to; put in or into

indesinénter, unceasingly
index, -icis, c., sign, token
Indi, -orum, m. pl., natives of India
Indiae, -arum, f. pl., Indies
indicáre, to tell; bespeak, indicate, show
indicíbilis, -e, unable to be told in words
indícium, -ii, n., sign, evidence
Indicus, -a, -um, Indian
indifferénter, not differently
índigens, -entis, needy
indigére, -ui, to need, stand in need of
indígnans, -antis, indignant, angry
indignári, dep., to be indignant, be angry
indignátio, -onis, f., indignation
indígne, indignantly; — ferre, to have indignation
indígnus, -a, -um, unworthy
indisciplinátus, -a, -um, unskillful
indissolúbilis, -e, imperishable
índitus, -a, -um, given or imposed (as a name)
indivíduus, -a, -um, undivided
indivísus, -a, -um, undivided
índoles, -is, f., talent, genius
indubitánter, indubitably
indubitátus, -a, -um, unwavering
indúcere, -duxi, -ductus, to lead; bring into
indúciae, -arum, f. pl., extension of time, truce
indúere, -ui, -utus, to put on; clothe
indulgéntia, -ae, f., pardon, forgiveness, indulgence
indulgére, -dulsi, -dultus, to grant; forgive
induméntum, -i, n., apparel
induráre, to harden; dry up
indúsium, -ii, n., shirt
indústria: de —, on purpose
indústrius, -a, -um, industrious
inebriáre, to water, soak; make drunk

inédia, -ae, f., fasting, abstinence, hunger
ineffábilis, -e, ineffable
ineffabíliter, in an unspeakable manner
inenarrábilis, -e, unspeakable
inéptus, -a, -um, stupid
inérmis, -e, unarmed, defenseless
ineruditio, -onis, f., ignorance
inésse, -fui, to be on or in
inexcusábilis, -e, inexcusable
inexháustus, -a, -um, inexhaustible
inexpectátus, -a, -um, unexpected
inexplébilis, -e, insatiable; extraordinary
inexplebíliter, insatiably
inexpugnábilis, -e, invincible
inextinguíbilis, -e, inextinguishable
inextricábilis, -e, inextricable
infallíbilis, -e, infallible
infámia, -ae, f., evil report
infans, -antis, m. and f., infant, child, babe; infántes expósiti, foundlings
infántia, -ae, f., childhood, infancy
infántula, -ae, f., babe
infántulus, -i, m., infant
infatigabíliter, indefatigably
infatuátus, -a, -um, tasteless
infecúndus, -a, -um, sterile
infelícitas, -atis, f., unhappiness, wretchedness
infélix, -icis, unhappy
infénsus, -a, -um, hostile, dangerous
inférior, -ius, lower, below
inférnus, -a, -um, of hell, infernal
inférnus, -i, m., grave, the underworld
inférre, -tuli, illátus, to bring, bear, carry in
ínferus, -a, -um, below; of hell
ínferus, -i, m., nether world, grave
infestátio, -onis, f., assault
inféstus, -a, -um, hostile
infícere, -feci, -fectus, (io) to infect, stain; pollute

infidélis, -e, unfaithful, unbelieving

infígere, -fixi, -fixus, to fasten in, stick fast

infinítus, -a, -um, infinite.

infirmáre, to weaken

infirmári, dep., to be weak, sick, diseased

infírmitas, -atis, f., sickness, infirmity, disease

infírmus, -a, -um, weak, sick, infirm

inflammáre, to kindle; inflame

infláre, to puff up

infléctere, -flexi, -flectus, to bend

informáre, to fashion

informátio, -onis, f., information

infra, prep. and adv., under, beneath

infrémere, -frémui, to groan

infríngere, -fregi, -fractus, to break; infringe upon

infructuósus, -a, -um, barren

infrunítus, -a, -um, bold

infúndere, -fudi, -fusus, to pour; water; infuse

infúsio, -onis, f., outpouring; infusion

ingemináre, to repeat

ingemíscere, -gémui, to groan, sigh

ingénitus, -a, -um, unbegotten

ingénium, -i, n., natural character

ingens, -entis, great, vast

ingérere, -gesse, -gestus, to pour into, infuse

ingraváre, to aggravate

ingravéscere, to become serious

íngredi, -gressus sum, dep. 3 (io), to walk along; come in

ingréssus, -us, m., procession

ingrúere, -ui, to assault

inguen, -inis, n., groin

inhabitábilis, -e, not inhabited; uninhabitable

inhabitáre, to dwell

inhaerére, -haesi, -haesus, to adhere to

inhiáre, to gape after; long for

inhonéste, adv., with dishonor

inhonoráre, to dishonor

inhonorátio, -onis, f., dishonor

inhumánus, -a, -um, brutal

inhumátus, -a, -um, unburied

ínibi, adv., in that place

inimicítia, -ae, f., enmity

inimícus, -a, -um, hostile

inimícus, -i, m., enemy

ininterpretábilis, -e, difficult to explain

iníque, wickedly, unjustly

iníquitas, -atis, f., iniquity

iníquus, -a, -um, unjust

iníre, -ivi and -ii, -itus, (eo), to enter; enter upon, undertake

initiáre, to initiate

inítium, -ii, n., beginning; corner

ínitus, -a, -um, begun, entered upon

injícere, -jeci, -jectus, (io), to lay upon

injúngere, -junxi, -junctus, to enjoin, impose

injúria, -ae, f., wrong, injury

injúste, unjustly

injustítia, -ae, f., iniquity, injustice

injústus, -a, -um, unjust

innátus, -a, -um, inborn, innate

inníti, -nixus sum, dep. 3, to lean upon; rely upon

ínnocens, -entis, innocent, clean, pure

Innocéntius, -ii, m., Innocent

innocénter, adv., innocently

innócuus, -a, -um, innocent, blameless

innotéscere, -nótui, to become known

innováre, to renew

innóxius, -a, -um, harmless, innocent

innúere, -ui, to make a sign or signal to

innumerábilis, -e, innumerable

innúmerus, -a, -um, without number, countless

innúptus, -a, -um, unmarried

inobediéntia, -ae, f., disobedience

inoffénsus, -a, -um, unhurt; inofénso pede, without tripping

inoléscere, -evi, -itus, to grow in or on

inólitus, -a, -um, ingrown

inópia, -ae, f., poverty, want

inopinátus, -a, -um, unexpected

inops, -opis, needy, destitute, afflicted

inordináte, adv., unequally

inquam, defect. verb, I say

inquietáre, to disquiet

inquiétus, -a, -um, unquiet

inquinaméntum, -i, n., stain, filthiness

inquináre, to stain, defile

inquinátus, -a, -um, defiled

inquírere, -sivi, -situs, to seek, search for, desire

inquisítio, -onis, f., inquiry; search; speculation

Inquisítio, -onis, f., Inquisition

inquisítor, -oris, m., inquisitor

inquit, defect. verb, he says

insanábilis, -e, incurable

insánia, -ae, f., madness, insanity

insaníre, to be mad, be outrageous

insánus, -i, m., madman

insatiábilis, -e, insatiable; ambitious

inscítia, -ae, f., lack of knowledge, ignorance

inscríbere, -scripsi, -scriptus, to write over

inscrutábilis, -e, unsearchable, inscrutable

inscúlpere, -sculpsi, -sculptus, to brand, carve, engrave

insecútor, -oris, m., pursuer, persecutor; tyrant foe

insensátus, -i, m., fool

insensíbilis, -e, insensible

inseparábilis, -e, inseparable

insepúltus, -a, -um, unburied

insérere, -sérui, -sertus, to enroll; entangle

insérere, -sevi, -situs, to implant

insértus, -a, -um, fixed, rooted

inservíre, to serve

insidére, -sedi, -sessus, to rest upon

insídia, -ae, f., deceit

insídiae, -arum, f. pl., snare, snares, ambush

insidiáre, to lay snares

insidiári, dep., to lie in wait

insidiátor, -oris, m., traitor

insigníre, to distinguish, honor, adorn, endow

insígnis, -e, noted, notable; notorious

insígniter, remarkably

insignítus, -a, -um, signed; known

insinuáre, to insinuate

insípiens, -entis, unwise, foolish

insipiéntia, -ae, f., folly, foolishness; in insipiéntia, foolishly

ínsitus, -a, -um, ingrafted

insoléscere, to become insolent, behave extravagantly

insolúbilis, -e, insoluble; that cannot be unlocked

insómnis, -e, sleepless

insonáre, to resound

insons, -ontis, innocent

insperátus, -a, -um, unhoped for, unexpected

inspérgere, -spersi, -spersus, to sprinkle

inspícere, -spexi, -spectus, to stare upon

inspiráre, to breathe into

inspirátio, -onis, f., inspiration; breath, blast

instábilis, -e, unstable, inconstant, having no fixed abode

instans, -antis, present; instant

instántia, -ae, f., instance

instar, indecl., n., image, likeness

instáre, -stiti, -statúrus, to insist; await; threaten

instauráre, to renew; strengthen; comprise

instaurátio, -onis, f., renewal

instaurátor, -oris, m., restorer

instínctus, -us, m., inspiration

ínstita, -ae, f., winding band

ínstitor, -oris, m., merchant

instituere, -ui, -utus, to institute, ordain

institútio, -onis, *f.*, institution; manner of life

institútor, -oris, *m.*, tutor; founder; creator

institútrix, -icis, *f.*, foundress

institútum, -i, *n.*, institute; institution

instrúctus, -a, -um, drawn up in order of battle

instrúere, -struxi, -structus, to draw up; instruct

Insúbria, -ae, *f.*, Lombardy

insudáre, to sweat at or in

insúere, -sui, -sutus, to sew up

insufflare, to blow; breathe upon

insufflátio, -onis, *f.*, a breathing upon or into

ínsula, -ae, *f.*, island; ínsulae Océani, Oceanic Islands

insulánus, -i, *m.*, islander

insultáre, to scoff at

insúmere, -sumpsi, -sumptus, to consume

ínsuper, *adv.*, in addition, moreover

insúrgere, -surréxi, -surréctus, to rise up

intáctus, -a, -um, inviolate

intaminátus, -a, -um, unspotted

ínteger, -gra, -grum, whole

integérrime, *adv.*, most rigidly

intégritas, -atis, *f.*, wholeness; health; integrity

intellectuális, -e, spiritual

intelléctus, -us, *m.*, sense, meaning; understanding, insight

intelligéntia, -ae, *f.*, knowledge, understanding, intelligence

intellígere, -lexi, -lectus, to perceive, understand; heed, attend to

intemerátus, -a, -um, spotless

intempestívus, -a, -um, untimely

intempéstus, -a, -um, unseasonable; intempésta nox, the dead of night

inténdere, -tendi, -tentus or -tensus, to mark, hearken, be attentive; direct; look steadfastly; look down mercifully upon; go forth; arcum —, to bend a bow

intentátor, -oris, *m.*, one who wars against, threatener; tempter

inténtio, -onis, *f.*, intention

inténtus, -a, -um, intent, anxious

inter, *prep.*, between, among

intercédere, -cessi, -cessus, to intercede

intercéssio, -onis, *f.*, intercession

intercéssor, -oris, *m.*, intercessor

intercídere, -cidi, -cisus, to divide, cleave

interdíctum, -i, *n.*, interdict

intérdiu, *adv.*, by day

intérea, *adv.*, in the meantime

intérere, -trivi, -tritus, to break, crumble

interésse, -fui, to be between; be different; take part in

interféctor, -oris, *m.*, slayer

interfícere, -feci, -fectus, (io), to kill, slay, put to death, destroy

ínterim, *adv.*, meanwhile

interímere, -emi, -emptus, to slay

intérior, -ius, inward; interióra, *n. pl.*, entrails

interíre, -ivi or -ii, -itus, (eo), to perish, die

interítio, -onis, *f.*, destruction

intéritus, -us, *m.*, destruction; overthrow

intérius, *adv.*, inwardly

interminátus, -a, -um, endless

intérminus, -a, -um, endless, infinite

intermíssio, -onis, *f.*, ceasing

intermíttere, -misi, -missus, to leave, let pass

internécio, -onis, *f.*, massacre, carnage

interpelláre, to make intercession

interpositio, -onis, *f.*, a bringing forward, introducing

ínterpres, -pretis, c., interpreter, ex-
pounder
interpretáre, to interpret
interpretári, dep., to expound
interpretátio, -onis, f., interpretation
interrogáre, to ask questions, inquire
interrogátio, -onis, f., question, argument, inquisition; pledge
interrúmpere, -rupi, -ruptus, to break
into; divide, cleave
intersérere, -sérui, -sertus, to place between or among
intersérere, -sevi, -situs, to sow or
plant between
intervállum, -i, n., space
intervéntio, -onis, f., intercession
intervéntor, -oris, m., intercessor
intervéntus, -us, m., intercession
intestínum, -i, n., entrail; intestína,
n. pl., bowels
intimáre, to tell, intimate
íntimus, -a, -um, inmost; íntima, n.
pl., bowels
intíngere, -tinxi, -tinctus, to dip in or
steep
intolerábilis, -e, overwhelming, un-
bearable
intonáre, -tónui, -tonátus, to thunder
intra, prep., among, within
intráre, to enter
intrínsecus, adv., within
intro, adv., in, within
introdúcere, -duxi, -ductus, to bring
into
intrógredi, -gressus sum, dep. 3 (io),
to go or come in
introíre, -ivi and -ii, -itus, (eo), to go
in or into, enter
intróitus, -us, m., going in, entering,
entrance, introit
intromíttere, -misi, -missus, to send
into; cast within or into
introspícere, -spexi, -spectus, (io), to
look in

intuéri, -túitus sum, dep. 2, to look at,
consider, behold earnestly
intúitus, -us, m., mind
intuméscere, -túmui, to swell
intus, adv., inwardly, within
inúltus, -a, -um, unpunished, unavenged
inundántia, -ae, f., inundation
inundáre, to overflow
inundátio, -onis, f., flood, multitude
inúngere, -unxi, -unctus, to anoint
inútilis, -e, useless, profitless
inutíliter, uselessly
invádere, -vasi, -vasus, to invade, usurp
invaléscere, -válui, to become strong,
be more earnest, prevail
invéhere, -vexi, -vectus, to attack
inveníre, -veni, -ventus, to come upon,
find, obtain; to bring about, effect
invéntio, -onis, f., finding
invéntor, -oris, m., inventor
inverecúndia, -ae, f., impudence
investigábilis, -e, unsearchable, unac-
countable
investigáre, to seek after, search out;
trace
inveteráre, to grow old
inveterátus, -a, -um, old, decrepit
ínvicem, adv., by turns, alternately;
ad —, reciprocally, among themselves
invíctus, -a, -um, invincible, uncon-
querable
invidére, -vidi, -visus, to envy
invídia, -ae, f., envy
ínvidus, -i, m., envious one
invigiláre, to watch over
inviolabíliter, inviolably
inviolátus, -a, -um, pure
invisáre, to go and see, visit
invisíbilis, -e, invisible
invisibíliter, invisibly
invitaméntum, -i, n., invitation
invitáre, to invite

invitátor, -oris, *m.*, one who invites
invitatórium, -ii, *n.*, invitatory
invítus, -a, -um, unwilling
ínvium, -ii, *n.*, trackless region, waste
land
ínvius, -a, -um, trackless, pathless, impassable, desert
invocáre, to call upon, invoke
invocátio, -onis, *f.*, invocation
involuménta, -orum, *n. pl.*, swaddling
clothes
invólvere, -volvi, -volútus, to wrap up;
shut up
iota, *indecl., n.*, iota, jot
ipse, -a, -um, *intensive pron.*, he (himself), etc.
ipsíssimus, -a, -um, one's very self;
ipsíssima verba, the very words
ira, -ae, *f.*, anger, wrath
iracúndia, -ae, *f.*, anger, wrath
iracúndus, -a, -um, angry
irásci, irátus sum, *dep. 3*, to be angry;
be kindled (of wrath)
irátus, -a, -um, angry
ire, ivi and ii, itus, (eo), to go
iris, -idis, *f.*, rainbow
irradiáre, to shine, illumine
irrationábilis, -e, irrational; irrationabília, *n. pl.*, irrational creatures,
animals
irrationabíliter, senselessly
irrépere, -repsi, -reptus, to creep into
irreprehensíbilis, -e, blameless, unspotted
irrevocábilis, -e, not to be turned back,
irrevocable
irridére, -risi, -risus, to laugh at
irrigátio, -onis, *f.*, watering, moistening
irríguus, -a, -um, watered
irrísor, -oris, *m.*, one who scorns, derider
irritáre, to provoke
irritátio, -onis, *f.*, provocation

irritátor, -onis, *m.*, provoker of anger
írritus, -a, -um, vain, void, unheard
irrogáre, to inflict, impose
irrúere, -ui, to rush or fall upon, beset, rush in, press upon
irrugíre, to roar out
irrúmpere, -rupi, -ruptus, to extirpate
is, ea, id, *demons. pron.*, that; he, she,
etc.
Isáacus, -i, *m.*, Isaac
Isáuricus, -i, *m.*, Isaurian
Iscarióta, -ae, *m.*, Iscariot
Iscariótes, -is, *m.*, Iscariot
Isidórus, -i, *m.*, Isidore
Islébium, -ii, *n.*, Eisleben
Ismaelítae, -arum, *m. pl.*, Ismaelites
Ismahelíta, -ae, *m.*, Ismaelite
Israëlíta, -ae, *m.*, Israelite
Israelíticus, -a, -um, Israelitish
iste, -a, -ud, *demons. pron.*, this, that
istinc, *adv.*, hence, from the place
ita, *adv.*, so, even
Ítali, -orum, *m. pl.*, Italians
Itália, -ae, *f.*, Italy
ítaque, *adv.*, therefore
item, *adv.*, likewise
iter, itíneris, *n.*, journey; departure;
way, wayside
iterátio, -onis, *f.*, renewal, repetition
íterum, *adv.*, again
ítidem, *adv.*, in like manner, likewise
Ituraéa, -ae, *f.*, Iturea

J

jacére, to lie, sleep
jácere, jeci, jactus, (io), to throw, cast
Jacóbus, -i, *m.*, James
Jacóbus de Flisco, -i, *m.*, Jacopo Fieschi
jactántia, -ae, *f.*, vainglory
jactáre, to cast
jactúra, -ae, *f.*, loss
jactus, -us, *m.*, cast, throw

jáculum, -i, *n.*, dart, arrow

jam, *adv.*, now; (with negative) no longer, no more

jamdúdum, *adv.*, now for a long time

jamjam, *adv.*, on the point of

jamprídem, *adv.*, now for a long time

jánitor, -oris, *m.*, gate keeper, porter

jánua, -ae, *f.*, door, gate

Januárius, -ii, *m.*, January; Januarius

Japon, -is, *m.*, Japan

Japónia, -ae, *f.*, Japan

Jarláthus, -i, *m.*, Jarlath

jaspis, -idis, *f.*, jasper

Jebusaéus, -i, *m.*, Jebusite

jecur, jécoris (jecínoris), *n.*, liver

jejunáre, to fast, abstain

jejúnium, -ii, *n.*, fast, fasting

jejúnus, -a, -um, *fasting*

Jerosólyma, -orum, *n. pl.*, Jerusalem

Jerosólymi, -orum, *m. pl.*, people of Jerusalem

Jerosolymitánus, -a, -um, of Jerusalem

Jesus Nave, Josue the son of Nun

Jezrahelítes, -is, *f.*, Jezrahelitess

Joánna, -ae, *f.*, Johanna, Jane, Joan

Joánnes, -is, *m.*, John

Joánnes Baptísta, -is, -ae, *m.*, John the Baptist

Joánnes Cántius, -is, -ii, *m.*, John Cantius

Jobus, -i, *m.*, Job

jocári, *dep.*, to jest

jod, the tenth letter of the Hebrew alphabet, corresponding to English *y*

Jojada, -ae, *m.*, Joiada

Jónathas, -ae, *m.*, Jonathan

Jordanis, -is, *m.*, the Jordan

Jósaphat (us) Kuncewítius, -i, -ii, *m.*, Jehoshaphat Kuncewicz

Jovis, -is, *m.*, Jove

jubar, -aris, *n.*, a beaming light, radiance

jubére, jussi, jussus, to command; ask

jubilaéus, -i, *m.*, jubilee

jubiláre, to shout, sing joyfully

jubilátio, -onis, *f.*, jubilee; gladness; festival cry

júbilum, -i, *n.*, jubilee, joy

jucundáre, to shout for joy

jucundári, *dep.*, to have joy, be glad

jucúnde, merrily

jucúnditas, -atis, *f.*, cheerfulness, joy

jucúndus, -a, -um, pleasing

Judaéa, -ae, *f.*, Judea

Judaéus, -i, *m.*, Jew

Judáicus, -a, -um, Jewish

judaizáre, to Judaize, convert to the doctrines or methods of the Jews

Judas, -ae, *m.*, Judas; Jude

judex, -icis, *m.*, judge

judicáre, to judge

judiciális, -e, judicial

judícium, -ii, *n.*, judgment, matter of judgment

jugális, -e, pertaining to a yoke; connecting

jugáre, to bind together; marry, espouse

júgerum, -i, *n.*, acre

jugis, -e, perpetual, continual

júgiter, *adv.*, ever, forever, always

juguláre, to cut the throat, slay

júgulum, -i, *n.*, throat

jugum, -i, *n.*, yoke, bond, fetter

Juliána de Falconnérii, -ae, *f.*, Juliana Falconieri

Juliánus, -i, *m.*, Julian

Juliánus Adúrnus, -i, -i, *m.*, Giuliano Adorno

Juliánus Apóstata, -i, -ae, *m.*, Julian the Apostate

Július, -ii, *m.*, July

jumentum, -i, *n.*, beast; (pl.) cattle

junctúra, -ae, *f.*, joint

juncus, -i, *m.*, bulrush

júngere, junxi, junctus, to join, bind, unite

júnior, -oris, young; younger

juníperus, -i, *f.*, juniper tree

Június, -ii, *m.*, June; Junius

juraméntum, -i, *n.*, oath

juráre, to swear

jurgáre, to contend in words, quarrel

jurgári, *dep.*, to quarrel

júrgum, -ii, *n.*, quarrel

jurisprudéntia, -ae, *f.*, law

jus, juris, *n.*, law

jusjurándum, jurisjurándi, *n.*, oath

jussio, -onis, *f.*, command

jussus, *m.*, used only in ablative, jussu, by command

juste, righteously, justly

justificáre, to justify; do justice to

justificátio, -onis, *f.*, statute, ordinance; justification

Justiniáni, -orum, *m. pl.*, Giustiniani

Justiniánus, -i, *m.*, Justinian

Justínus, -i, *m.*, Justin; Justinian

justítia, -ae, *f.*, justice

justus, -a, -um, right, righteous, just

juvámen, -inis, *n.*, help

Juvenális, -is, *m.*, Juvenal

juvéncula, -ae, *f.*, maiden

juvénculus, -i, *m.*, bullock

juvenéscere, -ui, to be young, to reach the age of youth

júvenis, -e, young; (as a noun) young man

juvénta, -ae, *f.*, youth

juvéntus, -utis, *f.*, youth

juxta, *prep.* and *adv.*, near, close to, by, at hand; according to

K

Kaléndae, -arum, *f. pl.*, calends, the first day of the Roman month

Kalendárius, -ii, *m.*, calendar

Kerriénsis, -e, of Kerry

Killéedy, Killadysert

Kiowénsis, -e, of Kieff

Kyrie (Greek), Lord

L

labáre, to totter, waver

labáscere, to begin to fall, totter

labes, -is, *f.*, stain, blemish

labi, lapsus sum, *dep. 3*, to fall

lábium, -ii, *n.*, lip

labor, -oris, *m.*, labor; mischief

laboráre, to labor

laboriósus, -a, -um, toilsome, laborious

labrúsca, -ae, *f.*, wild grape

labrum, -i, *n.*, lip

lac, lactis, *n.*, milk

lacer, -a, -um, torn, ragged

laceráre, to rend

lácrima, -ae, *f.*, tear

lacrimábilis, -e, woeful, worthy of tears

lacrimári, *dep.*, to weep

lacrimósus, -a, -um, tearful

lactáre, to give suck

lactens, -entis, *f.*, suckling

lactúca, -ae, lettuce

lacus, -us, *m.*, lake; pit; den

laédere, laesi, laesus, to do harm, injure

laetabúndus, -a, -um, full of joy

laetári, *dep.*, to rejoice

laetificáre, to give joy

laetítia, -ae, *f.*, gladness

laetus, -a, -um, joyful

laeva, -ae, *f.*, the left; left hand; ad laevam, on the left hand or arm

laevigátus, -a, -um, smooth, polished

lagéna, -ae, *f.*, pitcher

Lagénia, -ae, *f.*, Leinster

laicális, -e, lay

láicus, -a, -um, lay, common

láicus, -i, *m.*, layman

Lalovéscum, -i, *n.*, La Louvesc

lámbere, lambi, lámbitus, to lick

lamed, the twelfth letter of the Hebrew alphabet, corresponding to English *l*

lamentáre, to lament

lamentári, *dep.*, to lament

lamentátio, -onis, *f.*, lamentation

laméntum, -i, *n.*, wailing, lamentation

lámia, -ae, *f.*, sea monster

lámina, -ae, *f.*, metal plate

lampas, -adis, *f.*, lamp, torch; flame

Lampértus, -i, *m.*, Lampert

lana, -ae, *f.*, wool

láncea, -ae, *f.*, spear, lance

Lancellótus, -i, *m.*, Lancelot

lancináre, to mangle

lancis, -is, *f.*, event; aequa lance, likewise

Landúlfus, -i, *m.*, Landulf

Landúnum, -i, *n.*, Laon

láneus, -a, -um, woolen

Lanfráncus, -i, *m.*, Lanfranc

languens, -entis, sick

languére, -ui, to be faint or weak, swoon

lánguidus, -a, -um, infirm

lánguor, -oris, *m.*, disease, sickness, infirmity

laniáre, to mangle

laniátus, *m.*, mangling

lantérna, -ae, *f.*, lantern

lantgrávius, -ii, *m.*, landgrave

lapidáre, to stone

lapídeus, -a, -um, of stone; stony

lapíllus, -i, *m.*, gem

lapis, -idis, *m.*, stone

lapsus, -us, *m.*, slipping, falling

láquear, -aris, *n.*, panel, rafter, ceiling

láqueus, -i, *m.*, snare, halter

lárgiens, -entis, bountiful

largíri, *dep. 4*, to grant, bestow

lárgitas, -atis, *f.*, bounty

lárgitor, -oris, *m.*, one who grants

lárgius, *adv.*, more abundantly

largus, -a, -um, abundant

larva, -ae, *f.*, ghost

lassitúdo, -inis, *f.*, weariness

lassus, -a, -um, faint, tired

látebra, -ae, *f.*, concealment, subterfuge

laténter, secretly

later, -eris, *m.*, brick

Lateranénsis, -e, Lateran, of the Lateran

latére, -ui, to be hidden

latérna, -ae, *f.*, lantern

latex, -icis, *m.*, liquid; water

latíbulum, -i, *n.*, hiding place, covert

latíne, *adv.*, in Latin

latínus, -a, -um, Latin

latitáre, to lie hidden, be concealed

latitúdo, -inis, *f.*, breadth; a large place; in latitúdine, at liberty

latráre, to bark

latría, -ae, *f.*, worship

latro, -onis, *m.*, thief, robber

latrúnculus, -i, *m.*, robber, bandit; rover

latus, -eris, *n.*, side

latus, -a, -um, broad

laudábilis, -e, praiseworthy, laudable; glorious

laudabíliter, laudably

laudáre, to praise

laudátio, -onis, *f.*, praise

laudátor, -oris, *m.*, one who praises

laudes, -um, *f. pl.*, lauds

laura, -ae, *f.*, a kind of monastery

láurea, -ae, *f.*, laurel; laurel crown; triumph, victory

laureátus, -a, -um, crowned with laurel

Lauréntius, -ii, *m.*, Lawrence

Lauretánus, -a, -um, of Loreto

laus, laudis, *f.*, praise

lavácrum, -i, *n.*, laver; bath; water of baptism

laváre (lávere), lavi, lautus (lotus), to wash

Lavicánus, -a, -um, Lavican

laxáre, to let down, relax

laxus, -a, -um, loose

leaéna, -ae, *f.*, lioness

lebes, -etis, *m.*, wash basin; kettle

léctio, -onis, *f.*, reading; lesson

lector, -oris, *m.*, reader, lector

léctulus, -i, *m.*, small bed; couch

lectus, -a, -um, choice, eminent

lectus, -i, *m.*, bed

lécythus, -i, *m.*, flask

legális, -e, legal

legátio, -onis, *f.*, duty of a legate; legation, embassage

legátus, -i, *m.*, legate, ambassador

légere, legi, lectus, to read

légifer, -i, *m.*, lawgiver

légio, -onis, *f.*, band; legion

Légio, -onis, *f.*, Leon

legislátor, -oris, *m.*, lawgiver; master

legisperítus, -i, *m.*, lawyer

legítime, lawfully

legítimum, -i, *n.*, ordinance

legítimus, -a, -um, legal

legúmen, -inis, *n.*, pulse; bean; vegetable

leníre, to mitigate, relieve

lenis, -e, smooth; mild, easy

lénitas, -atis, *f.*, meekness

léniter, gently

lentéscere, to relax

lentícula, -ae, *f.*, little bottle; vial

leo, -onis, *m.*, lion

Leo, -onis, *m.*, Leo

Leonárdus, -i, *m.*, Leonard

leopárdus, -i, *m.*, leopard

Leópolis, -is, *f.*, Lemberg

Leovigíldus, -i, *m.*, Leovigild

lepra, -ae, *f.*, leprosy

leprósus, -a, -um, leprous

leprósus, -i, *m.*, leper

Leptinénsis, -e, of Lessines

lethális, -e, lethal

levámen, -inis, *n.*, consolation, alleviation

levaméntum, -i, *n.*, mitigation, rest

leváre, to lift up, raise

leúnculus, -i, *m.*, young lion

levigáre, to polish, furbish

levis, -e, light

Levíta, -ae, *m.*, Levite

lex, legis, *f.*, law; legem fácere, to keep the law

libámen, -inis, *n.*, libation, drink offering

líbanus, -i, *m.*, frankincense

libáre, to celebrate a religious rite

libátio, -onis, *f.*, libation; partaking

libatórium, -ii, *n.*, pouring vessel

libéllus, -i, *m.*, a writing, a bill

libénter, gladly

liber, -a, -um, free; fearless; abandoned

Liber, -i, *m.* Bacchus

liber, -bri, *m.*, book

líbera, -ae, *f.*, free woman

liberáre, to free, deliver

liberátor, -oris, *m.*, deliverer

líbere, *adv.*, freely; steadfastly

líberi, -orum, *m. pl.*, children

Liberiánus, -a, -um, Liberian

líbertas, -atis, *f.*, freedom

Libertíni, -orum, *m. pl.*, Libertines

libet (lubet), -buit, -bitum est, *impers.*, it pleases, is agreeable

libído, -inis, *f.*, lust

libra, -ae, *f.*, pound

libráre, to weigh, poise, balance

librárius, -ii, *m.*, copyist

libum, -i, *n.*, a cake offered to the gods; an offering

licet, lícuit, lícitum est, *impers.*, it is allowed or lawful; one may or can; licet, although

liciatórium, -ii, *n.*, beam

Liciniánus, -a, -um, Licinian

ligáre, to bind
lígneus, -a, -um, wooden
lignum, -i, *n.*, wood; stick; staff; tree
ligo, -onis, *m.*, spade
Ligórius, -ii, *m.*, Liguori
Ligúria, -ae, *f.*, Liguria; Piedmont
liliátus, -a, um, decorated with lilies; lily white
lílium, -ii, *n.*, lily
Limánus, -a, -um, of Lima
linátus, -a, -um, polished, furbished
limen, -inis, *n.*, threshold
Limericénsis, -e, of Limerick
limes, -itis, *m.*, boundary, limit
limpidíssimus, -a, -um, very smooth
limus, -i, *m.*, mud, mire, dirt
línea, -ae, *f.*, line
lineaméntum, -i, *n.*, feature, delineation
línere, livi and levi, litus, (io), to anoint
líneus, -a, -um, of flax; linen
língere, linxi, linctus, to lick
lingua, -ae, *f.*, tongue; language
linguósus, -a, -um, evil tongued
liníre, to smear, besmear, spread; anoint
linóstemus, -a, -um, linen
línquere, liqui, to leave
linteámen, -inis, *n.*, linen cloth
línteum, -i, *n.*, towel; linen cloth
linum, -i, *n.*, flax
Liparitánus, -a, -um, of Lipari
liquáre, to melt
liquefácere, -feci, -factus, (io), to melt
liquefactívus, -a, -um, melting
liquefáctus, -a, -um, melted
liquére, líqui or lícui, to be evident
liquéscere, lícui, to melt
liquor, -oris, *m.*, liquid
lis, litis, *f.*, debate, contention
litanía, -ae, *f.*, litany
litáre, to offer
Lithuáni, -orum, *m. pl.*, Lithuanians

litigáre, to quarrel, strive, wrangle
litigiósus, -a, -um, quarrelsome
líttera, -ae, *f.*, letter of the alphabet,
líterae, *pl.*, a letter; bill
litteratúra, -ae, *f.*, learning; writing
littus, -oris, *n.*, shore
litúra, -ae, *f.*, daubing
liturgía, -ae, *f.*, liturgy
lívidus, -a, -um, envious
livor, -oris, *m.*, bruise
locáre, to place; let out, rent, hire out
lóculus, -i, *m.*, coffin, bier; tomb; purse
lócuples, -etis, rich
locupletáre, to enrich
locus, -i, *m.* (*pl.* loca, -orum, *n.*),
place; position, station; room
locústa, -ae, *f.*, locust
locútio, -onis, *f.*, word
Londinénsis, -e, of London
Londínium, -ii, *n.*, London
longaévus, -a, -um, long-lived
longánimis, -e, longsuffering
longanímitas, -atis, *f.*, longsuffering
longe, *adv.*, afar; a longe, afar off; longe latéque, far and wide
longínquus, -a, -um, far, distant, afar off; de longínquo, from afar
longitúdo, -inis, *f.*, length
longitúrnitas, -atis, *f.*, length
Longobárdi, -orum, *m. pl.*, Lombards
loquéla, -ae, *f.*, saying; speech
loqui, locútus sum, *dep. 3*, to speak, converse; profess
loríca, -ae, *f.*, coat of mail; breastplate
lorum, -i, *n.*, leather strap, thong; scourge, whip
Lotharíngia, -ae, *f.*, Lorraine
lotus, -a, -um, washed
lúbricum, -i, *n.*, slipperiness
lúbricus, -a, -um, slippery; dangerous, impure
Lucas, -ae, *m.*, Luke
lucére, -luxi, to shine
lucérna, -ae, *f.*, candle, lamp

lucéscere, luxi, to begin to dawn
Lúcia, -ae, *f.*, Lucy
lúcidus, -a, -um, bright
lúcifer, -i, *m.*, day star, morning star
Lucílla, -ae, *f.*, Lucille
lucrári, *dep.*, to gain
lucratívus, -a, -um, profitable
lucrifácere, -feci, -factus, (io), to win
lucrum, -i, *n.*, lucre; gain
luctámen, -inis, *n.*, struggling, wrestling
luctátor, -oris, *m.*, wrestler
luctuósus, -a, -um, sorrowful
luctus, -us, *m.*, mourning
lucubrátio, -onis, *f.*, laborious study
luculénte, admirably
luculénter, excellently
luculéntus, -a, -um, bright
lucus, -i, *m.*, grove; sacred grove
lúdere, lusi, lusus, to play
ludíbrium, -ii, *n.*, mockery, scorn
Ludovícus, -i, *m.*, Louis
Ludúlphus, -i, *m.*, Ludolph
ludus, -i, *m.*, game
lues, -is, *f.*, disease
Lugdunénsis, -e, of Lyons
Lugdúnum, -i, *n.*, Lyons
lugére, luxi, luctus, to bewail, lament
Luitprándus, -i, *m.*, Luitprand
lumbus, -i, *m.;* (*pl.*) loins
lumen, -inis, *n.*, light
Lumílla, -ae, *f.*, Ludmilla
luminàre, -aris, *n.*, light
luna, -ae, *f.*, moon
lunáticus, -i, *m.*, lunatic
lupánar, -aris, *n.*, brothel
lupínus, -i, *m.*, lupine
lupínus, -a, -um, wolfish
lupus, -i, *m.*, wolf
Lusitánia, -ae, *f.*, Portugal
lustrális, -e, holy, blessed
lustráre, to purify
lustrum, -i, *n.*, a period of five years, a
luster

lusus, -us, *m.*, game
Lutétia Parisiórum, -ae, *f.*, Paris
lúteus, -a, -um, of clay
Lútherus, -i, *m.*, Luther
lutum, -i, *n.*, clay, dirt
lux, lucis, *f.*, light, dawn
luxúria, -ae, *f.*, dissipation, lust; luxury
luxuriári, *dep.*, to live riotously
luxurióse, riotously
luxus, -us, *m.*, lust
lychnus, -i, *m.*, lamp
lympha, -ae, *f.*, water
lyra, -ae, *f.*, lute
Lystrae, -arum, *f. pl.*, Lystra

M

Mácedo, -onis, *m.*, Macedonian
Macedónia, -ae, *f.*, Macedonia
maceráre, to afflict, mortify
macerátio, -onis, *f.*, mortification
macéria, -ae, *f.*, wall; fence
Machabaéi, -orum, *m. pl.*, Machabees
Machaéa, -ae, *m.*, Mahew
machaéra, -ae, *f.*, sword
máchina, -ae, *f.*, machine; device;
fabric, frame
mácies, -ei, *f.*, thinness, emaciation
maciléntus, -a, -um, thin, lean
mactáre, to offer as a sacrifice, kill;
punish
mácula, -ae, *f.*, stain, blemish
maculáre, to accuse
maculósus, -a, -um, spotted
madefácere, -feci, -factus, (io), to
make wet, soak
madére, mádui, to drink too much, be
drunk
madéscere, mádui, to become wet
Madianíti, -orum, *m. pl.*, Madianites
maerére, to be sorrowful
maestus, -ae, -um, sad
Magdeburgénsis, -e, of Magdeburg
Magdebúrgus, -i, *m.*, Magdeburg

Magdaléna (Magdaléne), -ae, *f.*, Magdalen

mágicus, -a, -um, magic

magis, *adv.*, rather; plus magis, far more

magíster, -tri, *m.*, master; teacher

magistérium, -ii, *n.*, office, power

magístra, -ae, *f.*, teacher; mistress

magistrátus, -us, *m.*, magistrate

magnália, -ium, *n. pl.*, wonderful works, wonders

magnátus, -i, *m.*, great man

magnes, -etis, *m.*, magnet, loadstone

Magnesiáni, -orum, *m. pl.*, Magnesians

magnificáre, to enlarge, magnify; glorify, exalt

magnífice, nobly, generously

magnificéntia, -ae, *f.*, magnificence, majesty

magníficus, -a, -um, glorious

magníloquus, -a, -um, boastful

magnitúdo, -inis, *f.*, greatness

magnópere, *adv.*, greatly

magnus, -a, -um, great; magna, *n.pl.*, great things

magus, -i, *m.*, wise or learned man; magician, sorcerer

Mahometáni (Mahumetáni) -orum, *m. pl.*, Mohammedans

májestas, -atis, *f.*, majesty

major, majus, greater; elder

Majórga, -ae, *f.*, Mayorga

Majus, -i, *m.*, May

Málaca, -ae, *f.*, Malacca

malágma, -atis, *n.*, plaster

Malcólmus, -i, *m.*, Malcolm

male, *adv.*, badly, ill; grievously

maledícere, -dixi, -dictus, to speak evil, revile, curse

maledíctio, -onis, *f.*, curse

maledíctum, -i, *n.*, abusive language, railing

malédicus, -a, -um, evil speaking

malédicus, -i, *m.*, railer

malefáctor, -oris, *m.*, malefactor, evildoer

malévolus, -a, -um, malicious

malígnans, -antis, malicious, wicked

malignáre (-ari), to do wickedly

malígnitas, -atis, *f.*, evil, malice

malígnus, -a, -um, malignant; (*as a noun*), evildoer

malítia, -ae, *f.*, malice; naughtiness; evil

malitióse, maliciously

malle, málui, to prefer

malleátor, -oris, *m.*, hammerer

málleus, -i, *m.*, hammer, mallet

malum, -i, *n.*, evil

malum, -i, *n.*, apple, — púnicum, pomegranate

malus, -a, -um, bad, evil, wicked

Mamertínus, -a, -um, Mamertine

mamílla, -ae, *f.*, breast, pap

mamma, -ae, *f.*, breast, pap

mammóna, -ae, *m.*, mammon

manáre, to flow, pour forth

mancipáre, to deliver up

mancípium, -ii, *n.*, slave

mandáre, to command, give charge over

mándere, mandi, mansus, to eat

mandátum, -i, *n.*, command, commandment

mandragóra, -ae, *f.*, mandrake

manducáre, to eat

manducátio, -onis, *f.*, eating

mane, *adv.*, in the morning, early morning; primo —, early in the morning; sumo —, valde —, very early in the morning

manére, mansi, mansus, to remain, abide, tarry, wait

Manéttus Antellénsis, -i, -is, *m.*, Manetto Antalli

mánica, -ae, *f.*, manicle

Manichaéi, -orum, *m. pl.*, Manichaeans

manifestáre, to make manifest, discover, reveal

manifestátio, -onis, *f.*, manifestation

maniféste, openly, plainly, manifestly

manípulus, -i, *m.*, handful; sheaf; maniple

manna, -ae, *f.*, manna

mánsio, -onis, *f.*, abode, dwelling

mansiúncula, -ae, *f.*, little room

mansuetúdo, -inis, *f.*, meekness

mansuétus, -a, -um, meek, mild, humble

mansúrus, -a, -um, enduring

mantéllum, -i, *n.*, cloak

manufáctus, -a, -um, made with hands

manus, us, *f.*, hand; power

marcére, to wither

marcéscere, to fade away, to wither, to decay

márchio, -onis, *m.*, marquis

márcidus, -a, -um, withered; delicate

Márcio, -onis, *f.*, Marcion

Marcus, -i, *m.*, Mark

Mardochaéus, -i, *m.*, Mardochai

mare, maris, *n.*, sea

margaríta, -ae, *f.*, pearl

Margaríta, -ae, *f.*, Margaret

María, -ae, *f.*, Mary

Mariális, -e, of Mary

marínus, -a, -um, sea, of the sea

maritális, -e, of wedlock, marital

maritáre, to marry, give in marriage

marítima, -orum, *n. pl.*, seacoast

marítus, -i, *m.*, husband

marmóreus, -a, -um, marble, of marble

Maróchius (Marróchius), -ii, *m.*, Morocco

marsúpium, -ii, *n.*, purse

Martiális, -is, *m.*, Martial

Martiniánus, -i, *m.*, Martinian

Martínus, -i, *m.*, Martin

Mártius, -ii, *m.*, March

martyr, -is, *m.*, martyr

martýrium, -ii, *n.*, martyrdom

martyrológium, -ii, *n.*, martyrology

masculínus, -a, -um, masculine

másculus, -a, -um, male

massa, -ae, *f.*, lump

Massília, -ae, *f.*, Marseilles

Massiliénsis, -e, of Marseilles

mater, -tris, *f.*, mother

materfamílias, matrisfamílias, *f.*, mistress of the house

matéria, -ae, *f.*, substance

matérnitas, -atis, *f.*, maternity

materiáliter, materially

matérnus, -a, -um, maternal

matértera, -ae, *f.*, mother's sister, maternal aunt

Matrítum, -i, *n.*, Madrid

matróna, -ae, *f.*, matron, lady

Matthaéus, -i, *m.*, Matthew

matúre, early

maturéscere, -ui, to ripen

matúritas, -atis, *f.*, fullness; early morning, dawn

matutínum, -i, *n.*, mattins; night watch

matutínus, -a, -um, morning, early

Mauri, -orum, *m. pl.*, Moors

Máuricus, -a, -um, Moorish

Maurítius, -ii, *m.*, Maurice

maxílla, -ae, *f.*, jaw; cheek

máxime, *adv.*, especially, chiefly

Maximiánus, -i, *m.*, Maximian

Maximínus, -i, *m.*, Maximin

maximópere, *adv.*, exceedingly

máximus, -a, -um, greatest; very great; most grievous

medéla, -ae, *f.*, healing remedy

medéri, *dep. 2*, to heal

mediáre, to be in the middle; festo mediánte, about the midst of the feast

mediátor, -oris, *m.*, mediator

mediátrix, -icis, *f.*, mediatrix

medicámen, -inis, *n.*, medicine

medicátio, -onis, *f.*, remedy, healing power

medicína, -ae, f., remedy
medicinális, -e, salutary, healing
médicus, -i, m., physician
medíetas, -atis, f., the half
Mediolanénsis, -e, of Milan, Milanese
Mediolánum, -i, n., Milan
meditáre (-ari), to meditate, devise
meditátio, -onis, f., thought, meditation
médium, -ii, n., the midst, middle
médius, -a, -um, middle, midst
médius, adv., in the midst
medúlla, -ae, f., marrow
medullátus ,-a, -um, full of marrow
medúllitus, adv., in the very marrow
Medus, -i, m., Mede
meípsum, me + ipsum, myself
mel, mellis, n., honey
Meldénsis, -e, of Meaux
Meletiánus, -a, -um, Meletian
mélior, -ius, better; in mélius, for the better
mellífluus, -a, -um, dripping with honey or sweetness
melos, -i, n., song, hymn, melody
melóta, -ae, f., sheepskin
melóte, -is, f., sheepskin coat
mem, the thirteenth letter of the Hebrew alphabet, corresponding to English m
membrána, -ae, f., parchment
membrátim, adv., limb from limb
membrum, -i, n., member, limb
meminísse, defect. verb, to be mindful
memor, -oris, mindful
memoráre, to recall, remember
memorári, dep., to remember
memorátus, -us, m., mention
memória, -ae, f., remembrance
memoriále, -is, n., memorial, remembrance
memoriális, -e, memorial
mendácium, -ii, n., lie, lying, falsehood

mendax, -acis, false
mendax, -acis, m., liar
mendicáre, to beg
mendícitas, -atis, f., want, poverty
mendícus, -a, -um, poor, needy
mendícus, -i, m., beggar
mens, mentis, f., mind; mente capti, lunatics
mensa, -ae, f., table; banquet; bank
mensis, -is, m., month
mensor, -oris, m., measurer
menstruáta, -ae, f., menstruous woman
menstruátus, -a, -um, menstruous
ménstruus, -a, -um, monthly
mensúra, -ae, f., measure
mensurábilis, -e, measurable; short
méntio, -onis, f., mention
mentíri, dep. 4, to lie
mentum, -i, n., chin; throat
merácus, -a, -um, pure
mercári, dep. 4, to buy
mercatúra, -ae, f., trade; mercatúram fácere, to engage in trade
mercátus, -us, m., traffic
mercenárius, -ii, m., hired servant; hireling
merces, -edis, f., reward, ransom; hire, pay, wages; Virgo de Mercéde, Our Lady of Ransom
Mercúrius, -ii, m., Mercury
meréri, dep. 2, to be worthy, merit, deserve
méretrix, -icis, f., harlot
mérgere, mersi, mersus, to sink
merídianus, -a, -um, noonday; of the south, southern
merídies, -ei, m., midday, noon; south; per merídiem, at noon
meridionális, -e, south
mérito, adv., deservedly
méritum, -i, n., merit
Merulánus, -a, -um, Merulan
merum, -i, n., wine (unmixed with water)

Messána, -ae, *f.*, Messina
messis, -is, *f.*, harvest
messor, -oris, *m.*, reaper
meta, -ae, *f.*, goal
metállum, -i, *n.*, mine
metáphora, -ae, *f.*, metaphor
métere, méssui, messus, to reap
méthodus, -i, *f.*, method
metíri, mensus sum, *dep. 4,* to measure
metréta, -ae, *f.*, a Greek liquid measure containing about nine English gallons
métricus, -a, -um, metrical
metrópolis, -is, *f.*, chief or capital city
metropolitánus, -a, -um, metropolitan
metropolitánus, -i, *m.*, metropolitan
metropolítus, -i, *m.*, metropolitan
metrum, -i, *n.*, meter, verse
metúere, -ui, -utus, to be afraid
metus, -us, *m.*, fear
Metýmna Campi, -ae, *f.*, Medina del Campo
meus, -a, -um, my, mine
Mexicánus, -a, -um, Mexican
mi, *voc.* of meus; fili mi, my son
mica, -ae, *f.*, crumb, morsel
micans, -antis, shining, radiant
micáre, -ui, to shine
Michaéas, -ae, *m.*, Micheas
migráre, to depart
migrátio, -onis, *f.*, departure
miles, -itis, *m.*, soldier
mílitans, -antis, militant; *as a noun,* soldier
militáre, to serve as a soldier; to war
milítia, -ae, *f.*, army; soldiers
mille, one thousand; *pl.,* mília
millésimus, -a, -um, thousandth
milliárium, -ii, *n.*, mile; milestone
míllies, a thousand times
milvus, -i, *m.*, stork
mináciter, *adv.*, threateningly; by threats
minae, -arum, *f. pl.*, threats

minax, -acis, threatening
Míncius, -ii, *m.*, Mincio
míngere, minxi, minctus, to urinate
mínimus, -a, -um, smallest, least; mínimum, a very small thing
miníster, -tri, *m.*, minister; servant; waiter; primarius sacrórum —, chaplain general
ministérium, -ii, *n.*, ministry
minístra, -ae, *f.*, servant
ministráre, to serve, minister
ministrátor, -oris, *m.*, one who serves, server
minitári, *dep.*, to threaten
minoráre, to decrease
minor, minus, less, lesser; younger; least; Fratres Minóres, Friars Minor
minúere, -ui, -utus, to abate, diminish, make less
minus, *adv.*, less; si quo —, if not; paulo —, *adv.*, almost
minúsculus, -a, -um, small
minútum, -i, *n.*, mite
mirábilis, -e, wonderful
mirabíliter, wonderfully
mirabílium, -ii, *n.*, wonder
miráculum, -i, *n.*, miracle
Miramolínus, -i, *m.*, Miramolin
mirandus, -a, -um, extraordinary, strange
mirári, *dep.*, to wonder; mira, behold
mirificáre, to make wonderful, to show forth wonderfully
mirus, -a, -um, wonderful
miscére, -cui, mixtus, to mix
Misénus, -ae, of Miseno
miser, -a, -um, wretched
miserári, *dep.*, to have pity on
miserátio, -onis, *f.*, mercy
miserátor, -oris, merciful, compassionate; *(as a noun)* one who shows mercy
miseréri, misértus sum, *dep. 2,* to have mercy on

miséria, -ae, *f.*, wretchedness; trouble
misericórdia, -ae, *f.*, mercy, kindness
misericórditer, mercifully
miséricors, -ordis, merciful
missa, -ae, *f.*, Mass
missale, -is, *n.*, missal
míssio, -onis, *f.*, mission
mistum (mixtum), -i, *n.*, mixture
mitéscere, to grow mild, subside
mitigáre, to diminish, weaken, subdue, mitigate
mitis, -e, tender, mild
míttere, misi, missus, to send; cast; put, lay
mitra, -ae, *f.*, bonnet; miter
mixtúra, -ae, *f.*, mixture
mixtus, -a, -um, mingled
mna, -ae, *f.*, a mina
Moabítidae, -arum, *f. pl.*, women of Moab
mobílitas, -atis, *f.*, changeability, fickleness
moderári, *dep.*, to govern, regulate
moderátor, -oris, *m.*, moderator, director, guide, adviser; confessor
modéstia, -ae, *f.*, modesty
módicum, -i, *n.*, a little while
módicus, -a, -um, little; módicum quid, a little something
módius, -ii, *m.*, bushel
modo, *adv.*, now, even now, presently, just
modulátio, -onis, *f.*, singing
módulus, -i, *m.*, melody, rhythm
modus, -i, *m.*, way, manner, fashion; measure; supra modum, above measure
moecha, -ae, *f.*, adulteress
moechári, *dep.*, to commit adultery
moechus, -i, *m.*, adulterer
moénia, -ium, *n. pl.*, ramparts
moeror, -oris, *m.*, grief, sorrow
moestítia, -ae, *f.*, sorrow
moestitúdo, -inis, *f.*, sadness

moestus, -a, -um, afflicted, sorrowful
Mogrovéjus, -a, -um, Mogrovejo
Mogúntia, -ae, *f.*, Mainz
Moguntínus, -a, -um, of Mainz
mola, -ae, *f.*, jaw tooth, molar; —
  asinária, millstone
moláris, -is, *m.*, cheek tooth, molar
Moldáva, -ae, *f.*, Moldau
molendínum, -i, *n.*, mill
mólere, -ui, -itus, to grind
moles, -is, *f.*, mass, bulk
molestári, *dep.*, to molest
moléstia, -ae, *f.*, trouble; harm
moléstus, -a, -um, grievous, troublesome
molímen, -inis, *n.*, effort; working
Molíni, -orum, *m. pl.*, Moulins
molíri, *dep. 4*, to plot; practice
molítio, -onis, *f.*, demolition
mollíre, to make smooth, soften
mollis, -e, soft
mólliter, gently
mollíties, -ei, *f.*, softness
mollítus, -a, -um, soft
momentáneus, -a, -um, fleeting
moméntum, -i, *n.*, movement, motion; change; weight; importance; moment
mónacha, -ae, *f.*, nun
mónachus, -i, *m.*, monk
monastérium, -ii, *n.*, monastery
monásticus, -a, -um, monastic
monére, to warn; teach
moniális, -is, *f.*, nun
moníle, -is, *n.*, necklace; jewel
monítio, -onis, *f.*, warning
mónitor, -oris, *m.*, adviser
mónitum, -i, *n.*, precept; admonition
mónitus, -us, *m.*, warning
Monothelítae, -arum, *m. pl.*, Monothelites
mons, montis, *m.*, hill, mount, mountain
Mons Major, -tis, -is, *m.*, Montemor

Mons Olivéti, -tis, *m.*, Mount of Olives

Mons Regális in Subalpínis, -tis, -is, *m.*, Mondovi

monstráre, to show; command

montána, -orum, *n. pl.*, hill country

Montanísta, -ae, *m.*, Montanist

Montereyénsis, -e, of Monterey

Montília, -ae, *f.*, Montilla

monuméntum, -i, *n.*, monument; sepulcher, grave

mora, -ae, *f.*, delay; hindrance

morális, -e, moral

morári, *dep.*, to delay; abide

Morasthítes, -is, *m.*, Morasthite

Morávi, -orum, *m. pl.*, Moravians

mórbidus, -a, -um, diseased, depraved

morbus, -i, *m.*, disease

mordax, -acis, stinging, piercing

mordére, mómordi, morsus, to bite; take hold upon

mori, mórtuus sum, *dep. 3,* (io), to die

morígerus, -a, -um, compliant, accommodating

mors, mortis, *f.*, death

morsus, -us, *m.*, bite, eating

mortális, -e, mortal

mortaríolum, -i, *m.*, little mortar

morticínum, -i, *n.*, corpse

mórtifer, -a, -um, deadly

mortificáre, to mortify; kill

mórtuus, -a, -um, dead; (*as a noun*) the dead

morus, -i, *f.*, mulberry tree

mos, moris, *m.*, custom, manner; action

Mosáicus, -a, -um, Mosaic

Moscóvia, -ae, *f.*, Moscow

motábilis, -e, moving

mótio, -onis, *f.*, movement, motion

motus, -us, *m.*, motion, moving; emotion; tempest; tumult

movére, movi, motus, to move; affect, influence; quake

movéri, motus sum, *dep. 2,* to move

Móyses, -i, *m.*, Moses

mucro, -onis, *m.*, sharp edge or point

mugíre, to low

mula, -ae, *f.*, mule

mulcére, mulsi, mulsus, to charm

mulcta, -ae, *f.*, fine

mulgére, mulsi, mulctus, to milk (out); to pour out as milk

muliebris, -e, feminine

múlier, -eris, *f.*, woman

muliércula, -ae, *f.*, a disgraceful woman

mulsum, -i, *n.*, sweet wine

multifáriam, *adv.*, at sundry times

multifórmis, -e, multiform, manifold

multifórmiter, *adv.*, in divers ways

multiplex, -icis, manifold

multiplicáre, to multiply

multiplicátio, -onis, *f.*, multiplicity

multipliciter, greatly; in many ways

multísonus, -a, -um, many sounding, loud

multitúdo, -inis, *f.*, multitude

multo, *adv.*, many

multum, *adv.*, much; long; very

multus, -a, -um, much, many; bountiful

mulus, -i, *m.*, mule

mundánus, -a, -um, of the world

mundáre, to cleanse

mundítia, -ae, *f.*, cleanliness

mundus, -i, *m.*, world; ornament

mundus, -a, -um, clean, pure, clear

muneráre, to bestow a gift upon

munerári, *dep.*, to present

múnia, -ium, *n. pl.*, services, gifts

muníficens, -entis, munificent

munímen, -inis, *n.*, protection

muníre, to defend, strengthen, preserve, fortify

munítio, -onis, *f.*, fort

munitiúncula, -ae, *f.*, little fortress

munus, -eris, *n.*, gift, offering, bounty; office; bribe

munúsculum, -i, *n.*, little gift
murénula, -ae, *f.*, necklace
murmur, -uris, *n.*, murmuring
murmuráre, to murmur
murmurátio, -onis, *f.*, murmur
Múrtia, -ae, *f.*, Murcia
murus, -i, *m.*, wall
mus, muris, *c.*, mouse
música, -ae, *f.*, music
música, -orum, *n. pl.*, music
músicus, -i, *m.*, musician
musívum, -i, *n.*, mosaic
mustum, -i, *n.*, new wine
mutabílitas, -atis, *f.*, change
mutáre, to change
mutátio, -onis, *f.*, change
mutatórium, -ii, *n.*, change
mutuári, *dep.*, to borrow
mútuo, *adv.*, mutually, to one another
mutus, -a, -um, dumb
mútuus, -a, -um, mutual
Myrénsis, -e, of Myra
myríca, -ae, *f.*, tamaric
myrrha, -ae, *f.*, myrrh
myrrháts, -a, -um, mingled with myrrh
mýrrheus, -a, -um, of myrrh
myrtétum, -i, *n.*, a grove or thicket of
  myrtle trees
mystérium, -ii, *n.*, mystery, secret
mýstice, *adv.*, mystically
mýsticus, -a, -um, of deep meaning,
  mystical

N

N. (nomen), name
Nabuthaéi, -orum, *m. pl.*, Nabutheans
nam, *conj.*, for
nancísci, nactus or nanctus sum, *dep.*
  3, to get, obtain
Narbonénsis, -e, of Narbonne
nardus, -i, *f.*, and nardum, -i, *n.*, spikenard; — spicátum, spikenard
nares, -ium, *f. pl.*, nostrils, nose

Narniénsis, -e, of Narni
narráre, to tell, relate
narrátor, -oris, *m.*, narrator
nasci, natus sum, *dep. 3*, to be born;
  spring up
natális, -e, natal
natális, -is, *m.*, birthday
natalítium, -ii, *n.*, feast, birthday; nata-
  lítia, *n. pl.*, birthday festival
natatória, -orum, *n. pl.*, pool
nátio, -onis, *f.*, nation; natiónes,
  heathen
natívitas, -atis, *f.*, birth, nativity
natúra, -ae, *f.*, nature
naturáliter, *adv.*, according to nature
natus, -i, *m.*, son
natus, -us, *m.*, birth; majóres natu,
  elders, ancients
naufrágium, -ii, *n.*, shipwreck
náufragus, -a, -um, shipwrecked
naulum, -i, *n.*, fare
náusea, -ae, *f.*, nausea, squeamishness
nauseáre, to vomit
nauta, -ae, *m.*, sailor, mariner
náuticus, -a, -um, of a ship, nautical
naváre, to do anything zealously
navícula, -ae, *f.*, boat
navigáre, to sail, be at sea
navígium, -ii, *n.*, ship
navis, -is, *f.*, ship
Naxus, -i, *f.*, Naxos
Názara, -ae, *f.*, Nazareth
Nazaraéus, -i, *m.*, Nazarene, Nazarite
Nazarénus, -a, -um, of Nazareth, Nazarene
Nazarethánus, -a, -um, of Nazareth
Nazianzénus, -a, -um, of Nazianzus
ne, *adv.* and *conj.*, and not; neither,
  nor; that not; lest
Neápolis, -is, *f.*, Naples
nébula, -ae, *f.*, cloud, mist
nec, neither; — non, and also, nor less
necáre, to kill, slay
necessário, *adv.*, necessarily

necessárius, -a, -um, needful

necésse, *adj.* and *n.,* necessary

necéssitas, -atis, *f.,* necessity; distress

nectar, -aris, *n.,* nectar

néctere, néxui and nexi, nexus, to weave

nedum, *adv.,* to say nothing of, much less

nefárius, -a, -um, shameful

negáre, to deny

negátio, -onis, *f.,* denial

neglégere, -lexi, -lectus, to neglect

negligéntia, -ae, *f.,* negligence

negotiári, *dep.,* to trade

negotiátio, -onis, *f.,* traffic; merchandise

negotiátor, -oris, *m.,* merchant

negótium, -ii, *n.,* business; pestilence

nemo, -inis, *m.* and *f.,* no one, nobody

nemorénsis, -e, of a grove or wood

nempe, *adv.,* namely; truly

nemus, -oris, *n.,* wood, forest, grove

Neocaesáraea, -ae, *f.,* Neocaesarea

Neocaesariénsis, -e, of Neocaesarea

neoménia, -ae, *f.,* new moon

neóphytus, -i, *m.,* novice, neophyte

Nepesínus, -a, -um, of Nepi

Nepomucénus, -a, -um, of Nepomuk

Nepómucum, -i, *n.,* Nepomuk

Nepotiánus, -i, *m.,* Nepotian

neptis, -is, *f.,* granddaughter

nepos, -otis, *m.* and *f.,* grandchild; nephew, niece, posterity

nequam, *indecl. adj.,* wicked, evil

nequándo, *conj.,* lest, lest at any time

nequáquam, *adv.,* no, not, by no means

neque, *adv.* and *conj.,* and not, neither, nor

néquior, -ius, more wicked

nequíre, -ivi and -ii, -tus, (eo), to be unable

nequíssmus, -i, *m.,* most wicked one

nequítia, -ae, *f.,* evil, malice

nere, nevi, netus, to spin

Neritonénsis, -e, of Nardo

nervus, -i, *m.,* nerve, sinew

nescíre, not to know, not to take notice

Nestórius, -ii, *m.,* Nestor, Nestorius

neuter, -tra, -trum, neither

nex, necis, *f.,* violent death

nexus, -us, *m.,* bond

ni, *conj.,* if not, unless

Nicaénus, -a, -um, of Nicaea, Nicene

Nicoláus, -i, *m.,* Nicholas

Nicoláitae, -orum, *m. pl.,* Nicolaites

Nicomediénsis, -e, of Nicomedia

nidificáre, to build a nest

nídulus, -i, *m.,* little nest

nidus, -i, *m.,* nest

nigríta, -ae, *m.* and *f.,* negro

Nigrítae, -arum, *m. pl.,* Negroes

nihil (nil), *n., indecl.,* nothing

nihilóminus, *adv.,* yet, nevertheless

níhilum, -i, *n.,* nothing

nimíetas, -atis, *f.,* excess, superfluity, redundancy

nimírum, *adv.,* certainly, truly

nimis, *adv.,* beyond measure, exceedingly; most diligently

nímius, -a, -um, excessive

Ninivíta, -ae, *f.,* Ninive

Ninivítae, -arum, *m. pl.,* Ninivites

Niniviti, -orum, *m. pl.,* Ninivites

nisi, *conj.,* if not, unless, except, but

Nisibénus, -a, -um, of Nisibis

nisus, -us, *m.,* striving, strength

nitens, -entis, shining

niti, nisus or nixus sum, *dep. 3,* to strive, endeavor

nítidus, -a, -um, smooth

nitor, -oris, *m.,* brightness, splendor. shining light

nitrum, -i, *n.,* natural soda; niter

níveus, -a, -um, snowy white

nix, nivis, *f.,* snow

nóbilis, -e, noble

nobilitáre, to ennoble, make known or illustrious, glorify

nocére, to hurt

noctúrnus, -a, -um, of the night, nocturnal

nodósus, -a, -um, knotted

Nolánus, -a, -um, of Nola

Noláscus, -i, m., Nolasco

nolle, nólui, to be unwilling, refuse

nomen, -inis, n., name

Nomentánus, -a, -um, of Nomentum

nomináre, to name

nominátim, adv., by name

nominátus, -a, -um, renowned

non, adv., not; no

nona, -ae, f., none

nonagenárius, -a, -um, being ninety years of age

nonagésimus, -a, -um, ninetieth

nonagésimus quintus, -a, -a, -um, -um, ninety-fifth

nonagintanóvem, ninety-nine

nondum, adv., not yet

nongentésimus, -a, -um, nine hundredth

Nonnátus, -i, m., Nonnatus (not born)

nonne, interrog. adv., introduces a question to which an affirmative answer is expected

nonnúllus, -a, -um, some

nonnúmquam, adv., sometimes

nonus, -a, -um, ninth

Norbértus, -i, m., Norbert

norma, -ae, f., rule, way of life

Normánnia, -ae, f., Normandy

Northmánnus, -i, m., Norman

nóscere, novi, notus, to know (how)

nosocómium, -ii, n., hospital

nosse, contraction of novísse, perfect infinitive of nóscere

noster, -tra, -trum, our, ours

nota, -ae, f., note, sign

notámen, -inis, n., sign, token

notáre, to mark; denote; prepare

notárius, -ii, m., scribe

notítia, -ae, f., knowledge; news

notus, -a, -um, known; nota fácere, to show

notus, -i, m., friend, acquaintance

novácula, -ae, f., razor

Novatiánus, -a, -um, Novatian

novélla, -orum, n. pl., young shoots

novéllus, -a, -um, young, new

novem, nine

novendiális, -e, lasting nine days; nine days' funeral rites

nóvies, nine times

novénnis, at the age of nine

novíssime, adv., last of all

novíssimus, -a, -um, latest, last; most abject; novíssima, n. pl., last state; in novíssimo die, at the last day

nóviter, adv., newly

nóvitas, -atis, f., newness, freshness; new thing, work, condition, or life

Novocómum, -i, n., Como

novus, -a, -um, new

nox, noctis, f., night

noxa, -ae, f., crime, sin; harm, offense

noxiális, -e, evil

nóxius, -a, -um, harmful, hurtful; sinful, guilty

núbere, nupsi, nuptus, to marry

nubes, -is, f., cloud

núbila, -orum, n. pl., clouds

Nucéria Paganórum, -ae, f., Nocera dei Pagani

núcleus, -i, m., kernel

nudáre, to lay bare, uncover

núdipes, -pedis, barefooted

núditas, -atis, f., nakedness

nudiustértius, adv., day before yesterday

nudus, -a, -um, naked, bare

nugácitas, -atis, f., trifling, frivolity, vanity

nullátenus, adv., not at all

núllibi, adv., nowhere, in no part

nullus, -a, -um, not any

num, *interr. adv.*, used when a negative answer is expected

numélla, -ae, *f.*, a kind of torture rack

numen, -inis, *n.*, divine power

numeráre, to number

numerósitas, -atis, *f.*, number, numbers

númerus, -i, *m.*, number

numísma, -atis, *n.*, coin, medal

nummulárius, -ii, *m.*, money changer

númmulus, -i, *m.*, small coin; paltry sum

nummus, -i, *m.*, coin

numquid, *interrog. adv.*, used when a negative answer is expected

nun, the fourteenth letter of the Hebrew alphabet, corresponding to English *n*

nunc, *adv.*, now

nuncupáre, to name, call

nuncupátio, -onis, *f.*, public offering or pronouncing of a vow

nuncupatíve, *adv.*, in name, nominally

núndinae, -arum, *f. pl.*, market day or place

nunquam (numquam), *adv.*, never

núntia, -ae, *f.*, herald

nuntiáre, to proclaim, announce, declare

núntium, -ii, *n.*, message, news

núntius, -ii, *m.*, messenger, herald; nuncio

nuper, *adv.*, recently, newly

núptiae, -arum, *f. pl.*, marriage, marriage feast

nuptiális, -e, wedding, nuptial

nuptus, -us, *m.*, marriage, wedlock

nuptus, -i, *m.*, married person, husband

nurus, -us, *f.*, daughter-in-law

nusquam, *adv.*, nowhere; in nothing; on no occasion

nutans, -antis, feeble, inconstant

nutáre, to waver, fail; wander

nutríre, to nourish, sustain

nutrítius (nutrícius), -ii, *m.*, foster father; guardian

nutrix, -icis, *f.*, nurse

nutus, -us, *m.*, nod; command; will

nux, nucis, *f.*, nut

nyctícorax, -acis, *m.*, a night raven

Nymphe, -es, *f.*, Santa Ninfa

Nyssénus, -a, -um, of Nyssa

O

ob, *prep.*, for, on account of, in consideration of

obarmátus, -a, -um, armed

obaudíre, to make or cause to be heard

obcaecátio, -onis, *f.*, blindness

obcaecátus, -a, -um, blinded

obdormíre, to sleep, fall asleep

obdúcere, -duxi, -ductus, to produce

obdúctio, -onis, *f.*, covering; cloudiness; doubt

obduráre, to harden

obdurátio, -onis, *f.*, stubbornness

obediéntia, -ae, *f.*, obedience

obedíre, to obey

obedítio, -onis, *f.*, obedience

oberráre, to wander about

obesse, -fui, to impede; be prejudicial to; injure

obférre, -tuli, -latus, to put to

obíre, -ivi and -ii, -itus, (eo), to die

óbitus, -us, *m.*, death

objéctus, -us, *m.*, obstacle

objícere, -jeci, -jectus, (io), to drive away; charge against, lay to the charge of

objurgátio, -onis, *f.*, injury

Oblátae, -arum, *m. pl.*, Oblates

oblátio, -onis, *f.*, oblation, offering

oblectaméntum, -i, *n.*, pleasure, amusement, allurement

oblectátio, -onis, *f.*, pleasure

obligare, to entangle

obligatio, -onis, *f.*, binding, entangling

oblitteráre, to blot out

oblívio, -onis, *f.*, forgetfulness; oblivion

obliviósus, -a, -um, forgetful

oblivísci, -litus sum, *dep. 3*, to forget

oblóngus, -a, -um, long

óbloqui, -locútus sum, *dep. 3*, to revile

obmutéscere, -mútui, to be dumb

obníxe, *adv.*, earnestly

obnóxius, -a, -um, subject to

obnubiláre, to darken

óbolus, -i, *m.*, a coin worth about four cents

obrépere, -repsi, -reptus, to crawl to; take by surprise

obrigéscere, -rígui, to become stiff

obrízus, -a, -um, finest (referring to gold)

obrúere, -rui, -rutus, to bury; drown; overwhelm

obscoénus, -a, -um, foul

obscuráre, to darken, obscure

obscúre, *adv.*, obscurely

obscúrus, -a, -um, dark; in obscúrum, into darkness

obsecráre, to implore, beseech

obsecrátio, -onis, *f.*, entreaty, supplication, prayer

obsecundáre, to comply with

óbsequens, -entis, dutiful

óbsequi, -secutus sum, *dep. 3*, to obey

obséquium, -ii, *n.*, homage, worship, service

obsérere, -sevi, -situs, to sow

Obsérvans, -antis, *m.*, Observant

observántia, -ae, *f.*, observance; abstinence

observáre, to observe; mark; watch

observátio, -onis, *f.*, observance

obses, -idis, *c.*, hostage

obsidére, -sedi, -sessus, to beset, inclose

obsídio, -onis, *f.*, siege

obsignáre, to seal

obsístere, -stiti, to resist

obsolétus, -a, -um, worn out, cast off

obsónium, -ii, *n.*, that which is eaten with bread; relish, sweetmeats

obstríngere, -strinxi, -strictus, to be indebted to

obstrúere, -struxi, -structes, to close, stop up

obstrúsus, -a, -um, covered, concealed

obstupefácere, -feci, -factus, (io), to astonish

obstupéscere, -stúpui and -stípui, to be astonished; to be set on edge (of teeth)

obtemperáre, to obey

obtenebrári, *dep.*, to be obscured

obténtus, -us, *m.*, pleading, prayer

obtestári, *dep.*, to entreat, implore, supplicate; call to witness

obtinére, -tínui, -tentus, to obtain; prevail

obtíngere, -tigi, to fall to the lot of

obtrectátio, -onis, *f.*, detraction

obtúndere, -tudi, -tusus, to make blunt, dull; weaken

obturáre, to stop up, close

obumbráre, to overshadow

obumbrátio, -onis, *f.*, shadow; overshadowing

óbviam, *adv.*, on the way

obviáre, to meet, go forth to meet

óbvius, -a, -um, in the way, meeting; óbvia venire, to come to meet

obvólvere, -volvi, -volútus, to wrap

occásio, -onis, *f.*, occasion

occásus, -us, *m.*, setting (of the sun)

occídens, -entis, deathly

óccidens, -entis, *m.*, the west; evening

occidentális, -e, western

occídere, -cidi, -casus, to set, go down (of the sun)

occídere, -cidi, -cisus, to put to death

occísio, -onis, *f.*, slaughter
occísor, -oris, *m.*, killer, murderer
occúbitus, -us, *m.*, setting
occúlere, -cúlui, -cultus, to conceal
occultáre, to hide
occúlte, *adv.*, privately
occúltum, -i, *n.*, hidden thing; secret or hidden sin
occúltus, -a, -um, hidden
occúmbere, -cúbui, -cúbitus, to fall, fall down
occupáre, to occupy; reach unto; cumber
occupátio, -onis, *f.*, occupation
occúrrens, -entis, of the day, current
occúrrere, -curri, -cursus, to meet, go to meet, come to; occur
occúrsus, -us, *m.*, meeting; course; occurrence; **vádere in occúrsum,** to go to meet
ócius, *adv.*, quickly
ócrea, -ae, *f.*, greave
octáva, -ae, *f.*, octave
octávus, -a, -um, eighth
octénnis, at the age of eight
octingentésimus, -a, -um, eight hundredth
octo, eight
octódecim, eighteen
octogenárius, -ii, *m.*, octogenarian
octogésimus quintus, -a, -a, -um, -um, eighty-fifth
octogínta, eighty; four score
oculáris, -e, ocular, eye
oculátus, -a, -um, sharp-eyed; many-eyed
óculus, -i, *m.*, eye; **ex óculis eórum,** from their sight
odíbilis, -e, hateful
odísse, *defect. verb*, to hate
ódium, -ii, *n.*, hatred
odor, -oris, *m.*, smell, odor; savor
odoraméntum, -i, *n.*, odor
odoráre, to smell

odorári, *dep.*, to smell
odorátus, -us, *m.*, smell; smelling
oecuménicus, -a, -um, ecumenical
offéndere, -fendi, -fensus, to dash against; stumble; offend
offendículum, -i, *n.*, stumbling block
offénsio, -onis, *f.*, offense
offérre, óbtuli, oblátus, to offer
offertórium, -ii, *n.*, offertory
offícium, -ii, *n.*, favor, kindness; office; duty; fulfillment
offúsus, -a, -um, spread around, concealing
ólea, -ae, *f.*, olive tree
oleáster, -tri, *m.*, wild olive tree
ólera, -orum, *n. pl.*, herbs
óleum, -i, *n.*, oil
olfácere, -feci, -factus, (io), to smell
olim, *adv.*, formerly, once
olíva, -ae, *f.*, olive tree
Olivétus, -i, *m.*, Olivet
olla, -ae, *f.*, pot; caldron; **ollas cárnium,** flesh pots
olus, -eris, *n.*, herb, pot herb
omega, omega, the last letter of the Greek alphabet
omnímodus, -a, -um, entire, complete
omníno, *adv.*, at all
omnípotens, -entis, almighty, omnipotent
omnipoténtia, -ae, *f.*, might
omnis, -e, all, every
omophórion (Greek), bishop's pallium
ónager (ónagrus), -i, *m.*, wild ass
onerátus, -a, -um, burdened
ónerus, -a, -um, burdensome
onus, -eris, *n.*, burden
onustátus, -a, -um, burdened, laden
onústus, -a, -um, burdened, laden
operári, *dep.*, to work; commit; trade
operárius, -ii, *m.*, laborer
operátio, -onis, *f.*, operation; work; working; virtue

operátor, -oris, *m.*, worker

operatórius, -a, -um, conducive to action, mightily working

operiméntum, -i, *n.*, covering

operíre, -pérui, -pertus, to cover; overwhelm

operósus, -a, -um, hard, laborious

opertórium, -ii, *n.*, cover, vesture

ópifex, -ficis, *c.*, worker

opifícium, -ii, *n.*, aid

opínio, -onis, *f.*, rumor

opituláre (-ari), to help

opitulátio, -onis, *f.*, help, assistance

oportére, *imperson. verb*, 2, to be proper, behoove; ought; must

oppétere, -ivi and -ii, -itus, to meet, meet with, encounter

oppidánus, -i, *m.*, townsman, citizen

oppídulum, -i, *n.*, little town, village

óppidum, -i, *n.*, town

oppignoráre, to pawn; pledge; give

oppiláre, to close up

opportúne, *adv.*, conveniently; in season

opportúnitas, -atis, *f.*, due time; want, need

opportúnus, -a, -um, due

opprímere, -pressi, -pressus, to oppress; lie upon; overlie; overwhelm

oppróbrium, -ii, *n.*, reproach

ops, opis, *f.*, help

optábilis, -e, desirable, desired

optáre, to desire

óptimas, -atis, *m.*, chief, best or most important man, aristocrat

óptime, *adv.*, very well

óptimus, -a, -um, best, perfect

óptio, -onis, *f.*, choice

opus, -eris, *n.*, deed; work; wages; image; — esse, to need, be necessary; — habére, to have need

opúsculum, -i, *n.*, little work

ora, -ae, *f.*, coast; border

oráculum, -i, *n.*, oracle, revelation

oráre, to pray, beseech

orátio, -onis, *f.*, prayer; discourse

oratórium, -ii, *n.*, oratory

orátus, -us, *m.*, entreaty

orbátus, -a, -um, bereaved

orbis, -is, *m.*, world, earth

orcus, -i, *m.*, infernal regions

ordináre, to ordain; set in array or in order; set up

ordinárium, -ii, *n.*, ordinary

ordinátio, -onis, *f.*, ordination; ordinance

ordinátus, -a, -um, orderly

ordíri, orsus sum, *dep. 4*, to begin

ordo, -inis, *m.*, order, rank

órganum, -i, *n.*, organ

óriens, -entis, *m.*, the orient; east; dawn

orientális, -e, oriental, east

originális, -e, original

orígo, -inis, *f.*, beginning, origin

Oríonas, -ae, *m.*, Orion

Oríones, -um, *m. pl.*, Orion

oríri, ortus sum, *dep. 4*, to spring up, come forth, appear, rise

ornaméntum, -i, *n.*, ornament

ornáre, to adorn, garnish

ornátus, -us, *m.*, adornment; furniture

órphanus, -i, *m.*, orphan

orphanotrophíum, -ii, *n.*, orphanage

orthodóxus, -a, -um, orthodox

ortus, -us, *m.*, rising (of the sun); the east

os, oris, *n.*, mouth; edge

os, ossis, *n.*, bone

Osca, -ae, *f.*, Huesca

oscitáre, to gape

osculári, *dep.*, to kiss

ósculum, -i, *n.*, kiss

Osea, -ae, *f.*, Osee

osténdere, -tendi, -tensus or tentus, to show, display, expose

osténsio, -onis, *f.*, show, showing, display; evidence

ostiária, -ae, f., portress
ostiárius, -ii, m., porter
ostiátim, adv., from door to door
Ostia Tiberína, -orum, m. pl., Ostia
Ostiénsis, -e, of Ostia
óstium, -ii, n., door, gate
Otho, -onis, m., Otto
otiósus, -a, -um, idle
ótium, -ii, n., sloth
ováre, to rejoice
Oveténsis, -e, of Oviedo
ovíle, -is, n., fold, sheepfold
ovínus, -a, -um, of a sheep
ovis, -is, f., sheep
ovum, -i, n., egg
Oxoménsis, -e, of Osma

P

pábulum, -i, n., food
pacátrix, -icis, f., peacemaker
pacátus, -a, -um, peaceful
pácifer, -a, -um, peace-bringing
pacificáre, to pacify, grant peace
pacífice, adv., peaceably
pacíficum, -i, n., peace offering
pacíficus, -a, -um, of peace, peaceful
pacísci, pactus sum, dep. 3, to cove-
    nant, make a bargain
pactum, -i, n., covenant
Padus, -i, m., Po River
paean, -anis, n., paean, hymn
paedagógus, -i, m., instructor
pagánus, -i, m., heathen, pagan
página, -ae, f., page
pagus, -i, m., village
Palaestína, -ae, f., Palestine
Palaestini, -orum, m. pl., Philistines
palaéstra, -ae, f., school, gymnasium
palam, adv., openly
palátium, -ii, n., palace
palátum, -i, n., palate, taste
pálea, -ae, f., straw
Paléntia, -ae, f., Palencia

palla, -ae, f., mantle; curtain
pallére, -ui, to grow pale, fade
palliáre, to soften, relieve
pállium, -ii, n., cloth; garment;
    mantle; pallium
pallor, -oris, m., paleness, pallor
palma, -ae, f., palm tree; palm of the
    hand
palmes, -itis, m., branch
palmus, -i, m., span
palpáre, to handle, feel
pálpebra, -ae, f., eyelid
palpitáre, to tremble; blink
palus, -i, m., stake, post
Pampelonénsis, -e, of Pamplona
Pancrátius, -ii, m., Pancras
pándere, pandi, pansus and passus, to
    lay bare, tell, announce
pángere, panxi, panctus and pegi or
    pépigi, pactus, to make; compose;
    sing
panífica, -ae, f., baker
panis, -is, m., bread; loaf
Pannónii, -orum, m. pl., Pannonians
pannus, -i, m., cloth; pannis, in swad-
    dling clothes
Panormitáni, -orum, m. pl., people of
    Palermo
Papa, -ae, m., Pope
Paphus, -i, f., Paphos
Papía, -ae, f., Pavia
papílio, -onis, m., tent
papílla, -ae, f., nipple; breast
par, paris, equal, like
par, paris, m., f., n., pair, couple
parábola, -ae, f., parable; byword
Paráclitus, -i, m., defender, comforter,
    Paraclete, Holy Ghost
paradígma, -atis, n., model, example
paradísus, -i, m., paradise
paralýticus, -a, -um, paralyzed
paráre, to prepare, provide
Parascéve, -es, f., day of preparation;
    Parasceve; Good Friday

parce, *adv.*, moderately, sparingly

párcere, peperci, párcitus, to spare; forbear; keep

parcimónia, -ae, *f.*, self-denial

párcitas, -atis, *f.*, frugality; temperance, sparing use

pardus, -i, *m.*, leopard

parens, -entis, *m.* and *f.*, parent

parére, to appear; obey

párere, péperi, partus, (io), to bear, bring forth, be delivered of a child

páries, -etis, *m.*, wall

Parisiénsis, -e, of Paris

Parísii, -orum, *m. pl.*, Paris

páriter, *adv.*, at the same time, together, with one accord

paróchia, -ae, *f.*, parish

párochus, -i, *m.*, parish priest; benefice

paroécia, -ae, *f.*, parish

parópsis, -idis, *f.*, dish

parricída, -ae, *c.*, murderer, murderer of one's own parent, parricide

pars, partis, *f.*, part, portion; **partes**, quarters; ex parte, in part

Parthi, -orum, *m. pl.*, Parthians

párticeps, -ipis, *m.* and *f.*, partaker; fellow, friend

participátio, -onis, *f.*, participation; a being compact

particula, -ae, *f.*, part; particle

partim, *adv.*, partly

partíri, *dep. 4*, to divide, part

parturíre, to travail

partus, -us, *m.*, bringing forth, birth, childbirth

parum, *adv.*, little

parvipéndere, -pépendi, -pensus, to esteem lightly

párvitas, -atis, *f.*, small quantity

párvulus, -a, -um, little; (*as a noun*) child

parvus, -a, -um, little, small

páscere, pavi, pastus, to feed, pasture; nourish

Pascha, -ae, *n.*, Pasch, Passover; Easter

paschális, -e, paschal

Paschális, -is, *m.*, Paschal

páscua, -ae, *f.*, pasture

pascuális, -e, of the pasture

páscuum, -i, *n.*, pasture; **páscua, *n. pl.*,** pasture, pastures

páscuus, -a, -um, relating to a pasture, grazing

passer, -eris, *m.*, sparrow

passíbilis, -e, susceptible to pain

passim, *adv.*, up and down, here and there, far and wide

Passiniánum, -i, *n.*, Passignano

pássio, -onis, *f.*, passion, suffering, martyrdom

passus, -us, *m.*, step, pace

pastophórium, -ii, *n.*, chamber adjoining the temple

pastor, -oris, *m.*, shepherd; pastor

pastorális, -e, of a shepherd, shepherd's; pastoral; watchful

pastus, -us, *m.*, food, sustenance

Patávium, -ii, *n.*, Padua

paténa, -ae, *f.*, paten

pater, -tris, *m.*, father

patére, -ui, to be open or extended

paterfamílias, patrisfamílias, *m.*, goodman of the house, householder, master of the house

patérnitas, -atis, *f.*, paternity

patérnus, -a, -um, paternal

patéscere, -ui, to lie open or extended

pati, passus sum, *dep. 3* (io), to suffer, to endure

patíbulum, -i, *n.*, gibbet; yoke; ignominy

pátiens, -entis, patient, long-suffering

patiéntia, -ae, *f.*, patience

Patrae, -arum, *f. pl.*, Patras

patráre, to perform, accomplish; commit

pátria, -ae, *f.*, country, fatherland; home

patriárcha, -ae, m., patriarch
patriarchális, -e, patriarchal
Patrícius; see vicus Patríci
patrícius, -a, -um, patrician
Patrícius, -ii, m., Patrick
pátrius, -a, -um, pertaining to a father, father's
patrocínium, -ii, n., protection, patronage
patróna, -ae, f., patroness, protectress
patrónus, -i, m., defender, advocate, patron
patruélis, -is, m., cousin
pátruus, -i, m., father's brother, uncle
pátulus, -a, -um, open, extended
páucitas, -atis, f., fewness
paucus, -a, -um, few, little
paulátim, adv., little by little
paulísper, adv., a little
paulo minus, adv., almost
páululum, adv., a very little
Paulus, -i, m., Paul
pauper, -eris, poor; páuperes, m. pl., the poor
paupérculus, -a, -um, poor
paupéries, -ei, f., poverty
páupertas, -atis, f., poverty, wretchedness
pausa, -ae, f., pause
pavére, pavi, to fear
pávidus, -a, -um, fearful, terrified
paviméntum, -i, n., floor; ground, dust
pavíre, to beat down
pavor, -oris, m., fear, terror
pax, pacis, f., peace; prosperity
paxíllus, -i, m., pin
peccáre, to sin
peccátor, -oris, m., sinner
peccátrix, -icis, sinful
peccátrix, -icis, f., sinner
peccátum, -i, n., sin
pecten, -inis, m., comb
pectus, -oris, n., breast
peculiáris, -e, peculiar

pecúlium, -ii, n., property
pecúnia, -ae, f., money
pecus, -oris, n., cattle, sheep
pecus, -udis, f., cattle (a single head)
pedáneus, -a, -um, pertaining to the foot; lignum pedáneum, altar step
pedes, -itis, m., foot soldier, infantryman
Pedrósum, -i, n., Pedroso
pejor, pejus, worse
Pelagiáni, -orum, m. pl., Pelagians
pélagus, -i, n., sea
Pelígni, -orum, m. pl., Abruzzo Citeriore
péllere, pépuli, pulsus, to cast out
pellicánus, -i, m., pelican
pellícere, -lexi, -lectus, (io), to seduce
pellíceus, -a, -um, of leather
pellícula, -ae, f., little skin
pellis, -is, f., skin, hide; tent cloth, tent
pelvis, -is, f., basin
pendére, pépendi, to hang; depend
péndulus, -a, -um, hanging
pene, adv., almost, well-nigh
penes, prep., with; before
penetrábilis, -e, sharp, piercing
penetrália, -orum, n. pl., inmost recesses; inner chambers, closets; inmost self, spirit
penetráre, to penetrate
pénitus, -a, -um, inward
pénitus, adv., wholly
penna, -ae, f., feather; wing
pennátus, -a, -um, feathered, winged
pensitáre, to weigh; pay
pentacontárchus, -i, m., captain over fifty men
Pentecóste, -es, f., Pentecost
per, through, by
pera, -ae, f., bag, wallet
perágere, -egi, -actus, to finish, accomplish; attain to; celebrate
peragráre, to travel, wander or pass through; visit

peramánter, *adv.*, very lovingly

perambuláre, to walk about

percéllere, -culi, -culsus, to daunt, repel

percéptio, -onis, *f.*, partaking

percípere, -cepi, -ceptus, (io), to take, partake, receive; attain; seize; experience; give ear to

pércitus, -a, -um, aroused, driven

percoláre, -cólui, -cultus, to honor, reverence

percontári, *dep.*, to inquire

percrebréscere, -crébrui, to spread abroad, be well known

percréscere, -crevi, -cretus, to increase greatly

percúlsus, -a, -um, struck, smitten

percúpidus, -a, -um, very desirous

percúrrere, -curri, and -cúcurri, -cursus, to run through; persevere to the end

percússio, -onis, *f.*, stroke, a beating, a striking

percussor, -onis, *m.*, striker; executioner, headsman

percútere, -cussi, -cussus, (io), to strike, strike down, smite; kill

pérdere, -didi, -ditus, to lose; destroy

perdítio, -onis, *f.*, waste; perdition; ruin, destruction

pérdolens, -entis, sorrowing

perdúcere, -duxi, -ductus, to bring to, lead to or through

péregre, *adv.*, abroad, into a strange country

peregrínans, -antis, *m.*, traveler, pilgrim

peregrinátio, -onis, *f.*, travel, pilgrimage

peregrínus, -a, -um, strange

peregrínus, -i, *m.*, stranger

perémptor, -oris, *m.*, slayer, destroyer

perénnis, -e, eternal

perénnitas, -atis, *f.*, eternity

perfécte, *adv.*, perfectly

perféctio, -onis, *f.*, perfection

perféctus, -a, -um, perfect

perférre, -tuli, -latus, to bring, bear, carry through, carry up

perfícere, -feci, -fectus, (io), to finish; perform; make perfect, perfect; accomplish; render; win

perfídia, -ae, *f.*, faithlessness

pérfidus, -a, -um, faithless

perfódere, -fodi, -fossus, (io), to dig through, break open

perforáre, to pierce

perfrícatio, -onis, *f.*, rubbing

pérfrui, -fractus sum, *dep. 3*, to enjoy

pérfuga, -ae, *m.*, deserter, fugitive

perfúnctio, -onis, *f.*, performance

perfúndere, -fudi, -fusus, to pour forth or over; overwhelm

pérgere, perréxi, perréctus, to go, go forward, continue

Pergis, -is, *f.*, Perga

perhibére, to report, bear witness

periclitári, *dep.*, to be in danger, be imperiled

periculósus, -a, -um, dangerous

perículum, -i, *n.*, danger, peril

perillústris, -e, shining

perímere, -emi, -emtus (-emptus), to slay, destroy

perínde, *adv.*, in a like manner

peripséma, -atis, *n.*, offscouring

períre, -ivi and -ii, -itus, (eo), to fail, be lost, perish

perítia, -ae, *f.*, skill

peritúrus, -a, -um, perishable

perizóma, -atis, *n.*, apron

perjuráre, to swear falsely

perliminária, -orum, *n. pl.*, lintels

perlínere, -livi and -levi, -litus, to besmear, anoint

perlúcidus, -a, -um, transparent

permanére, -mansi, -mansus, to remain, continue

permíttere, -misi, -missus, to suffer, permit

permíxtus, -a, -um, mingled

permovére, -movi, -motus, to arouse, agitate

permúltus, -a, -um, very much or many

permutáre, to change completely

pernícies, -ei, f., disaster

pernoctáre, to spend the night

perósus, -a, -um, hating

pérperam, adv., perversely

perpes, -etis, perpetual

perpéssio, -onis, f., suffering, endurance

pérpeti, -passus sum, dep. 3 (io), to suffer, endure, undergo

perpetráre, to do

pérpetim, adv., continually

perpetuáre, to make perpetual, continue

perpetúitas, -atis, f., perpetuity, eternity

perpétuo, adv., permanently

perpétuus, -a, -um, perpetual, everlasting, unfailing

perplúres, -ium, very many

perpúlcher, -chra, -chrum, very beautiful

perquírere, -sivi, -situs, to seek

Persa, -ae, m., Persian

perscríbere, -scripsi, -scriptus, to write down

perscrutátio, -onis, f., scrutiny

persecútio, -onis, f., persecution

persecútor, -oris, m., persecutor

pérsequi, -secutus sum, dep. 3, to persecute; pursue

perseveráre, to continue

Persi, -orum, m. pl., Persians

Persis, -idis, f., Persia

persístere, to resist

persólvere, -solvi, -solútus, to offer, render; discharge

persóna, -ae, f., person

personáre, -sónui, -sónitus, to proclaim, shout; resound; sing; ring again

personátus, -a, -um, masked, provided with a mask

perspícere, -spexi, -spectus, (io), to have regard to; look into

perspicúitas, -atis, f., clearness

perspícuus, -a, -um, evident

persuadére, -suasi, -suasus, to persuade

persuasíbilis, -e, persuasive

persuásio, -onis, f., doctrine

perstríngere, -strinxi, -strictus, to lay hold upon

pertaésus, -a, -um, thoroughly wearied

pertentáre, to put to the test

perterrefáctus, -a, -um, exceedingly terrified

pertérritus, -a, -um, terrified

pertiméscere, -timui, to fear greatly

pértinax, -acis, obstinate

pertinére, -tínui, to pertain to

pertíngere, to come to, extend to

pertractáre, to busy oneself with; study; celebrate

pertransíre, to go away; pierce; pass through

perturbátio, -onis, f., disturbance

pertúsus, -a, -um, with holes

Peruánus, -a, -um, Peruvian

perúngere, -unxi, -unctus, to anoint

perúrere, -ussi, -ustus, to burn up, parch

perurgére, -ursi, to urge forward

Perúsia, -ae, f., Perugia

perútilis, -e, very useful

pervagáre, to wander through

pervenire, -veni, -ventus, to come to, attain

pervéntio, -onis, f., coming, arrival

pervéntor, -oris, m., one who comes or arrives

pervérse, adv., perversely

pervérsitas, -atis, *f.,* perverse inclination

pervértere, -verti, -versus, to pervert

pervetústus, -a, -um, very old

pervicácia, -ae, *f.,* stubbornness

pérvigil, -ilis, ever watchful

pervigiláre, to watch

pervigílium, -ii, *n.,* watch; eve; vigil

pervíncere, -vici, -victus, to overcome

pérvius, -a, -um, accessible

pervulgáre, to make publicly known

pes, pedis, *m.,* foot

pessimáre, to oppress

péssimus, -a, -um, worst; wicked, evil

péstifer, -a, -um, pestilential

péstilens, -entis, pestilential

pestiléntia, -ae, *f.,* pestilence, plague

pétere, -ivi and -ii, -itus, to ask, request, entreat, beseech

petítio, -onis, *f.,* petition, request

petra, -ae, *f.,* rock

Petra Pertúsa, -a, -ae, *f.,* Pietra Pertusa

Petrus, -i, *m.,* Peter

Petrus Canísius, -i, -ii, *m.,* Peter Canisius

petulánter, *adv.,* wantonly, boldly

phalánga, -ae, *f.,* band

phaleráre, to adorn (with medals)

phantásia, -ae, *f.,* delusion

phantásma, -atis, *n.,* apparition, phantom

pháretra, -ae, *f.,* quiver

Pharisaéus, -i, *m.,* Pharisee

phármacum, -i, *n.,* remedy

phase, -es, *f.,* phase; rite

Phase, *indecl.,* Phase, Passover

Pherezaéus, -i, *m.,* Pherezite

phíala, -ae, *f.,* vial, phial

Philadélphii, -orum, *m. pl.,* Philadelphians

Philippénses, -ium, *m. pl.,* Philippians

Philippénsis, -e, of Philippi

Philippínae, -arum, *f. pl.,* Philippines

Philíppus, -i, *m.,* Philip; Philippian

Philíppus Benítius, -i, -ii, *m.,* Philip Benizi

Philíppus Nérius, -i, -ii, *m.,* Philip Neri

Philisthaéus, -i, *m.,* Philistine

Philisthíni, -orum, *m. pl.,* Philistines

Philístiim, Philistia

Philogónius, -ii, *m.,* Philogonius

philosophári, *dep.,* to philosophize

philosóphia, -ae, *f.,* philosophy

philosóphicus, -a, -um, philosophical

philósophus, -i, *m.,* philosopher

Phoeníce, -es and -is, *f.,* Phoenicia

phrenéticus, -a, -um, frantic

phthísicus, -a, -um, consumptive

phur, Purim, Jewish Feast of Lots that celebrates the deliverance of the Jews from the machinations of Aman

phylactérium, -ii, *n.,* phylactery

piaculáris, -e, expiatory, purifying

piáculum, -i, *n.,* sin, crime

Picárdia, -ae, *f.,* Picardy

Pictávi, -orum, *m. pl.,* Poitiers

Pictaviénsis, -e, of Poitiers

Picti, -orum, *m. pl.,* Picts

pictor, -oris, *m.,* painter

pictúra, -ae, *f.,* picture

pie, *adv.,* mercifully, piously

pientíssimus, -a, -um, most dutiful

píetas, -atis, *f.,* goodness, godliness; pity; loving kindness

piger, -gra, -grum, lazy, slothful

pigére, *impers. verb,* 2, to cause annoyance, weary, disgust

pignus, -oris and -eris, *n.,* pledge

pigráre, to be slothful

pigritári, *dep.,* to be slow or slothful

Pilátus, -i, *m.,* Pilate

pileátus, -a, -um, wearing a felt cap

pilósus, -a, -um, hairy

pincérna, -ae, *m.,* cupbearer

píngere, pinxi, pictus, to paint; adorn

pinguédo, -inis, *f.,* fatness; richness

pinguéscere, to grow fat; grow fertile

pinguis, -e, fat; strong; pínguia, n. pl., fat meats

pinnáculum, -i, n., pinnacle

Pipínus, -i, m., Pepin

piráta, -ae, m., pirate

Pisae, -arum, f. pl., Pisa

piscári, dep., to fish

piscátor, -oris, m., fisherman

piscículus, -i, m., little fish

piscína, -ae, f., tank for bathing; pool, pond; fish market

piscis, -is, m., fish

Pisis, -e, of Pisa

písticus, -a, -um, pure, genuine (of nard)

pius, -a, -um, pious, holy; just; pitying; merciful, tender, loving

pix, picis, f., pitch

placábilis, -e, appeased

placáre, to appease

placátio, -onis, f., a soothing, appeasing, propitiating, propitiation; ransom

Placéntia, -ae, f., Piacenza

placére, -ui or placátus sum, to please; placet, impers., it is pleasing

plácide, adv., peacefully

plácidus, -a, -um, favorable

Plácidus, -i, m., Placid

plácitus, -a, -um, acceptable

plaga, -ae, f., blow, stripe, scourge, stroke; wound; plague

plaga, -ae, f., flat surface, tract of land, district, zone, plain, desert

plagáre, to wound

plagátus, -a, -um, sore, wounded

planáre, to make plain

planctus, -us, m., mourning

plane, adv., surely

plángere, planxi, planctus, to bewail

planíties, -ei, f., plain

planta, -ae, f., sole of the foot

plantáre, to plant; set in place; create

plantárium, -ii, n., sole of the foot; foot

plantátio, -onis, f., plant; — rosae, rose plant

planum, -i, n., plain

planus, -a, -um, plain, flat

plasma, -atis, n., anything formed; creation

plasmáre, to form, fashion

plastes, -is, m., maker

plátanus, -i, f., plane tree

platéa, -ae, f., street

pláudere, plausi, plausus, to strike, clap

plaustrum, -i, n., cart

plausus, -us, m., applause

plebéjus, -a, -um, of the people, plebeian

plebs, -is, f., people

pléctere, to punish; cápite plecti, to be beheaded

pléctere, plexi and pléxui, plexus, to braid, plait

pléniter, adv., fully, completely

plenitúdo, -inis, f., fullness; fulfilling; full assembly

plénius, adv., more fully

plenus, -a, -um, full; plentiful

ploráre, to bewail, lament, weep

plorátus, -us, m., lamentation

plúere, plui or pluvi, to rain

plumbátum, -i, n., whip weighted with lead, plummet

plumbum, -i, n., lead

plurális, -e, plural

pluráliter, adv., in the plural

plúries, adv., frequently

plúrimus, -a, -um, very many; very great

plus, adj. and adv., more; — quam, more than

plúsculus, -a, -um, many

plúvia, -ae, f., rain

póculum, -i, n., goblet; drink

Pódium, -ii, *n.*, Le Puy

poena, -ae, *f.*, pain

poénitens, -entis, penitent

poeniténtia, -ae, *f.*, repentance; penance

poenitentiárius, -ii, *m.*, penitentiary

poenitére (paenitére), to repent; poénitet, *impers.*, one repents or is displeased

póesis, -is or -eos, *f.*, poetry

poëta, -ae, *m.*, poet

polítus, -a, -um, polite, polished

pollére, to be strong

pollicéri, *dep.* 2, to promise

pollicitátio, -onis, *f.*, promise

pollúere, -ui, -utus, to pollute, defile, profane

pollútio, -onis, *f.*, defilement

Polocénsis, -e, of Polotsk

Polónia, -ae, *f.*, Poland

Polónus, -a, -um, Polish

polus, -i, *m.*, sky, heaven

Polycárpus, -i, *m.*, Polycarp

Polychrónis, -is, *m.*, Polychron

polymítus, -a, -um, of divers colors

pomárium, -ii, *n.*, orchard

pómifer, -a, -um, fruit, fruit-bearing

pompa, -ae, *f.*, pomp

Pompéjus, -i, *m.*, Pompey

Pomposiánus, -a, -um, of Pomposia

pomum, -i, *n.*, apple

pomus, -i, *f.*, fruit tree

ponderáre, to weigh

ponderátor, -oris, *m.*, weigher

pondus, -eris, *n.*, load, weight, burden

pónere, pósui, pósitus, to put, set; lay down or aside; make

Póntia, -ae, *f.*, Ponza, Isola di Ponza

Pontiánis (de), de' Pontiani

Pontiánus, -i, *m.*, Pontian

Pónticus, -a, -um, Pontic; mare Pónticum, Black Sea

póntifex, -icis, *m.*, pontiff; bishop; high priest; — máximus, pope

pontificális, -e, pontifical

pontificátus, -us, *m.*, pontificate, reign

pontifícium, -ii, *n.*, pontifical power

pontíficus, -a, -um, pontifical, papal

Pontiniacénsis, -e, of Pontigni

Pontiniácum, -i, *n.*, Pontigni

Póntius Pilátus, -ii. -i, *m.*, Pontius Pilate

pontus, -i, *m.*, the deep, the sea

popína, -ae, *f.*, food, fare

populáres, -ium, *m. pl.*, the people

pópulus, -i, *m.*, people; in pópulis, among the nations

porcínus, -a, -um, of swine

porcus, -i, *m.*, pig

porósus, -a, -um, porous

Porphýrius, -ii, *m.*, Porphyry

porréctus, -a, -um, stretched out

porrígere, -rexi, -rectus, to stretch forth

porrígo, -inis, *f.*, dandruff; itch; lice

porro, *adv.*, but

porta, -ae, *f.*, gate; — aquárum, water gate

portáre, to carry; uphold

Portéllus, -i, *m.*, Portello

porténdere, -tendi, -tentus, to portend, presage

porténtum, -i, *n.*, wonder, portent

pórticus, -i, *m.*, porch

pórtio, -onis, *f.*, portion

pórtitor, -oris, *m.*, bearer, carrier

Portuénsis, -e, of Porto

portus, -us, *m.*, port, harbor

póscere, póposci, to ask, beseech

posse, pótui, to be able, can

posséssio, -onis, *f.*, possession

posséssor, -ris, *m.*, possessor

possíbilis, -e, possible

possibílitas, -atis, *f.*, possibility; power

post, *prep.*, after

postcommúnio, -onis, *f.*, postcommunion

póstea, *adv.*, afterward, hereafter

possidére, -sedi, -sessus, to possess, get possession of

pósteri, -orum, *m. pl.,* descendants, posterity

postérior, -ius, later, posterior; posterióra, *n. pl.,* hinder parts

postérius, *adv.,* afterward, later

posthabére, to esteem less

postícum, -i, *n.,* back door

postis, -is, *m.,* door post, side post

postliminium, -ii, *n.,* a return home

póstmodum, *adv.,* after, afterward

postpónere, -pósui, -pósitus, to put after

postquam, *conj.,* after, as soon as

postrémo, *adv.,* lastly

postuláre, to ask, pray for; require

postulátio, -onis, *f.,* entreaty, prayer; hope

potábilis, -e, fit to drink

potáre, to drink, give to drink

potátio, -onis, *f.,* drink; drinking

potens, -entis, mighty, powerful

potentátus, -us, *m.,* power, might

poténter, *adv.,* powerfully

poténtia, -ae, *f.,* power

potéstas, -atis, *f.,* power, authority, jurisdiction

pótior, -ius, better, greater, more excellent; preferable

potíri, *dep. 4,* to get possession of, obtain

potíssimus, *adv.,* chiefly, especially

pótius, *adv.,* rather

potus, -us, *m.,* drink

prae, *prep.,* before; because of

praeámbulus, -a, -um, going before

praebére, to grant, offer, furnish, afford

praecédere, -cessi, -cessus, to go before, precede

praecéllere, to excel

praeceps, -ipitis, headlong

praecéptor, -oris, *m.,* master

praecéptum, -i, *n.,* precept, command

praecéssor, -oris, *m.,* leader

praecídere, -cidi, -cisus, to cut, cut down or off

praecínere, -cécini and -cínui, -centus, to sing; sing or play before

praecíngere, -cinxi, -cinctus, to gird

praecípere, -cepi, -ceptus, (io), to teach, instruct; command

praecipitáre, to cast headlong

praecipitátio, -onis, *f.,* ruin

praecipítium, -ii, *n.,* precipice

praecípuus, -a, -um, special

praecláre, *adv.,* excellently, with distinction

praeclárus, -a, -um, excellent, glorious; goodly; in praecláris, in goodly places

praeco, -onis, *m.,* crier, herald

praecógnitus, -a, -um, known beforehand

praecónium, -ii, *n.,* praise; excellence

praecórdia, -orum, *n.pl.,* hearts

praecúrrere, -curri and -cucúrri, -cursus, to run before; take precedence over

praecúrsor, -oris, *m.,* one who runs before; precursor

praeda, -ae, *f.,* spoils of war, booty; prey

praedári, *dep.,* to plunder

praedátio, -onis, *f.,* taking of spoils, robbery

praedecéssor, -oris, *m.,* predecessor

praedestináre, to ordain

praedestinátio, -onis, *f.,* predestination

praedestinátus, -a, -um, predestinated

praedicábilis, -e, worthy of being spoken of

praédicans, -antis, *m.,* preacher

praedicáre, to shout, proclaim; declare; preach

praedicátio, -onis, *f.,* preaching; praise

praedicátor, -oris, *m.*, preacher

praedícere, -dixi, -dictus, to say before; foretell

praedíctus, -a, -um, aforesaid

praéditus, -a, -um, endowed

praédium, -ii, *n.*, farm, estate

praedocére, -dócui, -doctus, to teach beforehand

praedúlcis, -e, very sweet

praeelígere, -legi, -lectus, to choose before, forechoose

praeeminére, to excel, be remarkable

praeésse, -fui, to rule

praefátio, -onis, *f.*, preface

praefátus, -a, -um, aforesaid, above mentioned

praeféctus, -i, *m.*, prefect; overseer; governor

praéferox, -ocis, very cruel

praefiguráre, to prefigure

praefiníre, to appoint

praefinítio, -onis, *f.*, purpose

praefocáre, to suffocate; drown

praegnans, -antis, being with child

praegrándis, -e, very great

praegraváre, to weigh upon, oppress

praegustáre, to taste beforehand

praeintonátio, -onis, *f.*, intoning beforehand

praeíre, -ivi and -ii, -itus, (eo), to go before

praelátio, -onis, *f.*, bearing forward, guidance; preferment; dignity

praeliáre, to fight

praeliátor, -oris, warring; (*as a noun*) warrior

praelibátio, -onis, *f.*, oblation

praélium (proélium), -ii, *n.*, battle; war

praelucére, -luxi, to outshine, surpass

praelúdium, -ii, *n.*, eve

praematúrus, -a, -um, premature; eager

praemeditáre (-ari), to meditate before, premeditate

praémium, -ii, *n.*, gift, reward, prize

praemonstráre, to mark out, point out, indicate

Praemonstraténsis, -e, Premonstratensian

Praemonstrátus, -i, *m.*, Prémontré

Praenéste, -is, *n.* and *f.*, Palestrina

Praenestínus, -a, -um, of Palestrina

praenóbilis, -e, distinguished

praenóscere, -novi, -notus, to know beforehand, foreknow

praenotáre, to indicate, mark

praenuntiáre, to show before

praenúntius, -ii, *m.*, forerunner

praeoccupáre, to come before; overtake; take by surprise

praeordinátus, -a, -um, preordained

praeparáre, to prepare

praeparátio, -onis, *f.*, preparation

praepedíre, to fetter, shackle, obstruct

praepínguis, -e, very rich

praepónere, -pósui, -pósitus, to prefer

praepositúra, -ae, *f.*, archdeaconry

praepósitus, -i, *m.*, overseer, head, governor; prelate; Praepósitus Generális, general

praepósterus, -a, -um, inverted, reversed

praépotens, -entis, mighty

praepróperus, -a, -um, overhasty

praepútium, -ii, *n.*, prepuce, foreskin, uncircumcision

praerípere, -rípui, -reptus, (io), to carry off

praerogatíva, -ae, *f.*, privilege, prerogative

praesagíre, to foretell

praeságus, -a, -um, predicting

praesciéntia, -ae, *f.*, foreknowledge

praescíre, -scivi, -scitus, to foresee

praéscius, -a, -um, having a foreboding

praeseférre (prae se ferre), -tuli, -latus, to display; praeseferénte, bearing before himself, displaying

praesens, -entis, present

praesentáre, to present

praeséntia, -ae, f., presence

praesépe, -is, n., manger

praesépium, -ii, n., stall; manger

praesértim, adv., especially

praeses, -idis, m. and f., president; governor; abbess

praesidére, -sédi, to aid, protect

praesídium, -ii, n., defense

praesignáre, to foreshadow, represent

praestábilis, -e, remarkable, pre-eminent, powerful

praestans, -antis, gracious

praestántia, -ae, f., superiority, excellence

praestáre, -stiti, -stitus, to give, grant, bestow; accomplish

praestigiátor, -oris, m., juggler; deceiver

praesto, adv., here; ready

praestolári, dep., to wait for; perform

praestríngere, -strinxi, -strictus, to bind up

praesul, -is, c., protector

praesúmere, -sumpsi, -sumptus, to take before; presume

praeténdere, -tendi, -tentus, to stretch out before, extend; present to, grant

praeter, prep., besides, except, but

praetérea, adv., besides, further, and

praetérgredi, -gressus sum, dep. 3 (io), to go beyond, transgress; pass by

praeteríre, -ivi and -itus, (eo), to pass by or away; transgress

praetéritus, -a, -um, past

praetermíttere, -misi, -missus, to neglect, omit

praetérvehi, -vectus sum, dep. 3, to be carried past; sail past

praetor, -oris, m., praetor

praetórium, -ii, n., governor's hall; hall; palace

praetórius, -a, -um, pretorian

praevalére, to prevail

praevaricári, dep., to rebel, transgress; be guilty of collusion; prevaricate

praevaricátio, -onis, f., transgression; prevarication

praevaricátor, -oris, m., transgressor

praevéniens, -entis, prevenient, preceding

praeveníre, -veni, -ventus, to prevent, anticipate; guide; direct; look forward to; precede, go before

praevidére, -vidi, -visus, to foresee

praévius, -a, -um, going before, preceding

Praga, -ae, f., Prague

Pragénsis, -e, of Prague

prandére, prandi, pransus, 2, to eat

prándium, -ii, n., dinner

pratum, -i, n., meadow

právitas, -atis, f., evil, wickedness, guilt

pravus, -a, -um, crooked; perverse, evil

precári, dep., to pray, beseech

precátio, -onis, f., prayer

precátor, -oris, m., one who prays or entreats

precátus, -us, m., prayer, entreaty

predicátor, -oris, m., preacher

prémere, pressi, pressus, to press, press upon; oppress

préndere, prendi and préndidi, prensus, to catch

présbyter, -i, m., priest

presbyterátus, -us, m., priesthood

presentátio, -onis, f., presentation

pressáre, to press; distress

pressúra, -ae, f., distress, anguish, oppression

pretiósus, -a, -um, of great price, precious

prex, precis, *f.*, prayer; preces, *pl.*, prayer, prayers

prétium, -ii, *n.*, price, money; ransom money

prídie, *adv.*, on the day before

prima, -ae, *m.*, primate

prima, -ae, *f.*, prime

primaévus, -a, -um, youthful

primátus, -us, *m.*, chief place, primacy

primítiae, -arum, *f. pl.*, first fruits

primitívus, -a, -um, first, first-born

prímitus, *adv.*, first, for the first time

primogénitum, -i, *n.*, first birthright

primogenitúra, -ae, *f.*, primogeniture

primogénitus, -a, -um, first-born

primórdium, -ii, *n.*, the first beginning, origin

primum, *adv.*, first, at first; in the first place

primus, -a, -um, first; in primis, in the first place

primus, -i, *m.*, chief man

princeps, -ipis, *m.*, prince, chief, general, ruler; príncipes sacerdótum, chief priests

principális, -e, perfect; free

principálitas, -atis, *f.*, principality

principáliter, *adv.*, in the first place, from the beginning

principári, *dep.*, to begin

principátus, -us, *m.*, principality; marquisate; rule

princípium, -ii, *n.*, beginning, source, foundation; sovereignty; principality

prinus, -i, *f.*, holm tree

prior, -ius, first, former, previous

Priscillianístae, -arum, *m. pl.*, Priscillianists

priscus, -a, -um, original, ancient

prístinus, -a, -um, former

prius, *adv.*, before

priúsquam, *conj.*, before

priváre, to deprive, withhold

privátus, -a, -um, private

privilegiátus, -a, -um, privileged

privilégium, -ii, *n.*, privilege

pro, *prep.*, for; through; in behalf of; as a result of; instead of

probabílius, *adv.*, more probably

probáre, to prove; approve

probáticus, -a, -um, sheep cleansing; probatic

probátio, -onis, *f.*, proof, test, trial

probrum, -i, *n.*, shame, disgrace, reproach, sin

probus, -a, -um, happy

procédere, -cessi, -cessus, to come or go forth; proceed (from); — in diébus multis, to be far advanced in years

procélla, -ae, *f.*, tempest, storm

procer, -eris, *m.*, noble, prince

procídere, -cidi, to fall down

procínctus, -us, *m.*, preparation to set forth (a state of being girded)

procreáre, to beget

procónsul, -is, *m.*, proconsul

proconsuláris, -e, proconsular

procul, *adv.*, afar off

proculdúbio, *adv.*, without doubt

procuráre, to govern, administer

procurátor, -oris, *m.*, steward

procus, -i, *m.*, wooer, suitor

pródere, -didi, -ditus, to bring forth; become profitable; betray

prodésse (prosum), prófui, to avail, profit, benefit, be advantageous

prodígium, -ii, *n.*, wonder

pródigus, -a, -um, prodigal

prodíre, -ivi and -ii, -itus, (eo), to come out or forth

próditor, -oris, *m.*, traitor, betrayer

prodúcere, -duxi, -ductus, to shoot forth, produce; make grow

proélium (praélium), -ii, *n.*, battle; war

profanáre, to profane

profári, *dep.*, to speak in behalf of

proféctio, -onis, *f.*, journey; departure

profécto, *adv.*, truly, really, certainly, doubtless

proféctus, -us, *m.*, source

proférre, -tuli, -latus, to bring out or forth; lay before, display

proféssio, -onis, *f.*, profession

proféssor, -oris, *m.*, professor

profícere, -feci, -fectus, (io), to avail; advance, increase, contribute to; go forth; prevail

profícuus, -a, -um, profitable

profiscíci, -fectus sum, *dep. 3*, to go, set out or forth

profitéri, -fessus sum, *dep. 2*, to profess; be enrolled

profligáre, to scatter; overthrow; abolish

proflúere, -fluxi, -fluxus, to flow forth

proflúvium, -ii, *n.*, flowing, flowing forth

prófugus, -a, -um, fugitive

profúndum, -i, *n.*, depth

profúndus, -a, -um, deep

profúsio, -onis, *f.*, pouring out, profusion

profutúrus, -a, -um, profitable

progenerátor, -oris, *m.*, progenitor, ancestor

progénies, -ei, *f.*, progeny, offspring, generation; a generatióne et progénie, from generation to generation

prógredi, -gressus sum, *dep. 3* (io), to go further

proh!, *interj.*, oh! ah!

prohibére, to restrain, forbid

proínde, *adv.*, hence

projícere, -jeci, -jectus, (io), to cast away, down or upon

prolátio, -onis, *f.*, pronouncement

proles, -is, *f.*, offspring

prolíxe, *adv.*, freely, abundantly

prolíxitas, -atis, *f.*, fullness

prolíxius, *adv.*, the longer

prolongáre, to lengthen, prolong

prolongátus, -a, -um, long

próloqui, -locútus sum, *dep. 3*, to speak out, declare

prolúdere, -lusi, -lusus, to practice beforehand

prolúere, -ui, -utus, to wash out.

promanáre, to emanate or derive from

prómere, prompsi, promptus, to bring forth, utter

promerére (-éri), to merit, deserve; obtain

promicáre, to shine forth

promíssio, -onis, *f.*, promise

promíssum, -i, *n.*, promise

promíttere, -misi, -missus, to promise

promótor, -oris, *m.*, encourager, promoter, champion

promótus, -a, -um, promoted, raised

promptuárium, -ii, *n.*, storehouse; pantry

promptus, -a, -um, willing, ready

promptus, -us, *m.*, visibility, in promptu, manifest

promulgáre, to make known, publish

pronuntiáre, to speak, declare, pronounce; show; threaten

pronus, -a, -um, flat, prone; inclined, bent forward; on his side

Propagánda, -ae, *f.*, abbr. for the phrase de propagánda fide

propagáre, to spread

propagátio, -onis, *f.*, spreading, propagation

propagátor, -oris, *m.*, propagator

propágo, -inis, *f.*, shoot, branch; generation

propaláre, to make manifest

prope, *adv.*, near, at hand

propémodum, *adv.*, almost

propénsius, *adv.*, mercifully; speedily

propénsus, -a, -um, disposed to

properáre, to hasten

prophéta, -ae, *m.*, prophet

prophetális, -e, of a prophet, prophetical

prophetáre, to prophesy

prophétes, -is, *m.*, prophet

prophetía, -ae, *f.*, prophecy

prophéticus, -a, -um, prophetic

prophetíssa, -ae, *f.*, prophetess

propináre, to offer a drink to

propinquáre, to approach; attain

propínquitas, -atis, *f.*, nearness; relationship

propínquus, -a, -um, near of kin; near, approaching

própior, -ius, nearer

propitiábilis, -e, propitious

propitiáre, (-ari), to be merciful or favorable

propitiátio, -onis, *f.*, forgiveness, clemency, favor; propitiation

propitiatórium, -ii, *n.*, propitiatory, mercy seat

propítius, -a, -um, merciful, gracious, propitious

propónere, -pósui, -pósitus, to lay or set before

propositío, -onis, *f.*, setting forth, proposition; text; riddle

propósitum, -i, *n.*, plan, design, purpose

propríetas, -atis, *f.*, peculiarity, distinction

próprium, -ii, *n.*, proper

próprius, -a, -um, one's own

propter, *prep.*, for, because of, by reason of

proptérea, *adv.*, therefore

propugnáculum, -i, *n.*, rampart, bulwark

propugnátor, -oris, *m.*, defender

propulsáre, to repel

proripere, -rípui, -reptus, (io), to rush forth, escape

prorogáre, to defer, put off

prorsus, *adv.*, turned toward; wholly; at all

prosa, -ae, *f.*, prose

prosélytus, -i, *n.*, proselyte

prósequi, -secútus sum, *dep.* 3, to further; honor, regard, hear; look down upon

prosilíre, -ui, to spring, leap forth

prospéctor, -oris, *m.*, provider, guardian

prosperári, *dep.*, to prosper

próspere, *adv.*, prosperously

prospéritas, -atis, *f.*, prosperity

prósper, -a, -um, prosperous, well; próspera, *n. pl.*, prosperous things, prosperity; good tidings

prospícere, -spexi, -spectus, (io), to look; foresee

prostérnere, -stravi, -stratus, to strew or spread before; present; overthrow, prostrate, humble; (*reflexive*), to fall down, prostrate oneself

prostíbulum, -i, stews, brothel

prostitúere, -ui, -utus, to prostitute

prostitútio, -onis, *f.*, fornication

prostrátus, -a, -um, lying on the ground, humble, prostrate

Protásius, -ii, *m.*, Protase

protéctio, -onis, *f.*, protection

protéctor, -oris, *m.*, protector

protégere, -texti, -tectus, to cover; protect, help, defend

protén dere, -tendi, -tentus and -tensus, to hold up

protérere, -trivi, -tritus, to trample under foot

protérvus, -a, -um, stubborn

prótinus, *adv.*, constantly, immediately

protomártyr, -is, *m.*, protomartyr

protoplástus, -i, *m.*, the first man, Adam

protráhere, -traxi, -tractus, to draw out, extend; remain

prout, *conj.*, according as

provéctio, -onis, *f.*, advancement, progress

provéctus, -a, -um, advanced in age

provéhere, -vexi, -vectus, to lead on

proveníre, -veni, -ventus, to come for; be granted

provéntus, -us, *m.*, issue, result; crop; revenue

provérbium, -ii, *n.*, proverb

providéntia, -ae, *f.*, providence

providére, -vidi, -visus, to provide; set; see, behold

província, -ae, *f.*, province

Província, -ae, *f.*, Provence

provísor, -oris, *m.*, provider

provocáre, to provoke

provolútus, -a, -um, lying prostrate

provólvere, -volvi, -volútus, to throw oneself down

próximus, -a, -um, near, neighboring; in próximo, near at hand

próximus, -i, *m.*, neighbor

prudens, -entis, wise

prudénter, *adv.*, wisely

prudéntia, -ae, *f.*, prudence, wisdom, understanding

pruína, -ae, *f.*, hoar frost

pruna, -ae, *f.*, live coal

prúriens, -entis, itching

psállere, to sing, give praise

psalmísta, -ae, *m.*, psalmist

psalmódia, -ae, *f.*, singing of psalms, psalmody

psalmus, -i, *m.*, psalm

psaltérium, -ii, *n.*, psalter; psaltery

pseudochrístus, -i, *m.*, false Christ

pseudoprophéta, -ae, *m.*, false prophet

Ptolemaéus, -i, *m.*, Ptolemee

Ptoleménsis, -e, of Ptolemais; inhabitant of Ptolemais

publicánus, -i, *m.*, publican

publicáre, to publish; make a public example of

públice, *adv.*, openly; at public expense

públicus, -a, -um, public

pudére (usually impersonal), to be ashamed

pudicítia, -ae, *f.*, purity

pudícus, -a, -um, chaste

pudor, -oris, *m.*, modesty, purity, shame; maidenhood

puélla, -ae, *f.*, girl, maid, damsel

puéllus, -i, *m.*, boy, child

puer, -i, *m.*, boy, child; young man; servant

puerílis, -e, childish

puerítia, -ae, *f.*, childhood, boyhood, girlhood

puérpera, -ae, *f.*, child-bearer, mother

puérperus, -a, -um, child-bearing

pugilláris, -is, *m.*, writing tablet

pugíllus, -i, *m.*, handful

púgio, -onis, *f.*, dagger, sword

pugna, -ae, *f.*, battle

pugnáre, to fight, do battle

pugnátor, -oris, *m.*, fighter, warrior

pugnus, -i, *m.*, fist

pulcher, -chra, -chrum, fair, beautiful

pulchritúdo, -inis, *f.*, beauty

pulluláre, to sprout

pullus, -i, *m.*, young of animals; colt; chicken

pulmentárium, -ii, *n.*, anything to eat

pulméntum, -i, *n.*, savory meat; pottage

pulsáre, to knock; beset

pulvínar, -aris, *n.*, pillow

pulvis, -eris, *m.*, dust; ashes

púnctio, -onis, *f.*, pricking

punctum, -i, *n.*, a very small space; moment

púngere, púpugi, punctus, to pierce

Púnicus, -a, -um, Carthaginian, Punic

puníre, to punish

pupílla, -ae, *f.*, pupil of the eye

pupíllus, -i, *m.*, orphan

purgaméntum, -i, *n.*, refuse

purgáre, to purify, purge

purgátio, -onis, *f.*, purgation, expiation, purification

purgatórium, -ii, *n.*, purgatory

purgátus, -a, -um, cleansed

purificáre, to purify, cleanse

purificátio, -onis, *f.*, purification

púritas, -atis, *f.*, purity

púrpura, -ae, *f.*, purple; **regis púrpura,** royal purple

purpurátus, -a, -um, empurpled; clad in purple

purpúreus, -a, -um, purple

purus, -a, -um, pure, clean

pusillánimis, -e, fainthearted; feebleminded

pusillanímitas, -atis, fainteartedness

pusíllum, -i, *n.*, a little

pusíllus, -a, -um, little

putáre, to think; **puta,** for example, suppose

putátio, -onis, *f.*, pruning

putatíve, *adv.*, supposedly

putatívus, -a, -um, reputed

Puteolánus, -a, -um, of Pozzuolo

Putéoli, -orum, *m. pl.*, Pozzuolo

púteus, -i, *m.*, pit, well

putrédo, -inis, *f.*, rottenness

putrefáctus, -a, -um, rotten

putréscere, -ui, to become rotten

putris, -e, rotten, mortifying

pytho, -onis, *m.*, spirit of a diviner

Q

qua . . . qua, *adv.*, partly . . . partly

quacúmque, *adv.*, whatsoever

quadragenárius, -a, -um, of forty days

quadragéni, -ae, -a, forty each

quadragésima, -ae, *f.*, Lent

quadragesimális, -e, of forty days; Lenten

quadragínta, forty

quadráre, to fit exactly, correspond to

Quadratiánus, -a, -um, Quadratian

quadríga, -ae, *f.*, chariot

quadringénti, -ae, -a, four hundred

quádrupes, -edis, *m.* and *f.*, four-footed beast

quádruplum, fourfold

quaérere, -sivi or -sii, -situs, to seek; require; reason

quaésere, -ivi and -ii, -itus, to beseech

quaéstio, -onis, *f.*, question, inquiry

quaestor, -oris, *m.*, quaestor, pardoner

quaestuósus, -a, -um, profitable

quaestus, -us, *m.*, gain

qualis, -e, what manner? what sort? what kind?; as

quálitas, -atis, *f.*, quality

quáliter, *adv.*, how, in what manner; as, just as

quam, *adv.*, than, rather than; how!

quámdiu, *conj.*, as long as, while; until; how long?

quamóbrem, *adv.*, wherefore

quamplúrimi, -ae, -a, as many as possible

quamvis, *conj.*, although; *adv.*, even

quando, *adv.*, when

quandóquidem, *conj.*, since, because, seeing that

quantíllus, -a, -um, how little

quantócius, *adv.*, sooner, more quickly

quantum, *adv.*, as much as

quantus, -a, -um, what, how great, how much; **quanto . . . tanto,** the more . . . the more

quantúslibet, -tálibet, -túmlibet, however great

quaprópter, *adv.*, wherefore

quare, *adv.*, why

quartus, -a, -um, fourth

quartus décimus, -a, -a, -um, -um, fourteenth

Quarum, -i, *n.*, Quero

quasi, *adv.*, as if, like, as it were; about

quassátio, -onis, *f.*, affliction, scourge

quátenus, *adv.*, how far, in so far as; so that

quater, *adv.*, four times

quátere, quassi, quassus, (io), to shake

quatérnio, -onis, *f.*, quaternion; a body of four soldiers

quatriduánus, -a, -um, of four days

quatríduum, -i, *n.*, space of four days

quátuor, four

quatuórdecim, fourteen

-que, *conj., enclitic,* and

queis = quibus

quemádmodum, *adv.*, as, just as

quercus, -us, *f.*, oak

queréla, -ae, *f.*, complaint; blame

querimónia, -ae, *f.*, complaint

questus, -us, *m.*, complaint, lament

qui, quae, quod, who, which, what

quia, *conj.*, for, because; that

quid, what? why? ut quid, to what purpose

quidam, quaedam, quoddam and *subst.* quiddam, a certain person or thing; some, some one, something

quidem, *adv.*, indeed

quidnam, what then?

quies, -etis, *f.*, rest, quiet

quiéscens, -entis, of rest or quiet

quiéscere, -evi, -etus, to be still; cease

quiétus, -a, -um, quiet, peaceful

quílibet, quaélibet, quódlibet and *subst.* quídlibet, any, any one, anything whatsoever

quin, *conj.*, that not

quinárius, -a, -um, five

quíndecim, fifteen

quingentésimus, -a, -um, five hundredth

quingénti, -ae, -a, five hundred

quinímmo (quinímo), *adv.*, yea rather

quinquagenárius, -a, -um, fifty in number

quinquagésima: domínica in —, Quinquagesima Sunday

quinquagínta, fifty

quinque, five

quinquénnis, at the age of five

quinquénnium, -ii, *n.*, a period of five years

quínquies, five times

quintus, -a, -um, fifth

quintusdécimus, -a, -a, -um, -um, fifteenth

quippe, *conj.*, for, certainly

quíppiam (quídpiam), anyone (anything)

quire (queo), -ivi and -ii, -itus, to be able, can

quis, quid, *interrog. pron.*, who? what?

quis, quid, *indef. pron.*, anyone, anything

quisnam, quidnam, who then? what then?

quíspiam, quaépiam, quódpiam and *subst.* quídpiam or quíppiam, any one, anything, some one, something

quisquam, quaequam, quidquam, any person, anybody, any one, anything

quisque, quaeque, quidque and *adj.* quodque, each, every, every one, everybody, everything

quisquis, quaequae, quidquid, and *adj.* quodquod, any, each, whoever, whatever

quo, *adv.*, whither; so that

quoadúsque, *conj.*, until

quocírca, *adv.*, therefore, on that account

quocúmque, *adv.*, whithersoever, to whatever place

quod, that, which, what; because

quodámmodo, *adv.*, in a certain way; as it were

quodcúmque, whatsoever

quómodo, *adv.*, as, how?

quomodocúmque, *adv.*, in any way

quondam, *adv.*, formerly, once

quóniam, *conj.*, for, because, since; that

quoque, *adv.*, also

quot, how many; quotquot, however many

quotánnis, *adv.*, yearly

quotidiánus, -a, -um, daily

quotídie, *adv.*, daily, every day

quóties, *adv.*, how often

quotiescúmque, *adv.*, as often as

quoúsque, *adv.*, how long?

quum (cum), *conj.*, when, since, as often as

R

rabbi, rabbi, master

rábidus, -a, -um, mad

rábies, -ei, *f.*, ravening

raca, silly person

racémus, -i, *m.*, cluster

rádere, rasi, rasus, to scrape away

radicáre, to strike root

radicátus, -a, -um, rooted

radícitus, *adv.*, by the roots

rádius, -ii, *m.*, ray

radix, -icis, *f.*, root; radíces, *pl.*, base; in radícibus, at the foot

ramus, -i, *m.*, branch, bough

rana, -ae, *f.*, frog

rapax, -acis, ravening

rapax, -acis, *m.*, extortioner

rápere, -ui, raptus, (io), to seize, catch, take by force, take or carry up; pluck

rápiens, -entis, ravening

rapína, -ae, *f.*, robbery

raptor, -oris, *m.*, extortioner; robber

raptus, -a, -um, to be caught or carried up; rapt

rarus, -a, -um, strange

Rástislaus, -i, *m.*, Rastislav

ratis, -is, *f.*, raft, float

rátio, -onis, *f.*, reckoning, retribution; account; rule, way; reasoning

rationábilis, -e, reasonable, rational; rationabília, *n. pl.*, truths

rationális, -e, rational

ratus, -a, -um, settled, ratified, valid

ráucitas, -atis, *f.*, harshness

raucus, -a, -um, hoarse

Ravénnas, -atis, belonging to or an inhabitant of Ravenna

Ravennaténsis, -e, of Ravenna

Raymúndus, -i, *m.*, Raymund

Raymúndus Nonnátus, -i, -i, *m.*, Raymund Nonnatus

re-, *prefix* sometimes used for emphasis; reípsa cum carne, with the very flesh itself

reaedificáre, to rebuild

reális, -e, real

reamplécti, -plexus sum, *dep. 3*, to embrace again

reápse, *adv.*, indeed, in truth

reátus, -us, *m.*, guilt, fault

rebelláre, to rebel

rebéllio, -onis, *f.*, rebellion

rebéllis, -e, rebellious

recalcitráre, to kick

recapitulátio, -onis, *f.*, repetition

Reccarédus, -i, *m.*, Recared

recédere, -cessi, -cessus, to fall away, depart or stray from

recens, -entis, recent, new

recensére, to review, recall, celebrate

receptáculum, -i, *n.*, vessel, receptacle

receptíbilis, -e, acceptable

recéptor, -oris, *m.*, receiver

recípere, -cepi, -ceptus, (io), to receive, recover

recitáre, to recite

recitátio, -onis, *f.*, recitation

reclináre, to lay

recogitáre, to consider, reflect

recognítio, -onis, *f.*, recognition, examination

recólere, -cólui, -cultus, to contemplate, recollect

reconciliáre, to reconcile

reconciliátio, -onis, *f.*, reconciliation

reconciliátor, -oris, *m.*, intermediary

recóndere, -didi, -ditus, to lay up

recordári, *dep.*, to remember

recordátio, -onis, *f.*, memory, remembrance; record

recreáre, to refresh, treat

recte, *adv.*, rightly, well

rectitúdo, -inis, *f.*, rightness; righteousness

rector, -oris, *m.*, ruler

rectus, -a, -um, right, upright, righteous, straight

recubáre, to recline

recúbitus, -us, *m.*, seat

recúmbere, -cúbui, to lean; recline, sit down; be at table

recuperáre, to recover

recúrrere, -curri, -cursus, to occur

recusáre, to refuse

redamáre, to return love for love

redargútio, -onis, *f.*, retort

réddere, -didi, -ditus, to restore, render, pay

reddítio, -onis, *f.*, return, restoration

redémptio, -onis, *f.*, redemption, deliverance

redémptor, -oris, *m.*, redeemer

redígere, -egi, -actus, to bring down

redímere, -emi, -emptus, to redeem

redintegráre, to raise up, restore

redíre, -ivi and -ii, -itus, (eo), to return; pay

réditus, -us, *m.*, return; revenue

redonáre, to give back

redúcere, -duxi, -ductus, to bring back or again; draw back

redundáre, to overflow

redux, -ucis, returned

reféctio, -onis, *f.*, refreshment; refectory

reféllere, -felli, to refute, disprove

reférre, -tuli, -latus, to yield; tell, refer

refértus, -a, -um, crowded

refícere, -feci, -fectus, (io), to refresh; mend, repair

refléxus, -a, -um, crooked

refloréscere, -flórui, to flourish or bloom again

réfluus, -a, -um, flowing back

refocilláre, to relieve

reformáre, to renew, reform

reformátio, -onis, *f.*, reformation

reformidáre, to dread

refovére, -fovi, -fotus, to refresh, revive

refraenáre, to restrain

refragári, *dep.*, to oppose

refrenáre, to bridle

refrigeráre, to cool; refresh

refrigérium, -ii, *n.*, refreshment, recreation

refrigéscere, -frixi, to grow cold

réfuga, -ae, *m.*, forsaker

refúgium, -ii, *n.*, refuge

refulgére, -fulsi, to shine brightly

refúndere, -fudi, -fusus, to pour back, restore

regális, -e, regal, royal

regenerátio, -onis, *f.*, regeneration

regenerátor, -oris, *m.*, regenerator

régere, rexi, rectus, to govern

régimen, -inis, *n.*, government, direction

regína, -ae, *f.*, queen

régio, -onis, *f.*, region, country

régius, -a, -um, of a king, royal

regnáre, to reign

regnum, -i, *n.*, kingdom

régredi, -gressus sum, (io), to go back, return

régula, -ae, *f.*, rule

reguláris, -e, regular

régulus, -i, *m.*, nobleman, ruler; basilisk

reinveníre, -veni, -ventus, to find again

reípse, -a, -um, the very (re- is for emphasis)

relátus, -us, *m.,* narrative, recital

relaxáre, to loose, forgive

relegáre, to remove, banish

relégere, -legi, -lectus, to traverse again, collect

religáre, to fasten, hang

relígio, -onis, *f.,* religion, reverence; a religious order

religiósitas, -atis, *f.,* religiousness

religiósus, -a, -um, religious

relínquere, -liqui, -lictus, to leave behind

relíquiae, -arum, *f. pl.,* relics, remains; remnant

réliquus, -a, -um, remaining; et réliqua, and so forth

reluctári, *dep.,* to strive, contend or struggle against

remanére, -mansi, -mansus, to be left, remain

remeáre, to go back

remédium, -ii, *n.,* remedy

rememorári, *dep.,* to remember; be remembered

remetíri, -mensus sum, *dep. 4,* to measure again

remex, -igis, *m.,* rower

remigáre, to row

reminísci, *dep. 3,* to remember

remíssio, -onis, *f.,* remission, absolution, forgiveness

remíssus, -a, -um, negligent, slothful, remiss

remíttere, -misi, -missus, to send back; remit; forgive

remótus, -a, -um, far off

removére, -movi, -motus, to remove, to take away

remunerátio, -onis, *f.,* reward

remunerátor, -oris, *m.,* rewarder

renásci, -natus sum, *dep. 3,* to be regenerated

renes, -um and -ium, *m. pl.,* kidneys, loins, reins

renidére, to shine

reníti, *dep. 3,* to oppose

renováre, to renew, build anew

renovátio, -onis, *f.,* renovation

renúere, -ui, to refuse

renuntiáre, to relate, bring word; appoint; renounce

reosculári, *dep.,* to kiss again

repágulum, -i, *n.,* barrier; restraint

reparáre, to restore; anno reparátae salútis, in the year of Redemption

reparátio, -onis, *f.,* reparation; regeneration; healing

reparátrix, -icis, *f.,* restorer

repéllere, -puli, -pulsus, to cast off; overcome

rependere, -pendi, -pensus, to repay, return

repentínus, -a, -um, sudden

reperíre, -peri, -pertus, to find, obtain

repétere, -ivi and -ii, -itus, to exact of; repeat

repénte, *adv.,* suddenly

replére, -plevi, -pletus, to fill

replésti = replevísti, *perfect tense* of replére

replétus, -a, -um, filled

repónere, -pósui, -pósitus, to lay

reportáre, to bring back; receive, gain

repósitus, -a, -um, laid up

repraesentáre, to show, present; lead

reprehénsio, -onis, *f.,* censure

reprímere, -pressi, -pressus, to curb, repress

reprobáre, to refuse, reject

réprobus, -a, -um, good for nothing; reprehensible

réprobus, -i, *m.,* castaway

repromíssio, -onis, *f.,* promise

repromíttere, -misi, -missus, to promise in return

reptáre, to crawl, creep

réptile, -is, *n.*, creeping creature, reptile

repúdium, -ii, *n.*, divorce

repugnáre, to disagree with; resist

reputáre, to repute, esteem

réquies, -etis and -ei, *f.*, rest

requiéscere, -evi, -etus, to rest, be at rest

requiétio, -onis, *f.*, rest

requírere, -sivi, -situs, to seek; require; care for

réri, ratus sum, *dep. 2*, to think, esteem, suppose

res, rei, *f.*, thing; quem ab rem, wherefore; res familiáris, inheritance

rescíndere, -scidi, -scissus, to annul, repeal

rescíscere, -scivi and -scii, -scitus, to find out

rescríbere, -scripsi, -scriptus, to write back or again

rescríptum, -i, *n.*, copy of a writing

resecáre, to cut off; root out

reseráre, to open; reveal, make clear

reserváre, to save; preserve; reserve

residére, -sedi, -sessus, to sit up; remain; reside

resíduum, -i, *n.*, remainder

resíduus, -a, -um, remaining; left over

resína, -ae, *f.*, balm

resipíscere, -sípui, -sípii, and -sipívi, to come to one's right mind, repent

resístere, -stiti, to resist, withstand

resolútio, -onis, *f.*, dissolution

resolútus, -a, -um, careless

resólvere, -solvi, -solútus, to loosen

resonáre, to resound

respéctio, -onis, *f.*, esteem

respectivus, -a, -um, respective

respéctus, -us, *m.*, respect

respérgere, -spersi, -spersus, to sprinkle; scatter; shed; stain

respícere, -spexi, -spectus, (io), to look; receive one's sight

respiráre, to breathe; have life again; find relief

resplendére, -ui, to shine, be bright, show forth

respondére, -spondi, -sponsus, to answer, respond

responsórium, -ii, *n.*, responsory

respónsum, -i, *n.*, answer, response

respública, reipúblicae, *f.*, republic, commonwealth

respúere, -ui, to spit out; reject; despise

restáre, to remain

restauráre, to restore

restínguere, -stinxi, -stinctus, to quench, extinguish

restitúere, -ui, -utus, to set again; restore

restitútio, -onis, *f.*, restitution, restoration

restitútor, -oris, *m.*, restorer

restríctio, -onis, *f.*, restriction, restraint

resultáre, to resound, rebound

resúrgere, -surréxi, -surréctus, to rise again; awake

resurréctio, -onis, *f.*, rising up; resurrection

resuscitáre, to raise up

retardáre, to stop, check

rete, -is, *n.*, net

retéxere, -téxui, -tectus, to weave again; repeat

retiáculum, -i, *n.*, net

reticére, -ui, to be silent (about)

retinére, -tínui, -tentus, to keep, retain; remember; imitate

retráhere, -traxi, -tractus, to restrain; withdraw

retribúere, -ui, -utus, to render, repay; bring

retribútio, -onis, *f.*, reward, recompense, benefit, favor

retro, *adv.*, behind; back

retroáctus, -a, -um, past

retrógradus, -a, -um, going backward

retrórsum, *adv.*, back, backwards

retúndere, -tudi, -tusus, to blunt

reus, -i, *m.*, defendant, criminal, guilty one

reveláre, to reveal, disclose, make known, show

revelátio, -onis, *f.*, revelation

revéra, *adv.*, indeed, truly

reveréntia, -ae, *f.*, fear, reverence

reverénter, *adv.*, reverently

reveréri, *dep.* 2, to be ashamed

revérti, -versus sum, *dep. 3*, to return; depart

revincíre, -vinxi, -vinctus, to bind, bind fast

reviréscere, -vírui, to become green again

revívere, -vixi, -victus, to revive

revivíscere, -vixi, to come to life again, live again, revive

revocáre, to call back or away

rex, regis, *m.*, king

Reyi, -orum, *m. pl.*, the Rey family

Rhaeti, -orum, *m. pl.*, Rhaetians

Rhaétia, -ae, *f.*, Rhaetia, Tyrol

rhamnus, -i, *m.*, bramble, thornbush

rheda, -ae, *f.*, carriage with four wheels; chariot

Rhegiénsis, -e, of Reggio

Rheménsis, -e, of Rheims

Rhemi, -orum, *m. pl.*, Rheims

rhetórica, -ae, *f.*, rhetoric

rhetóricus, -i, *m.*, rhetorician

rhomphaéa, -ae, *f.*, sword

rhythmus, -i, *m.*, rhythm

rictus, -us, *m.*, open mouth, expanded jaws

ridére, risi, risus, to laugh, laugh at

rigáre, to water, sprinkle, wash

rigor, -oris, *m.*, rigor, stiffness

ripa, -ae, *f.*, bank

risus, -us, *m.*, laughter

rite, *adv.*, fitly, with suitable religious ceremonies

ritus, -us, *m.*, rite

rívulus, -i, *m.*, brook, rivulet

rivus, -i, *m.*, river, brook

rixa, -ae, *f.*, quarrel

rixári, *dep.*, to quarrel

Robértus, -i, *m.*, Robert

roboráre, to make strong, strengthen

roborátor, -oris, *m.*, strengthener

robur, -oris, *n.*, strength

robústus, -a, -um, mighty

Roccha Porrena, -ae, -ae, *f.*, Rocca Porena

Rodardénsis, -e, of Rodersdorf

Rodbódus, -i, *m.*, Rodbod

Rofténsis, -e, of Rochester

rogáre, to beseech

rogátio, -onis, *f.*, rogation

rogátus, -us, *m.*, request

Rogérius, -ii, *m.*, Roger

rogus, -i, *m.*, funeral pile

Roma, -ae, *f.*, Rome

Románus, -a, -um, of Rome, Roman

Romuáldus, -i, *m.*, Romuald

Romúleus, -a, -um, of Romulus

roráre, to cause dew to drop

ros, roris, *m.*, dew

rosa, -ae, *f.*, rose

Rosa, -ae, *f.*, Rose

rosárium, -ii, *n.*, rosary

róseus, -a, -um, roseate

rostrum, -i, *n.*, beak; prow

rota, -ae, *f.*, wheel

ruber, -bra, -brum, red

rubére, to redden

rubéscere, -ui, to become red

rúbeus, -a, -um, red

rubicúndus, -a, -um, ruddy

rubígo, -inis, *f.*, rust; mildew

rubor, -oris, *m.*, shame

rúbrica, -ae, *f.*, rubric

rubus, -i, *m.*, bush

rudis, -e, ignorant, illiterate, rough

rudus, -a, -um, brutish

rúere, rui, rutus, to rush, hasten; fall down; fail, be ruined

rufus, -a, -um, ruddy, red

ruga, -ae, f., wrinkle

rugíre, to roar

rugítus, -us, m., roaring

ruína, -ae, f., fall; invasion; breach; destruction

rumor, -oris, m., fame

rúmpere, rupi, ruptus, to break

rupes, -is, f., stony hill, sharp cliff, rock

rúptio, -onis, f., breaking open, an injuring

rurícola, -ae, c., peasant

rursum, adv., again, anew

rus, ruris, n., the country

Ruthéni, -orum, m. pl., Ruthenians

rutiláre, to glow

S

Sabaéus, -a, -um, Sabaean

Sábaoth (Hebrew), armies, hosts

Sabáudia, -ae, f., Savoy

sabbatísmus, -i, m., a day of rest; keeping of the Sabbath

sábbatum, -i, n., Sabbath; Saturday; week; sábbata, n. pl., Sabbath; una sabbatórum (sábbati), the first day of the week

sábulum, -i, n., sand

sácculus, -i, m., purse

saccus, -i, m., sackcloth

sacéllum, -i, n., chapel

sacer, -cra, -crum, sacred

sacérdos, -otis, m., priest; príncipes sacerdótum, chief priests

sacerdotális, -e, sacerdotal, priestly

sacerdótium, -ii, n., priestly function, priesthood

sacramentális, -e, sacramental

sacraméntum, -i, n., sacrament, sacramental grace

sacráre, to consecrate, hallow

sacrificáre, to sacrifice, offer up

sacrifícium, -ii, n., sacrifice

sacrosánctus, -a, -um, most sacred

sacrum, -i, n., holy thing; grace

Sadducaéi, -orum, m. pl., Sadducees

saeclum = saéculum

saeculáris, -e, worldly; saeculária, n. pl., feast, celebration

saéculum, -i, n., time, period, age; world; in saécula saeculórum, world without end; a saéculo, from the beginning, from everlasting; a saéculo et in saéculum, from eternity to eternity

saepe, adv., often

saéviens, -entis, fierce

saevíre, to rage

saevítia, -ae, f., fury, cruelty

saevus, -a, -um, cruel

sagéna, -ae, f., net

saginóre, to feed

saginátus, -a, -um, fatted

sagítta, -ae, f., arrow

sagittáre, to shoot with arrows

sagittárius, -ii, m., archer

Sahagúnum, -i, n., Sahagun

sal, -is, m. and n., salt

Salárius, -a, -um, Salarian

Salernitánus, -a, -um, of Salerno

Salérnum, -i, n., Salerno

Salésium, -ii, n., Sales

Salésius, -a, -um, of Sales

Sálicus, -a, -um, Salic

salínae, -arum, f. pl., salt pits

salíre, sálui, saltus, to spring up, leap

salíva, -ae, f., spittle, saliva

salix, -icis, f., willow

Sallustiánus, -a, -um, of Sallust

Salmántica, -ae, f., Salamanca

Salmanticénsis, -e, of Salamanca

Sálomon, -onis, m., Solomon

salsúgo, -inis, f., saltness; salt desert

saltáre, to dance

saltátio, -onis, *f.*, dancing, dance

saltátrix, -icis, *f.*, dancing girl

saltem, *adv.*, at least

saltus, -us, *m.*, forest

salúbris, -e, or salúber, -bris, -bre, strong; good, wholesome; useful

salúbritas, -atis, *f.*, health

salúbriter, *adv.*, wholesomely; profitably

salus, -utis, *f.*, salvation, deliverance; health; greeting

salutáre, to greet, salute

salutáre, -is, *n.*, health; salvation

salutáris, -e, wholesome, saving, salutary

salutáriter, *adv.*, beneficially

salutátio, -onis, f., salutation

salútifer, -a, -um, of salvation, saving

salváre, to save

salvátio, -onis, *f.*, salvation

salvátor, -oris, *m.*, savior

salve! (salvéte, salvéto), hail!

salvére, to be well

salvificáre, to save

Sálvius, -ii, *m.*, Salvi

salvus, -a, -um, saved, safe; whole

Samaritánus, -a, -um, Samaritan

Samaritánus, -i, *m.*, Samaritan

sambúca, -ae, *f.*, sackbut, a kind of musical instrument

samech, the fifteenth letter of the Hebrew alphabet, corresponding to English *s*

sanáre, to heal

Sanciánus, -i, *m.*, Sancian (a Chinese island)

sancíre, sanxi, sanctus, to make sacred; forbid

sancta, -ae, *f.*, saint

Sancta Fides, -ae, -ei, *f.*, Santa Fe

sanctificáre, to sanctify, hallow

sanctificátio, -onis, *f.*, holiness; sacred mystery; blessing; sanctuary

sanctificátor, -oris, *m.*, sanctifier

sanctifícium, -ii, *n.*, shrine, sanctuary

sanctimónia, -ae, *f.*, holiness

sanctimoniális, -e, pious

sanctimoniális, -is, *f.*, nun

sánctio, -onis, *f.*, sanction, rule

sánctitas, -atis, *f.*, sanctity

sanctitúdo, -inis, *f.*, holiness

sanctuárium, -ii, *n.*, sanctuary

sanctum, -i, *n.*, holy place; sanctuary

sanctus, -a, -um, holy, godly, saintly; sancta sanctórum, holy of holies

sanctus, -i, *m.*, saint

Sanctus Facúndus, -i, -i, *m.*, San Facondo

Sanctus Nicoláus de Portu, -i, -i, *m.*, San Nicola del Porto

sanguíneus, -a, -um, of blood

sanguis, -inis, *m.*, blood

sánies, -ei, *f.*, matter, pus

sánitas, -atis, *f.*, health

sanus, -a, -um, whole, healthy

sápere, -ii, (io), to understand; be wise; idípsum sápere, to be of one mind

sápiens, -entis, wise

sapiéntia, -ae, *f.*, wisdom

sapor, -oris, *m.*, taste

sapphírus, -i, *f.*, sapphire

Saracéni, -orum, *m. pl.*, Saracens

sárcina, -ae, *f.*, pack, burden

sarcíre, sarsi, sartus, to repair, restore

sárculum, -i, *n.*, hoe, spade

Sardicénsis, -e, of Sardis

sárdinis, -e: lapis sárdinis, sardine stone

sárdius, -ii, *f.*, sard

Sardus, -a, -um, Sardinian

sardónychus, -a, -um, sardonyx

sárdonyx, -nychis, *f.*, sardonyx

Sarépta (Saréphta), Sarephta

sartágo, -inis, *f.*, frying pan

sartatécta, -orum, *n. pl.*, repairs

sartus, -a, -um, repaired

Sásimi, -orum, *m. pl.*, people of Sasima

sat, *adv.*, enough

satágere, to be very busy; be in trouble

satagitáre, to be very busy or diligent

satan, *indecl.*, satan, adversary

Sátanas, -ae, *m.*, Satan

satélles, -itis, *c.*, guard; companion; servant; officer of justice

satiáre, to nourish, satisfy, fill, sate, feed

satis, *adv.*, enough, sufficiently; greatly, exceedingly

satisfácere, -feci, -factus, (io), to satisfy

satisfáctio, -onis, *f.*, satisfaction

sator, -oris, *m.*, sower; source; begetter, father

sátrapa, -ae, *m.*, noble, lord, satrap

saturáre, to fill

saturátio, -onis, *f.*, filling, satisfying

satúritas, -atis, *f.*, satisfaction, satiety, abundance, in saturitáte, to the full

satus, -i, *m.*, measure, sowing

sauciáre, to wound

sáucius, -a, -um, wounded

Saulus, -i, *m.*, Saul

sáxeus, -a, -um, stony

Saxónia, -ae, *f.*, Saxony

saxum, -i, *n.*, stone, rock

scabéllum, -i, *n.*, small stool, footstool

scala, -ae, *f.*, ladder

scalprum, -i, *n.*, chisel

scandalizáre, to scandalize

scándalum, -i, *n.*, scandal; trap, stumbling block

scándere, scandi, scansus, to climb, rise

scápulae, -arum, *f. pl.*, shoulders; wings

scapuláris, -e, scapular

scatére, to gush, gush forth; swarm; abound

scaturíre, to gush forth

scelerátus, -a, -um, wicked

sceléstus, -a, -um, wicked, shameless

scelus, -eris, *n.*, sin, crime

scenofactórius, -a, -um, tent making

Scenopégia, -ae, *f.*, Feast of Tabernacles

scéptriger, -a, -um, scepter bearing

sceptrum, -i, *n.*, scepter

schema, -atis, *n.*, form, scheme

schisma, -atis, *n.*, schism

schismáticus, -a, -um, schismatic

schinus, -i, *f.*, mastic tree

schola, -ae, *f.*, school

sciens, -entis, expert

sciénter, *adv.*, wisely

sciéntia, -ae, *f.*, knowledge, science

scílicet, *adv.*, actually

scíndere, scidi, scissus, to rend, cut; — médium, to cut in two

scintílla, -ae, *f.*, spark

scíre, -ivi and -ii, -itus, to know, know how

sciscitári, *dep.*, to inquire, inquire into

scissúra, -ae, *f.*, rending, splitting; piece

scissus, -a, -um, torn, rent, broken

scitum, -i, *n.*, decree, statute

scopa, -ae, *f.*, broom; scopis mundátus, swept

scópere, to search thoroughly

scópulus, -i, *m.*, rock, cliff

scória, -ae, *f.*, dross

scórpio, -onis, *m.*, scorpion; whip loaded with metal

scortári, *dep.*, to commit uncleanness

scortum, -i, *n.*, uncleanness, immorality

Scoti, -orum, *m. pl.*, Scots

Scótia, -ae, *f.*, Scotland

scriba, -ae, *m.*, scribe, scrivener, writer

scríbere, scripsi, scriptus, to write

scríptio, -onis, *f.*, writing

scriptor, -oris, *m.*, writer

scriptum -i, *n.*, writing, publication

scriptúra, -ae, *f.*, Scripture; writing

scrutáre (-ari), to search

scrutátio, -onis, *f.*, discerning

scrutátor, -oris, *m.*, searcher

scrutínium, -ii, *n.*, search

scúlptile, -is, *n.*, graven thing, idol

sculptura, -ae, *f.*, graven work, graving

sculptus, -a, -um, graven

scurrílitas, -atis, *f.*, scurrility

scutárius, -ii, *m.*, shield-bearer

scútulum, -i, *n.*, escutcheon

scutum, -i, *n.*, shield

scyphus, -i, *m.*, goblet, cup

Scýthia, -ae, *f.*, Scythia, southern Russia

Scythópolis, -is, *f.*, Beth-shean

se, *third person of the reflexive pronoun*, himself, herself, etc.

Sebastiánus, -i, *m.*, Sebastian

secáre, sécui, sectus, to cut; — médium, to cut in two; destroy, upset; terra non secta, untilled earth

secédere, -cessi, -cessus, to retire

secéssus, -us, *m.*, privy; retreat

seclúdere, -clusi, -clusus, to exclude

secretális, -e, hidden

secretárium, -ii, *n.*, place of retirement, secret place, solitude; private chapel

secréto, *adv.*, apart; silently

secrétum, -i, *n.*, secret

secrétus, -a, -um, secret, separate, apart

secta, -ae, *f.*, sect

sectári, *dep.*, to follow, pursue

sectátor, -oris, *m.*, follower, pursuer

secundáre, to direct favorably

secúndo, *adv.*, a second time

secúndum, *prep.*, according to

secundus, -a, -um, next, second

secúris, -is, *f.*, axe

secúritas, -atis, *f.*, safety, security

secúrus, -a, -um, secure; steadfast; quiet

secus, *prep.*, by, beside, along, near, on, at

secus, *adv.*, otherwise

sed, *conj.*, but, yet

sedáre, to soothe, still, calm, appease, settle, assuage

sedére, sedi, sessus, to sit

sedes, -is, *f.*, place, seat; throne; habitation; see

sedíle, -is, *n.*, seat; station

sedítio, -onis, *f.*, sedition

seditiósus, -a, -um, seditious

seditiósus, -i, *m.*, conspirator

sedúcere, -duxi, -ductus, to deceive, seduce

sedúctor, -oris, *m.*, deceiver

sédule, *adv.*, diligently

sedúlitas, -atis, *f.*, watchfulness

sédulo, *adv.*, industriously

sédulus, -a, -um, diligent, earnest

Sedúni, -orum, *m. pl.*, Seduni (Helvetian people near modern Sion in Switzerland)

seges, -etis, *f.*, harvest; corn

segméntum, -i, *n.*, piece, shaving

segnis, -e, slow, sluggish

segníties, -ei, *f.*, slothfulness

segregáre, to separate

Seguntínus, -a, -um, of Sigüenza

sejúngere, -junxi, -junctus, to separate from

selígere, -legi, -lectus, to choose

Selímus, -i, *m.*, Solyman

sella, -ae, *f.*, stool, chair

semel, *adv.*, once

semen, -inis, *n.*, seed; descendant

seméntis, -is, *f.*, seed

seméstris, -e, of six months

semetípsum, himself

semiánimis, -e, half-dead

semidúplex, -icis, semi-double

semimórtuus, -a, -um, half-dead

semináre, to sow

seminárium, -ii, *n.*, sowing; stock

seminátor, -oris, *m.*, sower

sémita, -ae, *f.*, path

sémitum, *gen. pl.*, seed

semiústus, -a, -um, half-burnt

semivívus, -a, -um, half-alive, half-dead

semovére, -movi, -motus, to separate; renounce

semper, adv., ever, always

sempitérnus, -a, -um, eternal, everlasting

Senánus, -i, m., the River Shannon

Senárius, -ii, m., Senario

senátor, -oris, m., senator

senatórius, -a, -um, senatorial

senátus, -i or -us, m., senate; parliament; college

senécta, -ae, f., old age

senéctus, -utis, f., old age

Senénsis, -e, of Siena

senére, to be old

senéscere, -ui, to grow old

senex, senis, old; (as a noun) old man, ancient

senílis, -e, aged

sénior, -oris, m., elder, ancient

sénium, -ii, n., old age

sensátus, -a, -um, wise

sensus, -us, m., sense, feeling; understanding, perception, mind

senténtia, -ae, f., sentence

sentína, -ae, f., the hold of a ship or the bilge water in the hold

sentíre, sensi, sensus, to feel, perceive, experience

seórsum, adv., apart, aside

separáre, to separate

separátim, adv., apart, separately

separátio, -onis, f., separation

sepelíre, -ivi or -ii, sepúltus, to bury

sepes, -is, f., hedge, fence

sepíre, sepsi, septus, to guard; fence in

sepónere, -pósui, -pósitus, to put apart or aside

septem, seven

septemplíciter, adv., sevenfold

septenárius, -a, -um, of the number seven, sevenfold

septénnis, at the age of seven

septentrionális, -e, north

sépties, adv., seven times

septifórmis, -e, sevenfold

séptimus, -a, -um, seventh

septuagenárius, -a, -um, of seventy years of age

Septuagésima: domínica in —, Septuagesima Sunday

septuágies, adv., seventy times

septuagínta, seventy

Septuagínta, -ae, f., Septuagint

séptuplum, adv., sevenfold

sepúlchrum (sepúlcrum), -i, n., sepulcher

sepultúra, -ae, f., burial; burying place

sequéla, -ae, m., follower

sequéntia, -ae, f., continuation

sequestráre, to separate

sequi, secutus sum, dep. 3, to follow

séquior, -ius, worse; lesser; ad sequióris sexus educatiónem, for the training of school teachers (lit., for the education of the lesser sex)

sera, -ae, f., bolt

seraph (Hebrew), pl. séraphim, seraph, seraphim

seráphicus, -a, -um, seraphic

sereníssimus, -a, -um, most serene, sovereign

serénitas, -atis, f., clearness, fair weather

serénus, -a, -um, serene, bright

sérere, sevi, satus, to sow

séries (no gen. or dat.), f., succession

sério, adv., seriously

sérius, adv., more earnestly

sermo, -onis, m., word; saying; speech; discourse, sermon

sermocinári, dep., to talk, converse

sermocinátio, -onis, f., discussion

sero, adv., in the evening

serótinus, -a, -um, late; lateward springing

serpens, -entis, creeping

serpens, -entis, m. and f., serpent

serpentínus, -a, -um, serpentlike

serrans, -antis, like a saw

serrátus, -a, -um, saw-toothed; Mons Serrátus, Monserrat

serta, -ae, f., wreath, garland of flowers

serváre, to keep, preserve; observe, watch

Servátor, -oris, m., Savior

Servi, -orum, m. pl., Servites

servílis, -e, servile

servíre, to serve; be obedient; be in bondage

servítium, -ii, n., service

sérvitus, -utis, f., servitude, serving, service, bondage, subjection; use

sérvulus, -i, m., young slave or servant, servant-lad

servus, -i, m., servant, bondman; slave

séssio, -onis, f., sitting down

sessor, -oris, m., rider

Sessoriánus, -a, -um, Sessorian

seu, conj., or

Sevísium, -ii, n., Sevis

sex, six

sexagésima: domínica in —, Sexagesima Sunday

sexagínta, sixty

sexcentésimus, -a, -um, six hundredth

sexcénti, -ae, -a, six hundred

séxdecim, sixteen

sexennális, -e, of six years

séxies, adv., six times

sexta, -ae, f., sext

Séxtias: Aquae Séxtiae, -arum, -arum, f. pl., Aix

sextus, -a, -um, sixth

sextusdécimus, -a, -a, -um, -um, sixteenth

sexus, -us, m., sex

si, conj., if

sibiláre, to hiss

síbilus, -i, m., hissing

Sibýlla, -ae, f., Sibyl, a prophetess of Apollo

sic, adv., so, thus

sicárius, -ii, m., assassin

siccáre, to dry up

síccitas, -atis, f., dryness, drought

siccum, -i, n., desert

siccus, -a, -um, dry

sícera, -ae, f., a strong drink; cider

Síchima, -ae, f., Sichem

Síchimi, -orum, m. pl., people of Sichem

Sicília, -ae, f., Sicily

siclus, -i, m., sicle

sícubi, adv., if anywhere

Sículus, -a, -um, Sicilian

sicut (sícuti), adv., as, like

sidéreum, -i, n., heavenly body, star; starry splendor

sidéreus, -a, -um, starry

Sidóni, -orum, m. pl., Sidonians

Sidónia, -ae, f., Sidon

Sidónius, -a, -um, of Sidon

sidus, -eris, n., star

sigillátim, adv., one by one

sigillatívus, -a, -um, of a seal

sigíllum, -i, n., seal

Sigmarínga, -ae, f., Sigmaringen

signáculum, -i, n., little seal; seal

signánter, adv., carefully; significantly

signáre, to sign, seal; signify

signátor, -oris, m., witness

sígnifer, -i, m., standard bearer

significáre, to signify

significátio, -onis, f., warning

signum, -i, n., sign, token; miracle; signet

siléntio, adv., secretly

siléntium, -ii, n., silence

silére, to be silent

silex, -icis, m., rock, flint

síliqua, -ae, f., husk

silva, -ae, f., wood, forest, grove

silvéster, -tris, -tre, woodland
Silvéster, -tri, m., Sylvester
Silvestríni, -orum, m. pl., Sylvestrines
símila, -ae, f., fine flour
similáre, to liken, compare
símilis, -e, like, similar
simíliter, adv., in like manner, likewise
similitúdo, -inis, f., likeness, similitude; parable
simoníacus, -a, -um, pertaining to simony, simoniacal, of the Simonians
simplex, -icis, simple, single, pure
simplícitas, -atis, f., simplicity
simplíciter, adv., simply
simplificáre, to simplify
simul, adv., together, at the same time; withal
simulácrum, -i, n., idol
simulátio, -onis, f., dissimulation; pretense, false show
simulátor, -oris, m., hypocrite
sin, conj., but if
Sina, Sinai
Sinae, -arum, f. pl., China
sinápis, -is, f., mustard, mustard seed
sincére, adv., sincerely
sincérus, -a, -um, sincere
sindon, -onis, f., linen cloth
sine, prep., without
sínere, sivi, situs, to suffer, permit, let alone; place
singillátim, adv., singly, one by one
singuláris, -e, unique, remarkable, excellent; single, hand to hand; solitary
singuláritas, -atis, f., oneness
singuláriter, adv., singularly; alone
singulátim, adv., one by one
síngulus, -a, -um, each (one), every (one); per síngulos dies, every day; per síngula, particularly
siníster, -tra, -trum, left; left hand
sinus, -us, m., bosom, breast

Sipontíni, -orum, m. pl., the people of Maria di Siponto
síquidem, conj., indeed; for
sístere, stiti or steti, status, to stand; to be, become
sistrum, -i, n., cornet
sitárcium, -ii, n., vessel
sítiens, -entis, thirsty
sitíre, to thirst
sitis, -is, f., thirst; drought
sive, conj., or; sive . . . sive; either . . . or; whether . . . or
Slavi, -orum, m. pl., Slavs
Slávicus, -a, -um, Slavic
Slavónicus, -a, -um, Slavonic
smarágdina, -ae, f., emerald
smarágdus, -i, m. and f., emerald
smegma, -atis, n., washing ball
Smyrnaéi, -orum, m. pl., Smyrnians
Smyrnaéus, -a, -um, of Smyrna
sóboles, -is, f., offspring
sóbrie, adv., soberly
sobríetas, -atis, f., sobriety
sóbrius, -a, -um, sober
socer, -i, m., father-in-law
sociáre, to share in; combine
sócietas, -atis, f., society, fellowship, union
sócius, -a, -um, together, allied
sócius, -ii, m., companion, ally
socórdia, -ae, f., indolence
socrus, -us, f., mother-in-law
sodális, -is, m., associate; companion, comrade
sodalítium, -ii, n., guild
Sódoma, -ae, f., Sodom
Sódomi, -orum, m. pl., people of Sodom
Sodomíta, -ae, m. and f., Sodomite
sol, -is, m., sun
solári, dep., to console
soláris, -e, of the sun, solar
solárium, -ii, n., top of a house
solátium, -ii, n., solace, comfort

solémne, -is, *n.*, solemnity, solemn festival

solémnis, -e, solemn

solémnitas, -atis, *f.*, solemnity

solémniter, *adv.*, solemnly

Solentíni, -orum, *m. pl.*, country of the Solentini, Calabria

solére, sólitus sum, *semidep.* 2, to be wont, be accustomed

solers, -ertis, adroit, skillful, watchful

solérter, *adv.*, skillfully, adroitly, cleverly

solículo: — monte, Monte Solicolo

solidáre, to strengthen; found; establish; comfort

solíditas, -atis, *f.*, steadfastness; solidity

sólidus, -a, -um, solid, massy

solitárius, -a, -um, solitary, lonely

solitárius, -ii, *m.*, solitary; contemplative

solitúdo, -inis, *f.*, solitude, wilderness, desert

sólium, -ii, *n.*, throne; flue (of a bathing tub)

sollicitúdo, -inis, *f.*, care, carefulness, solicitude

sollícitus, -a, -um, solicitous

solúmmodo, *adv.*, only

solus, -a, -um, only, alone

solútio, -onis, *f.*, loosening; dissolution; freedom

sólvere, solvi, solútus, to loose, set free; undo; fulfill; break, destroy; pay back, pay a debt

Sólymae, -arum, *f. pl.*, Jerusalem

Sólymus, -a, -um, belonging to Jerusalem or the Jews

Somáscha, -ae, *f.*, Somasca

somniáre, to dream

somniátor, -oris, *m.*, dreamer

sómnium, -ii, *n.*, dream

somnoléntia, -ae, *f.*, drowsiness

somnoléntus, -a, -um, sleepy, drowsy

somnus, -i, *m.*, sleep

sonáre, to sound, roar, make a tumult; mean

sónitus, -us, *m.*, sound, noise, crash

sonórus, -a, -um, loud

sons, -ontis, guilty

sonus, -i, *m.*, sound, noise

sopor, -oris, *m.*, sleep

soporáre, to put to sleep

soporari, *dep.*, to go to sleep

Sorácte, -is, *n.*, Soracte, now Monte di San Silvestro

Sorbónicus, -a, -um, of the Sorbonne

sordére, to be filthy

sordes, -is, *f.*, dirt, filth, defilement

soror, -is, *f.*, sister

sors, sortis, *f.*, lot; part; mittere sortem, to cast lots

sortiári, *dep.*, to cast lots

sortíri, *dep.*, to obtain

sortítio, -onis, *f.*, lot

sospes, -itis, safe

Sosteneús de Sosteneís, -i, *m.*, Sosteneo de' Sostenei

spado, -onis, *m.*, eunuch

spárgere, sparsi, sparsus, to fling, strew

sparsim, *adv.*, here and there, scattered

Spartiáni, -orum, *m. pl.*, Spartans

Spartiátes, -ae, *m.*, Spartan

spathárius, -ii, *m.*, sword-bearer

spatiósus, -a, -um, great, widespread

spátium, -ii, *n.*, space, extent

spátula, -ae, *f.*, branch

speciális, -e, special, individual, one's own

speciátim, *adv.*, especially

spécies, -ei, *f.*, loveliness, beauty; appearance; kind

spécimen, -inis, *n.*, mark, sign

speciósus, -a, -um, beautiful, fair

spectáculum, -i, *n.*, gazing-stock, spectacle, sight

spectáre, to behold

spectátrix, -icis, *f.*, spectator

speculátor, -oris, *m.*, watchman; eyewitness, observer

spéculum, -i, *m.*, glass, mirror

specus, -us, *m.*, *f.*, *n.*, hollow of a rock, cave

spelúnca, -ae, *f.*, den, cave

speráre, to hope, trust

spérnere, sprevi, spretus, to disdain, scorn, despise

spes, -ei, *f.*, hope

spica, -ae, *f.*, ear (of grain)

spiculátor, -oris, *m.*, executioner

spículum, -i, *n.*, dart, arrow; ray

spina, -ae, *f.*, thorn

spinétum, -i, *n.*, thorn bush

spíneus, -a, -um, of thorns

spiráculum, -i, *n.*, breath

spiráre, to breathe

spiritális, -e, spiritual

spirituális, -e, spiritual; spirituália, *n. pl.*, spirits

spirituáliter, *adv.*, spiritually

spíritus, -us, *m.*, spirit, ghost; breath; wind

splendéscere, -ui, to shine

spléndide, *adv.*, sumptuously

splendor, -oris, *m.*, brightness, splendor

spólia, -orum, *n. pl.*, spoils

spondére, spópondi, sponsus, to promise solemnly

spóngia, -ae, *f.*, sponge

spons, spontis, *f.*, will, free will

sponsa, -ae, *f.*, bride

sponsor, -oris, *m.*, sponsor; surety

sponsus, -i, *m.*, bridegroom, spouse

spontánee, *adv.*, freely, willingly

sponte, *adv.*, voluntarily

sporta, -ae, f., basket

spórtula, -ae, *f.*, basket

spuma, -ae, *f.*, foam

spumáre, to foam, foam at the mouth

spurcítia, -ae, *f.*, filthiness

spúrius, -a, -um, baseborn

sputum, -i, *n.*, spittle

squálidus, -a, -um, rough, bad looking

squalor, -oris, *m.*, roughness, neglect

squama, -ae, *f.*, scale

squamátus, -a, -um, with scales

Squillácum, -i, *n.*, Squillace

stabilíre, to establish

stábilis, -e, steadfast

stabílitas, -atis, *f.*, firm foundation

stabulárius, -ii, *m.*, innkeeper, host

stábulum, -i, *n.*, inn

stacte, -es, *f.*, oil of myrrh, myrrh

stádium, -ii, *n.*, race course; race; furlong

stagnum, -i, *n.*, pool; lake

stannum, -i, *n.*, tin

stare, steti, status, to stand, stand still

statéra, -ae, *f.*, balance, scales

Statiélli, -orum, *m. pl.*, people of Liguria

statim, *adv.*, immediately, presently

státio, -onis, *f.*, station; garrison; anchorage

státua, -ae, *f.*, statue

statuárius, -ii, *m.*, sculptor

statúere, -ui, -utus, to set, place, station; charge against

statúra, -ae, *f.*, stature, form

status, -us, *m.*, state; position

statútus, -a, -um, appointed

stella, -ae, *f.*, star

stellátus, -a, -um, starry

stéllifer, -a, -um, starry

Stéphanus, -i, *m.*, Stephen

stercus, -coris, *n.*, dung; dunghill

stérilis, -e, barren, unfruitful

sterílitas, -atis, *f.*, barrenness

stérnere, stravi, stratus, to spread; furnish; saddle

sterquilínium, -ii, *n.*, dunghill

stértere, to snore

stíbium, -ii, *n.*, antimony, stibic stone

stigma, -atis, *n.*, stigma (*pl.*, stigmata)

stilla, -ae, *f.*, drop

stilláre, to drop, drip

stillicídium, -ii, *n.*, raindrop

stímulus, -i, *m.*, sting, goad

stipáre, to surround, compass about

stipéndium, -ii, *n.*, recompense; stipén-
dia, *n. pl.*, wages

stipes, -itis, *m.*, stem, trunk of a tree

stípula, -ae, *f.*, stubble, straw

stirps, -pis, *f.*, stock

stiva, -ae, *f.*, plow handle

stola, -ae, *f.*, robe

stómachus, -i, *m.*, stomach

storax, -acis, *f.*, storax

strages, -is, *f.*, slaughter, massacre

stragulátus, -a, -um, made of tapestry

stramen, -inis, *n.*, straw, litter

straméntum, -i, *n.*, straw

stranguláre, to strangle

stratum, -i, *n.*, bed

Stremótium, -ii, *n.*, Estremoz

strénue, *adv.*, resolutely

strénuus, -a, -um, vigorous; steadfast

strépitus, -us, *m.*, din

stricte, *adv.*, severely

strictim, *adv.*, briefly

strictus, -a, -um, tight, close; strict,
severe

stridére, stridi, to gnash

Strido, -onis, *f.*, Sdrigni

stridor, -oris, *m.*, gnashing

Strigoniénsis, -e, of Gran

stríngere, strinxi, strictus, to hold tight

stropha, -ae, *f.*, strophe

stróphium, -ii, *n.*, girdle

structor, -oris, *m.*, builder

structúra, -ae, *f.*, building

strues, -is, *f.*, pile

strúthio, -onis, *m.*, ostrich

studére, to strive, be zealous; study

stúdium, -ii, *n.*, doing, striving; practice, deed

stultilóquium, -ii, *n.*, foolish talking

stultítia, -ae, *f.*, foolishness

stultus, -a, -um, foolish; stulta, *n. pl.*,
foolish things

stupefáctus, -a, -um, amazed

stupére, to be amazed, be struck, be
astonished

stupor, -oris, *m.*, astonishment

stuppa, -ae, *f.*, tow

stuprum, -i, *n.*, ravishing, violation,
lewdness

stylus, -i, *m.*, pen

suadére, suasi, suasus, to exhort

Suána, -ae, *f.*, Soana or Ravacum

suasor, -oris, *m.*, adviser

suasus, -us, *m.*, persuasion

suavídicus, -a, -um, soft, sweet

suavis, -e, sweet, kind, good

suávitas, -atis, *f.*, sweetness, goodness

suáviter, *adv.*, sweetly

sub, *prep.*, under

subarrháre, to give earnest money,
pledge

subaudíre, to hear, heed

subcinerícius: panis —, hearth cake

súbdere, -didi, -ditus, to subject

subdiáconus, -i, *m.*, subdeacon

súbditus, -i, *m.*, subject, servant; layman

súbdiu, *adv.*, in the open air

súbdolus, -a, -um, deceitful

subésse, -fui, to be under

subínde, *adv.*, immediately

subindicáre, to point out, indicate

subinférre, -íntuli, -illátus, to say, add

subintellígere, -lexi, -lectus, to understand

subintráre, to enter into

subintroíre, -ivi and -ii, -itus, (eo), to
enter stealthily

subíre, -ivi and -ii, -itus, (eo), to go up

subitátio, -onis, *f.*, suddenness

súbito, *adv.*, suddenly, unexpectedly

subjacére, to lie under, be subject to

subjéctio, -onis, *f.*, yielding; subjection

subjícere, -jeci, -jectus, (io), to set, place or put under; subdue, subject

subjugális, -e, used to the yoke

subjugáre, to subject

subjúngere, -junxi, -junctus, to say again, add, add to; unite to

Sublácum, -i, n., Subiaco

subleváre, to lift up; exalt

sublimáre, to exalt

sublímis, -e, lofty, sublime; on high; sublímia, n. pl., lofty things

sublímitas, -atis, f., height; high station; excellency

submérgere, -mersi, -mersus, to sink, be drowned

subministráre, to minister

subministrátio, -onis, f., ministration; aid; supply

submovére, -movi, -motus, to move or put away from

súbniger, -gra, -grum, somewhat black

subobscúrus, -a, -um, somewhat dark or obscure

subornáre, to instigate secretly

subrépere, -repsi, -reptus, to creep in

subréptio, -onis, f., deceit

subridére, -risi, -risus, to smile

subrúbeus, -a, -um, somewhat reddish

subsannáre, to mock, deride, have in derision

subsannátio, -onis, f., scorn, derision

subsedére, -sedi, -sessus, to rest against or under

súbsequi, -secútus sum, dep. 3, to follow after

subsidiárius, -a, -um, subsidiary

subsídium, -ii, n., help, aid

subsístere, -stiti, to stand; withstand

substántia, -ae, f., nature, substance; sure standing

substantiáliter, adv., in substance, substantially

substantíve, adv., in substance, actually

substérnere, -stravi, -stratus, to strew; spread out

subter, adv. and prep., under, beneath

subterfúgere, -fugi, (io), to evade, shun; spare

subterfúgium, -ii, n., subterfuge, deceit

subtéxere, -téxui, -textus, to subjoin, add

subtus, adv. and prep., under

suburbánum, -i, n., suburb

subvéhere, -vexi, -vectus, to bring up from below

subveníre, -veni, -ventus, to come in, upon or up to; relieve, assist

subvérsio, -onis, f., ruin, destruction

subvérsor, -oris, m., destroyer

subvértere, -verti, -versus, to pervert; upset, overthrow; destroy

succéndere, -cendi, -census, to heat; kindle; burn

successor, -oris, m., successor

succéssus, -us, m., succession, successive change

succídere, -cidi, -cisus, to cut off or down

succínum, -i, n., amber

succlamáre, to cry again

succréscere, -crevi, -cretus, to grow, increase

succúrrere, -curri, -cursus, to succor, aid

succúrsus, -us, m., help

succus, -i, m., juice, sap

sudárium, -ii, n., napkin

Suécia, -ae, f., Sweden

Suévia, -ae, f., Swabia

sufferéntia, -ae, f., patience

sufférre, to suffer, bear

suffícere, -feci, -fectus, (io), to be enough, be sufficient

sufficiénter, adv., enough, sufficiently

sufficiéntia, -ae, f., sufficiency, contentment

suffocáre, to choke, strangle, throttle
suffódere, -fodi, -fossus, (io), to dig up
suffrágans, -antis, favorable, helping
suffragári, *dep.*, to approve; aid
suffragátio, -onis, *f.*, prayer
suffrágium, -ii, *n.*, suffrage, vote, support
suffulcíre, -fulsi, -fultus, to support, support beneath
súgere, suxi, suctus, to suck
suggérere, -gessi, -gestus, to bring to mind; add
sulcus, -i, *m.*, furrow
sulphur, -uris, *n.*, brimstone
Sulpitiánus, -a, -um, of St. Sulpice
sum (esse), I am
súmere, sumpsi, sumptus, to take, receive, obtain
summa: in —, on the whole
summátim, *adv.*, briefly, in short
summe, *adv.*, highly, greatly
súmmitas, -atis, *f.*, top
summíttere (submittere), -misi, -missus, to let down
summópere, *adv.*, highly, exceedingly; ardently
summum, -i, *n.*, top, summit; end; brim
summus, -a, -um, highest, chief; summae manus, extremities of the hands
sumptus, -us, *m.*, cost, charges
Sunamítis, -idis, *m.* and *f.*, Sunamite
supéllex, -léctilis, *f.*, furniture
super, *prep.*, on, upon; above, over; toward; concerning
superabundánter, *adv.*, more abundantly
superadúltus, -a, -um, grown up
superaedificáre, to build up
superáre, to overcome; be left over, remain
supérbia, -ae, *f.*, pride
superbíre, to be proud
supérbus, -a, -um, proud

supercádere, -cécidi, to fall upon or over
supercaeléstis, -e, more than heavenly
supercertári, *dep.*, to contend
supercílium, -ii, *n.*, brow; arrogance
superéffluens, -entis, overflowing
supereffluére, -fluxi, to run over, overflow
superéminens, -entis, surpassing, unsurpassable
supereminére, to excel
supererogáre, to spend over and above
superésse, -fui, to remain over and above
superexténdere, -tendi, -tensus and -tentus, to stretch over, cover
superexaltáre, to exalt greatly
superextóllere, to exalt above
superférre, -tuli, -latus, to carry over; excel
superfícies, -ei, *f.*, surface, face
superflúitas, -atis, *f.*, excess, superfluity
supérfluus, -a, -um, superfluous
supergaudére, to rejoice over
supergloriósus, -a, -um, exceedingly glorious
supérgredi, -gressus sum, *dep. 3*, to go over; surpass; overreach
superimpéndere, -pendi, -pensus, to spend
superimplére, -plevi, -pletus, to fill to overflowing
superindúere, -ui, -utus, to put on over
supérior, -ius, upper
supérius, *adv.*, higher
superlaudabilis, -e, exceedingly to be praised
superliminária, *n. pl.*, upper door posts
superlucráre, to gain more or over and above
supérnus, -a, -um, heavenly, celestial; above
superplénus, -a, -um, brimful

superpónere, -pósui, -pósitus, to lay over

superscriptio, -onis, *f.*, superscription

supersemináre, to oversow

supersperáre, to hope or trust in greatly

superstitiósus, -a, -um, superstitious

súperus, -a, -um, higher, upper; supreme; divine

súperus, -i, *m.*, divine being, angel

supervacáneus, -a, -um, superfluous

supervácue, *adv.*, without cause

superveníre, to come in or upon, overtake

superventúrus, -a, -um, coming, approaching

supervestíre, to put clothes upon, clothe

supínus, -a, -um, lying upon the back

suppeditáre, to give abundantly

suppétere, -ivi and -ii, -itus, to be present, be in store

supplantáre, to supplant; overthrow

supplantátio, -onis, *f.*, treachery

suppleméntum, -i, *n.*, supply, reinforcement

supplére, -plevi, -pletus, to supply; use

supplex, -icis, suppliant, low

supplicáre, to beseech humbly

supplicátio, -onis, *f.*, supplication, prayer

suppíciter, *adv.*, suppliantly, humbly

supplícium, -ii, *n.*, punishment

suppónere, -póssui, -pósitus, to hold or put under

supportáre, to bear, bear with

supra, *prep.*, over, above, upon

supradíctus, -a, -um, aforesaid

suprémus, -a, -um, last

supputáre, to count, compute

súrculus, -i, *m.*, branch

surdus, -a, -um, deaf; surdi, *pl.*, the deaf

súrgere, surréxi, surréctus, to rise up, arise

surrípere, -rípui, -reptus, (io), to steal away; happen to; take by stealth

surrogáre, to grant

sursum, *adv.*, upward, above; — corda, lift up the hearts

suscéptio, -onis, *f.*, receiving; protection

suscéptor, -oris, receptive

suscéptor, -oris, *m.*, taker up, receiver; protector

suscípere, -cepi, -ceptus, (io), to receive; undertake; uphold

suscitáre, to raise up, raise to life, awake

suspéndere, -pendi, -pensus, to hang up

suspénsio, -onis, *f.*, suspension

suspicári, *dep.*, to suspect; dread

suspícere, -spexi, -spectus, (io), to look up

suspício, -onis, *f.*, suspicion

suspiráre, to sigh, long for

suspírium, -ii, *n.*, sigh; desire

sustáculum, -i, *n.*, prop, support

sustentáre, to maintain, support

sustentátio, -onis, *f.*, deferring, delay; forbearance

sustentátor, -oris, *m.*, supporter

sustinéntia, -ae, *f.*, enduring

sustinére, -tinui, -tentus, to sustain, endure, undergo; stand, wait for, wait upon; abide; rely

sustóllere, to lift up

susurráre, to murmur, whisper

susúrrus, -i, *m.*, whisperer

Sutrínus, -a, -um, of Sutri

suus, -a, -um, his, her, hers, it, its, their, theirs

Swéynus, -i, *m.*, Sweyn

Sybillínus, -a, -um, Sibylline

sycómorus, -i, *f.*, sycamore tree

sycophánta, -ae, *m.*, sycophant, flatterer

Sylla (Sulla), -ae, *m.*, Sulla

sýllaba, -ae, *f.*, syllable
sýmbolum, -i, *n.*, symbol; creed
symphónia, -ae, *f.*, music, symphony
Symphoriánus, -i, *m.*, Symphorian
synagóga, -ae, *f.*, synagogue, congregation, assembly
Synicénsis, -e, of Synica
synódicus, -a, -um, synodal
sýnodus, -i, *f.*, synod, council
Syracúsae, -arum, *f. pl.*, Syracuse
Syracusánus, -a, -um, of Syracuse
Syri, -orum, *m. pl.*, Syrians
Syrophoeníssus, -a, -um, Syrophoenician
syrtis, -is, *f.*, sandbank
Syrus, -a, -um, Syrian
systéma, -atis, *n.*, system

T

tabernáculum, -i, *n.*, tabernacle; dwelling; tent
tabéscere, -ui, to melt; languish, pine away
tábidus, -a, -um, decaying, melting
tábula, -ae, *f.*, writing-tablet
tabulátum, -i, *n.*, board
tacére, to be silent, hold one's peace
tacitúrnitas, -atis, *f.*, silence
tácitus, -a, -um, silent
tactus, -us, *m.*, touch; blemish
taeda, -ae, *f.*, torch
taedére, taéduit, *impers, 2,* to be heavy; be disgusted
taédium, -ii, *n.*, weariness, heaviness, care
taláris, -e, reaching to the ankles; túnica —, outside coat
taléntum, -i, *n.*, talent (a sum of money, about $1,000)
tálio, -onis, *f.*, retaliation
talis, -e, such
táliter, *adv.*, thus, so
talus, -i, *m.*, ankle

tam, *adv.*, so, to such a degree
támdiu, *adv.*, so long
tamen, *adv.*, yet, nevertheless
tamétsi, *conj.*, although
tamquam (tanquam), *adv.*, like, as, just as, as it were
Tanchélmus, -i, *m.*, Tanchelm
tángere, tétigi, tactus, to touch
tantísper, *adv.*, meanwhile
tantúmmodo, *adv.*, only
tantus, -a, -um, such, so much, so great, of such size; only; tanto . . . quanto, so much . . . as
Taráscum, -i, *n.*, Tarascon
Tarbiénsis, -e, of Tarbes
tardáre, to delay, tarry
tárditas, -atis, *f.*, slowness
tardus, -a, -um, slow
Tarpéjus, -a, -um, Tarpeian
Tarracína, -ae, *f.*, Terracina
Tarraconénsis, -e, of Tarragona
Tarsénsis, -e, of Tarsus
tártarus, -i, *m.*, hell
Tarvisínus, -a, -um, of Treviso
Tarvísium, -ii, *n.*, Treviso
Taurínas: Aquae Taurínae, -arum, -arum, *f. pl.*, Acquapendente
Taurunénsis, -e, of Belgrade
taurus, -i, *m.*, bull, bullock, ox; beef
tectum, -i, *n.*, roof, house top
tégere, texi, tectus, to cover
tegmen, -inis, *n.*, shelter
tégula, -ae, *f.*, tile
teguméntum, -i, *n.*, covering; shadow
teípsum, thyself
tela, -ae, *f.*, web; warp (of cloth)
teloneárius, -ii, *m.*, tax collector
telum, -i, *n.*, dart
tellus, -uris, *f.*, earth
teméritas, -atis, *f.*, rashness
temetípsum, thyself; propter —, for thy own sake
temperaméntum, -i, *n.*, tempered mortar

temperáre, to be temperate; learn to avoid; mingle; govern

temperatúra, -ae, *f.,* tempering

tempéries, -ei, *f.,* tempering; refreshment

tempéstas, -atis, *f.,* storm

templum, -i, *n.,* temple, church

temporális, -e, temporal, earthly

temporáliter, *adv.,* temporally; in time

temporáneus, -a, -um, early, timely

tempus, -oris, *n.,* time; season; quanto témpore, as long as; ad tempus, for a while; quátuor témporum, of Ember week

temuléntus, -a, -um, drunk

tenax, -acis, niggardly; firm, steadfast

téndere, tétendi, tentus or tensus, to stretch, extend; direct one's course; conform one's life

tendícula, -ae, *f.,* snare

ténebrae, -arum, *f. pl.,* darkness

tenebricósus, -a, -um, dark

tenebrósus, -a, -um, dark

tener, -a, -um, tender

tenére, -ui, tentus, to hold, have, possess, keep

teneritúdo, -inis, *f.,* tenderness

tenor, -oris, *m.,* course

tentaméntum, -i, *n.,* trial

tentáre, to tempt; prove

tentátio, -onis, *f.,* temptation

tentátor, -oris, *m.,* tempter

tentórium, -ii, *n.,* tent; hanging, drapery

tenuáre, to lessen, diminish

ténuis, -e, small, little, weak

tepefáctus, -a, -um, warm

Tepejacénsis, -e, of Tepeyac

tepéscere, -ui, to become tepid or lukewarm

ter, *adv.,* thrice

tercénties, *adv.,* three hundred times

terebínthus, -i, *f.,* terebinth or turpentine tree; Terebinth

térere, trivi, tritus, to rub away; smooth; bruise, afflict

Terésia, -ae, *f.,* Theresa

térgere, tersi, tersus, to wipe

tergum, -i, *n.,* back

términus, -i, *m.,* end; border, boundary; quarter

terni, -ae, -a, three, three apiece

terra, -ae, *f.,* earth, ground, land; dust

terraemótus, -us, *m.,* earthquake

terrénus, -a, -um, earthly; terréna, *n. pl.,* earthly things

terrére, to frighten, affright, terrify

terréster, -tris, -tre, earthly; on earth

térreus, -a, -um, earthly

terríbilis, -e, terrible, fearful

terribíliter, *adv.,* fearfully

terrígena, -ae, *c.,* earthborn

terror, -oris, *m.,* terror

tértia, -ae, *f.,* terce

tértio, *adv.,* a third time

tértius, -a, -um, third

tertiusdécimus, -a, -a, -um, -um, thirteenth

téssera, -ae, *f.,* token, distinguishing mark

testa, -ae, *f.,* clay; potsherd

testáceus, -a, -um, of brick or tile

testaméntum, -i, *n.,* testament, covenant

testári, *dep.,* to testify, bear witness

testátor, -oris, *m.,* one that makes a will, testator

testificáre, to witness

testificári, *dep.,* to testify; charge

testificátio, -onis, *f.,* witness, testimony

testimónium, -ii, *n.,* witness, evidence

testis, -is, *m.,* a witness

téstula, -ae, *f.,* potsherd

teter, -tra, -trum, foul, filthy, hideous

teth, the ninth letter of the Hebrew alphabet, corresponding to English *t*

tetrárcha, -ae, *m.,* tetrarch

texens, -entis, *m.,* weaver

téxere, -ui, textus, to weave
textrínus, -a, -um, weaving
textus, -us, m., context
Thaboríti, -orum, m. pl., Thaborites
thálamus, -i, m., bedroom, bridal chamber
Tharsaéas, -ae, m., Tharseas
Tharsis, Tartessus
thaumatúrgus, -i, m., wonderworker
Theatínus, -a, -um, of Chieti
theátrum, -i, n., theater; show
Thebaéi, -orum, m. pl., Thebans
Thébais, -idis, f., Thebes
theca, -ae, f., case, covering, sheath
Thecuítis, -is, of Thecua
thema, -atis, n., theme
Theobáldus, -i, m., Theobald
Theodóricus, -i, m., Theodoric
Theodórus, -i, Theodore
theológia, -ae, f., theology
theológicus, -a, -um, theological
theólogus, -i, m., theologian
Theopaschítae, -arum, m. pl., Theopaschites
Therésia, -ae, f., Theresa
thesaurizáre, to heap as a treasure, lay up treasure
thesáurus, -i, m., treasure; treasury, storehouse
Thésbites, -is, m., Thesbite
Thessalonicénses, -ium, m. pl., Thessalonians
Theutónicus, -a, -um, German
Thienaéus, -a, -um, of Tiené
thorax, -acis, m., breast plate
Thrácia, -ae, f., Thrace
Thrácius, -a, -um, Thracian
thrónus, -i, m., throne
thorus (torus), -i, m., bed, marriage couch
thuríbulum, -i, n., censer
thus, thuris, n., frankincense
thyínus, -a, -um, of the thyine tree
tiára, -ae, f., cap, tiara

Tiberínus, -a, -um, of the Tiber
Tíberis, -is, m., the Tiber River
tíbia, -ae, f., shinbone; leg; pipe, flute
tibícen, -inis, m., piper, minstrel
Tibilitánus, -a, -um, of Tibilis
Tiburtínus, -a, -um, Tiburtine; of Tivoli
Ticínum, -i, n., Ticino; Pavia
tignum, -i, n., beam
tigris, -is, m., tiger
timére, to fear, be afraid
tímidus, -a, -um, fearful
timor, -oris, m., fear, terror
timorátus, -a, -um, devout
Timótheus, -i, m., Timotheus, Timothy
tinctúra, -ae, f., dye, dyeing
tínea, -ae, f., moth
tíngere, tinxi, tinctus, to dye
tinníre, to tinkle
Tirconaília, -ae, f., Tirconail
tirocínium, -ii, n., noviceship, novitiate; apprenticeship
titio, -onis, m., firebrand
titubáre, to stagger; waver
tituláris, -e, titular
títulus, -i, m., title; inscription; pledge
Tolentínum, -i, n., Tolentino
tolerábilis, -e, bearable, light
toleráre, to bear
Toletánus, -a, -um, of Toledo
tóllere, sústuli, sublátus, to lift up; take away; hold in suspense
Tolósa, -ae, f., Toulouse
Tolosánus, -a, -um, of Toulouse
Tolosátes, -ium, m. pl., people of Toulouse
tomus, -i, m., volume
tonáre, -ui, to resound; thunder
tondens, -entis, m., shearer
tondére, tótondi, tonsus, to shear
tonítruum, -i, n., thunder
tonsúra, -ae, f., tonsure
topázion (topázus), -i, n., topaz

tórcular, -aris, *n.*, wine or oil press

torméntum, -i, *n.*, torment; engine; — béllicum, gun, blunderbuss (lit., war engine)

torpére, to be torpid, listless or sluggish

torpor, -oris, *m.*, dullness, torpor

torquére, torsi, tortus, to twist; torment

torquis, -is, *m.* and *f.*, collar, chain

torrens, -entis, *m.*, torrent, brook, stream

torrére, -ui, tostus, to burn, roast, parch

torta, -ae, *f.*, roll

tortor, -oris, *m.*, tormenter, torturer

torus, -i, *m.*, bed, marriage couch

tot, *adv.*, so many

totáliter, *adv.*, wholly

tótidem, just as many, so many

totus, -a, -um, all, the whole; per totum, throughout

trábea, -ae, *f.*, robe

trabs, -is, *f.*, beam

tractábilis, -e, that can be handled, manageable

tractáre, to treat; behave toward; celebrate

tractátus, -us, *m.*, tract, treatise

trádere, -didi, -ditus, to deliver up; betray

traditio, -onis, *f.*, surrender; tradition

tráditor, -oris, *m.*, betrayer, traitor

tradúcere, -duxi, -ductus, to lead; expose publicly

tradux, -ucis, *m.*, transmission; tradition

tragoédia, -ae, *f.*, tragic scene

tráhere, traxi, tractus, to draw, drag; contract; catch

Trajánus, -i, *m.*, Trajan

Trallénses, -ium, *m. pl.*, Trallians

trames, -itis, *m.*, crossroad, course, road, path

tranquilláre, to pacify, to make calm or still

tranquíllitas, -atis, *f.*, calm, tranquillity

tranquíllius, *adv.*, peacefully

tranquíllus, -a, -um, tranquil

trans, *prep.*, over, across, beyond, on the other side of

transcénsus, -us, *m.*, passage

transférre, -tuli, -latus, to move, remove; transform; translate

transfígere, -fixi, -fixus, to pierce

transfiguráre, to transfigure

transfigurátio, -onis, *f.*, transfiguration

transfíxio, -onis, *f.*, piercing

transformatívus, -a, -um, transforming

transfóssus, -a, -um, pierced

transfretáre, to pass over; cross the sea

tránsgredi, -gressus sum, *dep. 3* (io), to transgress; pass over

transgréssor, -oris, *m.*, transgressor

transígere, -egi, -actus, to get along

transilíre, -ui, -ivi, and -ii, to leap or skip over

transire, -ivi and -ii, -itus, (eo), to pass through, go over or across to; pass by or away; depart hence

transitórius, -a, -um, passing, transitory

tránsitus, -us, *m.*, a passing over or by; passage; brink

translátio, -onis, *f.*, transferring; translation

transmeáre, to go or come across

transmigráre, to flee

transmigrátio, -onis, *f.*, carrying away; transmigration

transmíttere, -misi, -missus, to send

transmutáre, to change, turn

transmutátio, -onis, *f.*, change

transplantáre, to plant

transvádere, to ford, pass over

transvéhere, -vexi, -vectus, to carry over, convey

transverberáre, to pierce, transfix

transvérsim, *adv.*, across; obliquely

transvértere, -verti, -versus, to overturn

Trebnicénsis, -e, of Trebnitz

trecénti, -ae, -a, three hundred

trédecim, thirteen

tremefáctus, -a, -um, terrified

treméndus, -a, -um, tremendous, awful

trémere, -ui, to tremble

tremor, -oris, *m.*, fear, trembling

trepidáre, to be busy; swarm about; be afraid; tremble

tres, three

Tréveri, -orum, *m. pl.*, Treves (Trier)

Trias, -adis, *f.*, Trinity

tribúere, -ui, -utus, to give, grant

tríbulans, -antis, *m.*, oppressor

tribuláre, to afflict

tribulári, *dep.*, to be in trouble

tribulátio, -onis, *f.*, tribulation, trouble

tríbulus, -i, *m.*, thorn, brier, thistle

tribúnal, -is, *n.*, place of judgment

tribúnus, -i, *m.*, tribune; captain over a thousand men

tribus, -us, *m.*, tribe

tribútum, -i, *n.*, tribute

tricári, *dep.*, to trifle

tricésimus, -a, -um, thirtieth

triclínium, -ii, *n.*, parlor; bedchamber; stewardship, charge of the table

tridens, -entis, having three teeth or prongs

Tridentínus, -a, -um, of Trent

triduánus, -a, -um, of three days

tríduo, *adv.*, three days

tríduum, -i, *n.*, a space of three days

triennális, -e, three years

triénnium, -ii, *n.*, space of three years

trigésimus, -a, -um, thirtieth

trigínta, thirty

trini, -ae, -a, three each; thrice

Trínitas, -atis, *f.* Trinity

trinus, -a, -um, three, trine, triune

triplex, -icis, threefold

triplicáre, to triple

tripudiáre, to dance

trirémis, -is, *f.*, galley

tristári, *dep.*, to be sad

tristéga, -ae, *f.*, sewer

tristis, -e, sad, sorrowful, cast down

tristítia, -ae, *f.*, sorrow

tritíceus, -a, -um, wheaten

tríticum, -i, *n.*, wheat

tritúra, -ae, *f.*, threshing

trituráre, to thresh

triumpháre, to triumph

triumphátor, -oris, *m.*, conqueror

triúmphus, -i, *m.*, triumph

Troas, -adis, *m.*, Troas

trophaéum, -i, *n.*, trophy; monument of victory; triumph

trucidáre, to cut to pieces, slay

trúdere, trusi, trusus, to push, thrust

truncus, -i, *m.*, trunk, stump

truncus, -a, -um, maimed, mutilated

trux, -cis, savage, rough, grim

Tryphónis, -is, *m.*, Tryphon

tu, thou

tuba, -ae, *f.*, trumpet

Tuder, -ertis, *f.*, Todi

tuéri, túitus and tutus sum, *dep.* 2, to protect, uphold, defend

tugúrium, -ii, *n.*, peasant's hut; lodge

tuítio, -onis, *f.*, protection, defense

tum, *adv.*, then, at that time; tum . . . tum, at one time. . . .at another time; now . . . now

tumére, to swell, be swollen; be puffed up

tumetípse, you yourself

túmidus, -a, -um, puffed up

túmor, -oris, *m.*, tumor, swelling; pride, bombast

tumuláre, to bury

tumultuáre (-ari), to make a tumult

tumultuárie, *adv.*, suddenly, in a disorderly manner

tumúltus, -us, *m.*, tumult
túmulus, -i, *m.*, grave
tunc, *adv.*, then; ex tunc, from olden times
Tuniátus Mons, -i, -tis, *m.*, Montagnate
túnica, -ae, *f.*, coat; shirt
túnsio, -onis, *f.*, striking, beating
turba, -ae, *f.*, crowd, multitude
turbáre, to trouble, disturb
turbátio, -onis, *f.*, fear
turben, -inis, *n.*, whirlwind
túrbidus, -a, -um, confused, disordered
turbo, -inis, *m.*, gale, whirlwind
Turcae, -arum, *m. pl.*, Turks
turma, -ae, *f.*, squadron, troop
Turonénsis, -e, of Tours
Túroni, -orum, *m. pl.*, Tours; Plessis-les-Tours
turpis, -e, filthy, foul; shameful
turpitúdo, -inis, *f.*, obscenity; disgrace
turris, -is, *f.*, tower
Turris Formosa, -is, -ae, *f.*, Torre Hermosa
turtur, -uris, *m.*, turtle dove
tutaméntum, -i, *n.*, safety
tutáre, to defend
tutéla, -ae, *f.*, safety, guard, protection
turor, -oris, *m.*, tutor
tuus, -a, -um, thy, thine
tympanístria, -ae, *f.*, accompaniment of a timbrel; a female drummer
týmpanum, -i, *n.*, drum, timbrel
týpice, *adv.*, prefiguratively
týpicus, -i, *m.*, figure, emblem
týpicus, -a, -um, typical
typus, -i, *m.*, type, figure
tyránnis, -idis, *f.*, tyrannical act or command; tyranny
tyránnus, -i, *m.*, ruler, tyrant
Týrii, -orum, *m. pl.*, Tyrians
tyrocínium, -ii, *n.*, novitiate, apprenticeship
Tyrrhénus, -a, -um, Etruscan
Tyrus, -i, *f.*, Tyre

U

uber, -eris, *n.*, breast, pap
uber, -eris, fruitful, rich
úbertas, -atis, *f.*, fullness, fruitfulness, abundance
úbertim, *adv.*, abundantly
ubi, *adv.*, where, when
úbinam, *adv.*, where
ubíque, *adv.*, everywhere, in all places
udus, -a, -um, moist; tearful
Ugúccio Ugucciónum, -onis, *m.*, Uguccio de' Guccioni
ulcerátus, -a, um, covered with sores
ulcísci, ultus sum, *dep. 3*, to avenge
ulcus, -eris, *n.*, boil, sore, ulcer
ullus, -a, -um, any
ulna, -ae, *f.*, arm
últimus, -a, -um, farthest, last
últio, -onis, *f.*, revenge, vengeance
ultor, -oris, *m.*, avenger
ultra, *adv.*, furthur, beyond; any more
Ultrajecténsis, -e, of Utrecht
Ultrajéctum, -i, *n.*, Utrecht
ultro, *adv.*, spontaneously, of itself
ululátus, -us, *m.*, wailing
Ulýssipo, -onis, *f.*, Lisbon
Umber, -bra, -brum, Umbrian
Umber, -bri, *m.*, the Humber River
umbilícus, -i, *m.*, navel
umbra, -ae, *f.*, shadow, shade
umbráculum, -i, *n.*, shade, bower, covert
umbrósus, -a, -um, shady; Umbrósa Valles, -ae, -is, *f.*, Vallombrosa
umquam, *adv.*, ever, at any time
unánimis, -e, of one mind
unanímiter, *adv.*, with one accord
unánimus, -a, -um, unanimous, of one mind, with one voice
úncia, -ae, *f.*, ounce
únctio, -onis, *f.*, unction, anointing
unda, -ae, *f.*, wave; water, moisture; stream

unde, *adv.*, wherefore, thence, whereupon; whence
undequáquam, *adv.*, from everywhere
úndecim, eleven
undécimus, -a, -um, eleventh
úndique, *adv.*, on all sides, on every
side
úngere, unxi, unctus, to anoint
unguentária, -ae, *f.*, maker of un-
guents, confectionery
unguéntum, -i, *n.*, ointment
unguis, -is, *m.*, nail, claw
úngula, -ae, *f.*, hoof; claw, talon; onyx
única, -ae, *f.*, only one, darling
unicórnis, -is, *m.*, unicorn
únicus, -a, -um, only, alone, lonely
unígena, -ae, *m.*, only-begotten
unigénitus, -a, -um, only-begotten
únio, -onis, *f.*, union
uníre, to unite
únitas, -atis, *f.*, unity
universális, -e, universal
univérsitas, -atis, *f.*, wholeness, com-
pleteness; the whole world, the universe; university; company
univérsum, -i, *n.*, the whole world, the
universe
univérsus, -a, -um, all, entire
unquam, *adv.*, ever, at any time
unus, -a, -um, one; in unum, as one,
together, in unity; unus post unum,
one by one; una cum, together with
unusquísque, every one
urbánitas, -atis, *f.*, good breeding
Urbánus, -i, *m.*, Urban
Urbínas, -atis, of Urbino
urbs, urbis, *f.*, city, town
Urbs, -bis, *f.*, Rome
úrceus, -i, *m.*, earthenware jug, pitcher,
vessel
úrere, ussi, ustus, to burn; (in the
passive voice) to be on fire
urgére, ursi, to press hard, be urgent;
to shut

Uritánum, -i, *n.*, Oria
urna, -ae, *f.*, pot
Ursiánus, -a, -um, Ursian
ursus, -i, *m.*, bear
úrtica, -ae, *f.*, nettle
usitáre, to use
usque, *adv.*, as far as, over to, all the
way; — ad, even until
usquequáque, *adv.*, everywhere; ut-
terly
úsquequo, *adv.*, how long? wherefore?
ustuláre, to singe, burn
usúra, -ae, *f.*, usury; interest
usurpáre, to make use of; assert one's
right to; usurp
usus, -us, *m.*, use
ut (uti), *conj.*, that, in order that; as;
after, when; — quid, to what purpose? why?
utcúmque, *adv.*, however; after a sort
utensília, -orum, *n. pl.*, utensils, fur-
nishings
uter, -tris, *m.*, wine-skin
uterínus, -a, -um, of the same mother
utérque, -tra, -trum, each of two, both
úterus, -i, *m.*, and úterum, -i, *n.*,
womb
útilis, -e, profitable
utílitas, -atis, *f.*, benefit, profit
utíliter, *adv.*, usefully
útinam, *adv.*, would that! oh that!
útique, *adv.*, indeed, doubtless
útpote, *adv.*, inasmuch as, since
utrínque, *adv.*, on both sides, in both
cases
utrobíque, *adv.*, in both places, on
both sides; both . . . and
utrum, *adv.*, whether
uva, -ae, *f.*, grape, a bunch of grapes
Uváda, -ae, *f.*, Ovada
uxor, -oris, *f.*, wife

V

vacans, -antis, empty, vacant
vacáre, to desist, leave off
vacca, -ae, f., cow; — foeta, milch cow
vacilláre, to doubt
vacúitas, -atis, f., vanity
vácuus, -a, -um, empty, void; in vacuum, in vain
vádere, to go
vae! interj., woe!
vafer, -fra, -frum, crafty, sly
vagína, -ae, f., scabbard, sheath
vagíre, to whimper, cry
vagus, -a, -um, wandering, harborless
vagus, -i, m., wanderer, vagrant, tramp
vah! (interj. of contempt), oh! ah! bah!
valde, adv., greatly, exceedingly
valénter, adv., strongly; with a strong voice
Valéntia, -ae, f., Valencia
Valentínus, -a, -um, of Valencia
Valentínus, -i, m., Valentine
valére, to be well or strong; have strength; be able; be worthy
Valeriánus, -i, m., Valerian
Valésii, -orum, m. pl., Valois
Valésius, -a, -um, of Valois; Felix—, icis, -ii, m., Felix de Valois
valetudinárium, -ii, n., hospital
valetúdo, -inis, f., health, strength
válide, adv., strongly, powerfully
válidus, -a, -um, mighty
valláre, to enclose, make a hedge about; fortify; besiege
vallis (-es), -is, f., valley, vale
Vallisolétum, -i, n., Valladolid
vallum, -i, n., trench
valvae, -arum, f. pl., doors
Vándali, -orum, m. pl., Vandals
Vándalus, -i, m., the Vistula River
vane, adv., vainly, in vain
vanilóquium, -ii, n., vain babbling

vaníloquus, -i, m., vain talker
vánitas, -atis, f., vanity, vain thing
vanus, -a, -um, vain; vana, n. pl., vain things
vapor, -oris, m., vapor
vaporáre, to perfume
vapuláre, to cry out; be beaten
Varállus, -i, m., Varallo
várie, adv., variously, in various ways
várietas, -atis, f., variety, changing thing
várius, -a, -um, various, varied, divers
vas, vasis (pl., vasa, -orum), n., vessel; vasa psalmi, harps
vásculum, -i, n., small vessel
Vastanénsis, -e, of Vadstena
vastáre, to spoil, lay waste
vastátor, -oris, m., destroyer
vástitas, -atis, f., waste, desolation
vastus, -a, -um, vast
vates, -is, m., prophet, seer
Vaticánus, -i, m., Vatican
vaticináre, to prophesy
vaticínium, -ii, n., prophecy, revelation
vau, the sixth letter of the Hebrew alphabet, corresponding to English w
-ve, enclitic, or
vecórdia, -ae, f., foolishness, folly
vectátio, -onis, f., carrying
vectígal, -alis, n., revenue, custom; rent
vectis, -is, m., bar, bolt, stave
vector, -oris, m., sailor, passenger
vegetáre, to stir up, quicken, nourish
vegetátio, -onis, f., new life
végetus, -a, -um, strong, vigorous
véhemens, -entis, mighty, violent
veheménter, adv., greatly, exceedingly
vehículum, -i, n., conveyance; chariot
Veitúrium, -ii, n., Voltaggio
vel, conj., or
velámen, -inis, n., veil, cloak
velaméntum, -i, n., veil; shelter

veláre, to cover; blindfold
Veláunus, -a, -um, of Velay
Veldkírchium, -ii, n., Feldkirch
Velitérnus, -a, -um, Velletri
velle (volo), volui, to desire, wish, will; like, be pleased, delight in; choose; mean
véllere, velli or vulsi, vulsus, to pluck
vellus, -eris, n., fleece
velóciter, adv., swiftly, speedily
velox, -ocis, swift
velum, i, n., veil; sail
velut, adv., like, as
vena, -ae, f., vein
venális, -e, for sale
venans, -antis, m., fowler, hunter
venátio, -onis, f., hunting; venison
venátor, -oris, m., hunter
venátus, -us, m., hunting
véndere, -didi, -ditus, to sell
vendítio, -onis, f., selling
venefícium, -ii, n., witchcraft
venéficus, -i, m., sorcerer, wizard
venenátus, -a, -um, poisonous, venomous, envenomed
venenósus, -a, -um, venomous
venénum, -i, n., poison
venerábilis, -e, venerable
venerándus, -a, -um, venerable
veneráre (-ari), to hold in honor, venerate, worship
venerátio, -onis, f., honor
Venétia, -ae, f., Vannes
Venétiae, -arum, f. pl., Venice
Vénetus, -a, -um, Venetian
vénia, -ae, f., pardon
veniábilis, -e, pardonable
veníre, veni, ventus, to come
veníre, -ivi (-ii), -ítus, to be sold
venter, -tris, m., womb; belly; bowels
ventiláre, to toss, scatter; winnow
ventitáre, to come often
ventúrus, -a, -um, to come, coming
ventus, -i, m., wind

venúmdare, -dedi, -datus, to sell
Venus, -eris, f., Venus
venústas, -atis, f., beauty
vepres, -is, m., briar, briar bush
ver, -is, n., spring
veráciter, adv., truly, truthfully
verax, -acis, true, truthful; (as a noun) a true speaker
Veránus, -a, -um, of Verus, Veranian
verber, -eris, n., blow, lash, stripe; lashing, scourging
verberáre, to beat
verberátio, -onis, f., chastisement
verbósus, -a, -um, verbose, wordy
verbum, -i, n., word
Vercéllae, -arum, f. pl., Vercelli
Vercellénsis, -e, of Vercelli
Verdúnum, -i, n., Verdun
vere, adv., in truth, truly, indeed
verecúndia, -ae, f., shame; modesty
veréri, dep. 2, to fear; reverence
vérgere, versi, to bend
véritas, -atis, f., truth, fidelity
vermiculátus, -a, -um, inlaid
vermículus, -i, m., crimson
vermis, -is, m., worm
vernáculus, -i, m., domestic, servant born in one's house, homeborn slave
vernans, -antis, springlike
vernus, -a, -um, of the springtime, spring
vero, adv., but, in truth
Veronénsis, -e, of Verona
vérrere, versus sum, semidep. 3, to sweep
versáre, to turn, change
versátilis, -e, revolving
versátus, -a, -um, versed
versículus, -i, m., little verse
versus, -us, m., verse
versútia, -ae, f., craftiness, subtlety
vértere, verti, versus, to turn; use; construe as; put to flight; verténte

anno, at the return of the year

vertex, -icis, *m.,* top; top or crown of the head

verúmtamen, *adv.,* but, nevertheless; surely

verus, -a, -um, true

vesánia, -ae, *f.,* madness, wild rage

vesánus, -a, -um, furious, insane

vesci, *dep. 3,* to eat

Vespasiánus, -i, *m.,* Vespasian

vesper, -eri and **-eris,** *m.,* evening

véspera, -ae, *f.,* evening

vésperae, -arum, *f. pl.,* vespers

vesperáscere, to become evening

vespertínus, -a, -um, evening

vester, -tra, -trum, your, yours

vestíbulum, -i, *n.,* porch, court

vestígium, -ii, *n.,* footstep; foot

vestiméntum, -i, *n.,* garment, robe; raiment

Vestíni, -orum, *m. pl.,* the Abruzzi

vestíre, to clothe; put on

vestis, -is, *f.,* garment; clothing, vesture

vestítus, -us, *m.,* providing of clothing; vesture

veteránus, -a, -um, veteran

veteráscere, to grow old; vanish

veternósus, -a, -um, dull, lethargic

vetáre, to forbid

vétitus, -a, -um, forbidden

vetus, -eris, old; original

vetústas, -atis, f., old age, old man, old life; antiquity; former ways

vetústus, -a, -um, old

vexáre, to trouble, oppress, afflict

vexátio, -onis, *f.,* annoyance; ill-treatment

vexíllum, -i, *n.,* standard, banner

via, -ae, *f.,* way, highway

viáre, to travel

viárius, -a, -um, wayfarer

viáticum, -i, *n.,* viaticum

viátor, -oris, *m.,* wayfarer, traveler

Vibiána, -ae, *f.,* Bibiana

vibráre, to brandish

vicárium, -ii, *n.,* vicariate; office or jurisdiction of a vicar

vicárius, -ii, *m.,* vicar

vicéni, -ae, -a, twenty

vicénnis, at the age of twenty

Vicéntia, -ae, *f.,* Vicenza

vicínus, -a, -um, neighboring, nearby

vicinus, -i, *m.,* neighbor

vicis (*gen.; no nom.*), change, alteration; time, instance; course; return; **vices,** *pl.,* punishment; **in** or **ad vicem,** instead of

vicíssim, *adv.,* in return; in turn, by turns

vicissitúdo, -inis, *f.,* alteration

victima, -ae, *f.,* victim

victitáre, to live upon

victor, -oris, *m.,* victor, conqueror

victória, -ae, *f.,* victory

victrix, -icis, victorious, conquering

victrix, -icis, *f.,* conqueror

victus, -us, *m.,* food, feeding; life, way of living

vicus, -i, *m.,* town; district; street, lane, way; **vicus Patrici,** a district of Rome

vidélicet, *adv.,* namely, to wit

viden = vidésne? seest thou?

videns, -entis, *m.,* seer

vidére, vidi, visus, to see, behold

vidéri, visus sum, to seem

vídua, -ae, *f.,* widow

viduáre, to deprive of

vidúitas, -atis, *f.,* widowhood

Viennénsis, -e, of Vienne

vigére, to live, flourish; be raised to power

vigésimus, -a, -um, twentieth

vigil, -ilis, watchful

vigilánter, *adv.,* vigilantly

vigiláre, to watch, be awake; resort

vigília, -ae, *f.,* watch, watching; vigil

vigínti, twenty

vigintiquatuor, twenty-four
vigintiquinque, twenty-five
vigor, -oris, *m.*, strength, vigor, force
viléscere, to become valueless
vilis, -e, vile, cheap
vílitas, -atis, *f.*, baseness
villa, -ae, *f.*, village; farm, country
place, country
Villácum, -i, *n.*, Villach
illicáre, to be or serve as a steward
illicátio, -onis, *f.*, stewardship
íllicus, -i, *m.*, steward
Vilnénis, -e, of Vilna (or Wilno)
inárius, -a, -um, wine, of wine
Vincéntius, -ii, *m.*, Vincent
víncere, vici, victus, to overcome,
conquer
vincla = víncula, bonds, chains
vinctus, -i, *m.*, prisoner, captive
vinculum, -i, *n.*, bond; string; chain;
in vínculis, in prison
vindémia, -ae, *f.*, vintage, wine
vindemiáre, to gather grapes, pluck
vindemiátor, -oris, *m.*, grape gatherer
vindex, -icis, *c.*, avenger
vindicáre, to avenge; claim
vindícta, -ae, *f.*, revenge, vengeance;
punishment
vínea, -ae, *f.*, vineyard; vine
vínitor, -oris, *m.*, vinedresser
vinoléntus, -a, -um, given to wine
drinking
Vintoniénsis, -e, of Winchester
vinum, -i, *n.*, wine
violáre, to ravish; defile
violátor, -oris, *m.*, violater, profaner
vípera, -ae, *f.*, viper
vir, -i, *m.*, man, husband
virágo, -inis, *f.*, heroine
virens, -entis, green
viréscere, to grow green
virétum, -i, *n.*, greensward, glade
virga, -ae, *f.*, rod, scepter
Virgiliánus, -a, -um, Vergiliano

virginális, -e, of a virgin, virginal
virgíneus, -a, -um, virginal
virgínitas, -atis, *f.*, virginity
virgo, -inis, *f.*, virgin, maiden; **Mons**
Virginis, Monte Vergine
virgúltum, -i, *n.*, slip for planting;
tender plant; plant; shrub, thicket
víridis, -e, green
viríliter, *adv.*, manfully
virítim, *adv.*, individually
viror, -oris, *m.*, verdure; freshness
virtuóse, *adv.*, virtuously
virtus, -utis, *f.*, virtue, excellence;
power, strength; host
vis, vis, *f.*, force, violence
víscera, -orum, *n. pl.*, bowels, innermost parts
vísere, visi, visus, to behold
visíbilis, -e, outward, visible
visibíliter, *adv.*, outwardly, visibly
Visigóthi, -orum, *m. pl.*, Visigoths
vísio, -onis, *f.*, vision
visitáre, to visit; survey
visitátio, -onis, *f.*, visiting, visitation
Visográdum, -i, *n.*, Wisgrade
visum, -i, *n.*, dream
visus, -us, *m.*, vision, sight
vita, -ae, *f.*, life
vitális, -e, life-giving, of life
vitáre, to avoid; withstand
Vitépscum, -i, *n.*, Vitebsk
Vitérbium, -ii, *n.*, Viterbo
vitiátor, -oris, *m.*, corrupter
vitióse, *adv.*, viciously
vitis, -is, *f.*, vine
vítium, -ii, *n.*, fault, sin, vice
vítreus, -a, -um, of glass
vitrum, -i, *n.*, glass
vitta, -ae, *f.*, ribbon, band, lace
vítula, -ae, *f.*, heifer
vítulus, -i, *m.*, calf, bullock, bull
vituperáre, to blame
vituperátio, -onis, *f.*, slander, defama-
tion

Vivariénsis, -e, of Vivarais
vivax, -acis, long-lived, vigorous
vívere, vixi, victus, to live
vívidus, -a, -um, living, healthy
vivíficans, -antis, life-giving
vivificáre, to bring to life, quicken
vivicátio, -onis, f., a new life
vivificátrix, -icis, f., quickener, vivifier
vivus, -a, -um, living, alive
vix, adv., scarcely, with difficulty
Vladimíria, -ae, f., Wlodzimierz
vobiscum, with you
vobismetípsis, dat. pl.; see tumetipse
vocábulum, -i, n., name
vocáre, to call
vocátio, -onis, f., calling, vocation, a
  summons
vociferátio, -onis, f., loud shouting,
  jubilation
voláre, to fly
Volatérrae, -arum, f. pl., Volterra
volátile, -is, n., fowl, winged fowl
volátus, -us, m., flight
volens, -entis, willing
Volhínia, -ae, f., Wolyń
volitáre, to fly about
volo (velle), I wish or will
vólucris, -is, f., bird, fowl
volúmen, -inis, n., volume, book
voluntárie, adv., voluntarily, of one's
  own will
voluntárium, -ii, n., free-will offering
voluntárius, -a, -um, voluntary
volúntas, -atis, f. will
volúptas, -atis, f., pleasure, delight
Volusiánus, -a, -um, Volusian
volutáre (ari), to roll about, wallow
vólvere, volvi, volútus, to meditate
vomer, -eris, m., plowshare
vorágo, -inis, f., breach
voráre, to eat, devour
vosmetípsos, acc.; see tumetipse
votívus, -a, -um, votive

votum, -i, n., vow; prayer, desire
vovére, vovi, votus, to vow, promise
  solemnly
vox, vocis, f., voice; sound; voce
  magna, with a loud voice
Vratislaviénsis, -e, of Wratislaw
vulgáre, to publish
vulgáris, -e, plain, common, coarse
vulgo, adv., commonly
vulgus, -i, n. people, multitude
vulneráre, to wound
vulnus, -eris, n., wound
vulpes, -is, f., fox
vultus, -us, m., countenance, face
vulva, -ae, f., womb

W

Wándali, -orum, m. pl., Vandals
Willélmus, -i, m., William
Willibrórdus, -i, m., Willibrord
Winfrídus, -i, m., Winfred
Wiremuthénsis, -e, of Wearmouth
Wolphárdus, -i, m., Wolphard

X

Xamphána, -ae, f., Champagne
Xavérius, -ii, m., Xavier
xenodóchium, -ii, n., hospital
Xystus, -i, m., Sixtus

Y

Ypsílon, Greek letter y

Z

zábulus, -i, m., devil
zain, the seventh letter of the Hebrew
  alphabet, corresponding to English
  z
Zatécium, -ii, n., Zatec

Zebedaéus, -i, *m.,* Zebedee
zeláre, to be jealous, envy
zelári, *dep.,* to be zealous for
zelátor, -oris, *m.,* zealot, enthusiast

zelus, -i, *m.,* zeal
Ziphaéi, -orum, *m. pl.,* Ziphites
zizánia, -orum, *n. pl.,* cockle
zona, -ae, *f.,* girdle

INDEX

A (*ab*), 56, 140, 151
Ablative absolute, 120, 150
Ablative case, 2, 3: prepositions governing, 55; uses of, 150
Accompaniment, how expressed, 150
Accusative case, 2, 3: prepositions governing, 55; of subject in indirect discourse, 130; uses of, 164
Active periphrastic, 48
Active voice, 17, 33, 81: deponent verbs, 98; semideponents, 98
Ad, 55, 149, 164: gerundive with, 64
Adjectives: comparison of, 149, 150; declension of, 2, 7, 12; demonstrative, 75; different forms of, 7; of first declension, 3; indefinite, 108; position of, 3; of second declension, 7; of special declension, 139; of third declension, 12
Adverbs, comparison of, 149, 150
Agent: with the passive periphrastic, 140; with the passive voice, 151
Agreement: of adjectives, 1, 3, 7, 12; of participles, 47
Aio, 163
Aliquis and *aliqui*, 108
Alius, 140
Alter, 140
An, 162
Ante, 55, 140, 164
Apud, 55, 164
Articles, 3

Bene, comparison of, 150

Capere, 90
Cardinal numerals, 175
Causa, gerundive with, 64
Causal clause with *cum*, 82
Cause, how expressed, 151
Circum, 55, 140, 164

Coepisse, 163
Comparative of adjectives and adverbs, 149; ablative with, 151; degree of difference, 151; irregular, 149, 150
Compounds of *capere, facere, jacere*, 90
Con-, compounded with verbs, 140
Concessive clause with *cum*, 82
Conditional clauses of doubt and contrary to fact, 82
Contra, 55, 164
Coram, 56
Cum: accompaniment with, 150; as conjunction, 82; to express manner, 151; governing ablative, 56, 152; with pronouns, 24

Dative case, 2, 3: uses of, 140
De, 56, 151, 152
Decere, impersonal verb, 139
Declension, 1: of adjectives, 12; fifth, 47; first, 2; fourth, 40; irregular, 139; second, 6; third, 11
Defective verbs, 163
Degree of difference, how expressed, 151
Demonstratives, pronouns and adjectives, 75
Deponent verbs, 98: governing the ablative case, 152
Description, how expressed, 151
Direct object, 2, 3, 164
Double questions, 162
Duration of time, how expressed, 164

E (*ex*), 151, 56
Emphatic pronouns, 75: verb forms, 18
Esse: future of, 41; future imperative of, 34; future participle of, 48; imperatives of, 34; imperfect of, 34, 81; perfect indicative of, 55; possession with, 140; present of, 8, 63

331

4

If you have enjoyed this book, consider making your next selection from among the following . . .

Prices subject to change.

Prices subject to change.

At your Bookdealer or direct from the Publisher.
Toll-Free 1-800-437-5876   *Fax 815-226-7770*

Prices subject to change.

Companion volume to **LATIN GRAMMAR**

SECOND LATIN

by

CORA CARROLL SCANLON, A.M.

and

CHARLES L. SCANLON, A.M.

This second-year Latin course supposes the previous study of *Latin Grammar,* by the same authors. It is intended for students who can devote only two years to the study of Latin and who must be prepared to read intelligently Latin textbooks of philosophy, theology, and canon law. Therefore the vocabularies, word studies, exercises, and connected passages have been selected with this practical purpose in mind.

The first half of the book is based on philosophical texts; the second half is drawn from works of theology and from the Code of Canon Law. At the end of the volume is a vocabulary of 3,000 words, which may serve the purpose of a concise dictionary.

TAN BOOKS AND PUBLISHERS, INC.
P.O. Box 424
Rockford, Illinois 61105

NOTES

NOTES